THAT TIME I GOT REINCARNATED AS A

SLIME

10

Author: **FUSE**

Artist: **TAIKI KAWAKAMI**

Character design: **MITZ VAH**

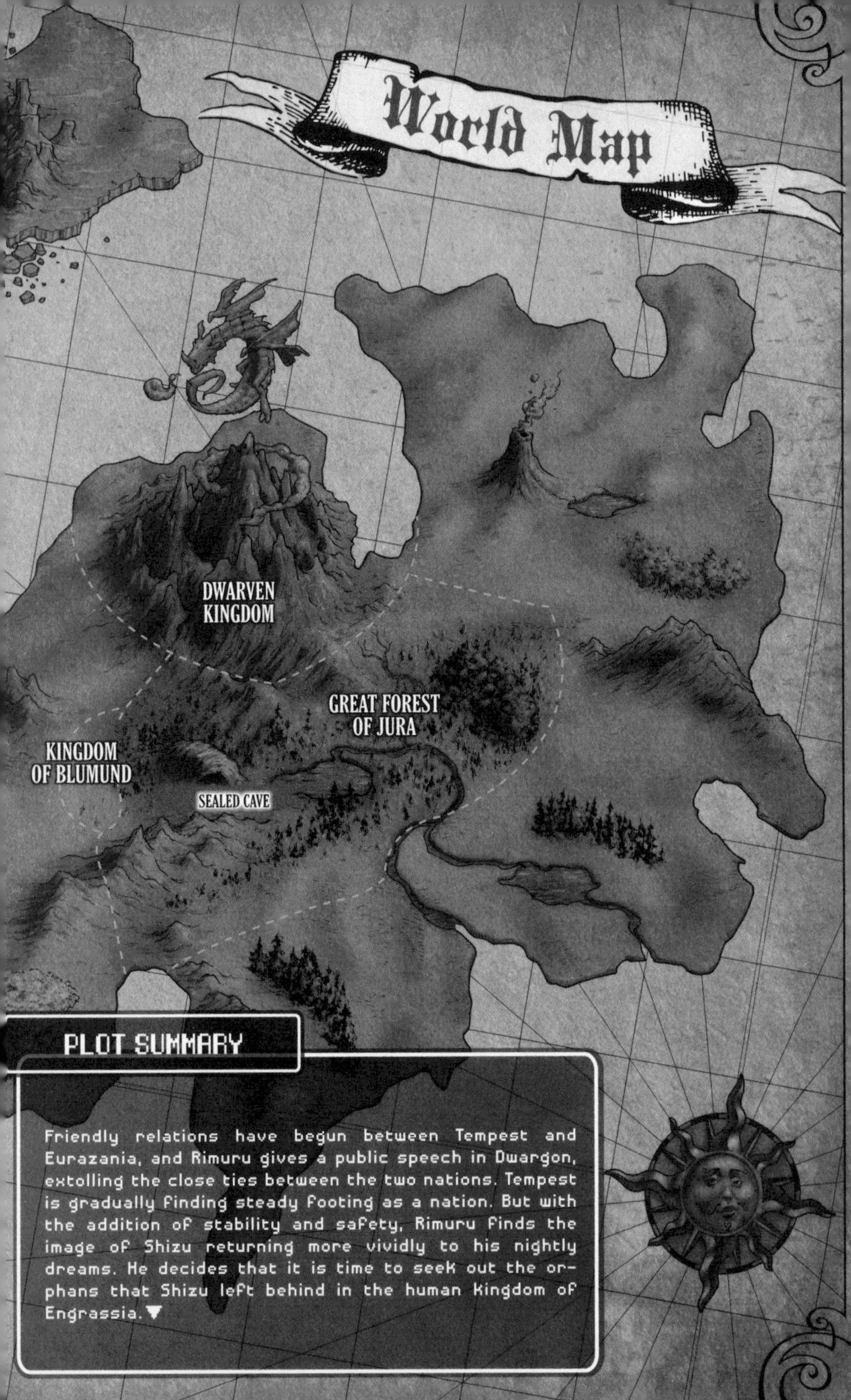
World Map
DWARVEN KINGDOM
GREAT FOREST OF JURA
KINGDOM OF BLUMUND
SEALED CAVE

PLOT SUMMARY

Friendly relations have begun between Tempest and Eurazania, and Rimuru gives a public speech in Dwargon, extolling the close ties between the two nations. Tempest is gradually finding steady footing as a nation. But with the addition of stability and safety, Rimuru finds the image of Shizu returning more vividly to his nightly dreams. He decides that it is time to seek out the orphans that Shizu left behind in the human kingdom of Engrassia. ▼

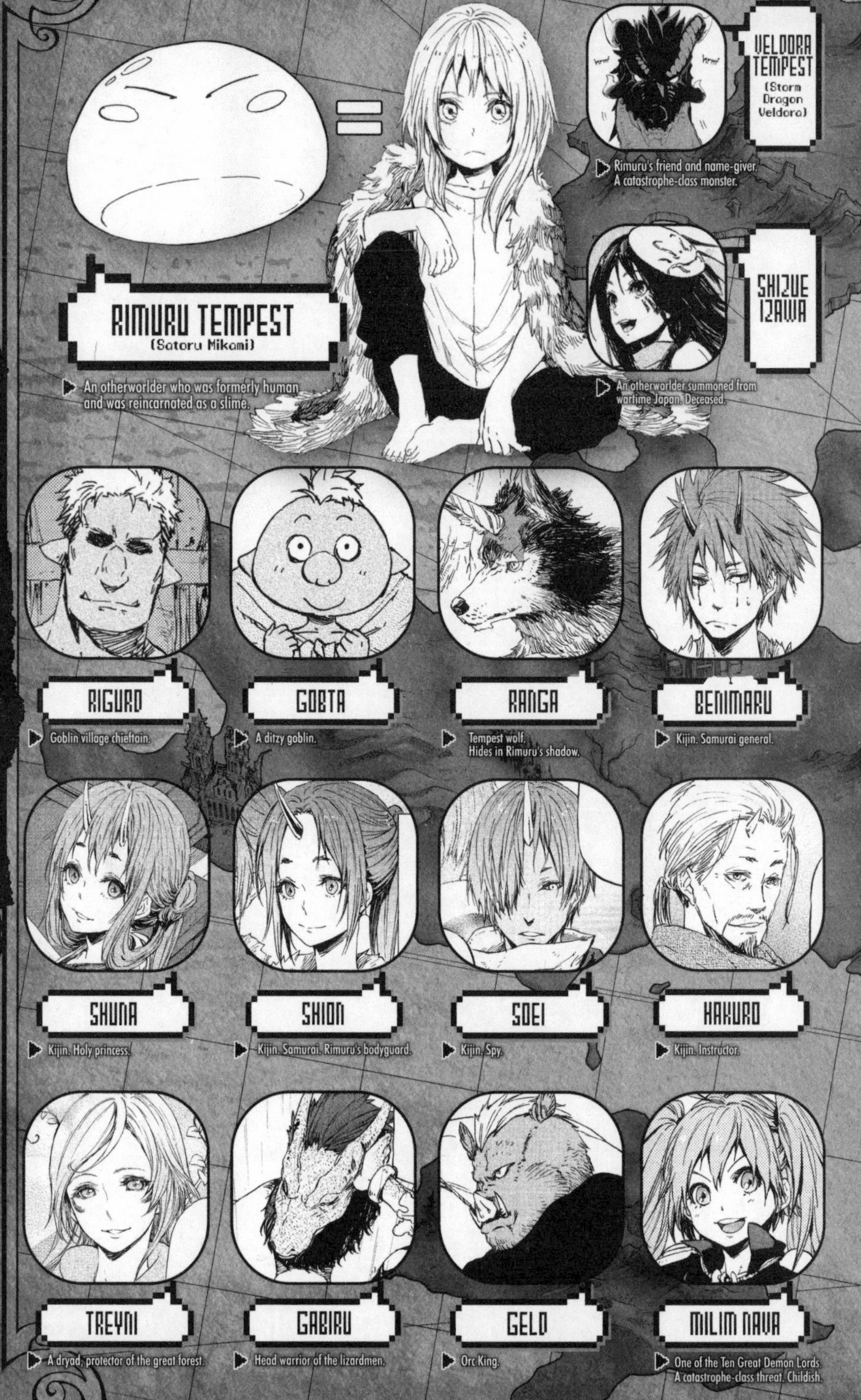
VELDORA TEMPEST
(Storm Dragon Veldora)
Rimuru's friend and name-giver. A catastrophe-class monster.
RIMURU TEMPEST
(Satoru Mikami)
An otherworlder who was formerly human and was reincarnated as a slime.
SHIZUE IZAWA
An otherworlder summoned from wartime Japan. Deceased.
BENIMARU
Kijin. Samurai general.
RANGA
Tempest wolf. Hides in Rimuru's shadow.
GOBTA
A ditzy goblin.
RIGURD
Goblin village chieftain.
HAKURO
Kijin. Instructor.
SOEI
Kijin. Spy.
SHION
Kijin. Samurai. Rimuru's bodyguard.
SHUNA
Kijin. Holy princess.
MILIM NAVA
One of the Ten Great Demon Lords. A catastrophe-class threat. Childish.
GELD
Orc King.
GABIRU
Head warrior of the lizardmen.
TREYNI
A dryad, protector of the great forest.

CONTENTS

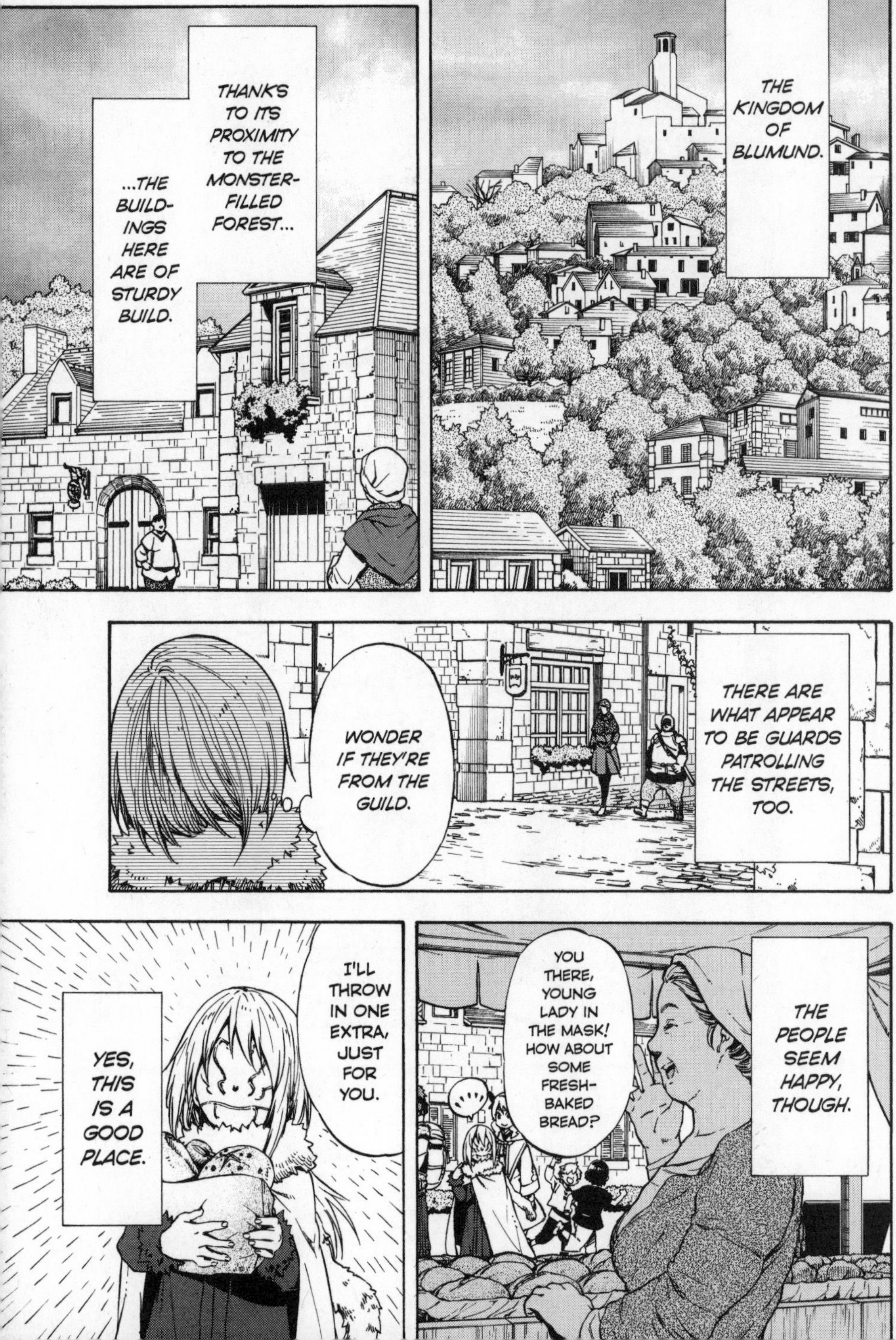
THE KINGDOM OF BLUMUND.
THANKS TO ITS PROXIMITY TO THE MONSTER-FILLED FOREST...
...THE BUILD-INGS HERE ARE OF STURDY BUILD.
THERE ARE WHAT APPEAR TO BE GUARDS PATROLLING THE STREETS, TOO.
WONDER IF THEY'RE FROM THE GUILD.
THE PEOPLE SEEM HAPPY, THOUGH.
YOU THERE, YOUNG LADY IN THE MASK! HOW ABOUT SOME FRESH-BAKED BREAD?
I'LL THROW IN ONE EXTRA, JUST FOR YOU.
YES, THIS IS A GOOD PLACE.

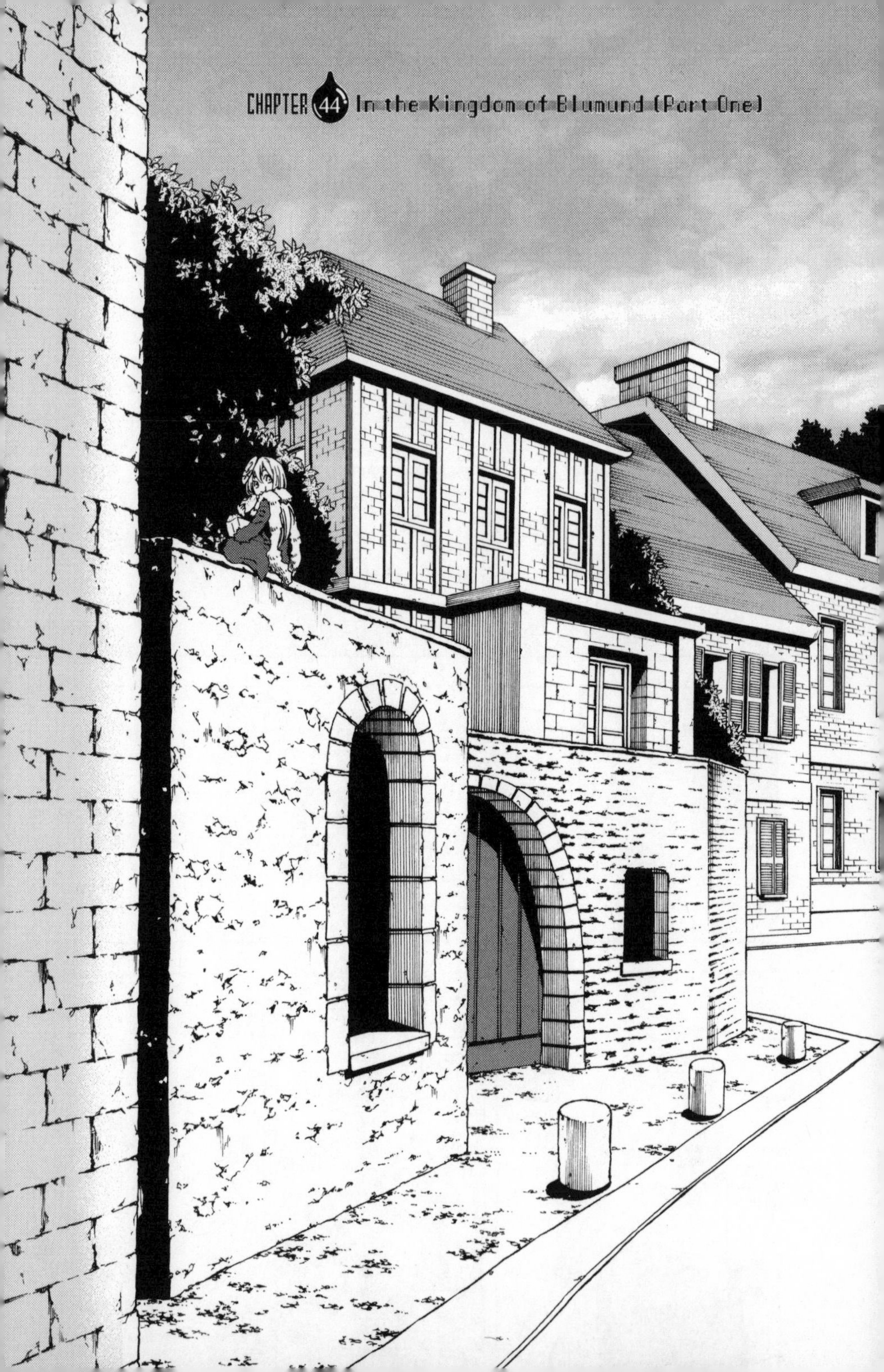
CHAPTER 44 In the Kingdom of Blumund (Part One)

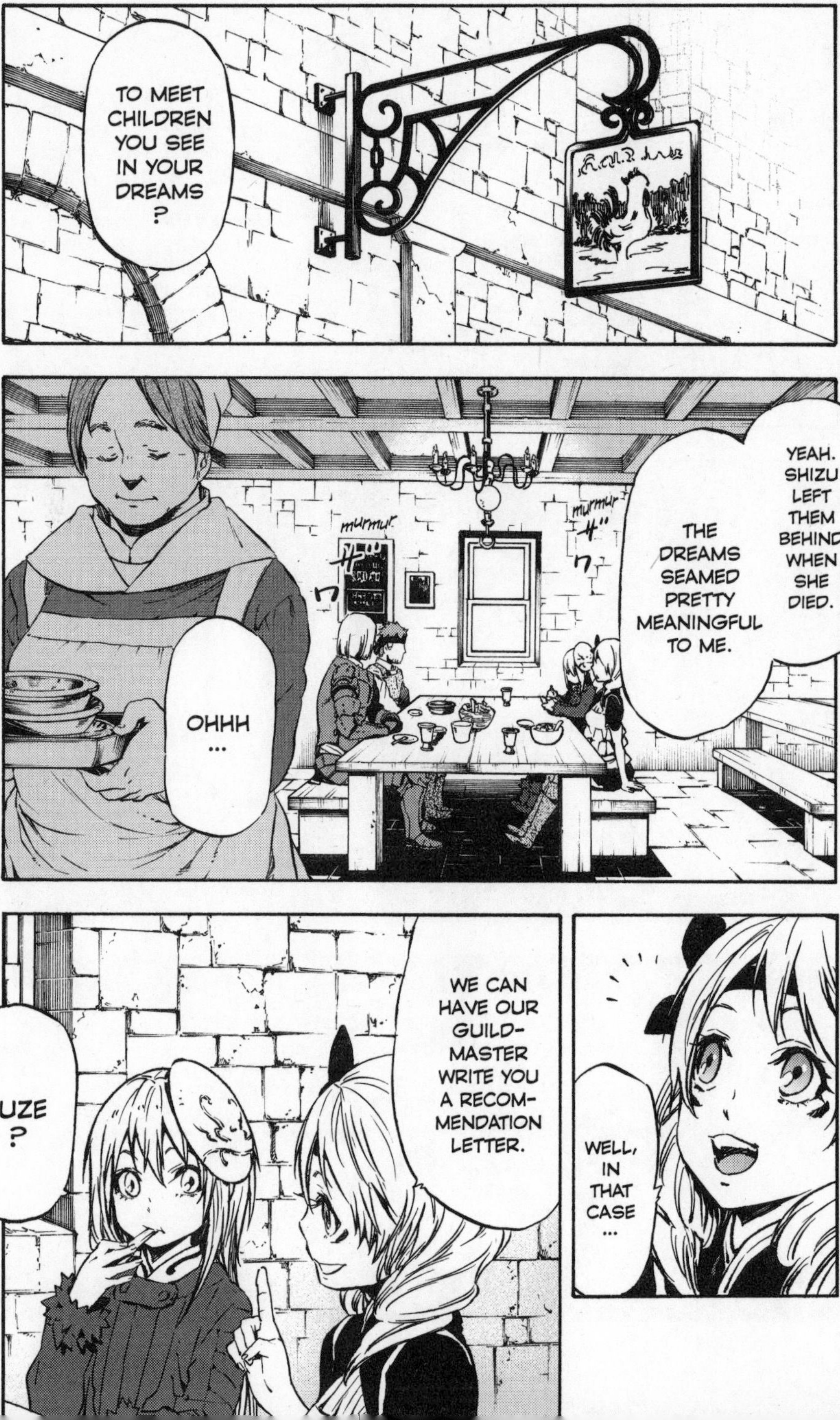
TO MEET CHILDREN YOU SEE IN YOUR DREAMS ?
YEAH. SHIZU LEFT THEM BEHIND WHEN SHE DIED.
THE DREAMS SEAMED PRETTY MEANINGFUL TO ME.
murmur
murmur
OHHH ...
WELL, IN THAT CASE ...
WE CAN HAVE OUR GUILD-MASTER WRITE YOU A RECOMMENDATION LETTER.
FUZE ?

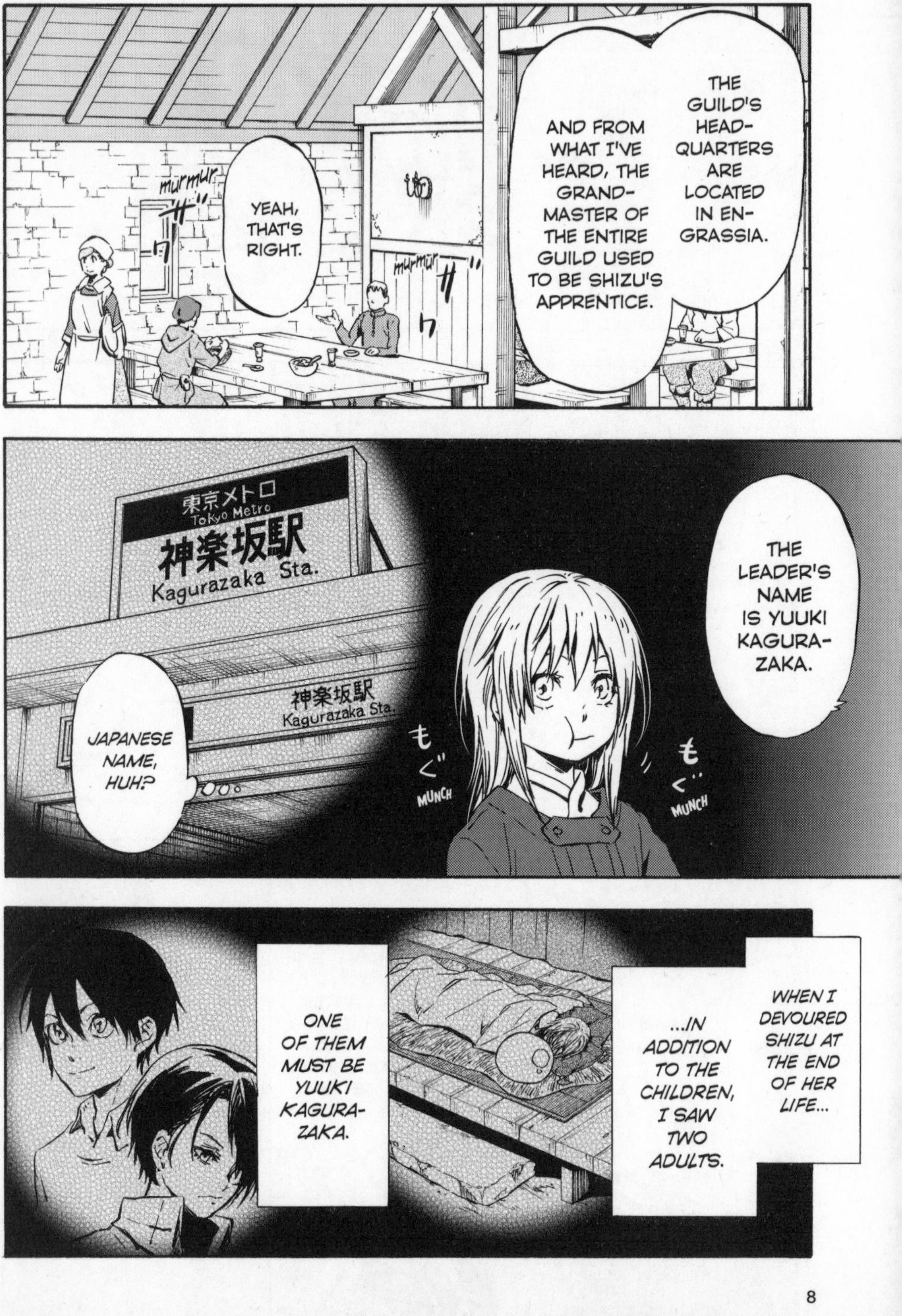
THE GUILD'S HEAD-QUARTERS ARE LOCATED IN EN-GRASSIA.
AND FROM WHAT I'VE HEARD, THE GRAND-MASTER OF THE ENTIRE GUILD USED TO BE SHIZU'S APPRENTICE.
murmur
YEAH, THAT'S RIGHT.
murmur
東京メトロ
Tokyo Metro
神楽坂駅
Kagurazaka Sta.
THE LEADER'S NAME IS YUUKI KAGURA-ZAKA.
もぐ
MUNCH
もぐ
MUNCH
神楽坂駅
Kagurazaka Sta.
JAPANESE NAME, HUH?
WHEN I DEVOURED SHIZU AT THE END OF HER LIFE...
...IN ADDITION TO THE CHILDREN, I SAW TWO ADULTS.
ONE OF THEM MUST BE YUUKI KAGURA-ZAKA.

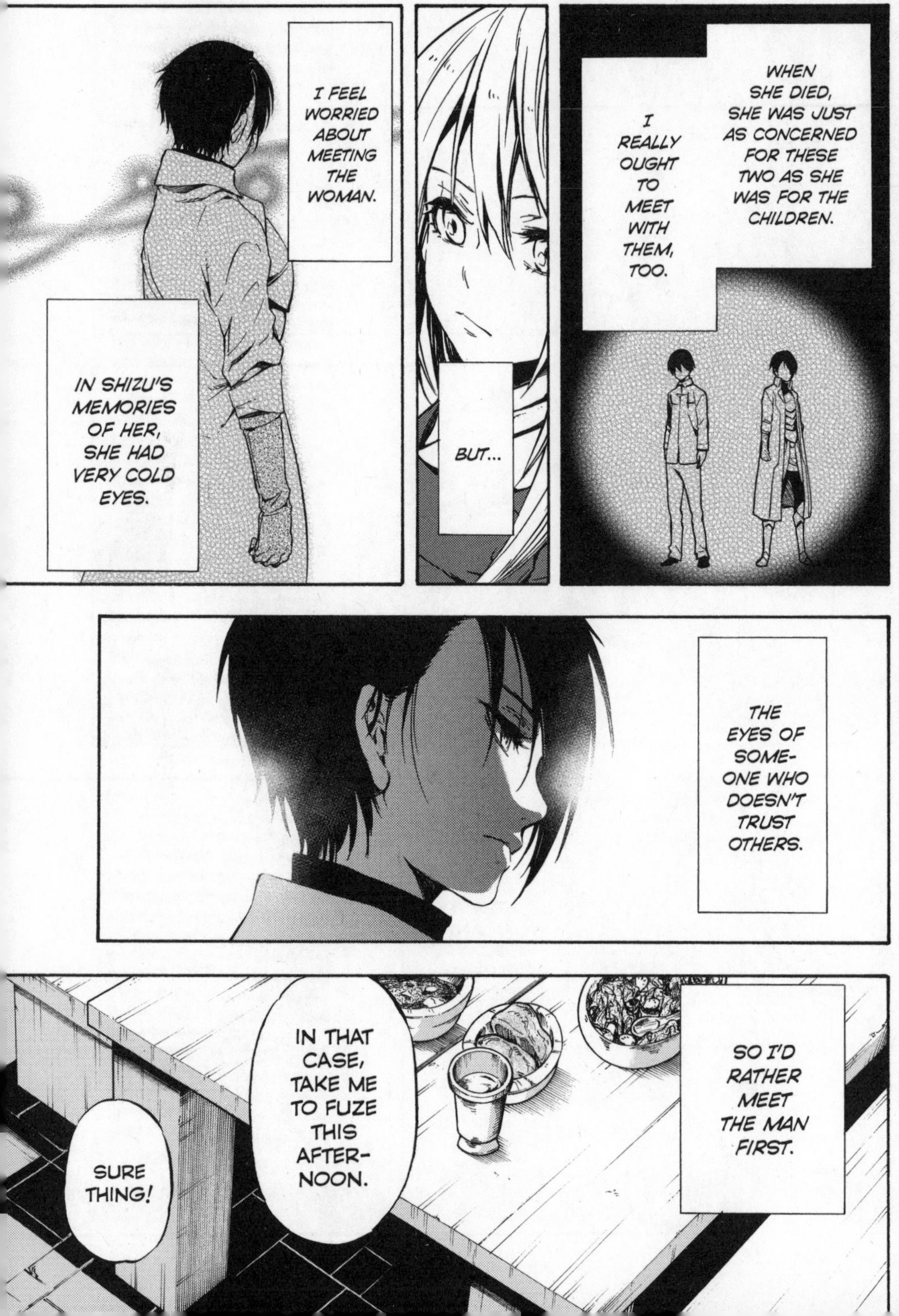
WHEN SHE DIED, SHE WAS JUST AS CONCERNED FOR THESE TWO AS SHE WAS FOR THE CHILDREN.
I REALLY OUGHT TO MEET WITH THEM, TOO.
BUT...
I FEEL WORRIED ABOUT MEETING THE WOMAN.
IN SHIZU'S MEMORIES OF HER, SHE HAD VERY COLD EYES.
THE EYES OF SOME-ONE WHO DOESN'T TRUST OTHERS.
SO I'D RATHER MEET THE MAN FIRST.
IN THAT CASE, TAKE ME TO FUZE THIS AFTER-NOON.
SURE THING!

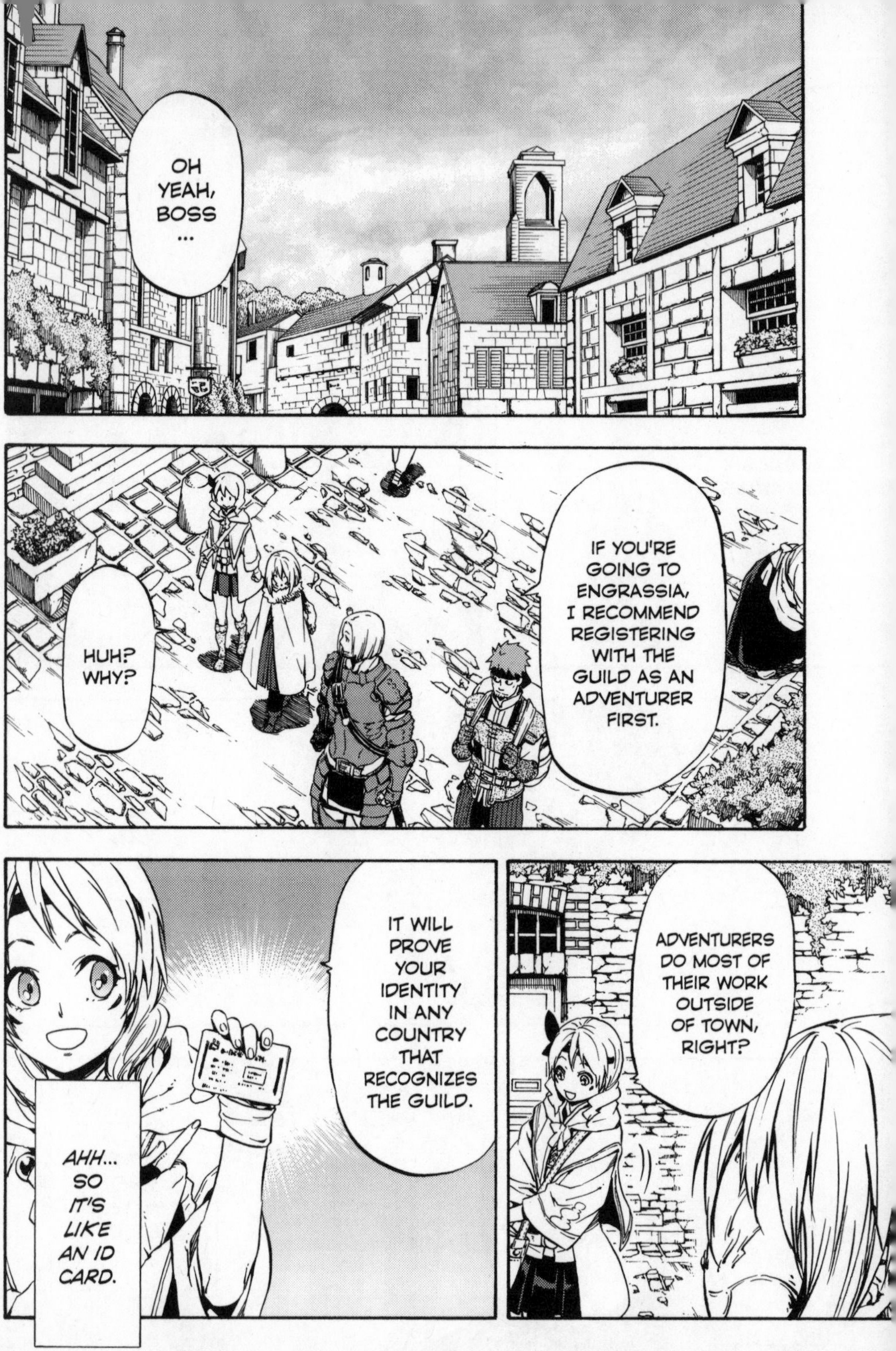
OH YEAH, BOSS ...
IF YOU'RE GOING TO ENGRASSIA, I RECOMMEND REGISTERING WITH THE GUILD AS AN ADVENTURER FIRST.
HUH? WHY?
ADVENTURERS DO MOST OF THEIR WORK OUTSIDE OF TOWN, RIGHT?
IT WILL PROVE YOUR IDENTITY IN ANY COUNTRY THAT RECOGNIZES THE GUILD.
AHH... SO IT'S LIKE AN ID CARD.

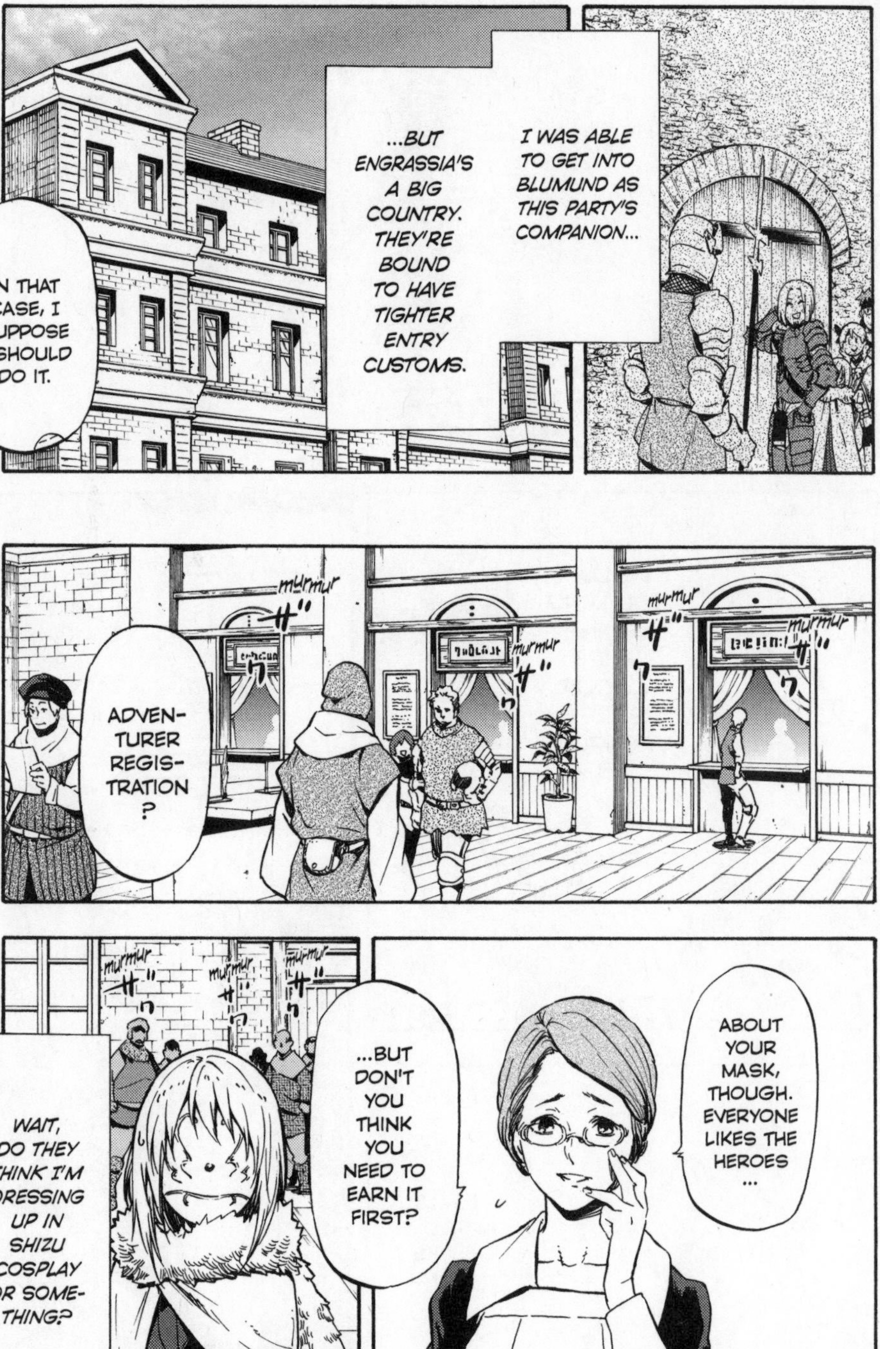
I WAS ABLE TO GET INTO BLUMUND AS THIS PARTY'S COMPANION...
...BUT ENGRASSIA'S A BIG COUNTRY. THEY'RE BOUND TO HAVE TIGHTER ENTRY CUSTOMS.
IN THAT CASE, I SUPPOSE I SHOULD DO IT.
murmur
murmur
murmur
murmur
ADVENTURER REGISTRATION?
ABOUT YOUR MASK, THOUGH. EVERYONE LIKES THE HEROES ...
...BUT DON'T YOU THINK YOU NEED TO EARN IT FIRST?
murmur
murmur
murmur
WAIT, DO THEY THINK I'M DRESSING UP IN SHIZU COSPLAY OR SOMETHING?

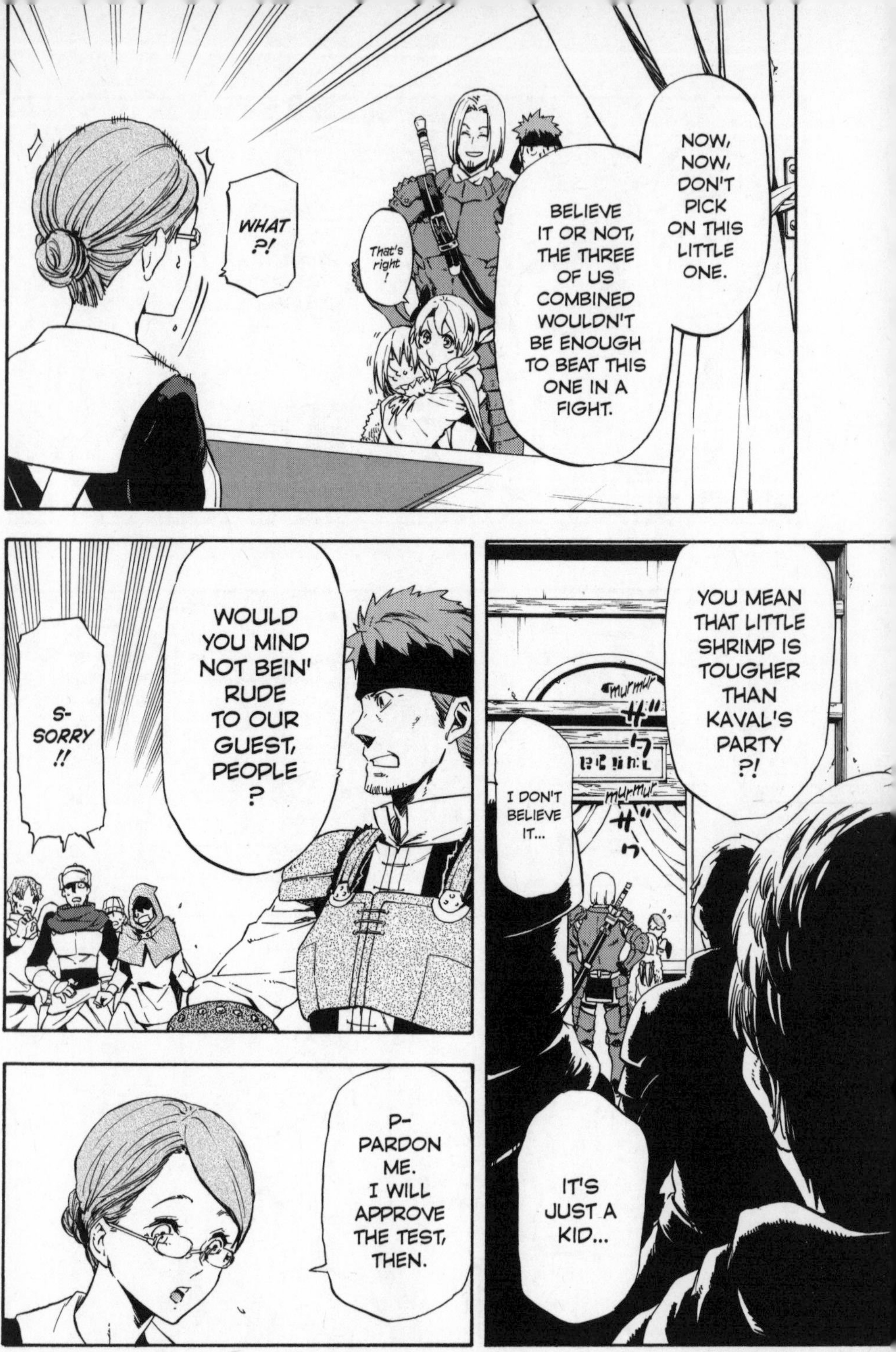
NOW, NOW, DON'T PICK ON THIS LITTLE ONE.
BELIEVE IT OR NOT, THE THREE OF US COMBINED WOULDN'T BE ENOUGH TO BEAT THIS ONE IN A FIGHT.
That's right!
WHAT?!
YOU MEAN THAT LITTLE SHRIMP IS TOUGHER THAN KAVAL'S PARTY?!
murmur ザワ
murmur ザワ
I DON'T BELIEVE IT...
IT'S JUST A KID...
WOULD YOU MIND NOT BEIN' RUDE TO OUR GUEST, PEOPLE?
S-SORRY!!
P-PARDON ME. I WILL APPROVE THE TEST, THEN.

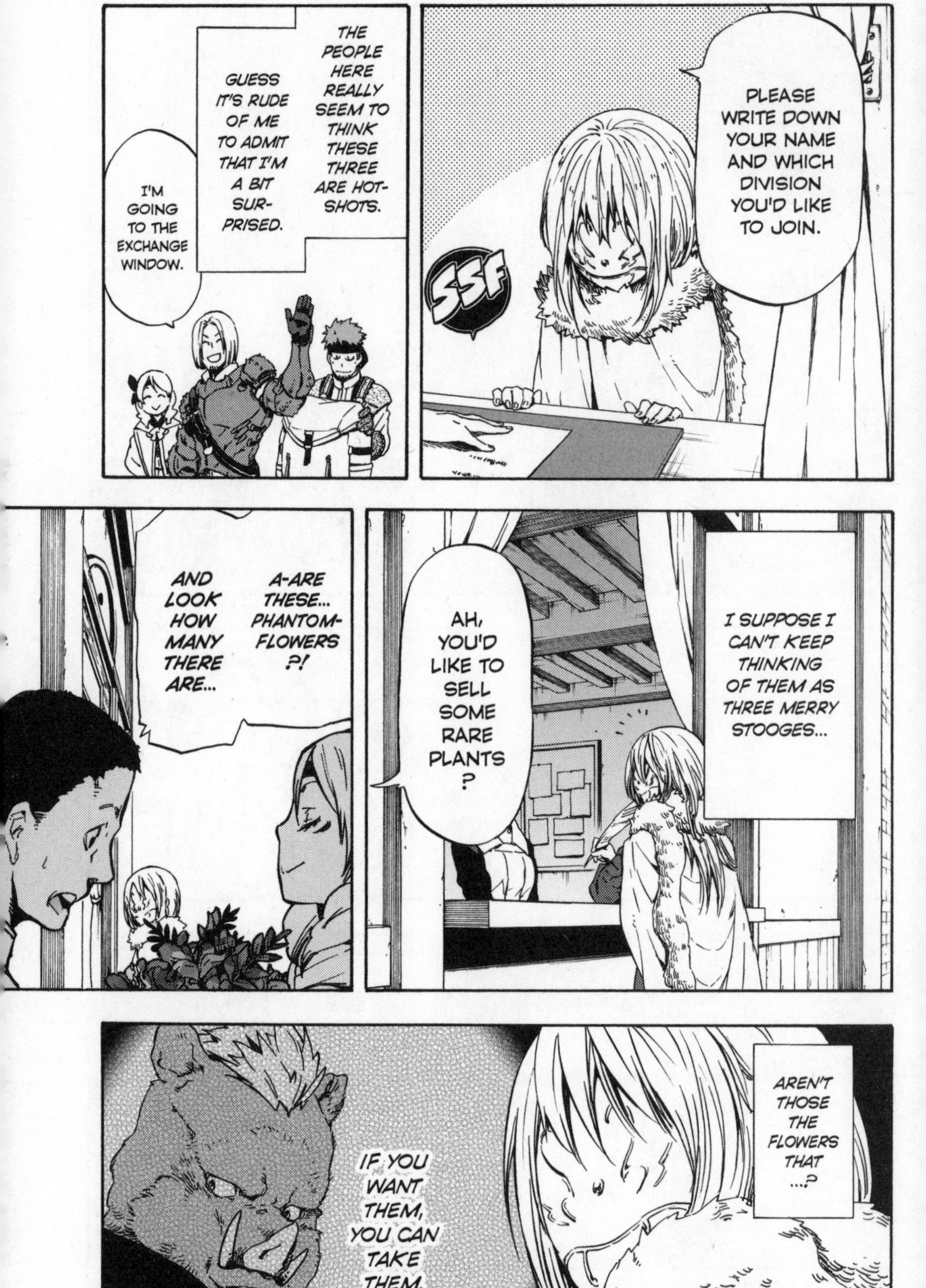
PLEASE WRITE DOWN YOUR NAME AND WHICH DIVISION YOU'D LIKE TO JOIN.
SSF
THE PEOPLE HERE REALLY SEEM TO THINK THESE THREE ARE HOT-SHOTS.
GUESS IT'S RUDE OF ME TO ADMIT THAT I'M A BIT SUR-PRISED.
I'M GOING TO THE EXCHANGE WINDOW.
I SUPPOSE I CAN'T KEEP THINKING OF THEM AS THREE MERRY STOOGES...
AH, YOU'D LIKE TO SELL SOME RARE PLANTS?
A-ARE THESE... PHANTOM-FLOWERS?!
AND LOOK HOW MANY THERE ARE...
AREN'T THOSE THE FLOWERS THAT ...?
IF YOU WANT THEM, YOU CAN TAKE THEM.

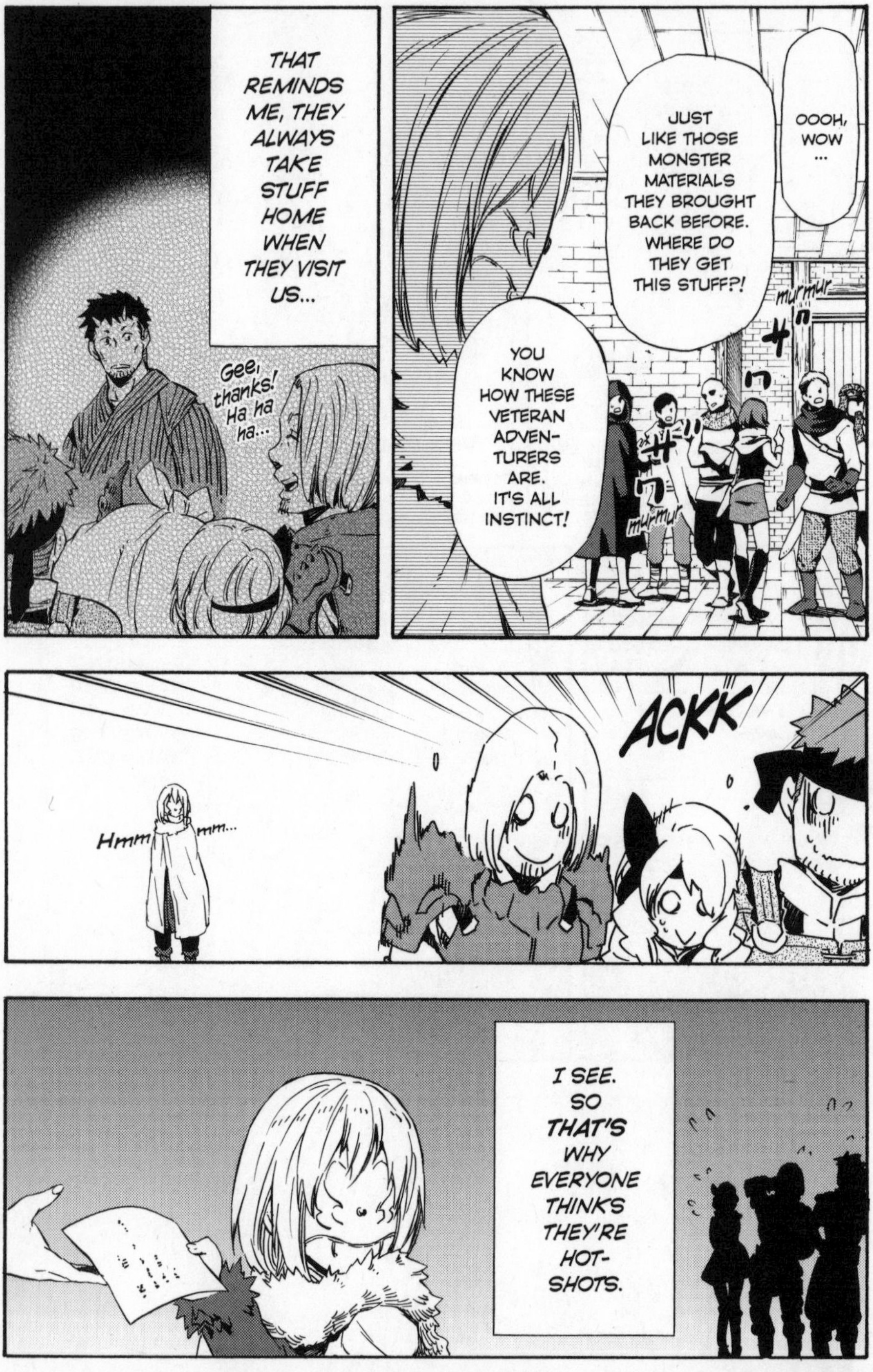
OOOH, WOW ...
JUST LIKE THOSE MONSTER MATERIALS THEY BROUGHT BACK BEFORE. WHERE DO THEY GET THIS STUFF?!
murmur
YOU KNOW HOW THESE VETERAN ADVEN-TURERS ARE. IT'S ALL INSTINCT!
murmur
THAT REMINDS ME, THEY ALWAYS TAKE STUFF HOME WHEN THEY VISIT US...
Gee, thanks! Ha ha ha...
ACKK
Hmmmmm...
I SEE. SO THAT'S WHY EVERYONE THINKS THEY'RE HOT-SHOTS.

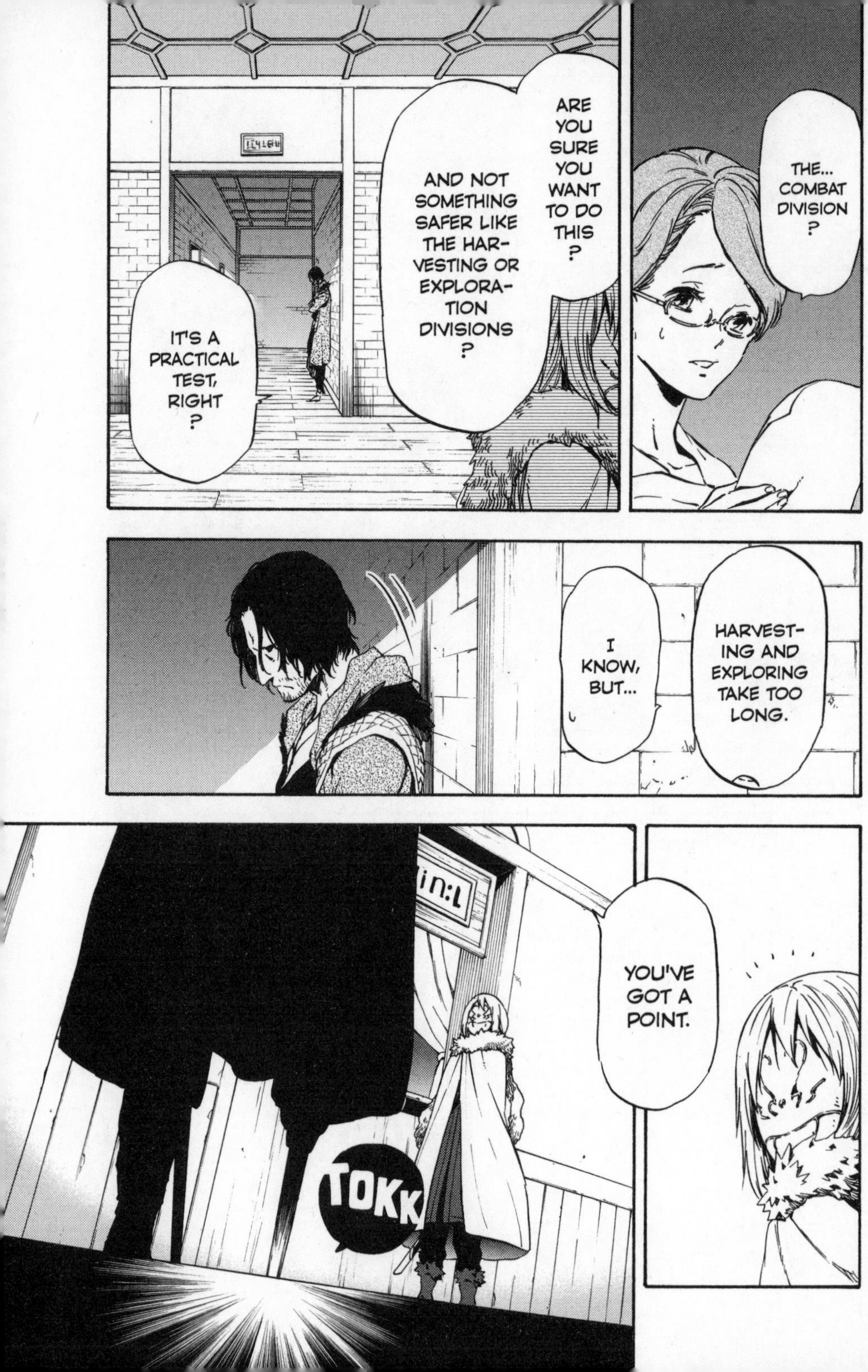
THE... COMBAT DIVISION?
ARE YOU SURE YOU WANT TO DO THIS?
AND NOT SOMETHING SAFER LIKE THE HARVESTING OR EXPLORATION DIVISIONS?
IT'S A PRACTICAL TEST, RIGHT?
HARVESTING AND EXPLORING TAKE TOO LONG.
I KNOW, BUT...
YOU'VE GOT A POINT.
TOKK

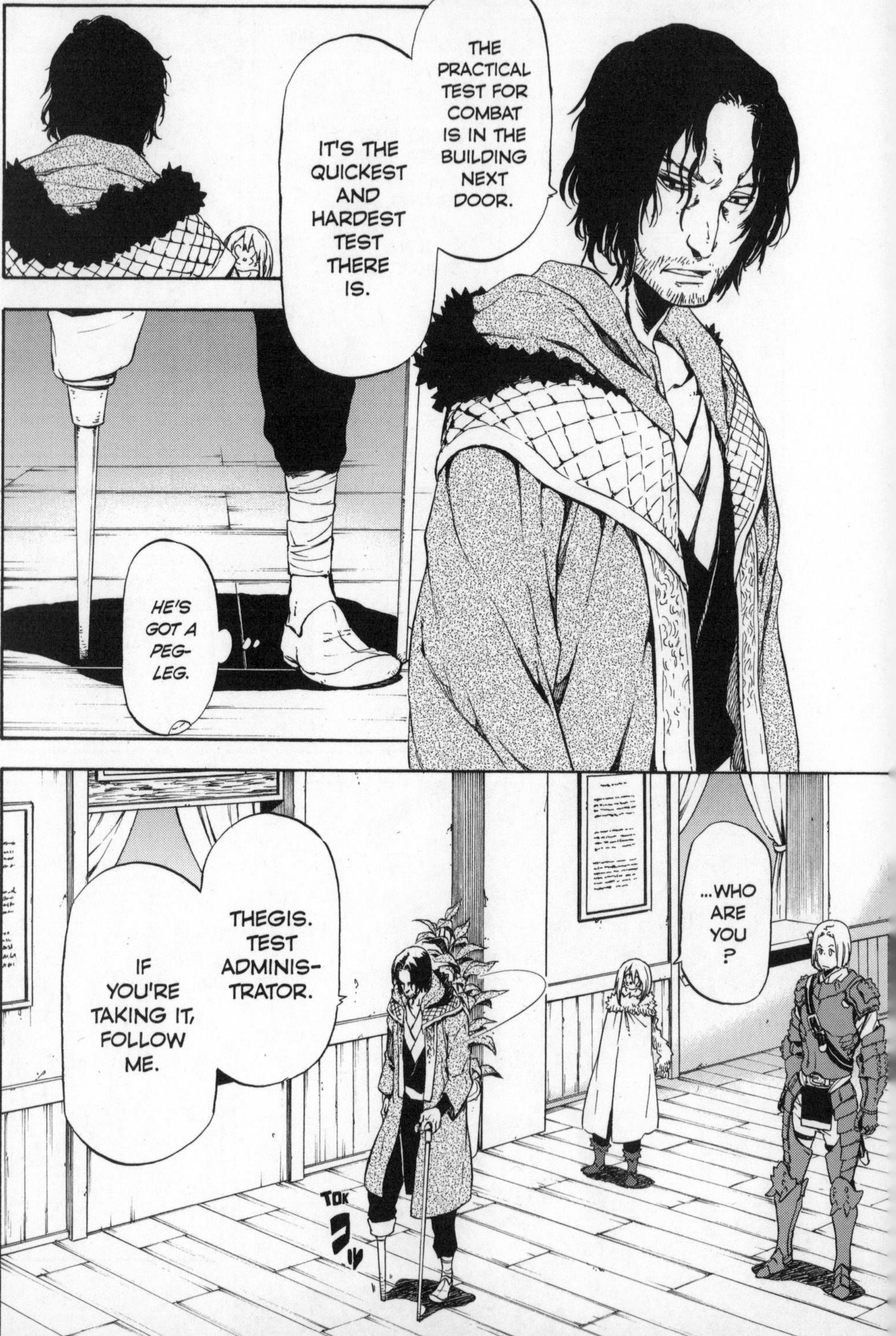
THE PRACTICAL TEST FOR COMBAT IS IN THE BUILDING NEXT DOOR.
IT'S THE QUICKEST AND HARDEST TEST THERE IS.
HE'S GOT A PEG-LEG.
...WHO ARE YOU?
THEGIS. TEST ADMINISTRATOR.
IF YOU'RE TAKING IT, FOLLOW ME.
TOK

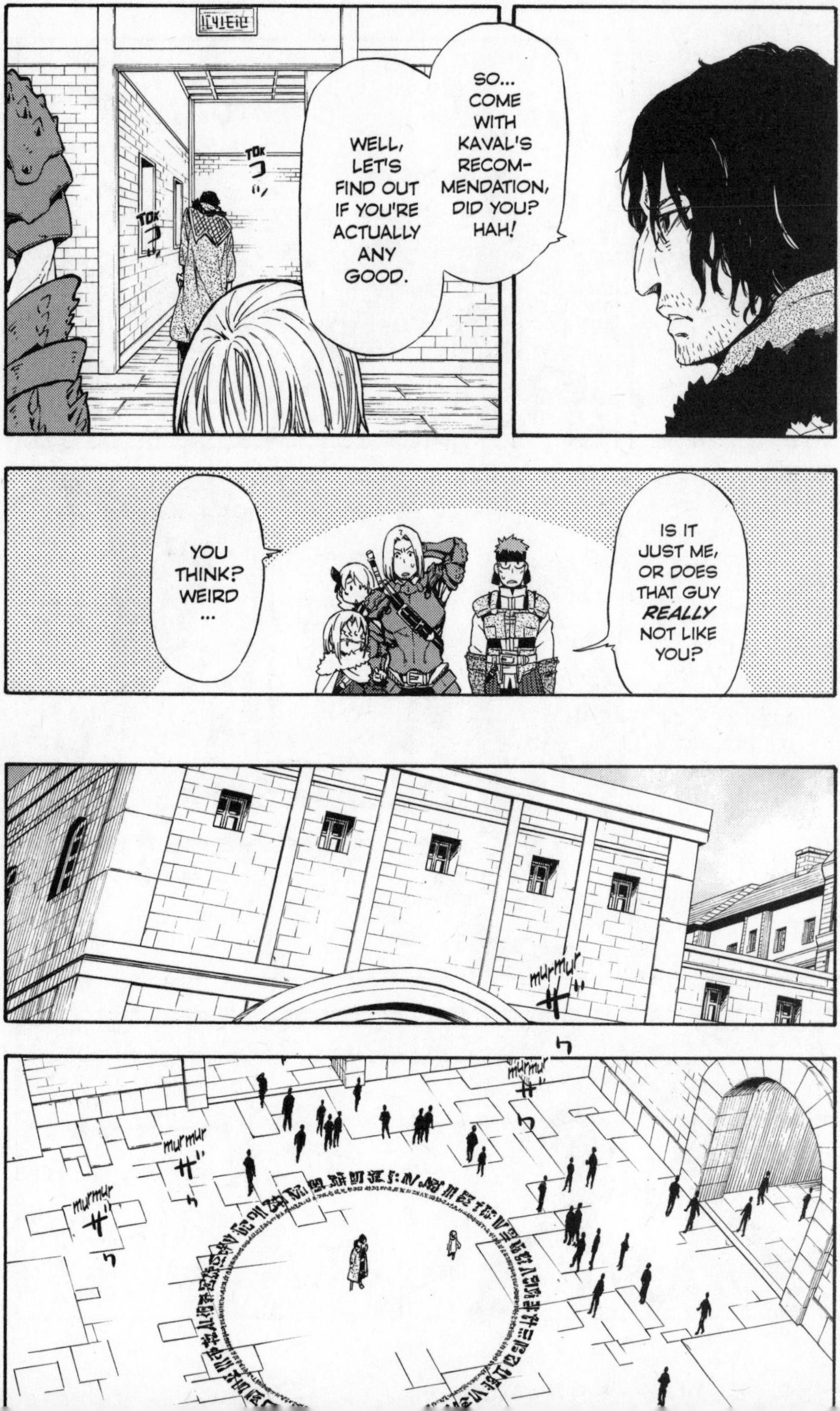
SO... COME WITH KAVAL'S RECOM-MENDATION, DID YOU? HAH!
WELL, LET'S FIND OUT IF YOU'RE ACTUALLY ANY GOOD.
TOK
TOK
IS IT JUST ME, OR DOES THAT GUY *REALLY* NOT LIKE YOU?
YOU THINK? WEIRD ...
murmur
murmur
murmur
murmur

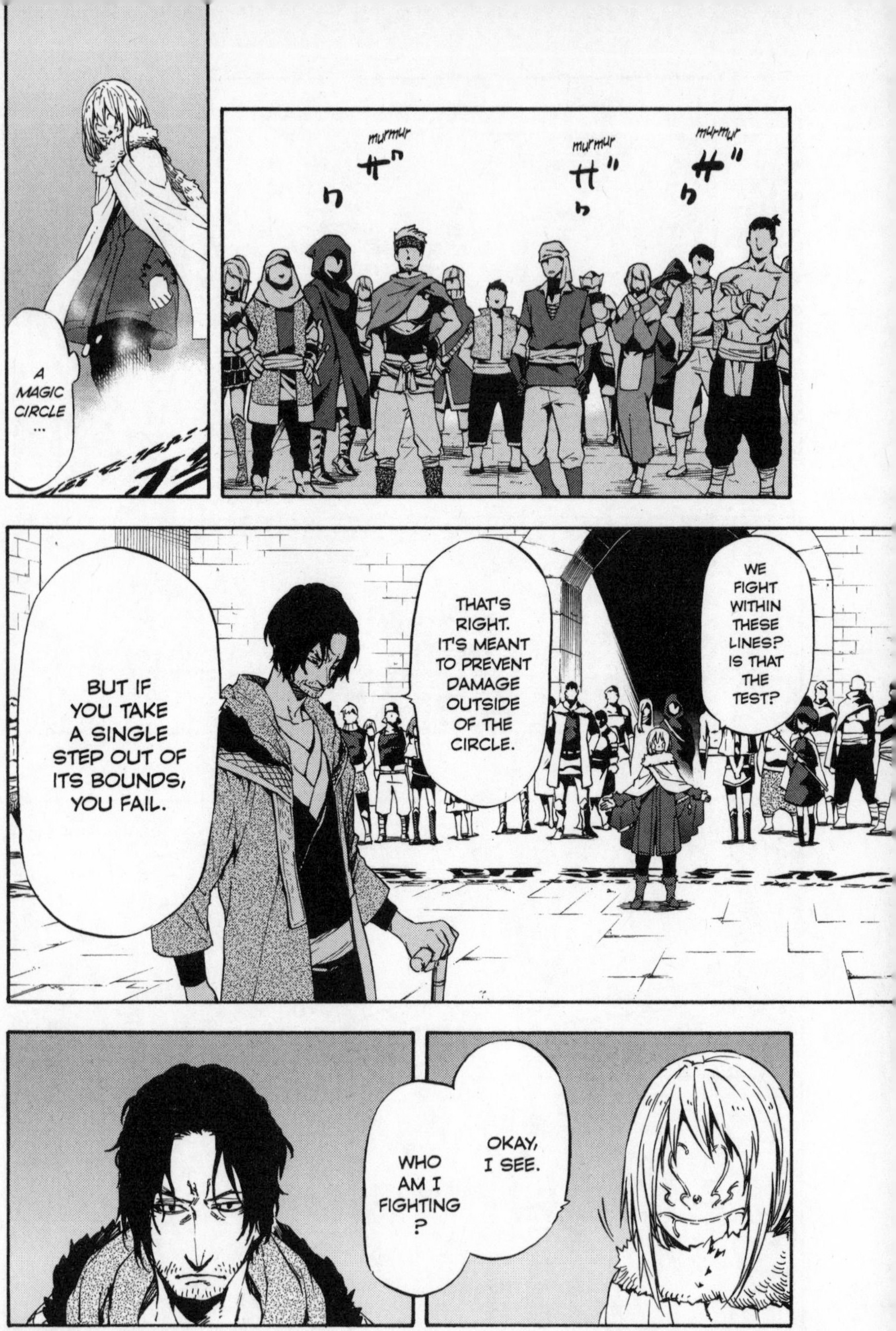
murmur
murmur
murmur
A MAGIC CIRCLE ...
WE FIGHT WITHIN THESE LINES? IS THAT THE TEST?
THAT'S RIGHT. IT'S MEANT TO PREVENT DAMAGE OUTSIDE OF THE CIRCLE.
BUT IF YOU TAKE A SINGLE STEP OUT OF ITS BOUNDS, YOU FAIL.
OKAY, I SEE.
WHO AM I FIGHTING?

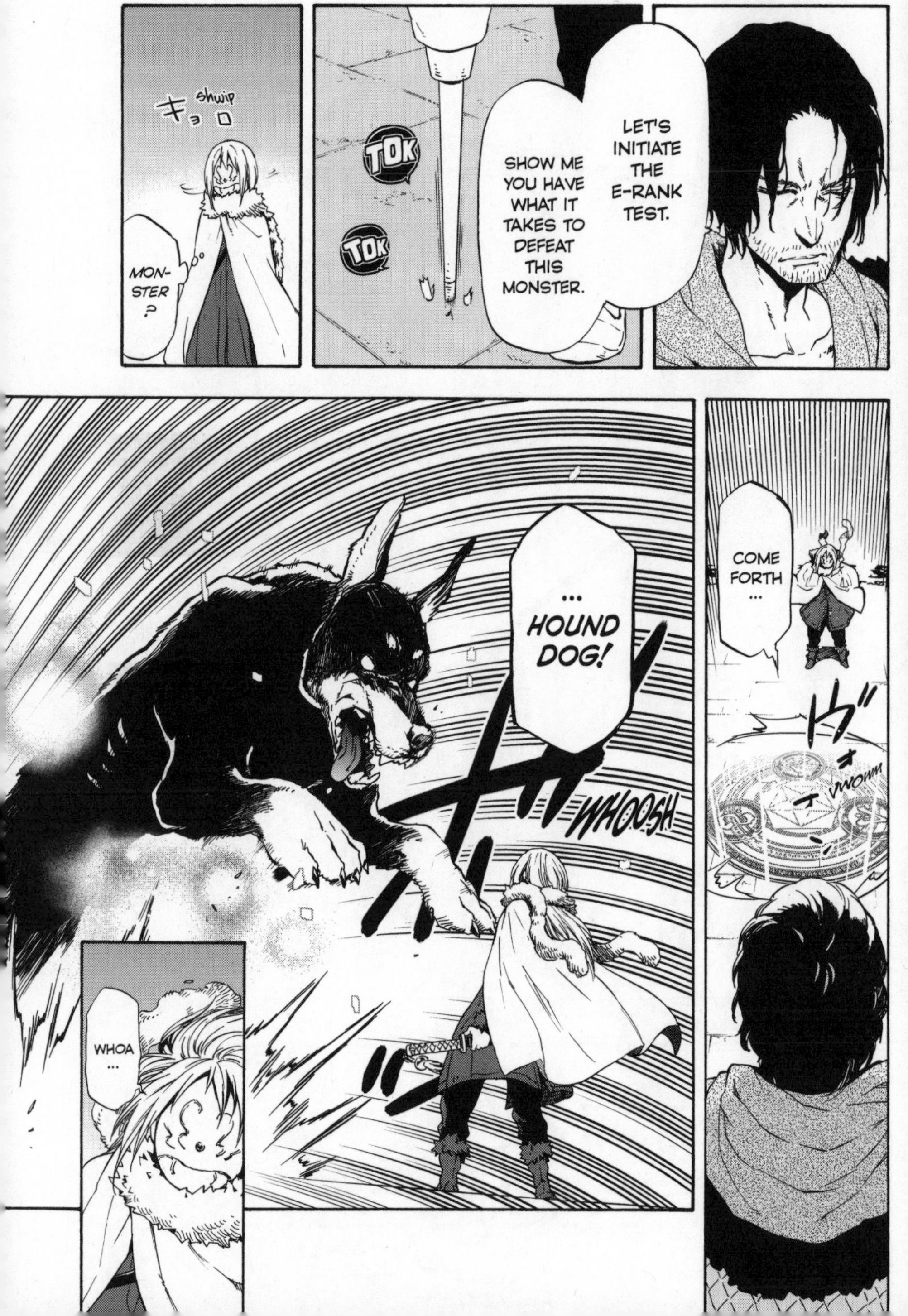
LET'S INITIATE THE E-RANK TEST.
SHOW ME YOU HAVE WHAT IT TAKES TO DEFEAT THIS MONSTER.
TOK
TOK
キョロ
shwip
MON-STER?
COME FORTH...
VWOWM
...HOUND DOG!
WHOOSH
WHOA...

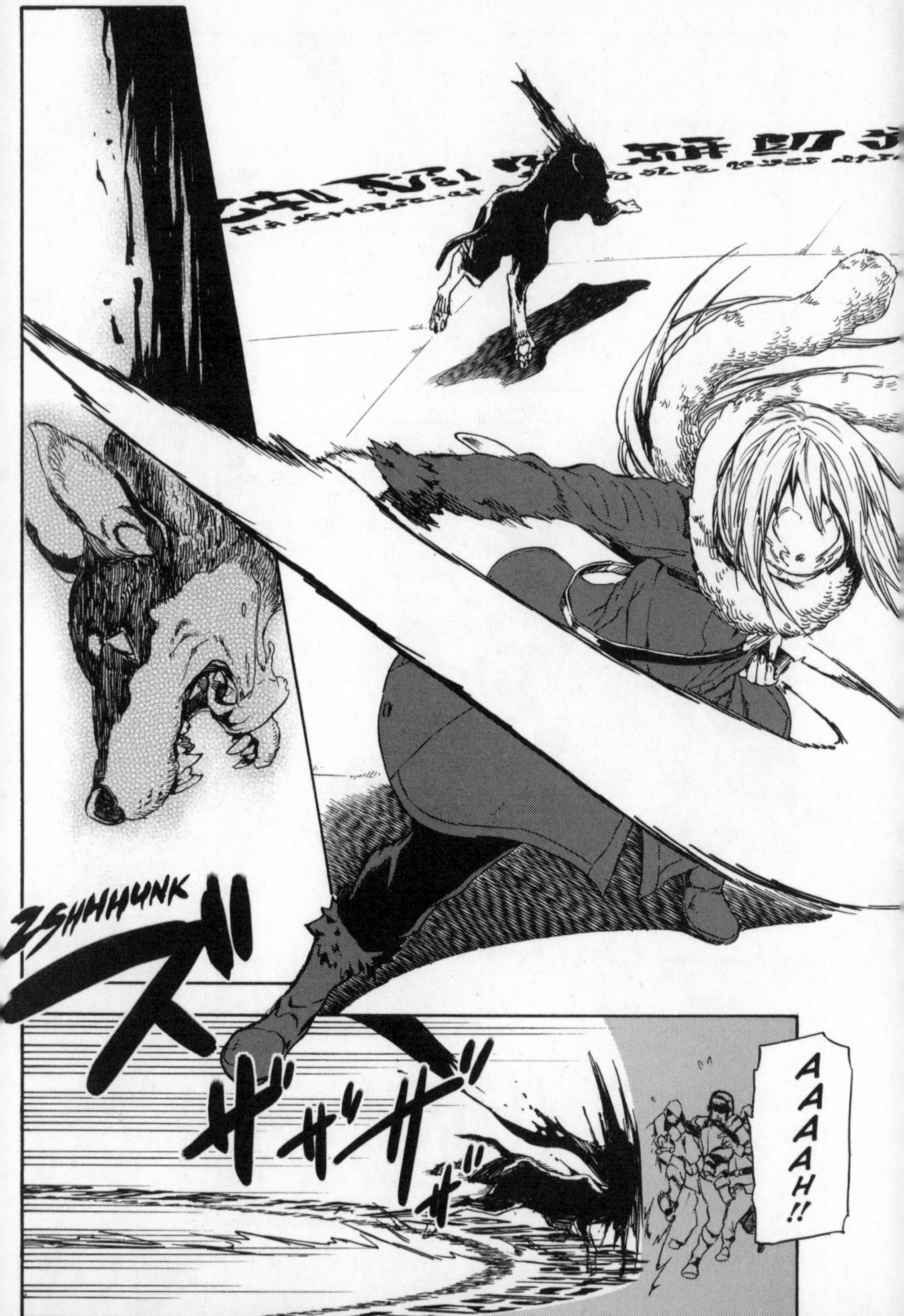
ZSHHHUNK
ズ
AAAAH!!
ザザザザ

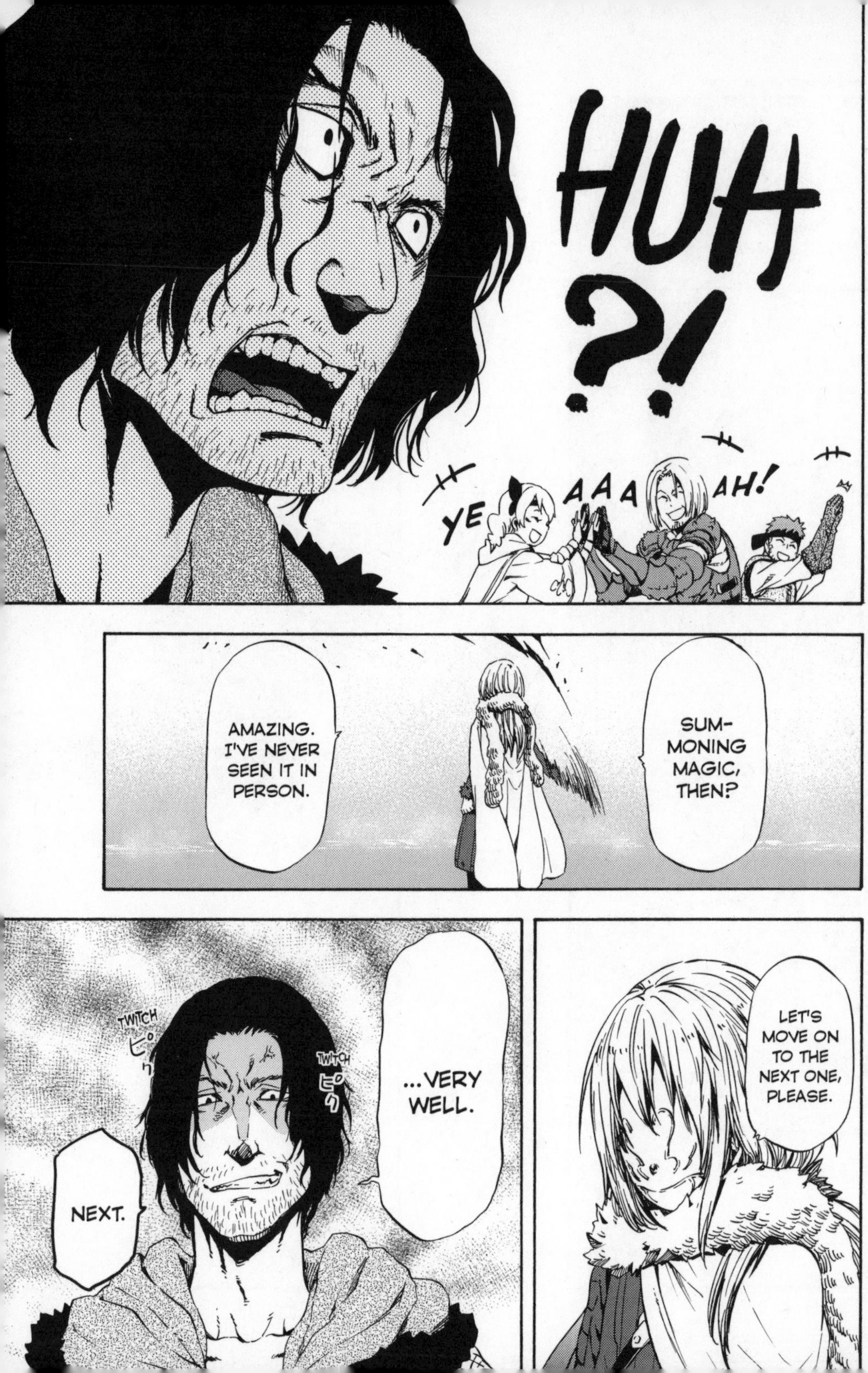
HUH?!
YEAAAAAH!
SUM-MONING MAGIC, THEN?
AMAZING. I'VE NEVER SEEN IT IN PERSON.
LET'S MOVE ON TO THE NEXT ONE, PLEASE.
TWITCH
ピク
...VERY WELL.
TWITCH
ピク
NEXT.

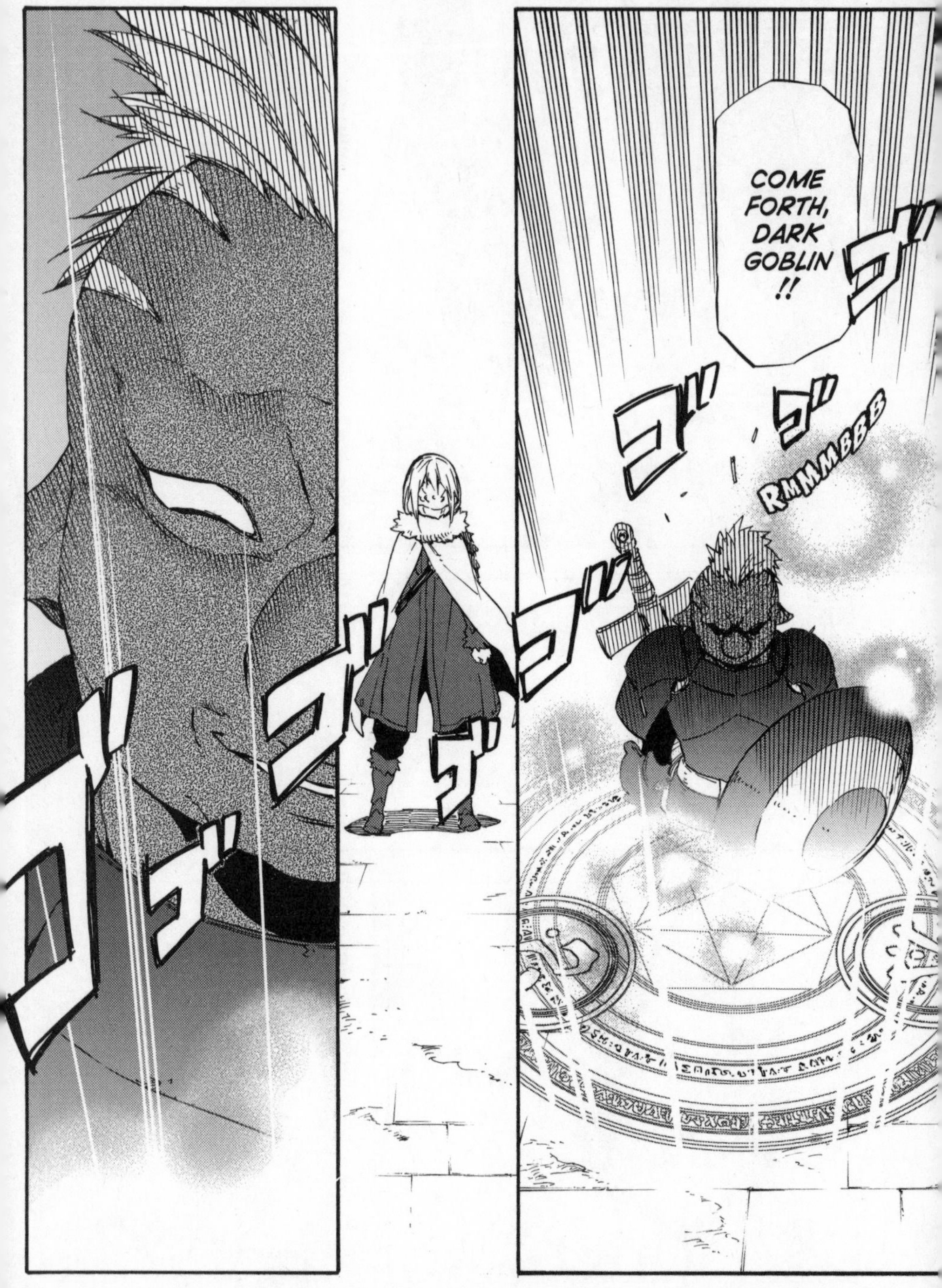
COME FORTH, DARK GOBLIN !!
RMMMBBB

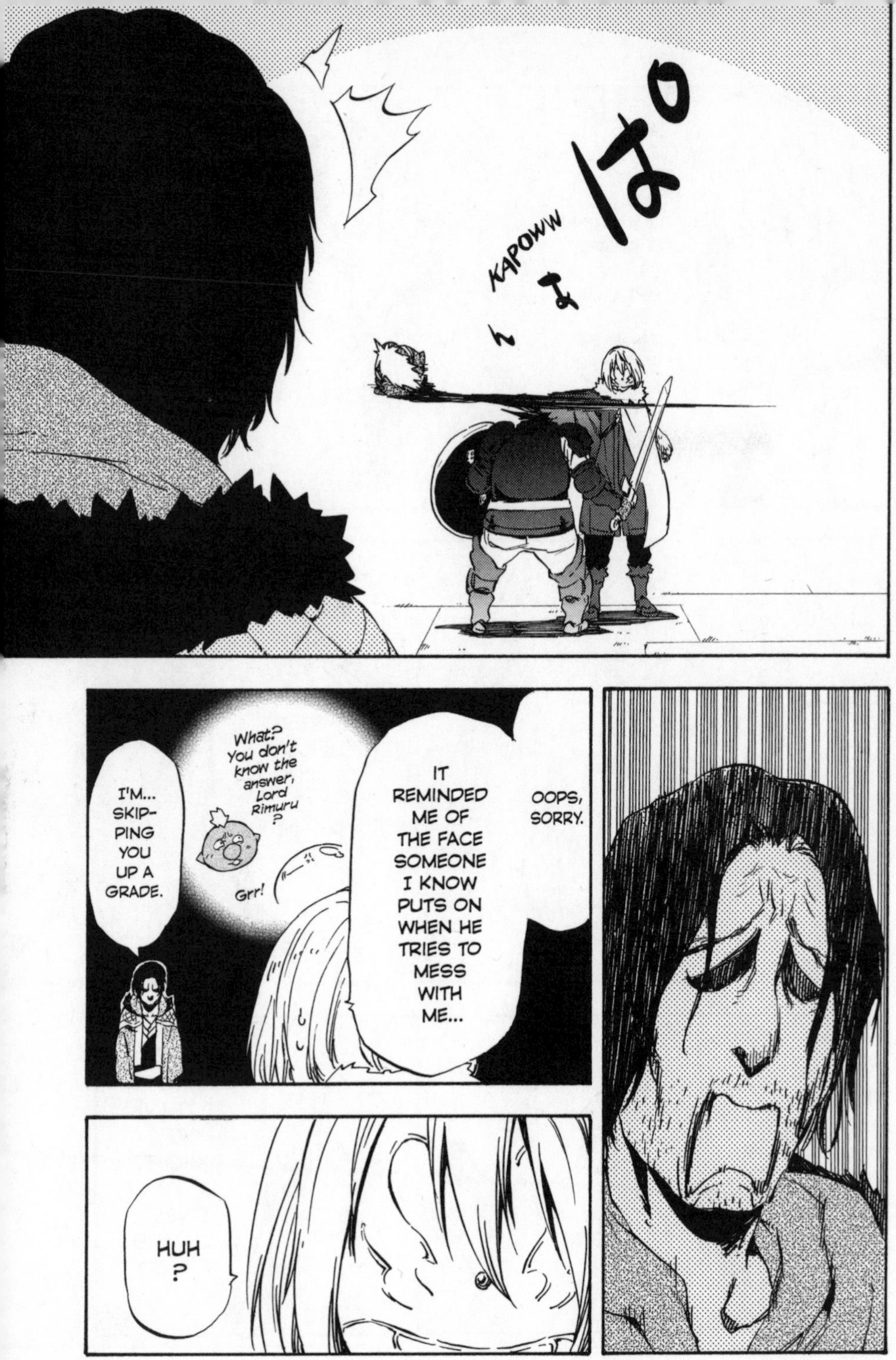
KAPOWW
OOPS, SORRY.
IT REMINDED ME OF THE FACE SOMEONE I KNOW PUTS ON WHEN HE TRIES TO MESS WITH ME...
What? You don't know the answer, Lord Rimuru?
Grr!
I'M... SKIPPING YOU UP A GRADE.
HUH?

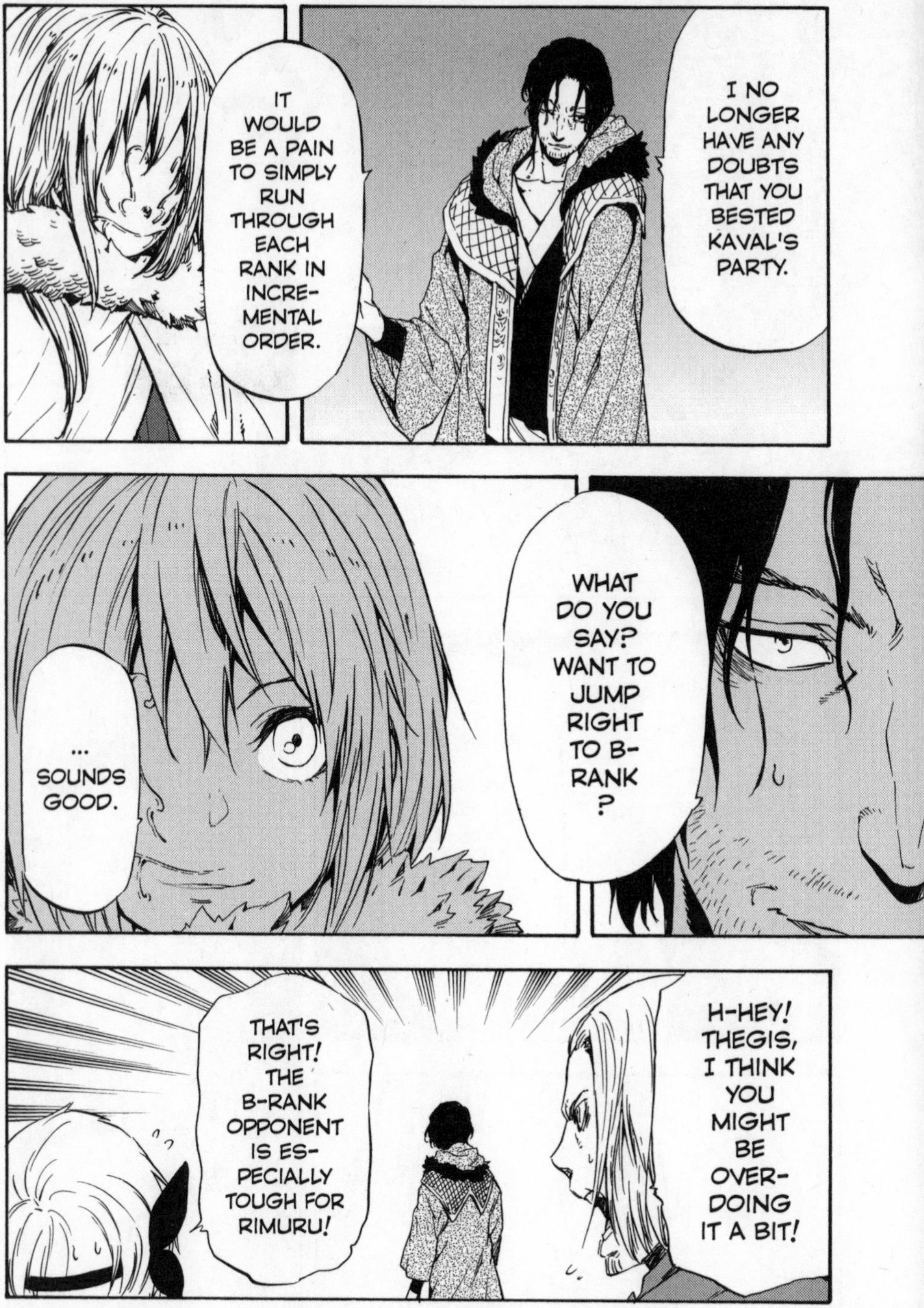
I NO LONGER HAVE ANY DOUBTS THAT YOU BESTED KAVAL'S PARTY.
IT WOULD BE A PAIN TO SIMPLY RUN THROUGH EACH RANK IN INCRE-MENTAL ORDER.
WHAT DO YOU SAY? WANT TO JUMP RIGHT TO B-RANK ?
... SOUNDS GOOD.
H-HEY! THEGIS, I THINK YOU MIGHT BE OVER-DOING IT A BIT!
THAT'S RIGHT! THE B-RANK OPPONENT IS ES-PECIALLY TOUGH FOR RIMURU!

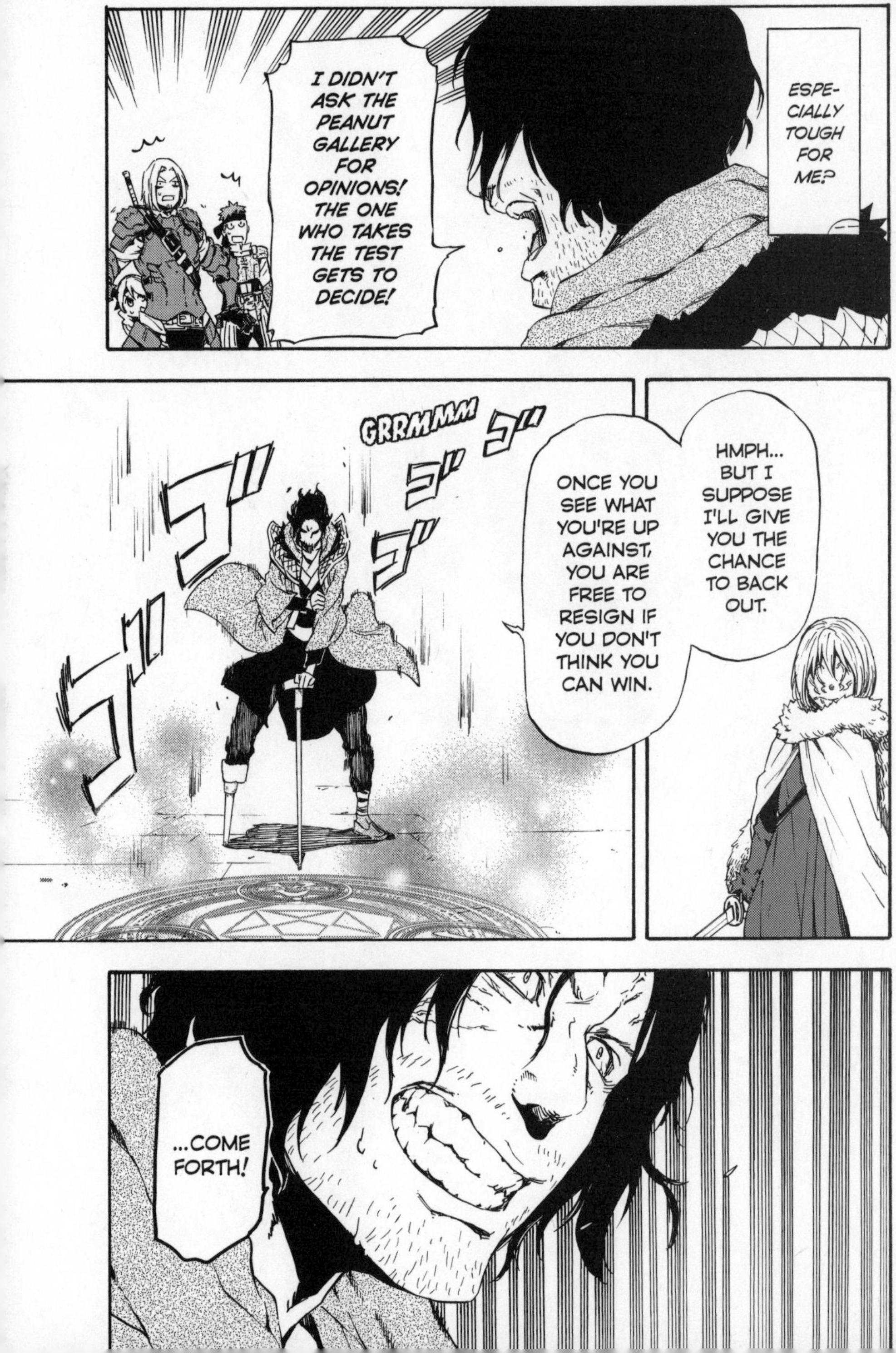
ESPE-CIALLY TOUGH FOR ME?
I DIDN'T ASK THE PEANUT GALLERY FOR OPINIONS! THE ONE WHO TAKES THE TEST GETS TO DECIDE!
HMPH... BUT I SUPPOSE I'LL GIVE YOU THE CHANCE TO BACK OUT.
ONCE YOU SEE WHAT YOU'RE UP AGAINST, YOU ARE FREE TO RESIGN IF YOU DON'T THINK YOU CAN WIN.
GRRMMM
...COME FORTH!

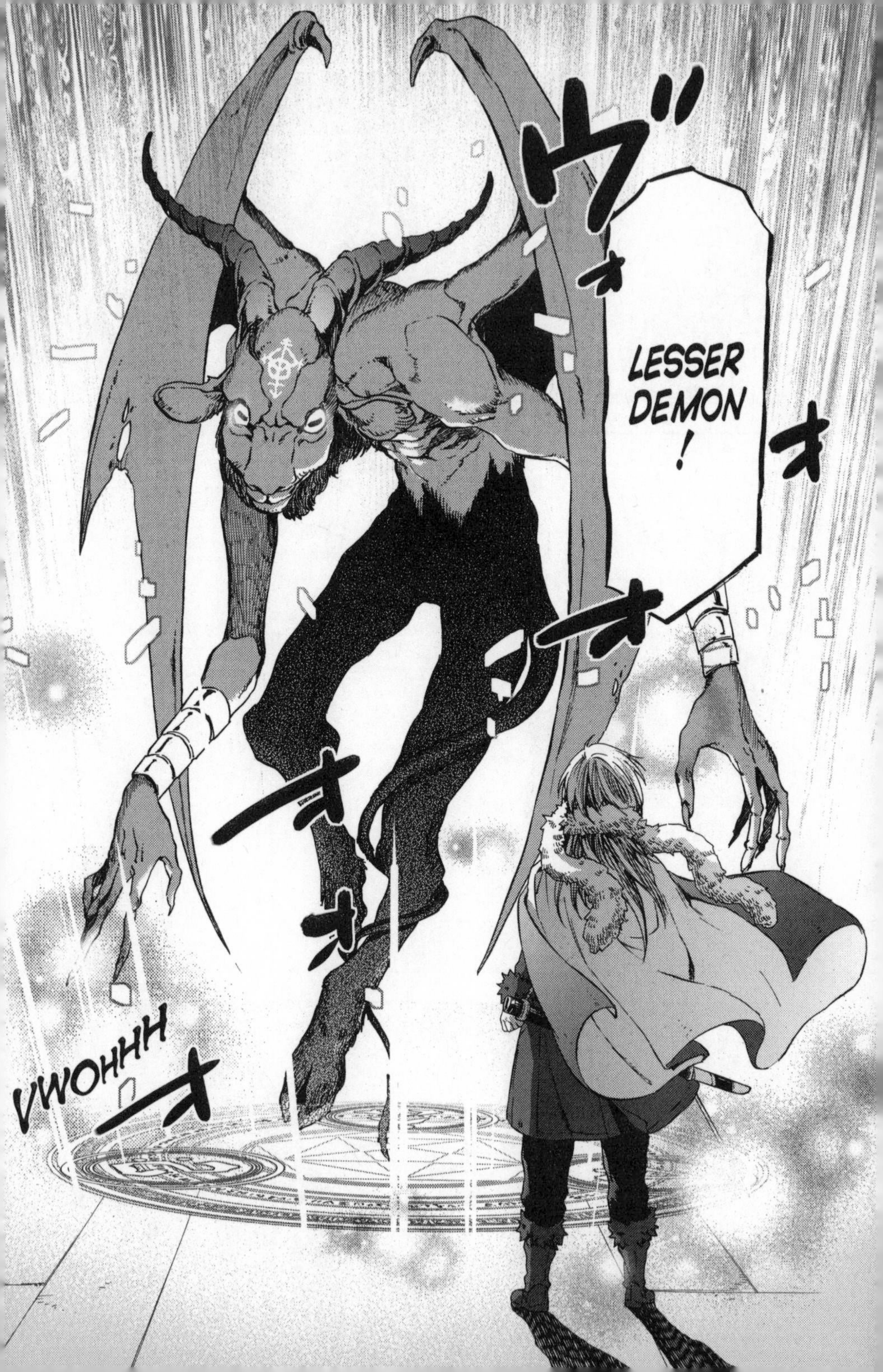
LESSER DEMON!
VWOHHH

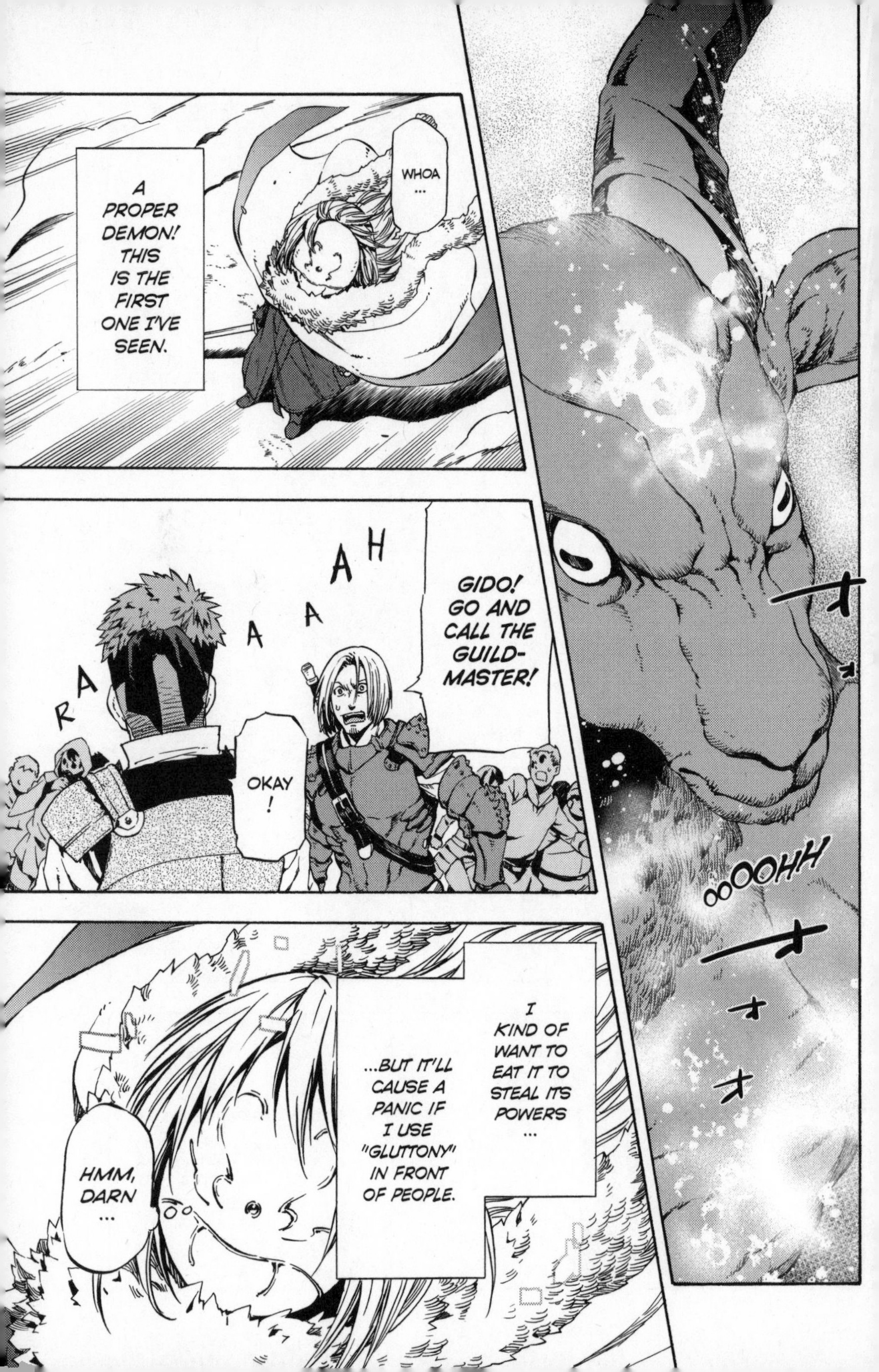
ooOOHH
WHOA ...
A PROPER DEMON! THIS IS THE FIRST ONE I'VE SEEN.
GIDO! GO AND CALL THE GUILD-MASTER!
RAAAAH
OKAY!
I KIND OF WANT TO EAT IT TO STEAL ITS POWERS ...
...BUT IT'LL CAUSE A PANIC IF I USE "GLUTTONY" IN FRONT OF PEOPLE.
HMM, DARN ...

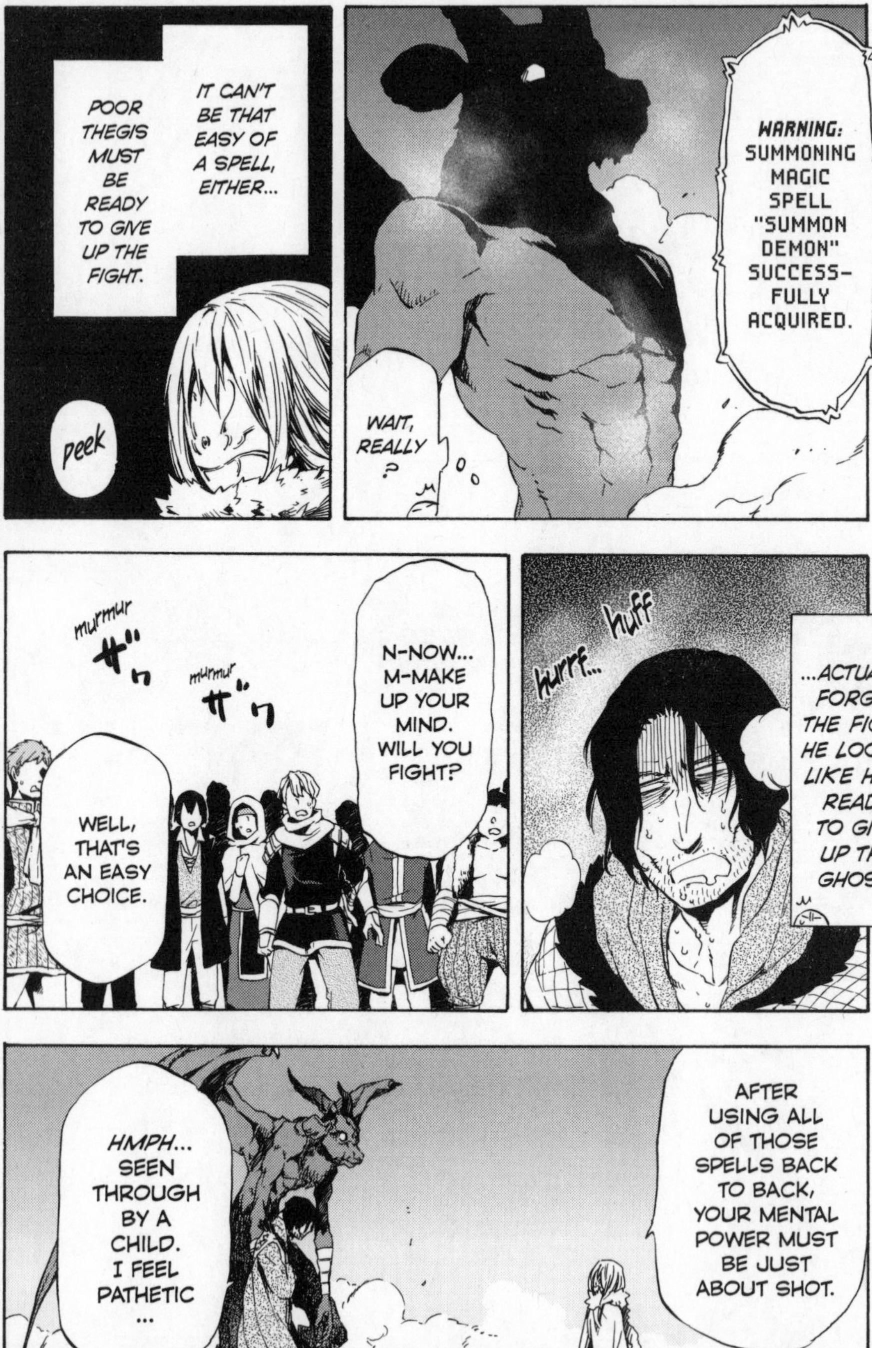
WARNING: SUMMONING MAGIC SPELL "SUMMON DEMON" SUCCESSFULLY ACQUIRED.
...
WAIT, REALLY?
IT CAN'T BE THAT EASY OF A SPELL, EITHER...
POOR THEGIS MUST BE READY TO GIVE UP THE FIGHT.
peek
huff
hurff...
...ACTUALLY, FORGET THE FIGHT. HE LOOKS LIKE HE'S READY TO GIVE UP THE GHOST!
N-NOW... M-MAKE UP YOUR MIND. WILL YOU FIGHT?
murmur
murmur
WELL, THAT'S AN EASY CHOICE.
AFTER USING ALL OF THOSE SPELLS BACK TO BACK, YOUR MENTAL POWER MUST BE JUST ABOUT SHOT.
HMPH... SEEN THROUGH BY A CHILD. I FEEL PATHETIC...

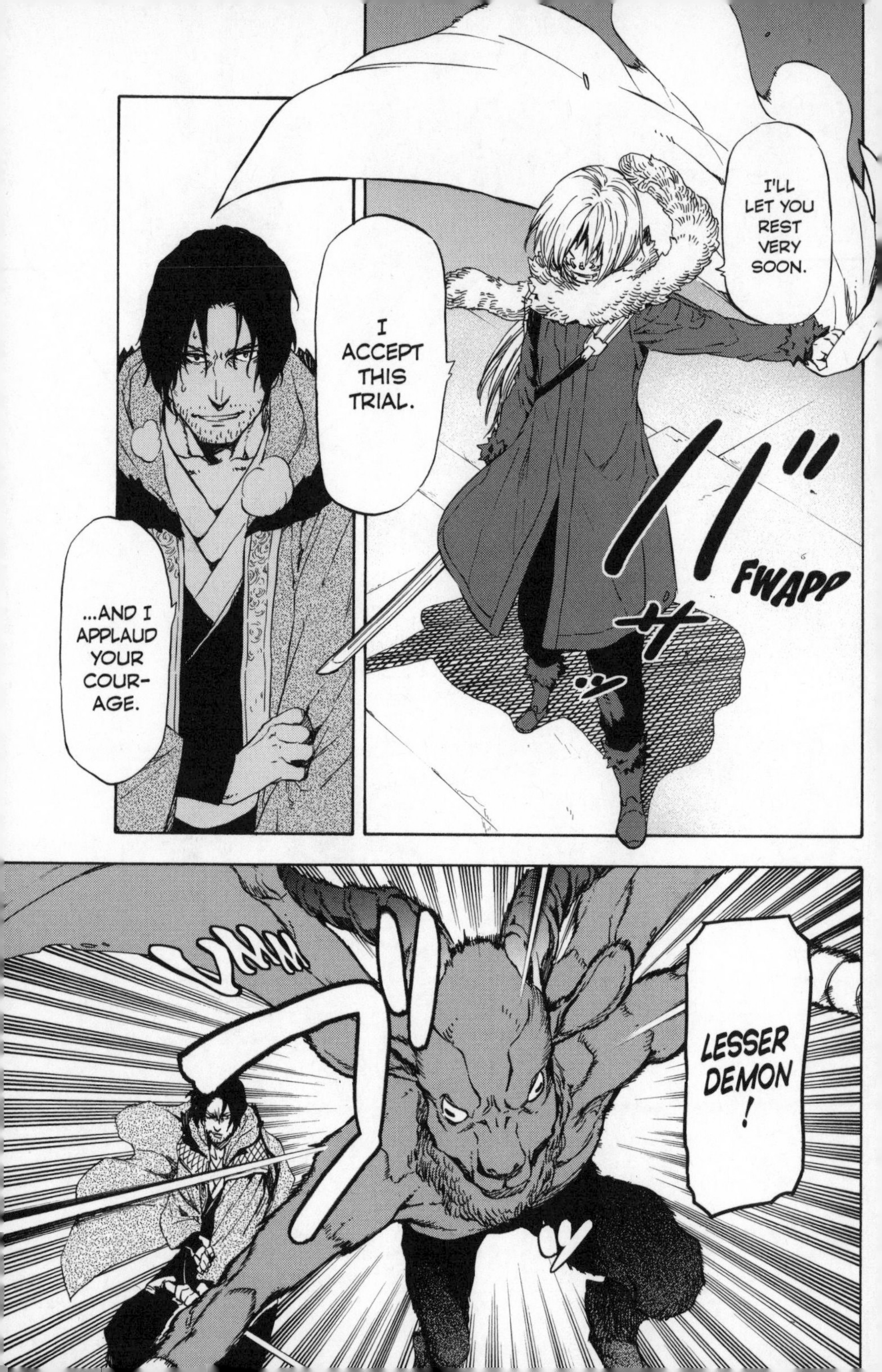
I'LL LET YOU REST VERY SOON.
FWAPP
I ACCEPT THIS TRIAL.
...AND I APPLAUD YOUR COURAGE.
LESSER DEMON!

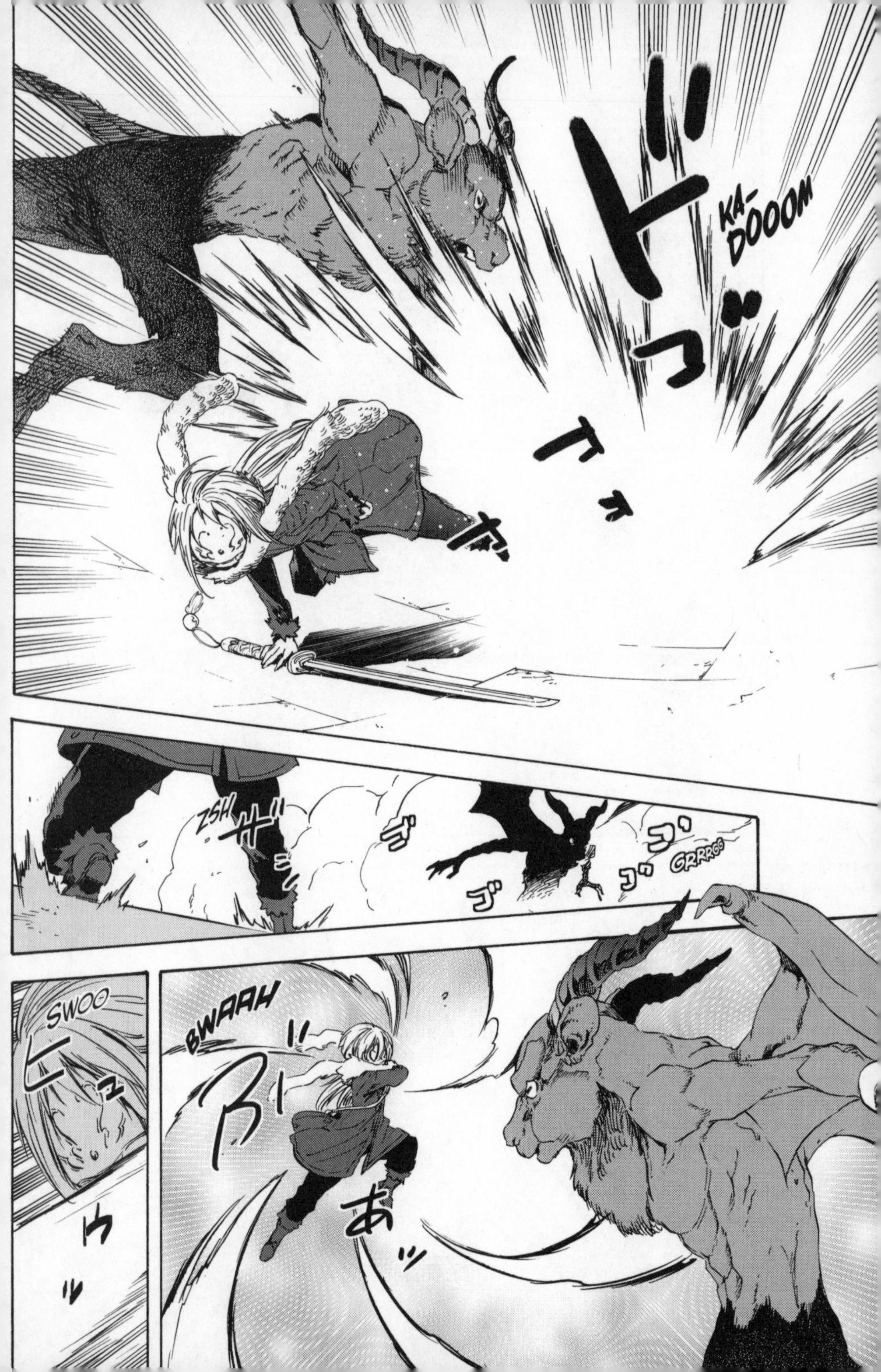

ドゴッ
KA-DOOOM
ZSH
GRRRGG
BWAAH
あッ
SWOO

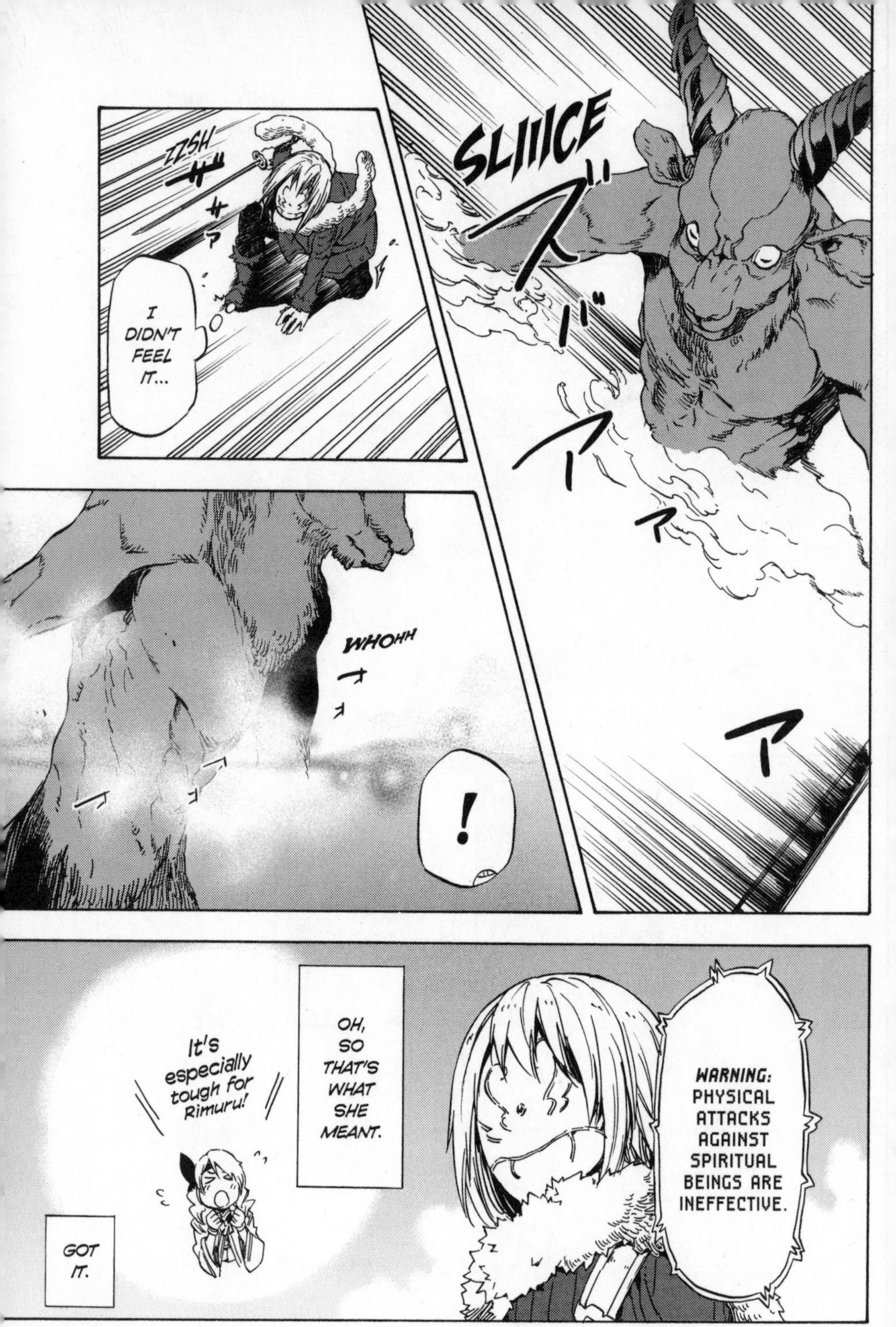
SLIIICE
ZZSH
I DIDN'T FEEL IT...
WHOHH
!
WARNING: PHYSICAL ATTACKS AGAINST SPIRITUAL BEINGS ARE INEFFECTIVE.
OH, SO THAT'S WHAT SHE MEANT.
It's especially tough for Rimuru!
GOT IT.

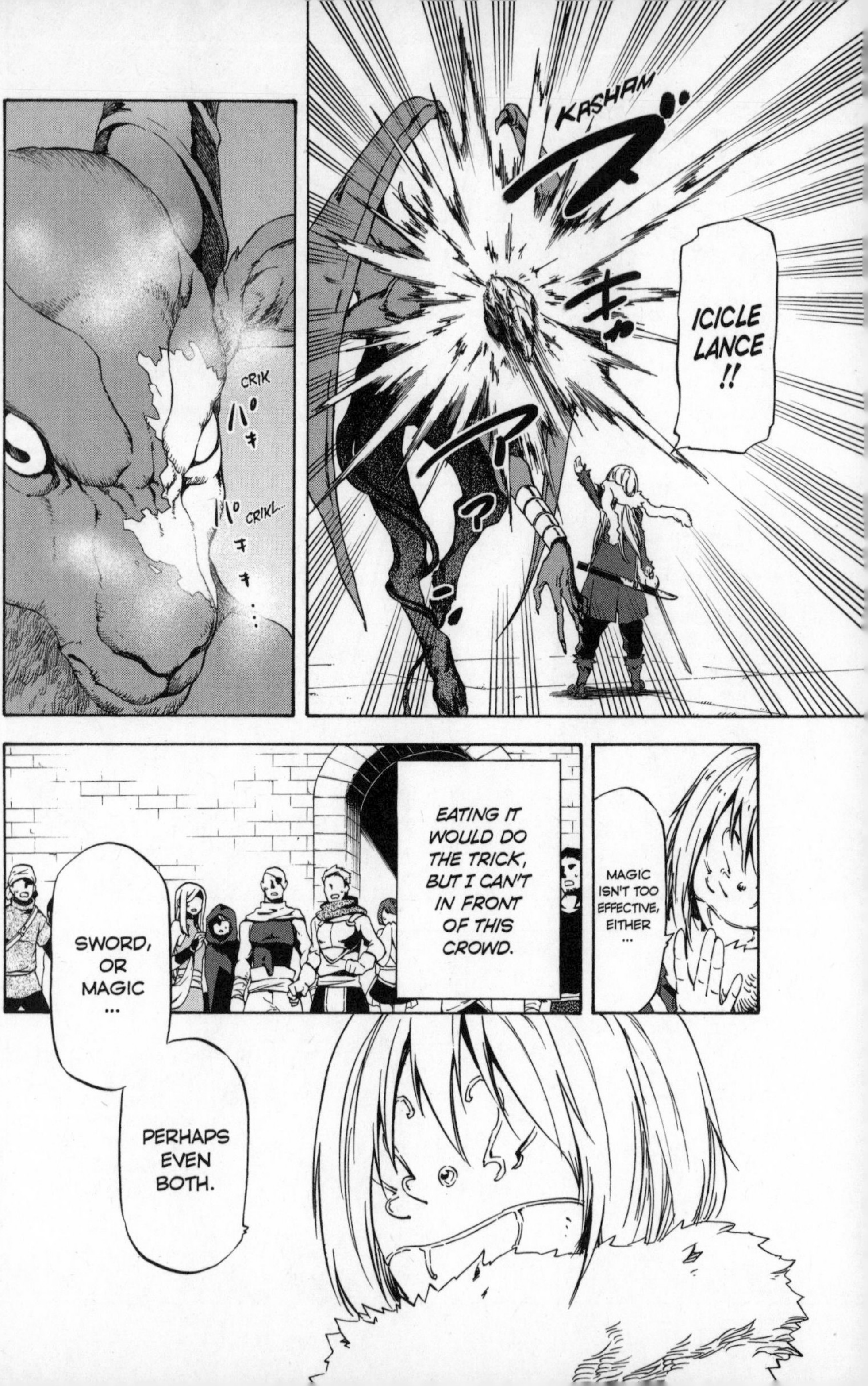
KASHAM
ICICLE LANCE !!
CRIK
CRIKL...
MAGIC ISN'T TOO EFFECTIVE, EITHER ...
EATING IT WOULD DO THE TRICK, BUT I CAN'T IN FRONT OF THIS CROWD.
SWORD, OR MAGIC ...
PERHAPS EVEN BOTH.

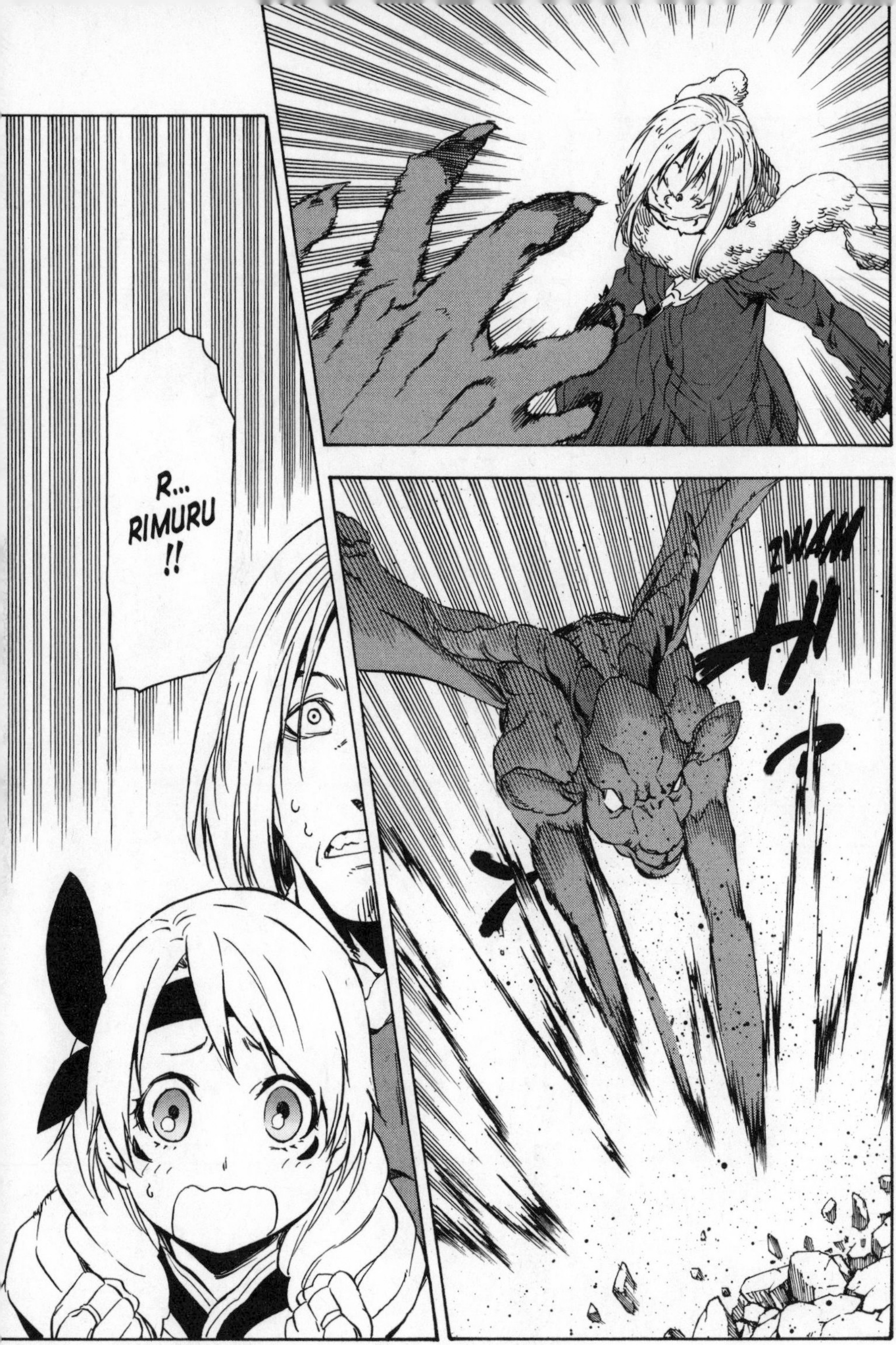
ZWAM
R... RIMURU !!

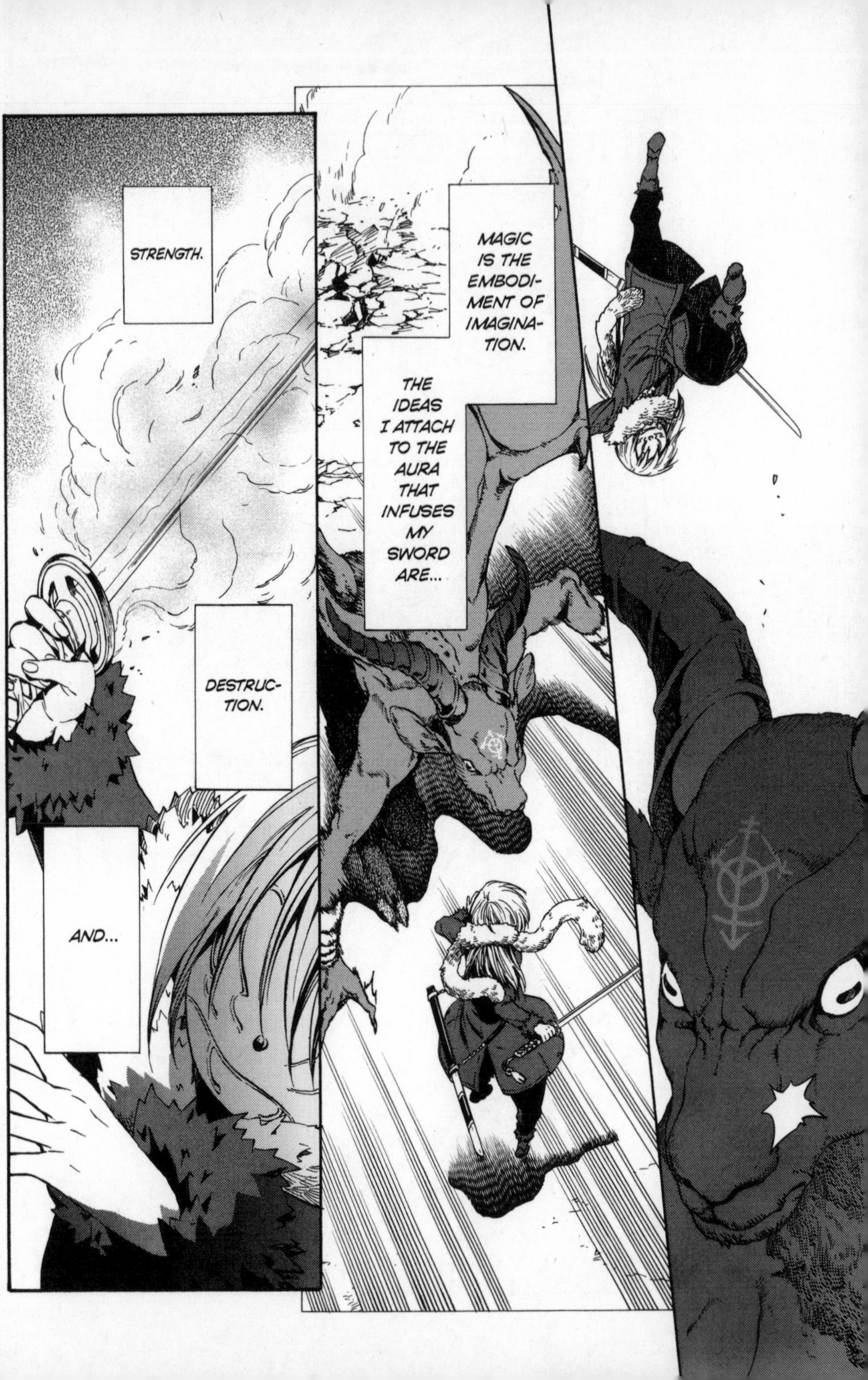
MAGIC IS THE EMBODIMENT OF IMAGINATION.
THE IDEAS I ATTACH TO THE AURA THAT INFUSES MY SWORD ARE...
STRENGTH.
DESTRUCTION.
AND...

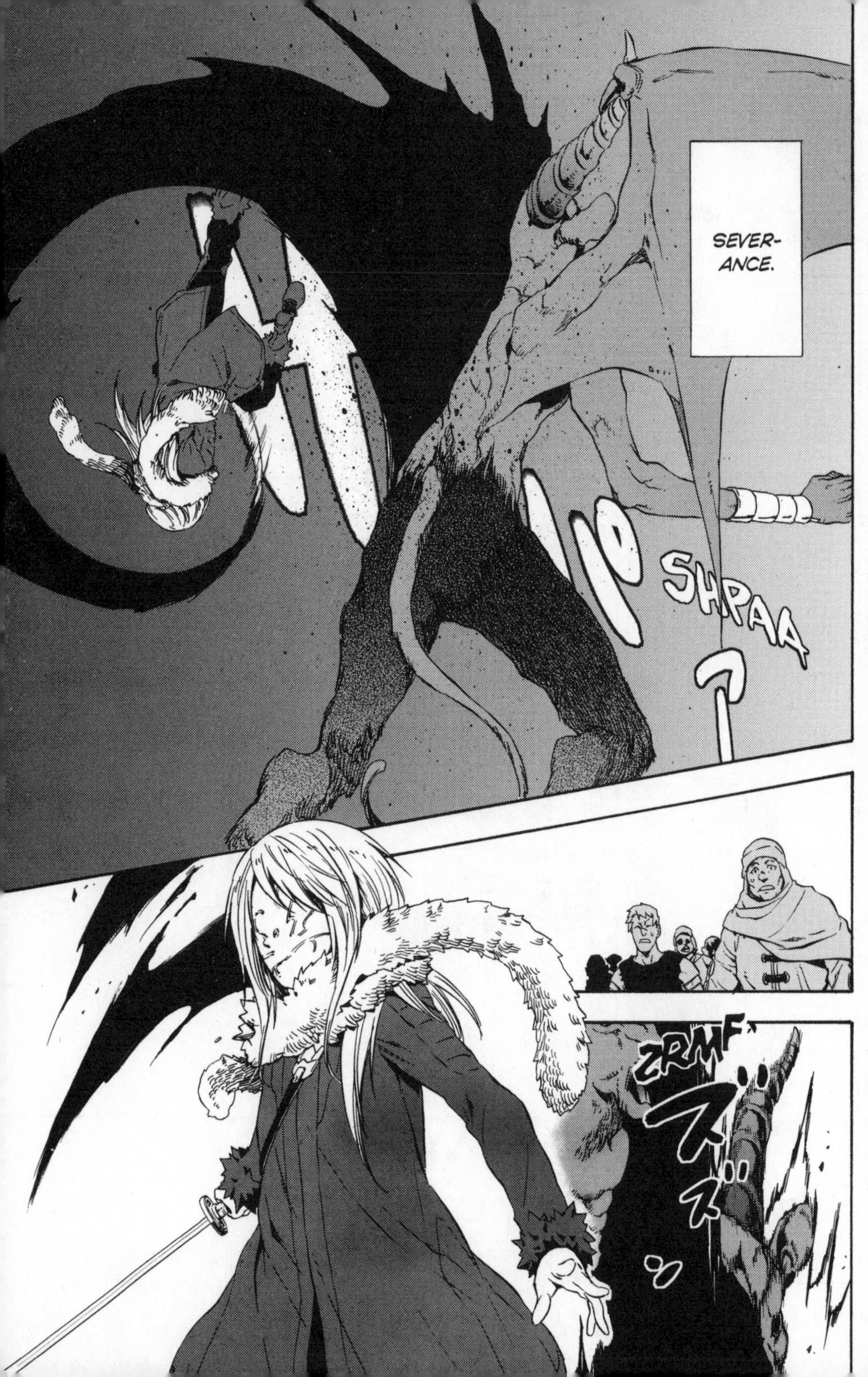
SEVER-
ANCE.
SHPAA
ZRMF

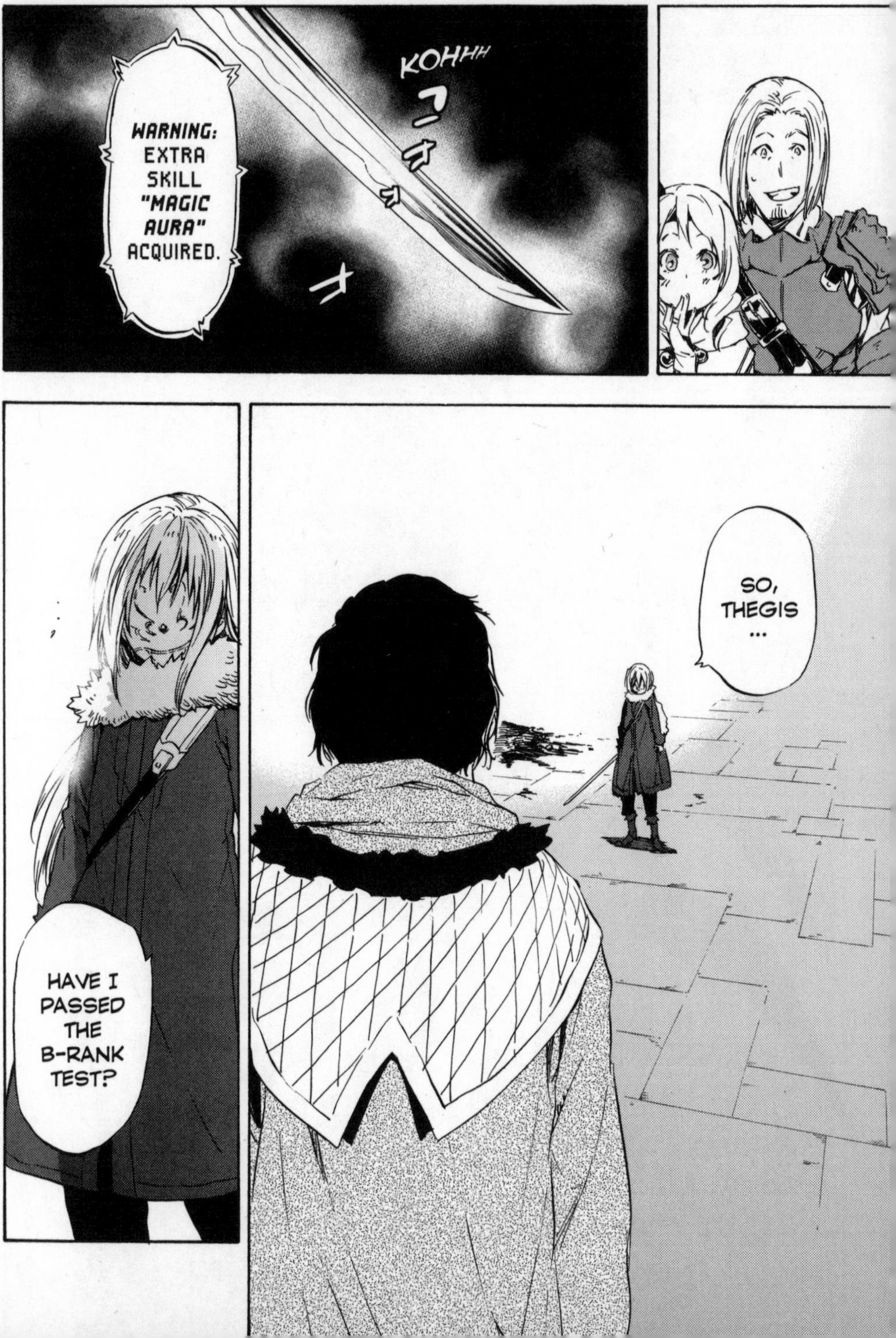
KOHHH
WARNING: EXTRA SKILL "MAGIC AURA" ACQUIRED.
SO, THEGIS ...
HAVE I PASSED THE B-RANK TEST?

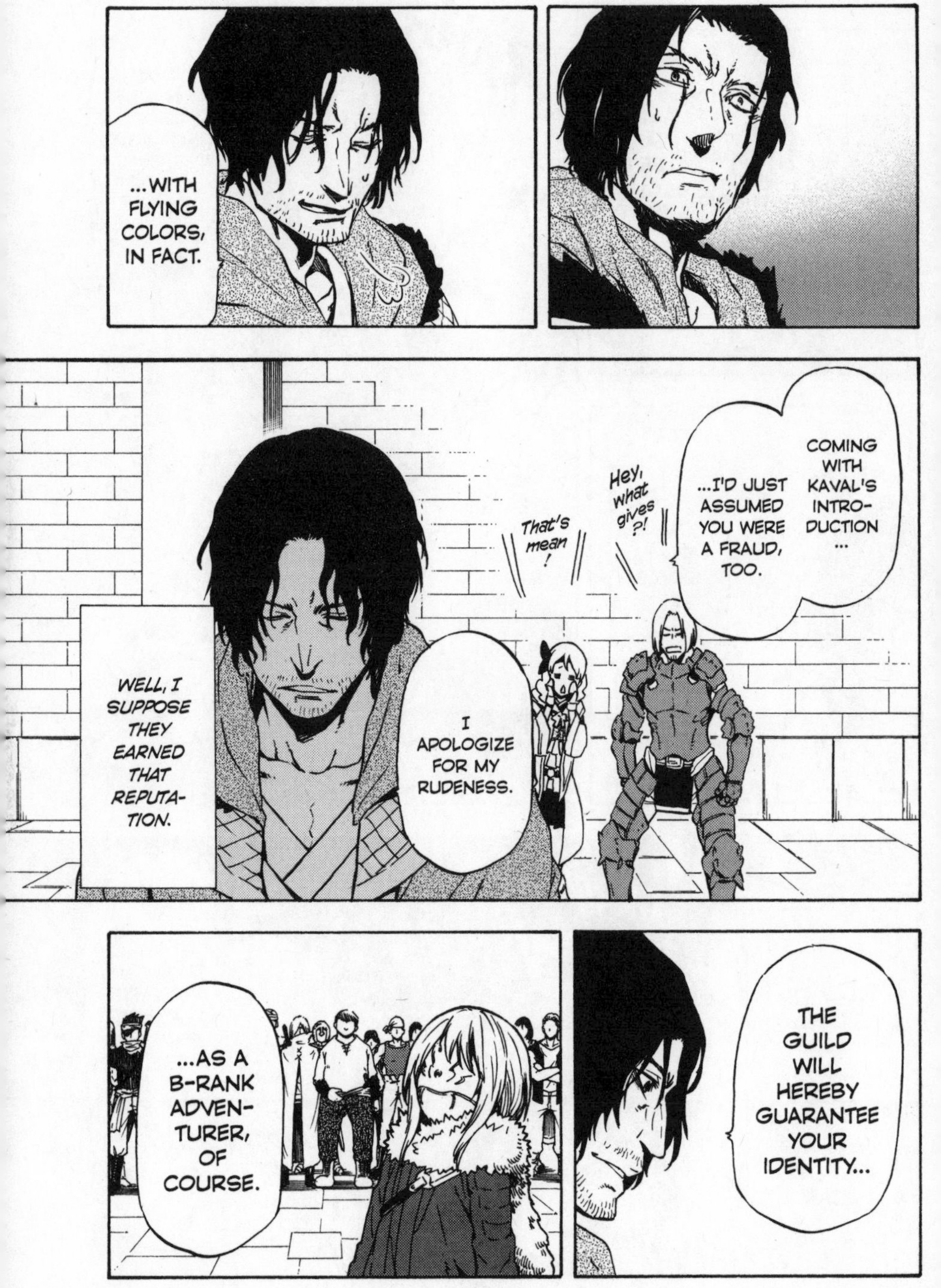
...WITH FLYING COLORS, IN FACT.
COMING WITH KAVAL'S INTRO-DUCTION...
...I'D JUST ASSUMED YOU WERE A FRAUD, TOO.
Hey, what gives?!
That's mean!
I APOLOGIZE FOR MY RUDENESS.
WELL, I SUPPOSE THEY EARNED THAT REPUTA-TION.
THE GUILD WILL HEREBY GUARANTEE YOUR IDENTITY...
...AS A B-RANK ADVEN-TURER, OF COURSE.

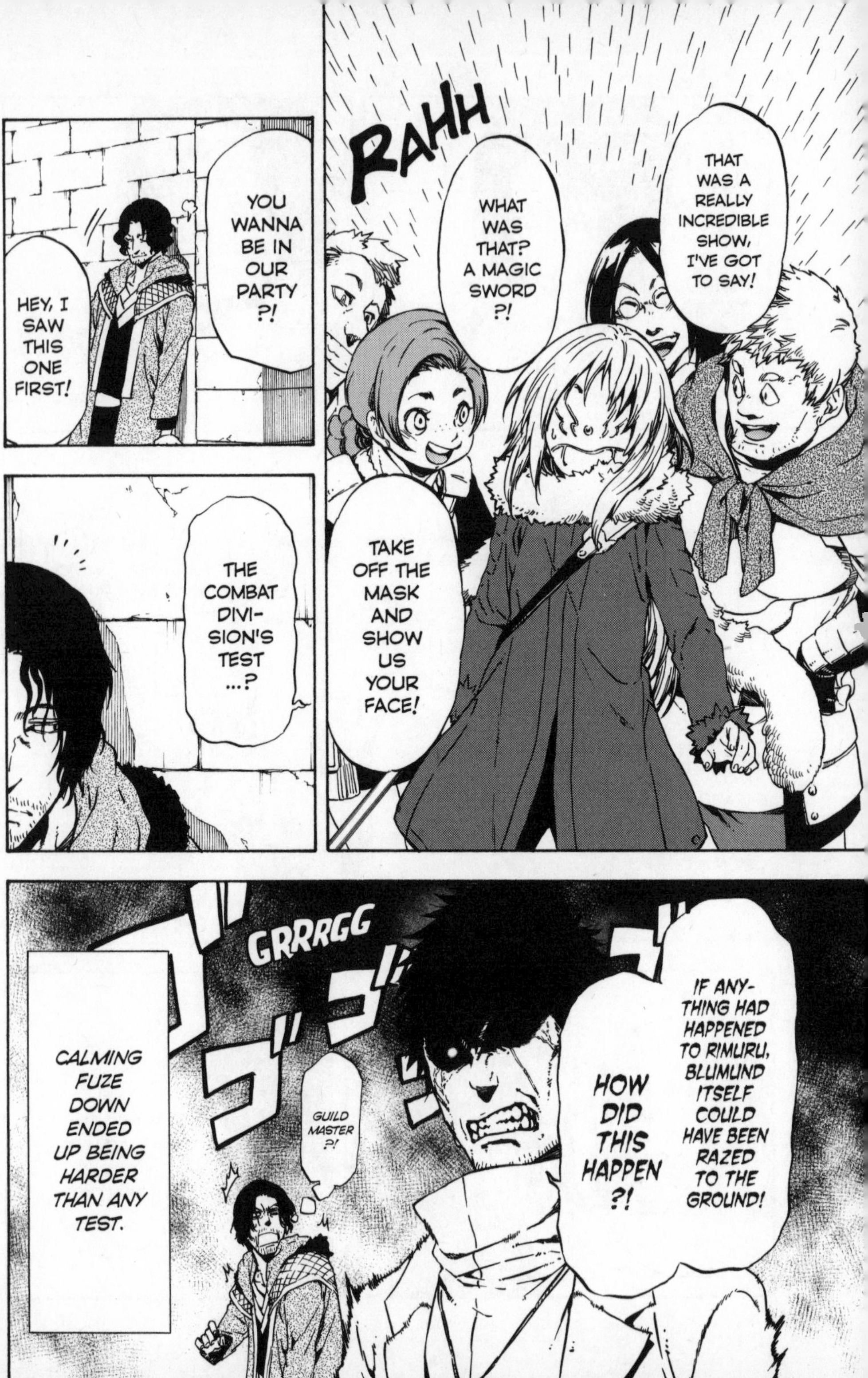
THAT WAS A REALLY INCREDIBLE SHOW, I'VE GOT TO SAY!
WHAT WAS THAT? A MAGIC SWORD?!
RAHH
TAKE OFF THE MASK AND SHOW US YOUR FACE!
YOU WANNA BE IN OUR PARTY?!
HEY, I SAW THIS ONE FIRST!
THE COMBAT DIVI-SION'S TEST ...?
IF ANY-THING HAD HAPPENED TO RIMURU, BLUMUND ITSELF COULD HAVE BEEN RAZED TO THE GROUND!
HOW DID THIS HAPPEN?!
GRRRGG
GUILD MASTER?!
CALMING FUZE DOWN ENDED UP BEING HARDER THAN ANY TEST.

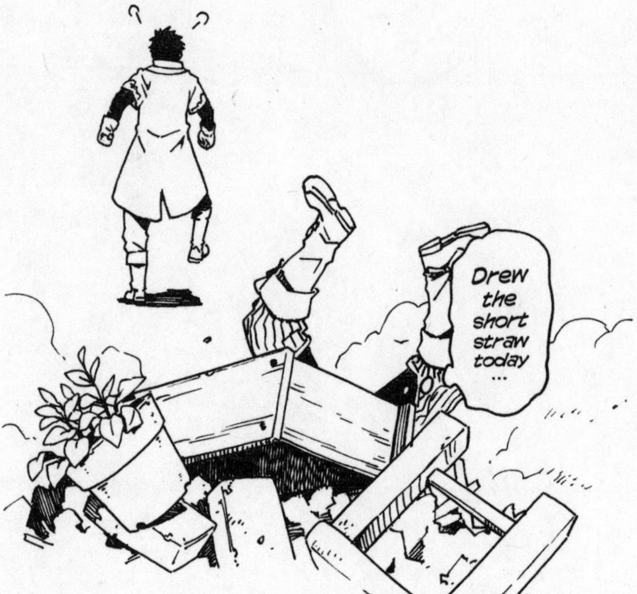
Drew the short straw today ...

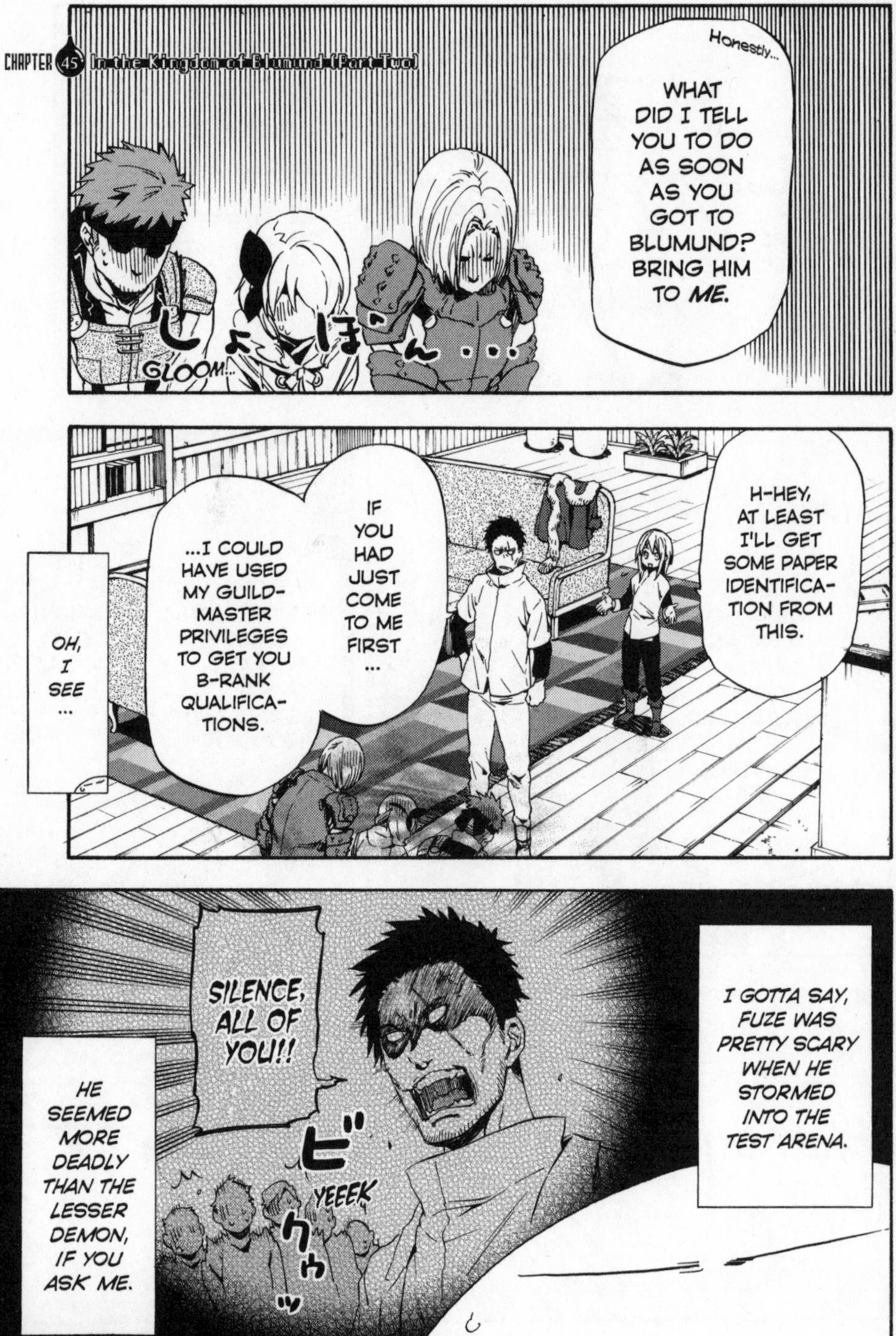
CHAPTER 45 In the Kingdom of Blumund (Part Two)
Honestly...
WHAT DID I TELL YOU TO DO AS SOON AS YOU GOT TO BLUMUND? BRING HIM TO ME.
しょぼん...
GLOOM...
H-HEY, AT LEAST I'LL GET SOME PAPER IDENTIFICATION FROM THIS.
IF YOU HAD JUST COME TO ME FIRST...
...I COULD HAVE USED MY GUILD-MASTER PRIVILEGES TO GET YOU B-RANK QUALIFICATIONS.
OH, I SEE...
I GOTTA SAY, FUZE WAS PRETTY SCARY WHEN HE STORMED INTO THE TEST ARENA.
SILENCE, ALL OF YOU!!
ビクゥッ
YEEEK
HE SEEMED MORE DEADLY THAN THE LESSER DEMON, IF YOU ASK ME.

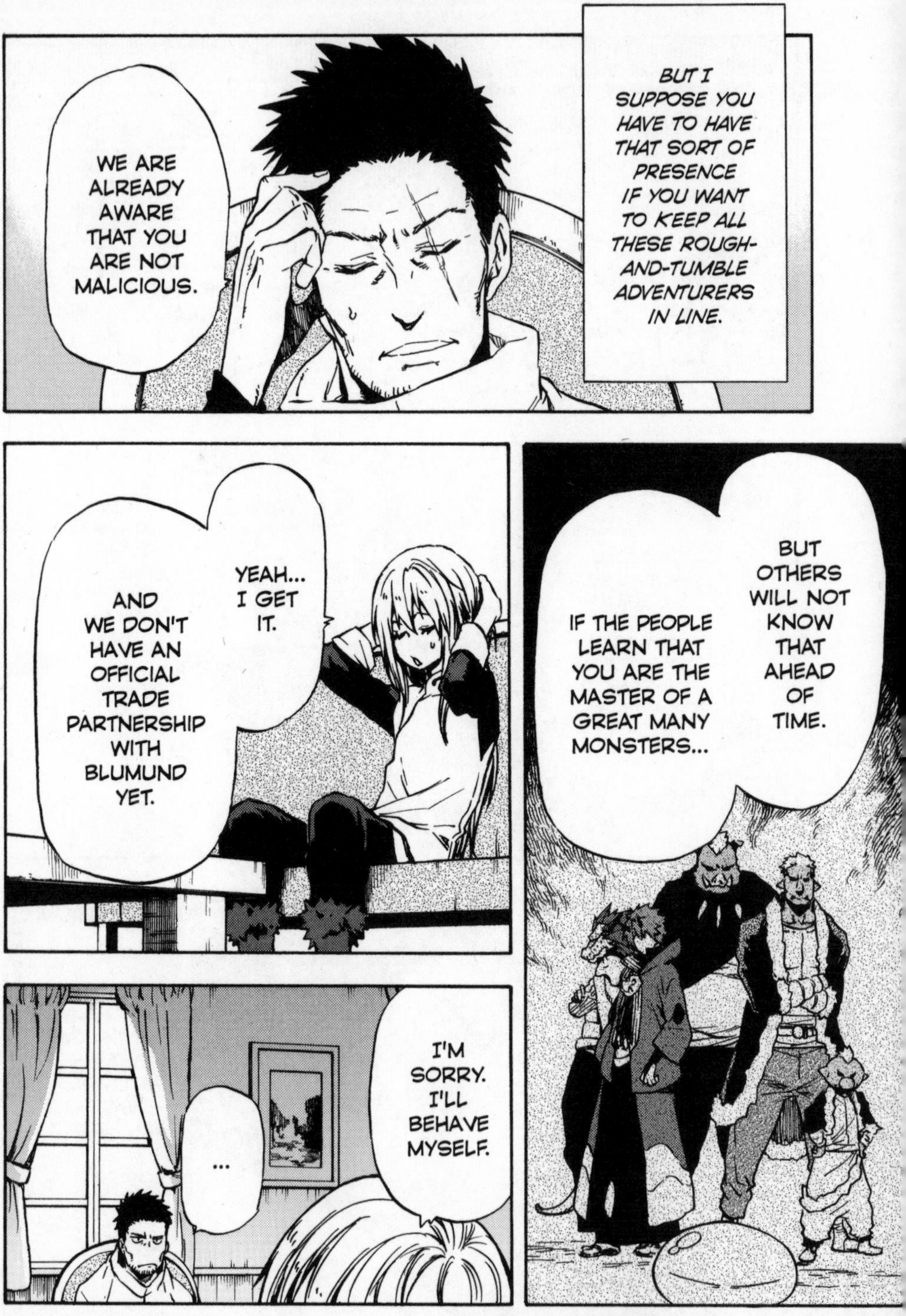
BUT I SUPPOSE YOU HAVE TO HAVE THAT SORT OF PRESENCE IF YOU WANT TO KEEP ALL THESE ROUGH-AND-TUMBLE ADVENTURERS IN LINE.
WE ARE ALREADY AWARE THAT YOU ARE NOT MALICIOUS.
BUT OTHERS WILL NOT KNOW THAT AHEAD OF TIME.
IF THE PEOPLE LEARN THAT YOU ARE THE MASTER OF A GREAT MANY MONSTERS...
AND WE DON'T HAVE AN OFFICIAL TRADE PARTNERSHIP WITH BLUMUND YET.
YEAH... I GET IT.
I'M SORRY. I'LL BEHAVE MYSELF.
...

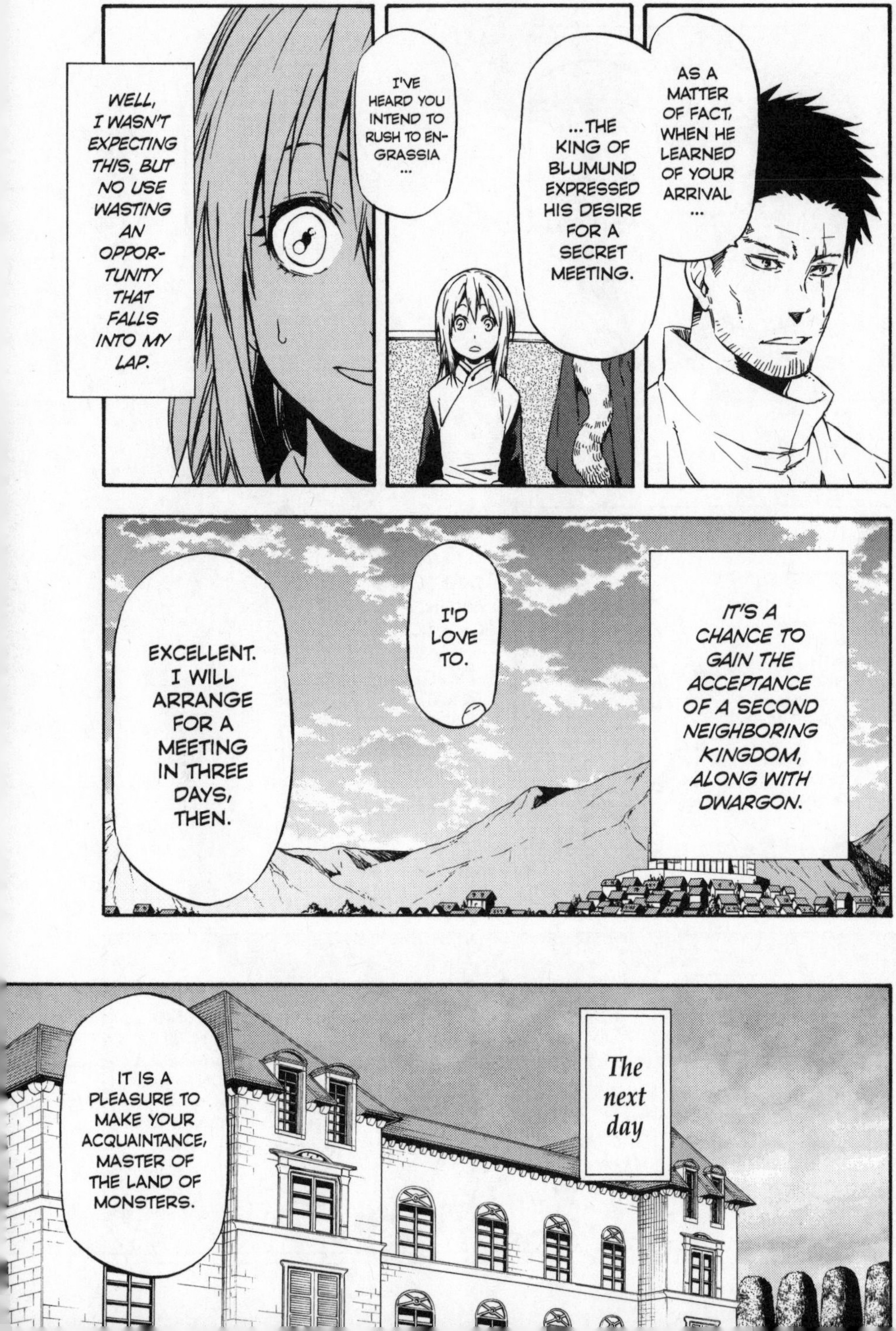

AS A MATTER OF FACT, WHEN HE LEARNED OF YOUR ARRIVAL ...
...THE KING OF BLUMUND EXPRESSED HIS DESIRE FOR A SECRET MEETING.
I'VE HEARD YOU INTEND TO RUSH TO EN-GRASSIA ...
WELL, I WASN'T EXPECTING THIS, BUT NO USE WASTING AN OPPOR-TUNITY THAT FALLS INTO MY LAP.
IT'S A CHANCE TO GAIN THE ACCEPTANCE OF A SECOND NEIGHBORING KINGDOM, ALONG WITH DWARGON.
I'D LOVE TO.
EXCELLENT. I WILL ARRANGE FOR A MEETING IN THREE DAYS, THEN.
The next day
IT IS A PLEASURE TO MAKE YOUR ACQUAINTANCE, MASTER OF THE LAND OF MONSTERS.

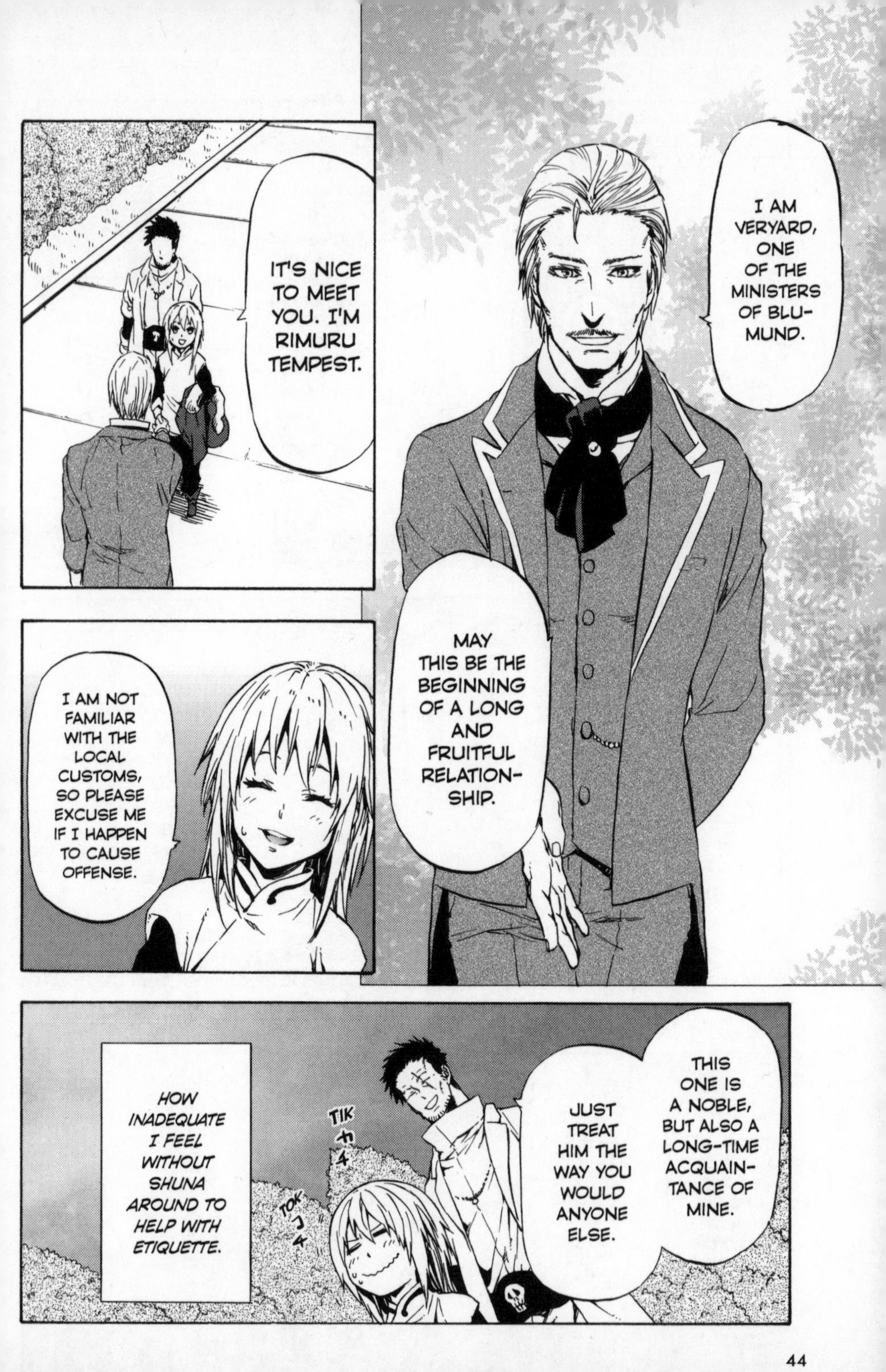
I AM VERYARD, ONE OF THE MINISTERS OF BLUMUND.
MAY THIS BE THE BEGINNING OF A LONG AND FRUITFUL RELATIONSHIP.
IT'S NICE TO MEET YOU. I'M RIMURU TEMPEST.
I AM NOT FAMILIAR WITH THE LOCAL CUSTOMS, SO PLEASE EXCUSE ME IF I HAPPEN TO CAUSE OFFENSE.
THIS ONE IS A NOBLE, BUT ALSO A LONG-TIME ACQUAINTANCE OF MINE.
JUST TREAT HIM THE WAY YOU WOULD ANYONE ELSE.
TIK
TOK
HOW INADEQUATE I FEEL WITHOUT SHUNA AROUND TO HELP WITH ETIQUETTE.

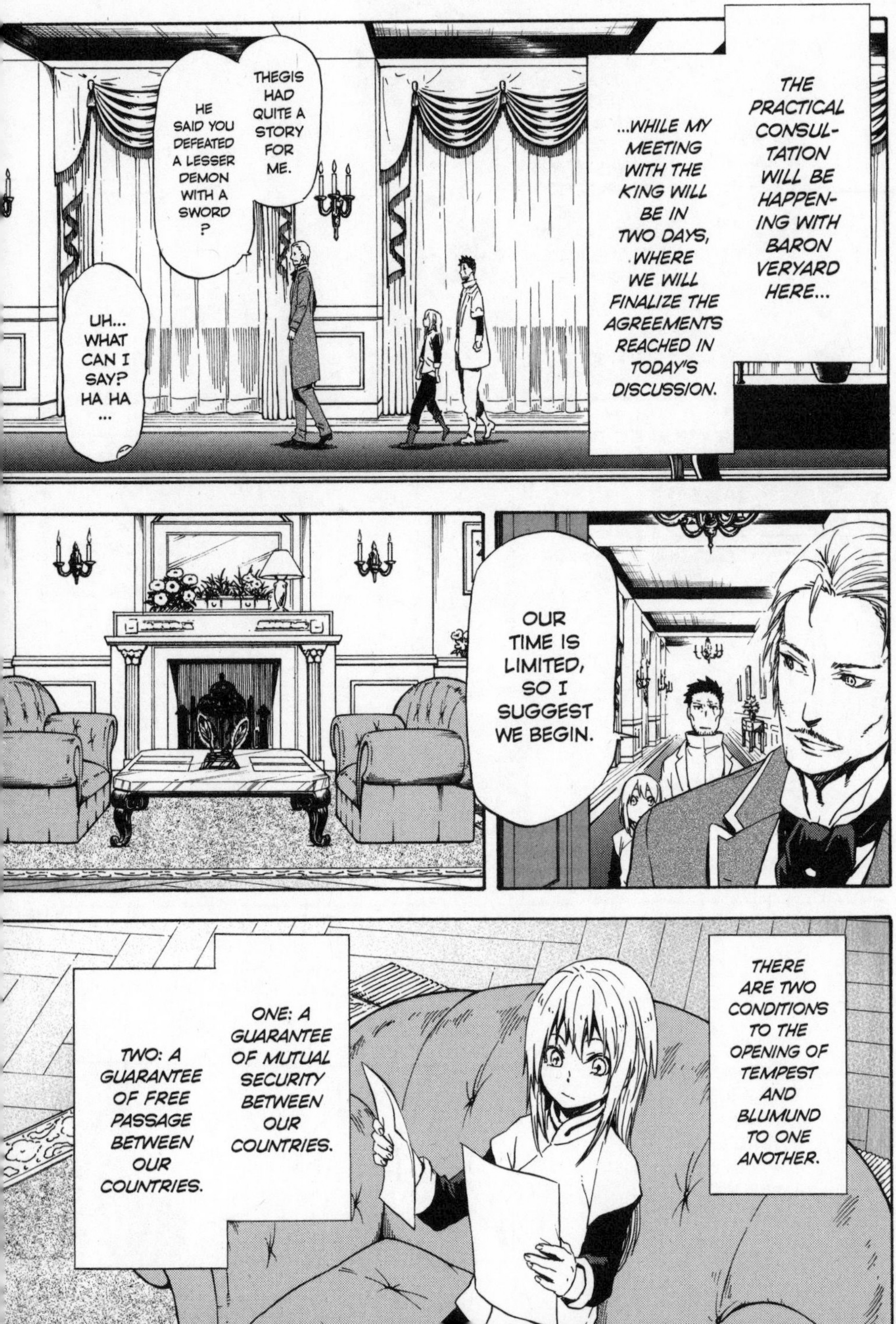
THE PRACTICAL CONSULTATION WILL BE HAPPENING WITH BARON VERYARD HERE...
...WHILE MY MEETING WITH THE KING WILL BE IN TWO DAYS, WHERE WE WILL FINALIZE THE AGREEMENTS REACHED IN TODAY'S DISCUSSION.
THEGIS HAD QUITE A STORY FOR ME.
HE SAID YOU DEFEATED A LESSER DEMON WITH A SWORD?
UH... WHAT CAN I SAY? HA HA...
OUR TIME IS LIMITED, SO I SUGGEST WE BEGIN.
THERE ARE TWO CONDITIONS TO THE OPENING OF TEMPEST AND BLUMUND TO ONE ANOTHER.
ONE: A GUARANTEE OF MUTUAL SECURITY BETWEEN OUR COUNTRIES.
TWO: A GUARANTEE OF FREE PASSAGE BETWEEN OUR COUNTRIES.

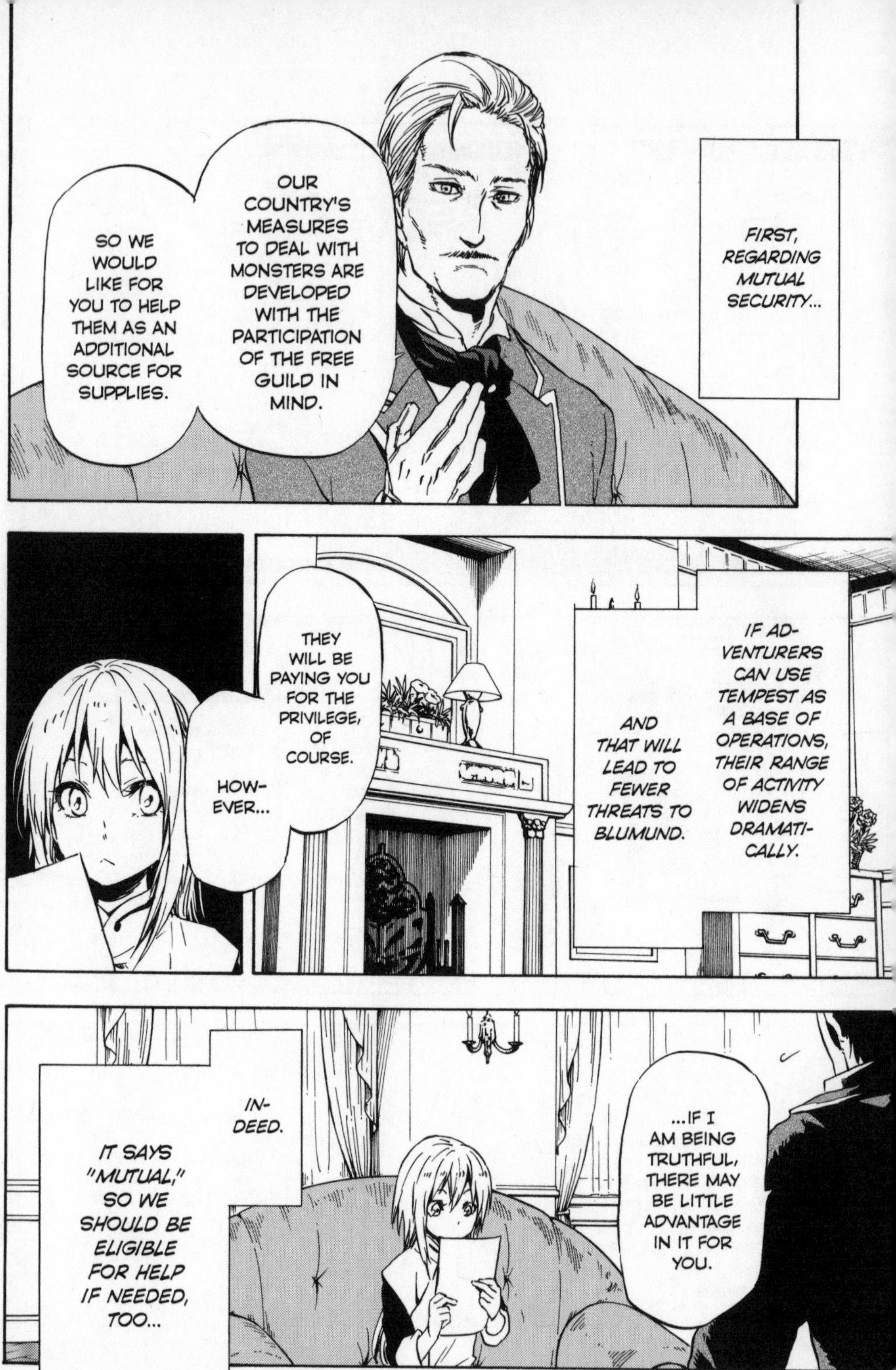
FIRST, REGARDING MUTUAL SECURITY...
OUR COUNTRY'S MEASURES TO DEAL WITH MONSTERS ARE DEVELOPED WITH THE PARTICIPATION OF THE FREE GUILD IN MIND.
SO WE WOULD LIKE FOR YOU TO HELP THEM AS AN ADDITIONAL SOURCE FOR SUPPLIES.
IF ADVENTURERS CAN USE TEMPEST AS A BASE OF OPERATIONS, THEIR RANGE OF ACTIVITY WIDENS DRAMATICALLY.
AND THAT WILL LEAD TO FEWER THREATS TO BLUMUND.
THEY WILL BE PAYING YOU FOR THE PRIVILEGE, OF COURSE.
HOWEVER...
...IF I AM BEING TRUTHFUL, THERE MAY BE LITTLE ADVANTAGE IN IT FOR YOU.
INDEED.
IT SAYS "MUTUAL," SO WE SHOULD BE ELIGIBLE FOR HELP IF NEEDED, TOO...

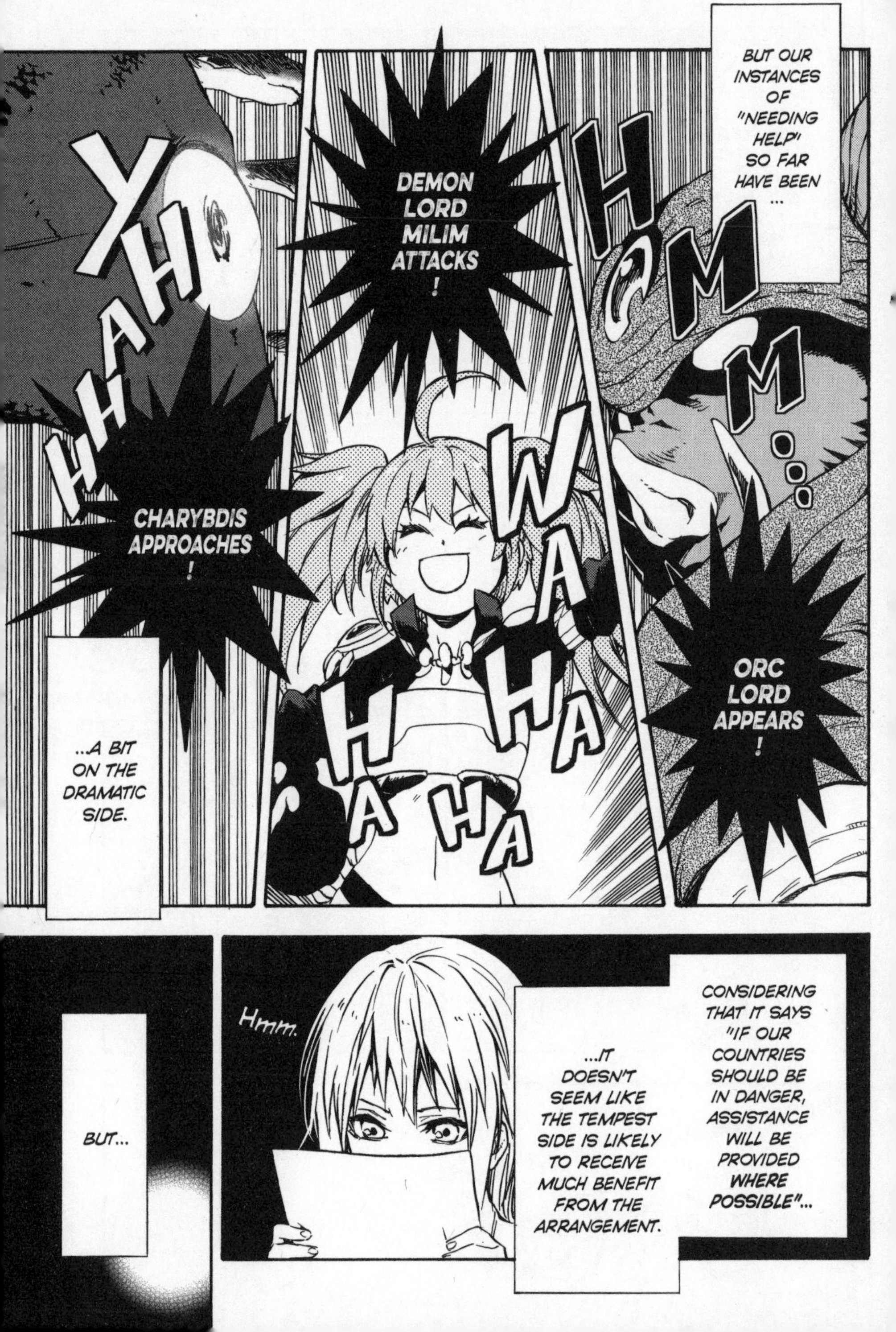
BUT OUR INSTANCES OF "NEEDING HELP" SO FAR HAVE BEEN ...
ORC LORD APPEARS!
DEMON LORD MILIM ATTACKS!
CHARYBDIS APPROACHES!
...A BIT ON THE DRAMATIC SIDE.
CONSIDERING THAT IT SAYS "IF OUR COUNTRIES SHOULD BE IN DANGER, ASSISTANCE WILL BE PROVIDED WHERE POSSIBLE"...
...IT DOESN'T SEEM LIKE THE TEMPEST SIDE IS LIKELY TO RECEIVE MUCH BENEFIT FROM THE ARRANGEMENT.
Hmm.
BUT...

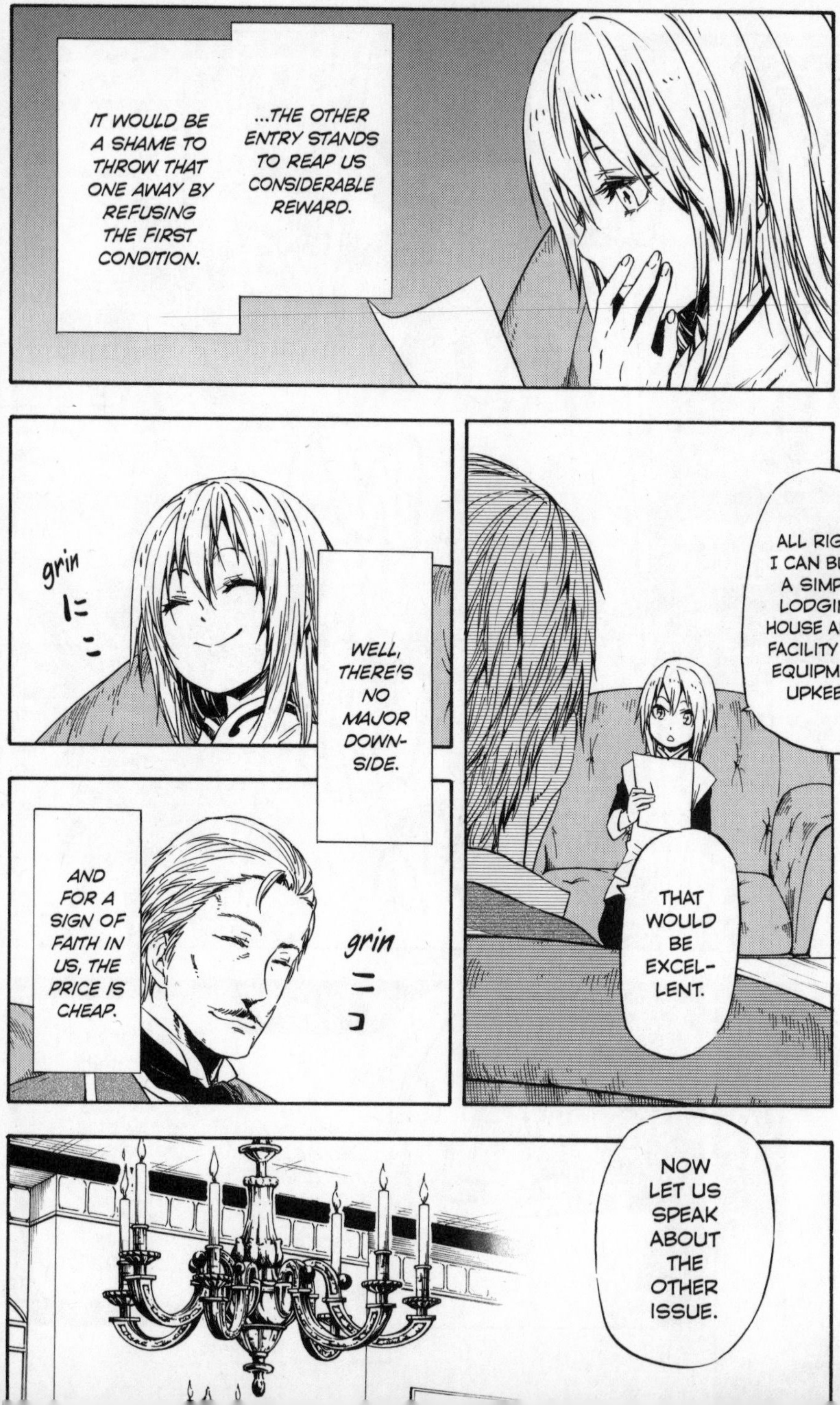
...THE OTHER ENTRY STANDS TO REAP US CONSIDERABLE REWARD.
IT WOULD BE A SHAME TO THROW THAT ONE AWAY BY REFUSING THE FIRST CONDITION.
ALL RIGHT. I CAN BUILD A SIMPLE LODGING HOUSE AND A FACILITY FOR EQUIPMENT UPKEEP.
THAT WOULD BE EXCEL-LENT.
WELL, THERE'S NO MAJOR DOWN-SIDE.
grin
にこ
AND FOR A SIGN OF FAITH IN US, THE PRICE IS CHEAP.
grin
ニコ
NOW LET US SPEAK ABOUT THE OTHER ISSUE.

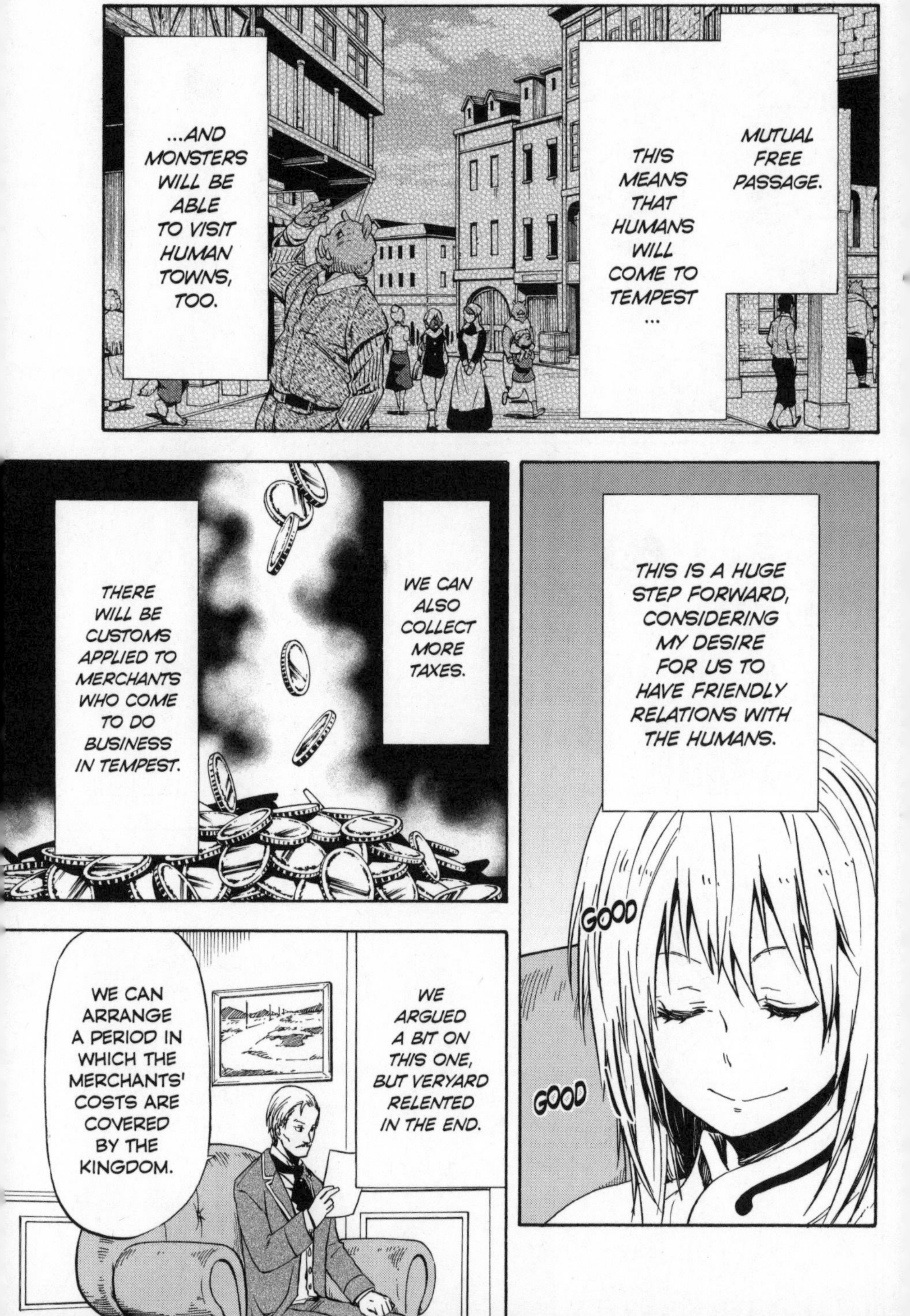
MUTUAL FREE PASSAGE.
THIS MEANS THAT HUMANS WILL COME TO TEMPEST ...
...AND MONSTERS WILL BE ABLE TO VISIT HUMAN TOWNS, TOO.
THIS IS A HUGE STEP FORWARD, CONSIDERING MY DESIRE FOR US TO HAVE FRIENDLY RELATIONS WITH THE HUMANS.
GOOD
GOOD
WE CAN ALSO COLLECT MORE TAXES.
THERE WILL BE CUSTOMS APPLIED TO MERCHANTS WHO COME TO DO BUSINESS IN TEMPEST.
WE ARGUED A BIT ON THIS ONE, BUT VERYARD RELENTED IN THE END.
WE CAN ARRANGE A PERIOD IN WHICH THE MERCHANTS' COSTS ARE COVERED BY THE KINGDOM.

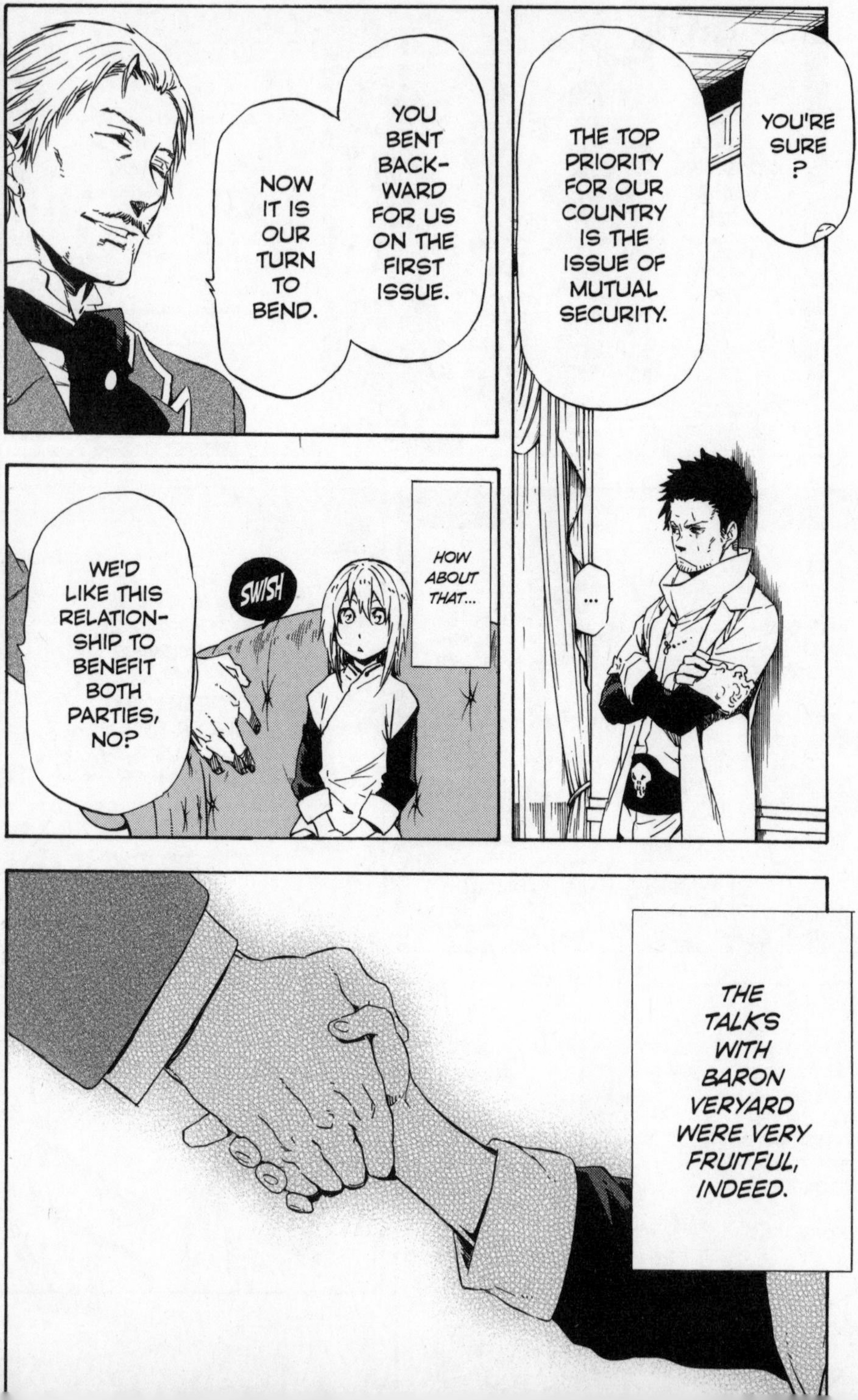
YOU'RE SURE ?
THE TOP PRIORITY FOR OUR COUNTRY IS THE ISSUE OF MUTUAL SECURITY.
...
YOU BENT BACKWARD FOR US ON THE FIRST ISSUE.
NOW IT IS OUR TURN TO BEND.
HOW ABOUT THAT...
SWISH
WE'D LIKE THIS RELATIONSHIP TO BENEFIT BOTH PARTIES, NO?
THE TALKS WITH BARON VERYARD WERE VERY FRUITFUL, INDEED.

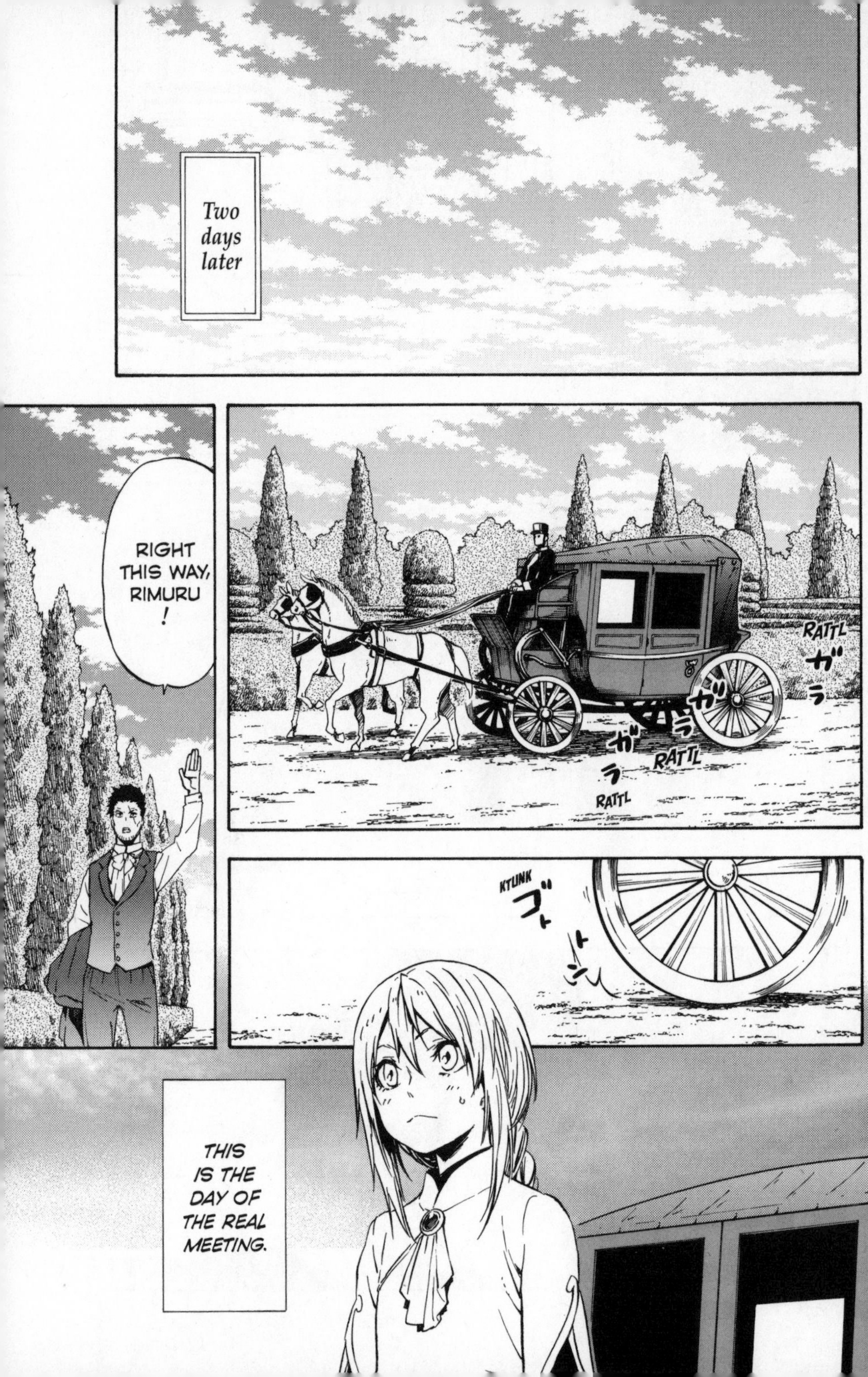
Two days later
RATTL
ガラ
ガリ
ラ
RATTL
ガ
ラ
RATTL
KTUNK
ゴト
トン
RIGHT THIS WAY, RIMURU!
THIS IS THE DAY OF THE REAL MEETING.

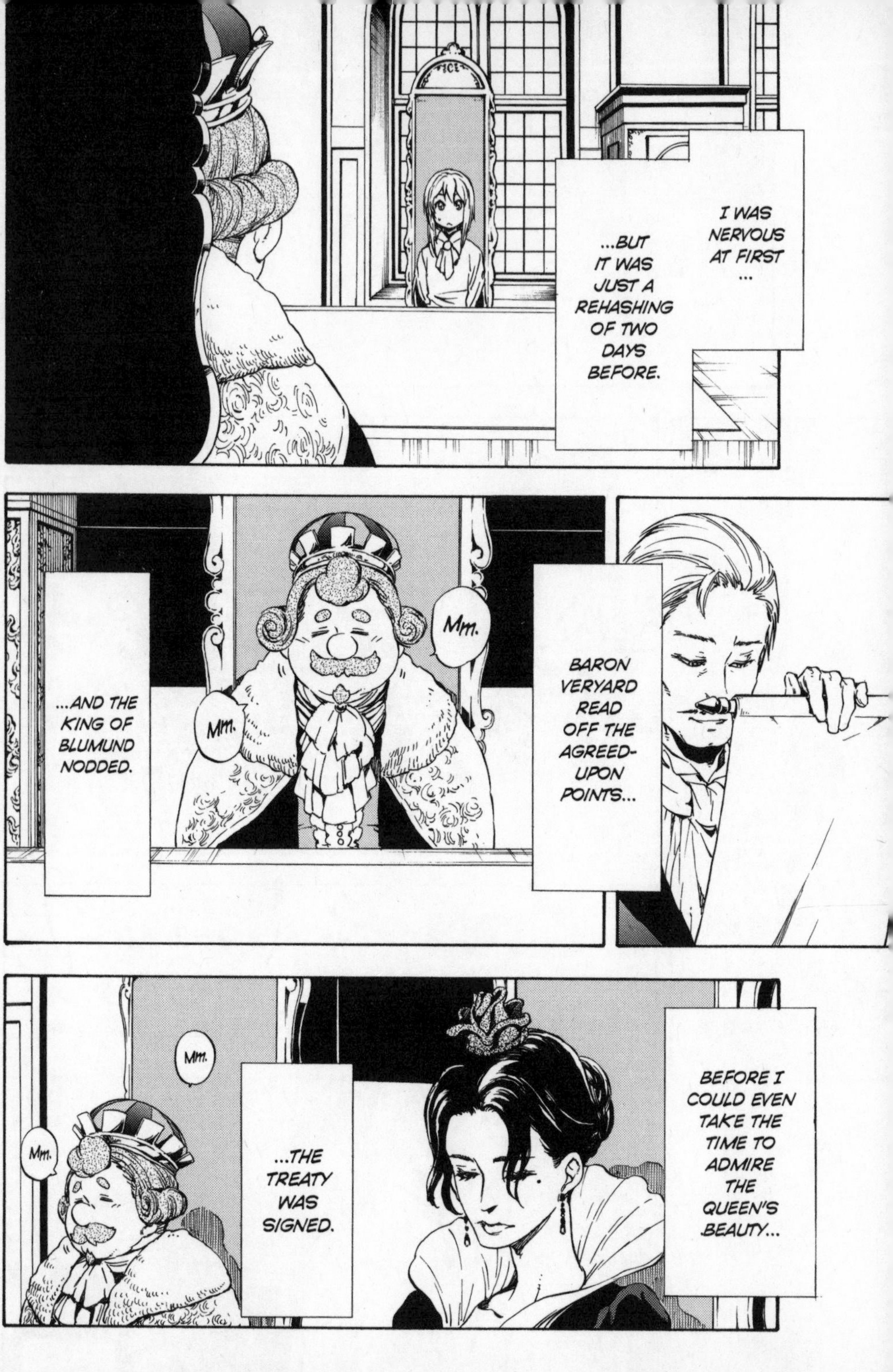
I WAS NERVOUS AT FIRST ...
...BUT IT WAS JUST A REHASHING OF TWO DAYS BEFORE.
BARON VERYARD READ OFF THE AGREED-UPON POINTS...
Mm.
...AND THE KING OF BLUMUND NODDED.
Mm.
BEFORE I COULD EVEN TAKE THE TIME TO ADMIRE THE QUEEN'S BEAUTY...
...THE TREATY WAS SIGNED.
Mm.
Mm.

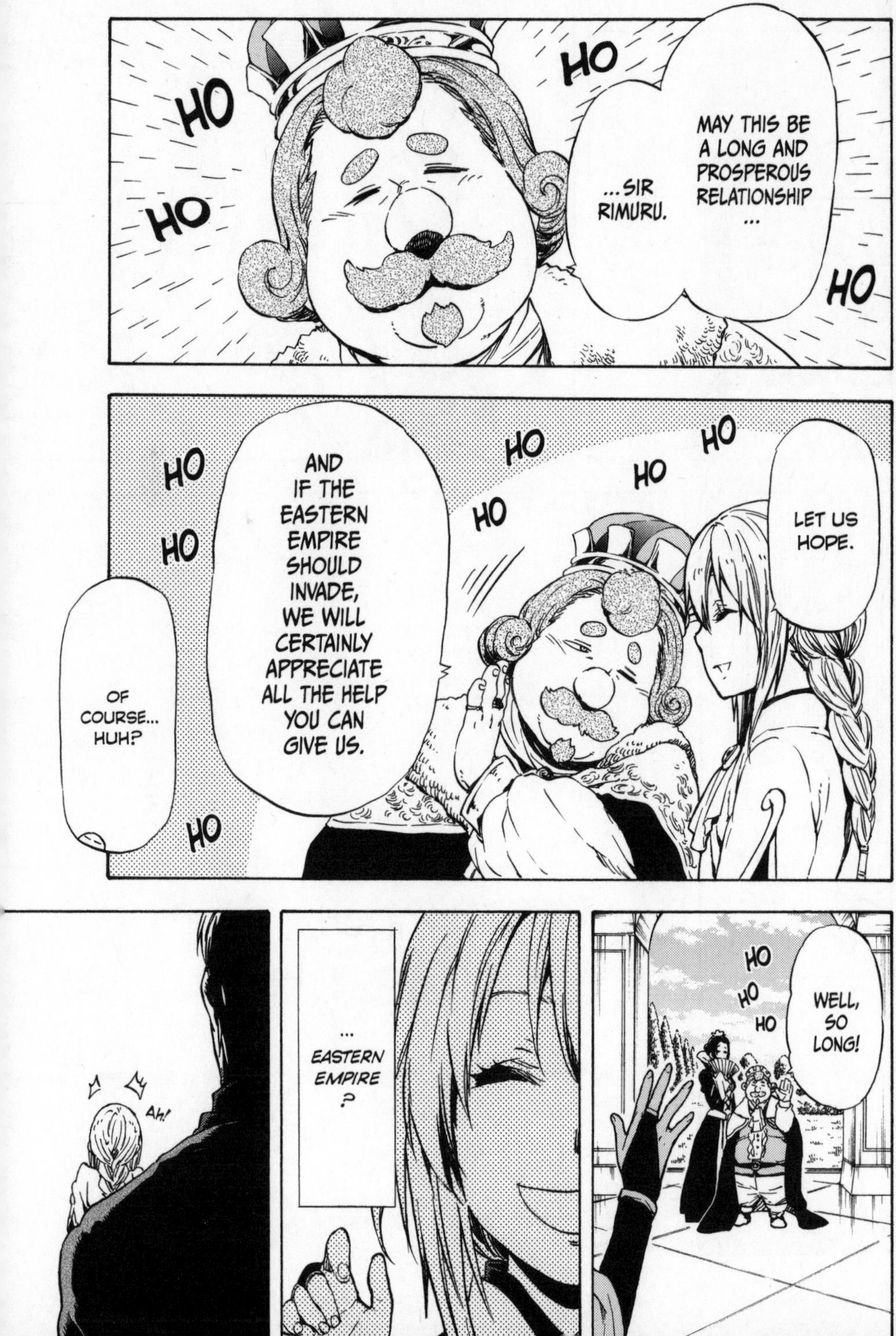
HO
MAY THIS BE A LONG AND PROSPEROUS RELATIONSHIP ...
...SIR RIMURU.
HO
HO
HO
HO
LET US HOPE.
HO
HO
HO
AND IF THE EASTERN EMPIRE SHOULD INVADE, WE WILL CERTAINLY APPRECIATE ALL THE HELP YOU CAN GIVE US.
HO
HO
HO
OF COURSE... HUH?
WELL, SO LONG!
HO
HO
HO
... EASTERN EMPIRE ?
Ah!

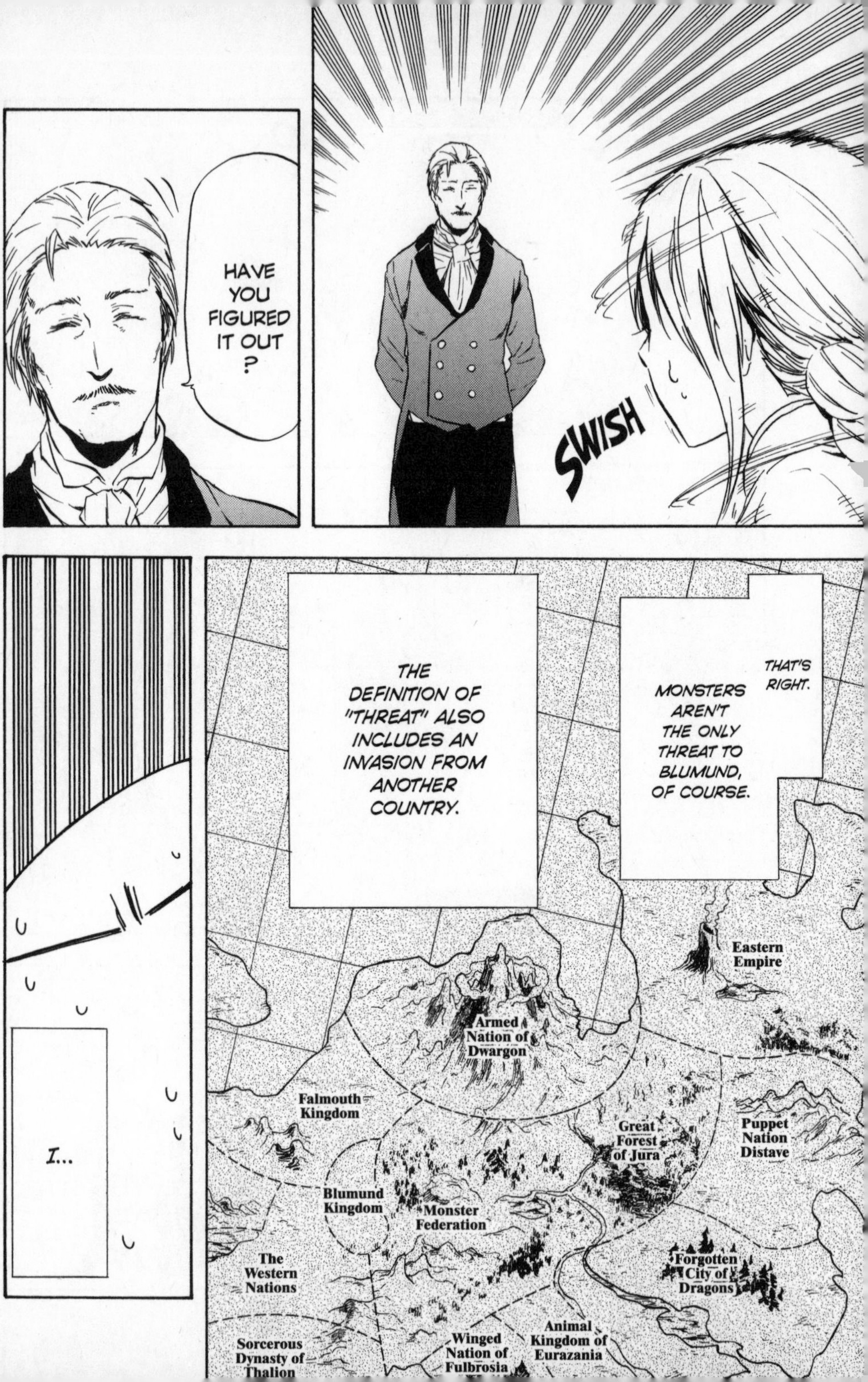
SWISH
HAVE YOU FIGURED IT OUT?
THAT'S RIGHT.
MONSTERS AREN'T THE ONLY THREAT TO BLUMUND, OF COURSE.
THE DEFINITION OF "THREAT" ALSO INCLUDES AN INVASION FROM ANOTHER COUNTRY.
Eastern Empire
Armed Nation of Dwargon
Falmouth Kingdom
Great Forest of Jura
Puppet Nation Distave
Blumund Kingdom
Monster Federation
The Western Nations
Forgotten City of Dragons
Sorcerous Dynasty of Thalion
Winged Nation of Fulbrosia
Animal Kingdom of Eurazania
I...

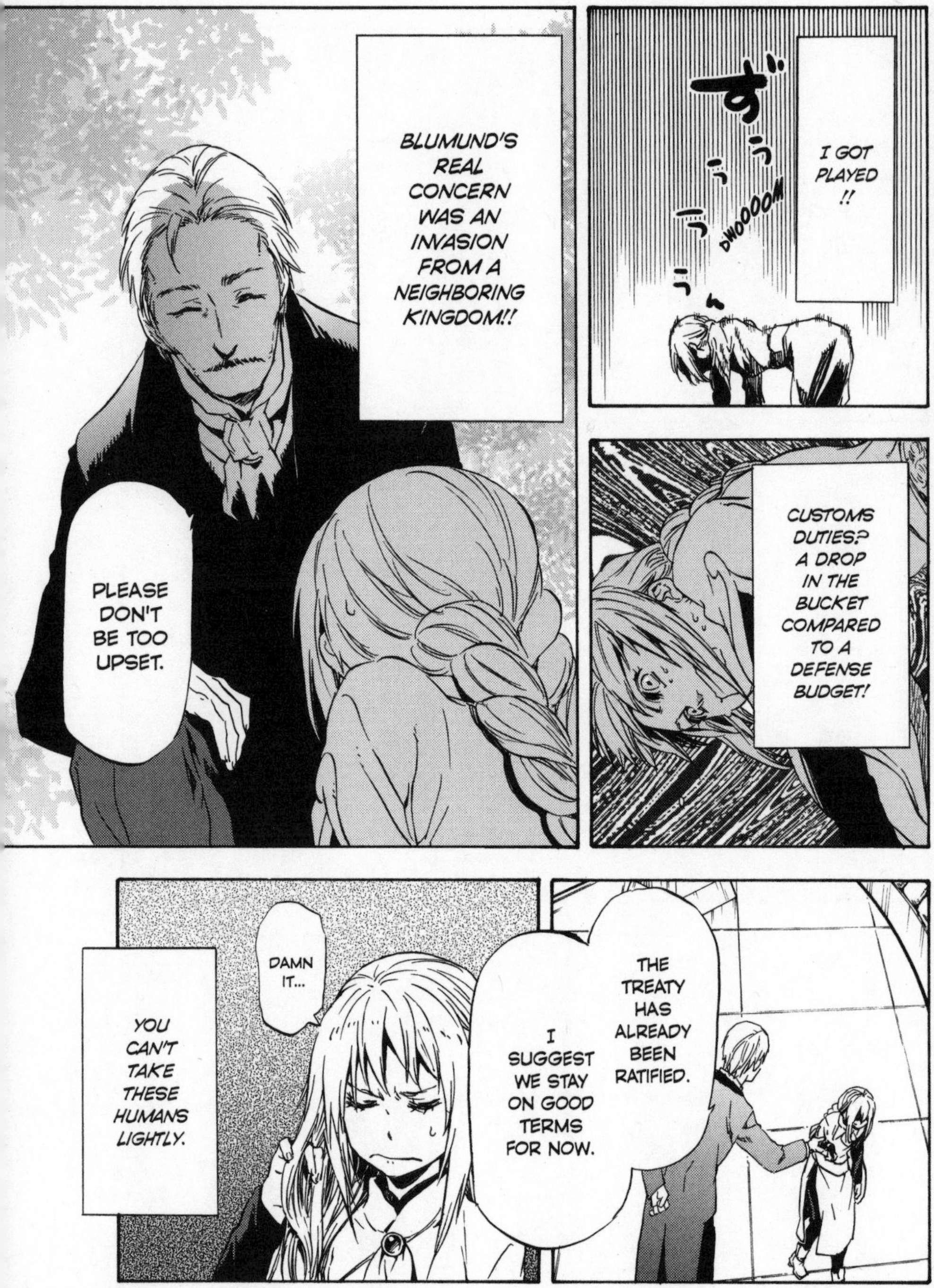
I GOT PLAYED!!
DWOOOOM
CUSTOMS DUTIES? A DROP IN THE BUCKET COMPARED TO A DEFENSE BUDGET!
BLUMUND'S REAL CONCERN WAS AN INVASION FROM A NEIGHBORING KINGDOM!!
PLEASE DON'T BE TOO UPSET.
THE TREATY HAS ALREADY BEEN RATIFIED.
I SUGGEST WE STAY ON GOOD TERMS FOR NOW.
DAMN IT...
YOU CAN'T TAKE THESE HUMANS LIGHTLY.

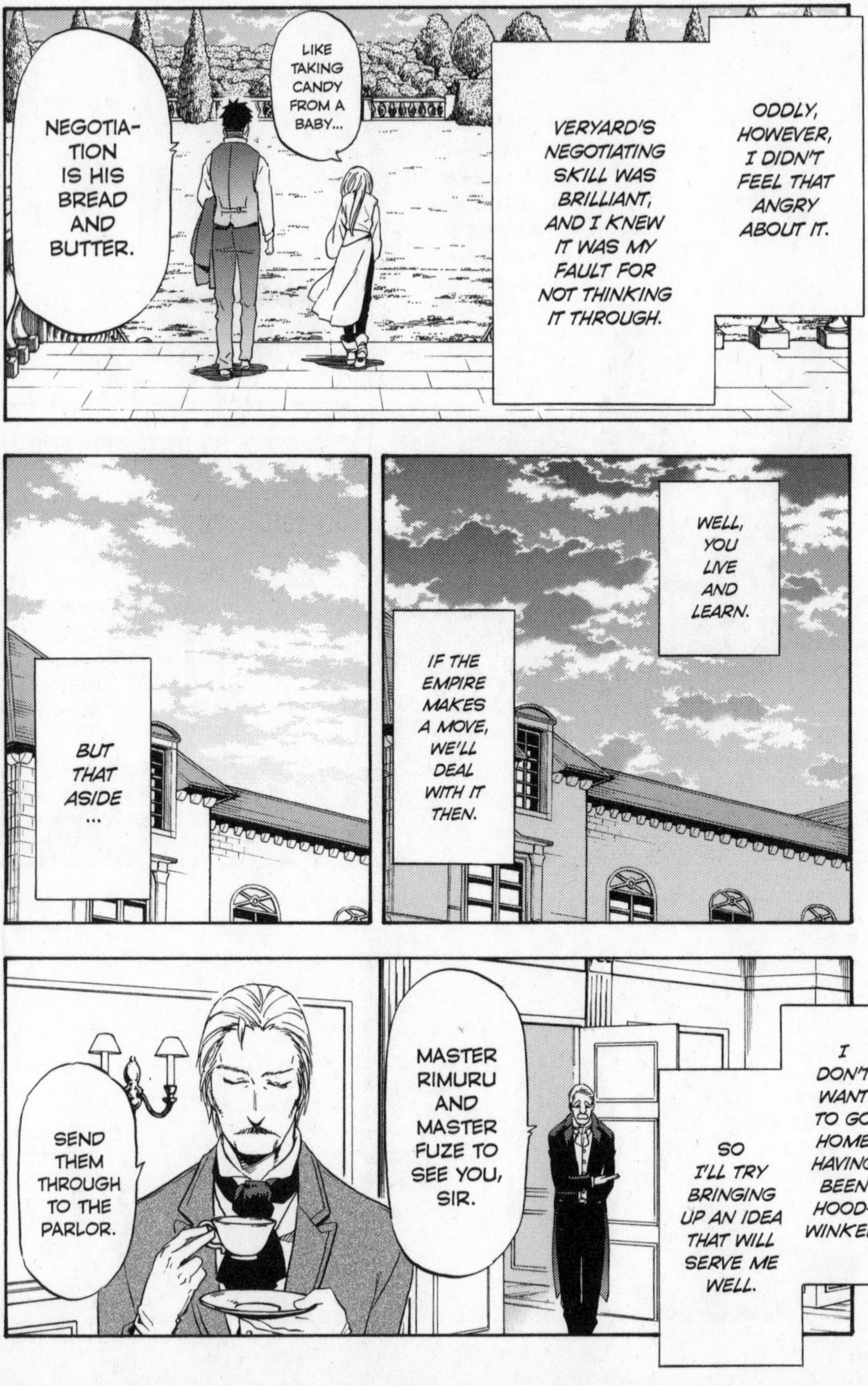
VERYARD'S NEGOTIATING SKILL WAS BRILLIANT, AND I KNEW IT WAS MY FAULT FOR NOT THINKING IT THROUGH.
ODDLY, HOWEVER, I DIDN'T FEEL THAT ANGRY ABOUT IT.
LIKE TAKING CANDY FROM A BABY...
NEGOTIATION IS HIS BREAD AND BUTTER.
WELL, YOU LIVE AND LEARN.
IF THE EMPIRE MAKES A MOVE, WE'LL DEAL WITH IT THEN.
BUT THAT ASIDE...
I DON'T WANT TO GO HOME HAVING BEEN HOODWINKED.
SO I'LL TRY BRINGING UP AN IDEA THAT WILL SERVE ME WELL.
MASTER RIMURU AND MASTER FUZE TO SEE YOU, SIR.
SEND THEM THROUGH TO THE PARLOR.

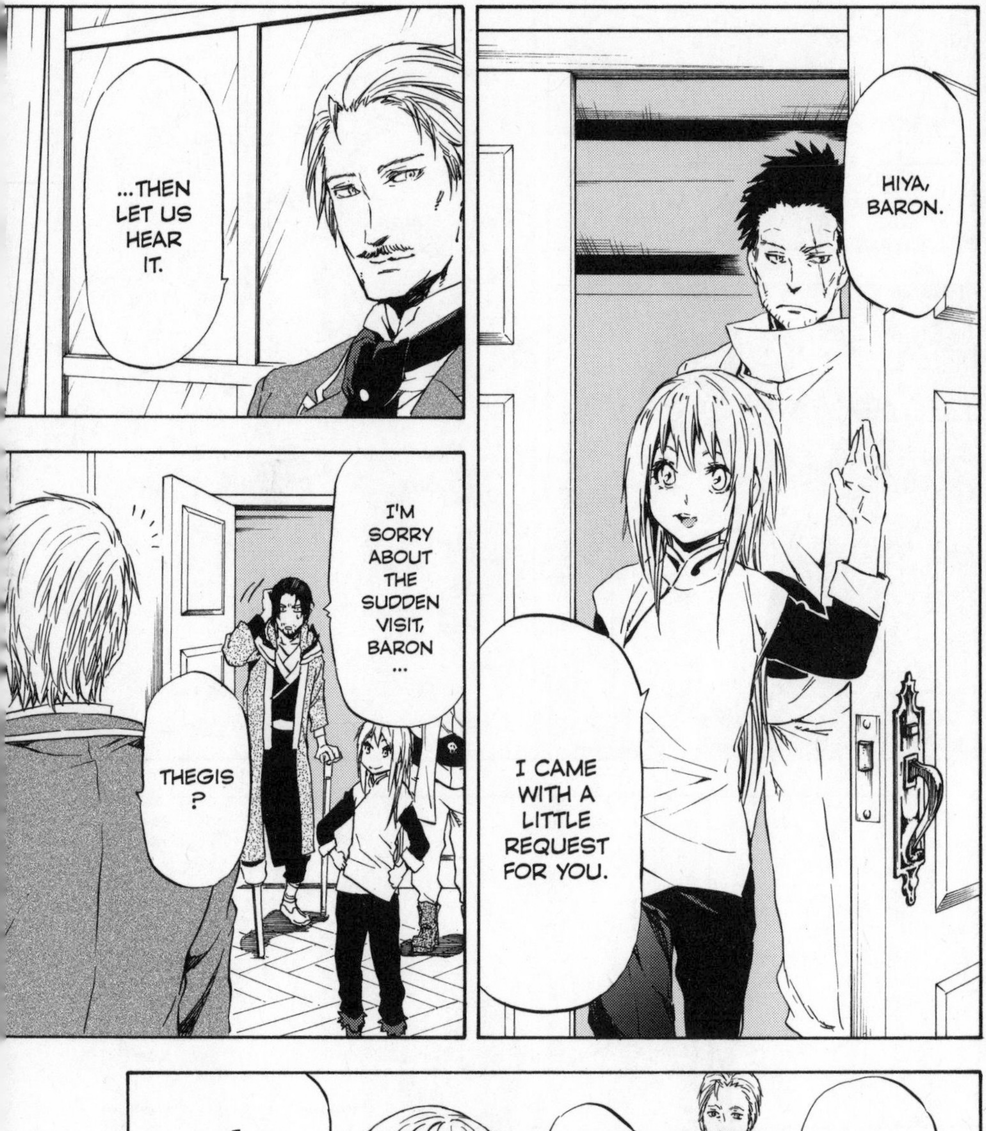
HIYA, BARON.
I CAME WITH A LITTLE REQUEST FOR YOU.
...THEN LET US HEAR IT.
I'M SORRY ABOUT THE SUDDEN VISIT, BARON...
THEGIS?
WHY IS HE HERE?
ACTUALLY...
...I THOUGHT I'D ENGAGE IN A LITTLE SALES PITCH DEMONSTRATION.

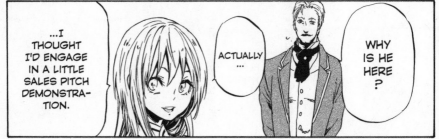

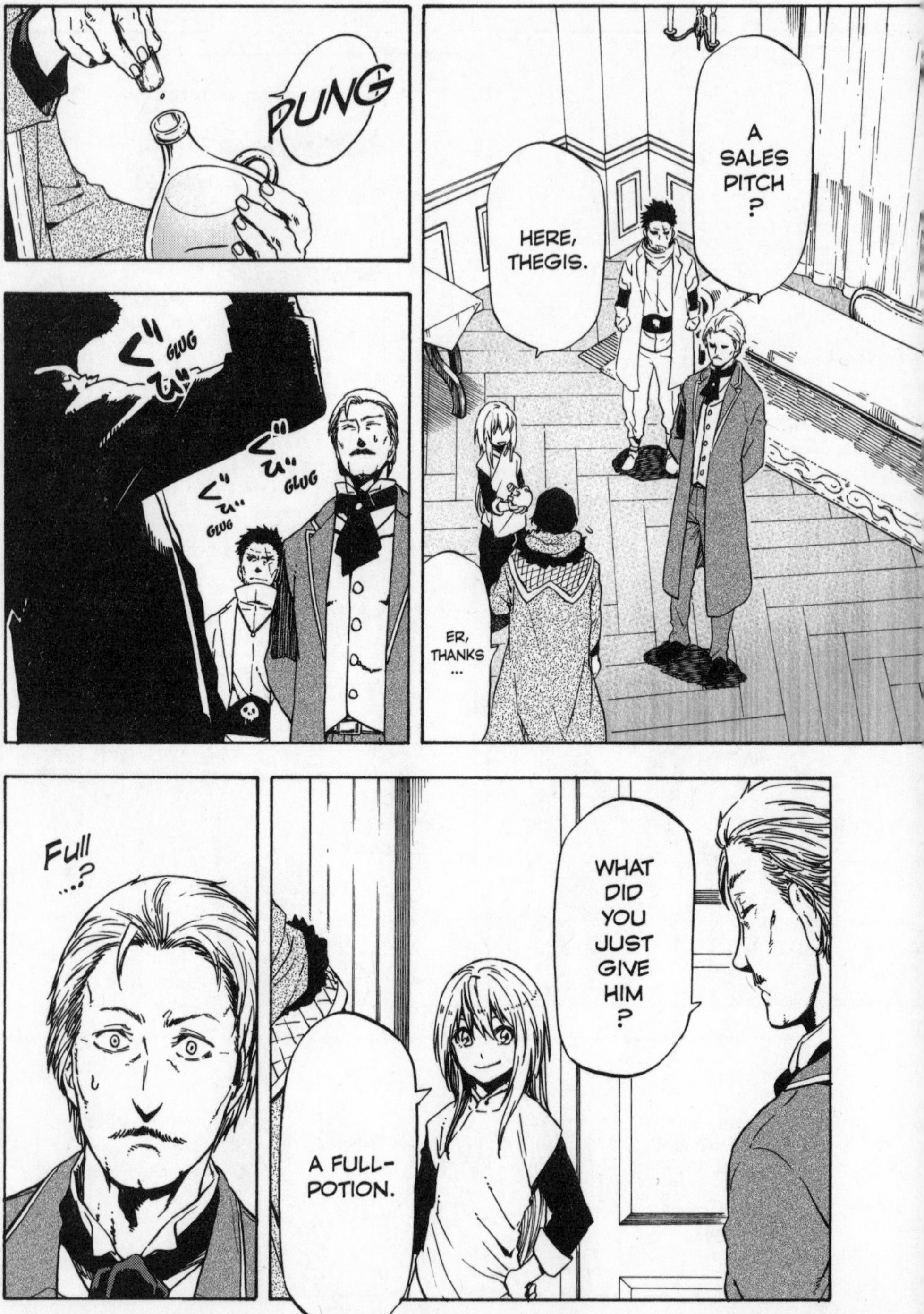
A SALES PITCH?
HERE, THEGIS.
ER, THANKS...
PUNG
ぐび GLUG
ぐび GLUG
ぐび GLUG
WHAT DID YOU JUST GIVE HIM?
A FULL-POTION.
Full...?

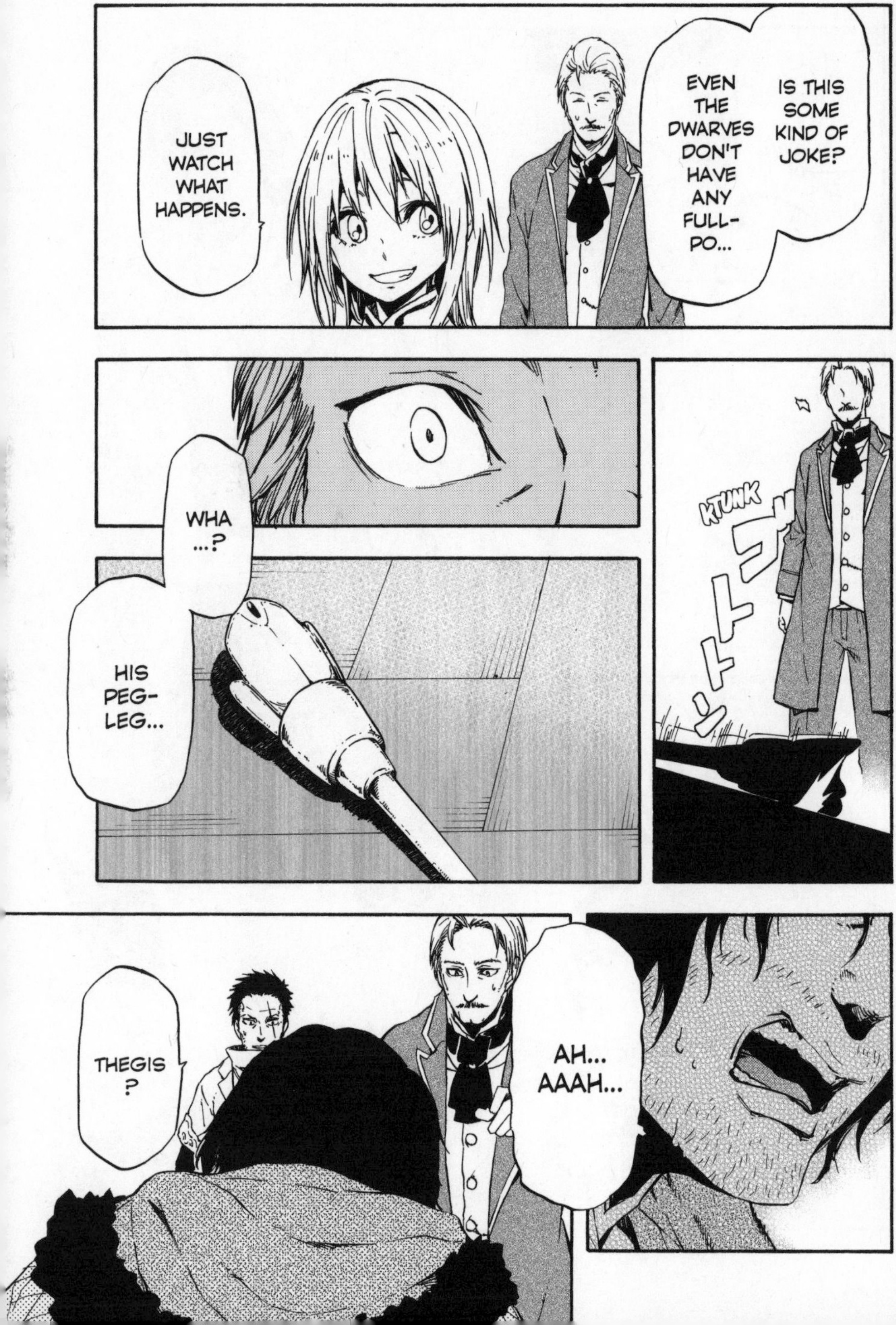
IS THIS SOME KIND OF JOKE?
EVEN THE DWARVES DON'T HAVE ANY FULL-PO...
JUST WATCH WHAT HAPPENS.
KTUNK
WHA ...?
HIS PEG-LEG...
AH... AAAH...
THEGIS ?

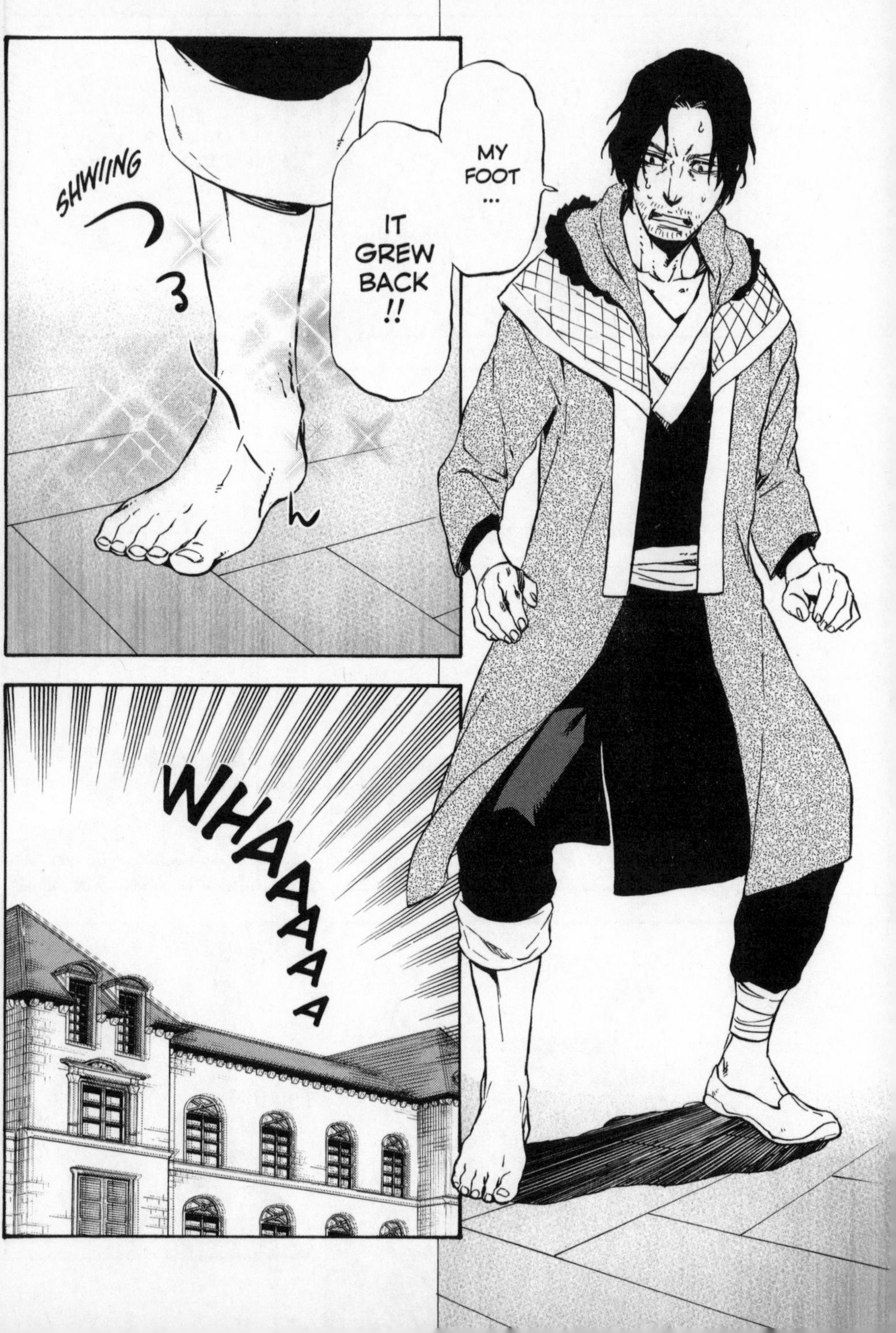
MY FOOT ...
IT GREW BACK !!
SHWIING
WHAAAAAA

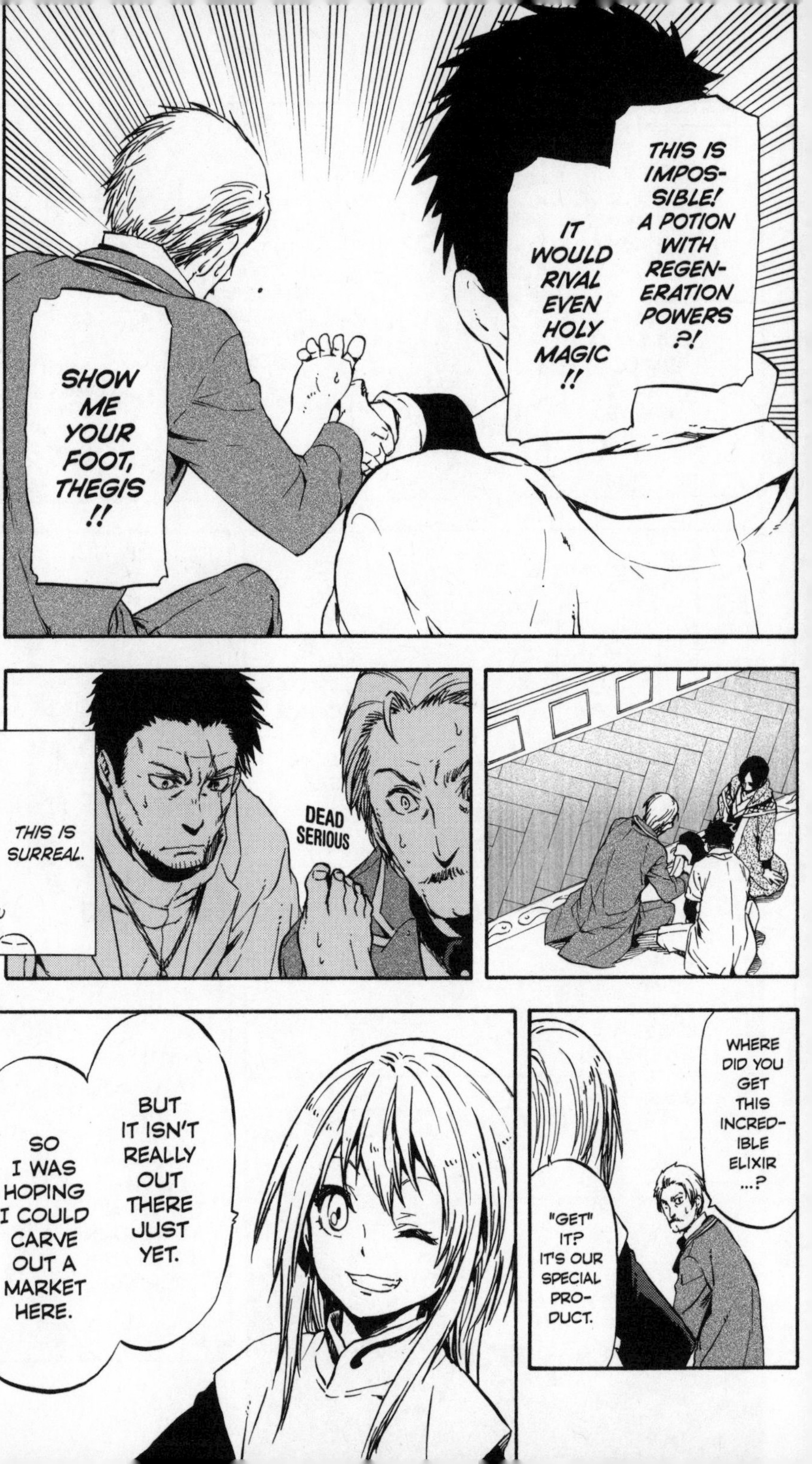
THIS IS IMPOSSIBLE! A POTION WITH REGENERATION POWERS?!
IT WOULD RIVAL EVEN HOLY MAGIC!!
SHOW ME YOUR FOOT, THEGIS!!
DEAD SERIOUS
THIS IS SURREAL.
WHERE DID YOU GET THIS INCREDIBLE ELIXIR...?
"GET" IT? IT'S OUR SPECIAL PRODUCT.
BUT IT ISN'T REALLY OUT THERE JUST YET.
SO I WAS HOPING I COULD CARVE OUT A MARKET HERE.

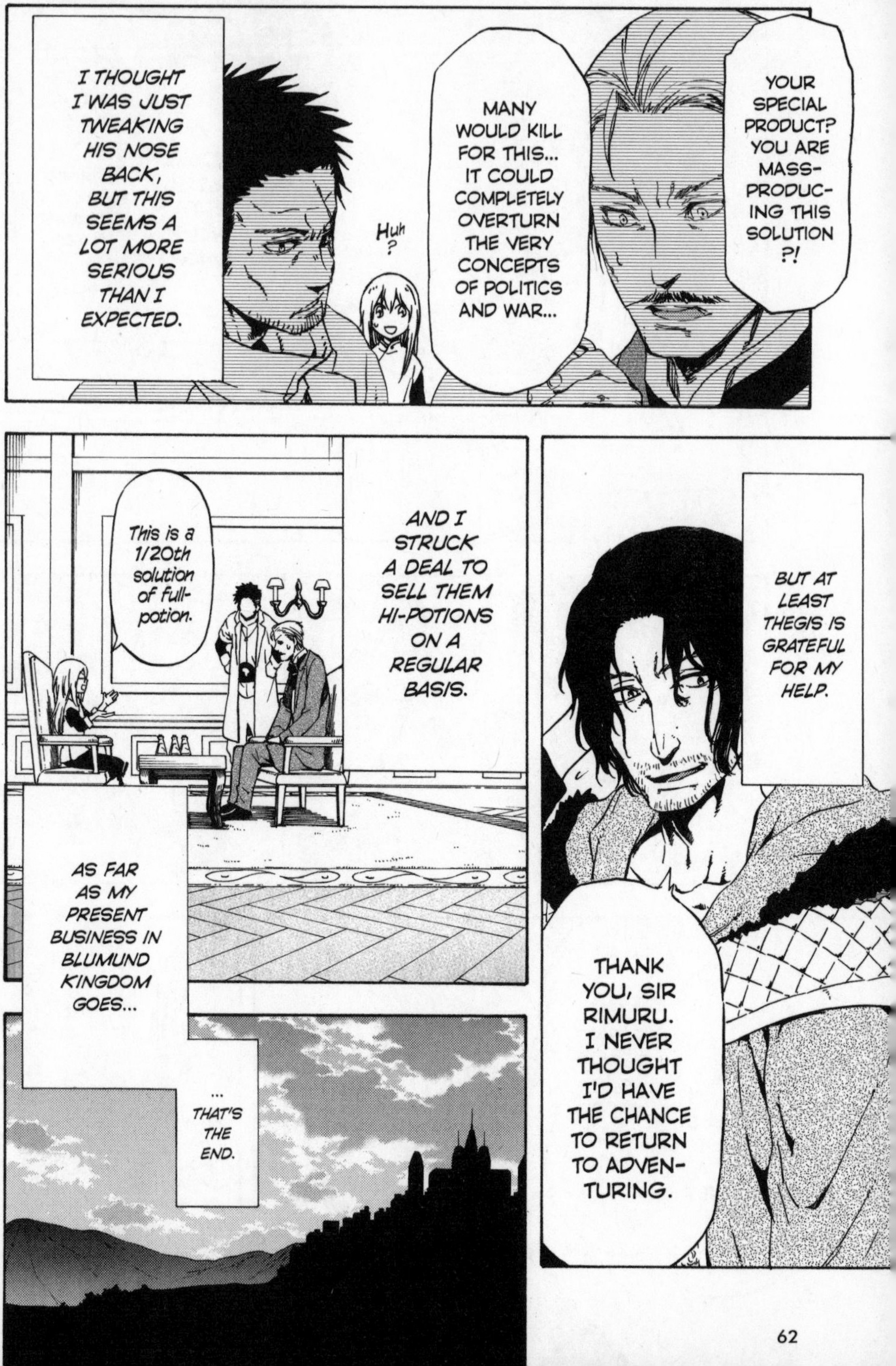
YOUR SPECIAL PRODUCT? YOU ARE MASS-PRODUCING THIS SOLUTION?!
MANY WOULD KILL FOR THIS... IT COULD COMPLETELY OVERTURN THE VERY CONCEPTS OF POLITICS AND WAR...
Huh?
I THOUGHT I WAS JUST TWEAKING HIS NOSE BACK, BUT THIS SEEMS A LOT MORE SERIOUS THAN I EXPECTED.
BUT AT LEAST THEGIS IS GRATEFUL FOR MY HELP.
THANK YOU, SIR RIMURU. I NEVER THOUGHT I'D HAVE THE CHANCE TO RETURN TO ADVENTURING.
AND I STRUCK A DEAL TO SELL THEM HI-POTIONS ON A REGULAR BASIS.
This is a 1/20th solution of full-potion.
AS FAR AS MY PRESENT BUSINESS IN BLUMUND KINGDOM GOES...
...THAT'S THE END.

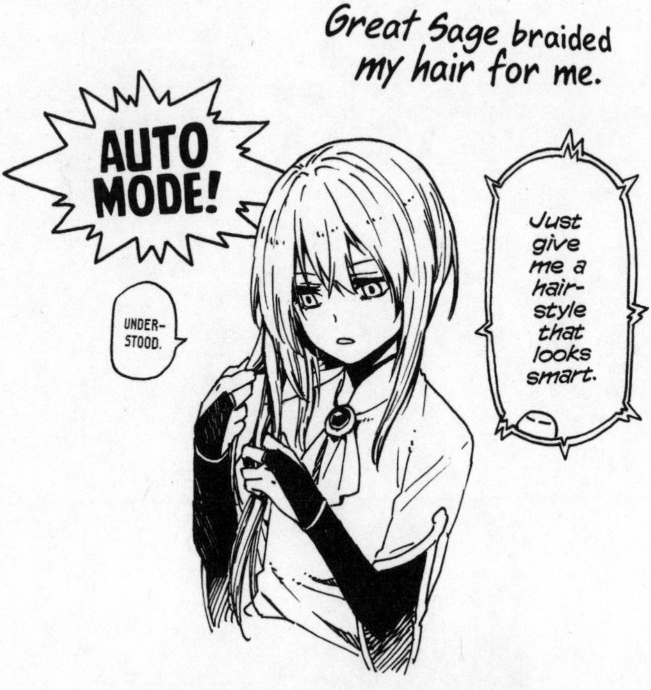
Great Sage braided my hair for me.
Just give me a hair-style that looks smart.
AUTO MODE!
UNDER-STOOD.

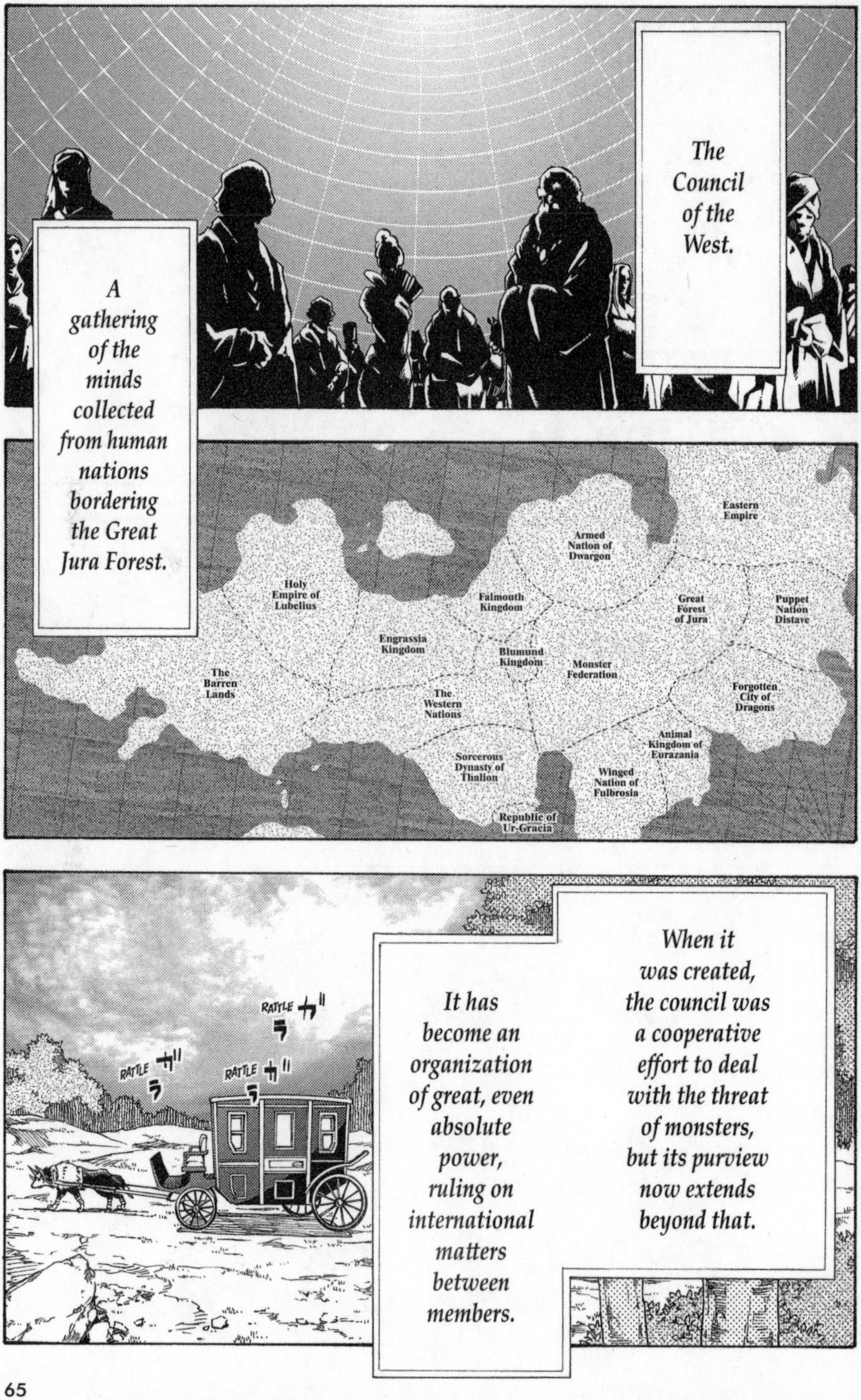
The Council of the West.
A gathering of the minds collected from human nations bordering the Great Jura Forest.
Eastern Empire
Armed Nation of Dwargon
Puppet Nation Distave
Great Forest of Jura
Falmouth Kingdom
Holy Empire of Lubelius
Engrassia Kingdom
Blumund Kingdom
Monster Federation
Forgotten City of Dragons
The Barren Lands
The Western Nations
Animal Kingdom of Eurazania
Sorcerous Dynasty of Thalion
Winged Nation of Fulbrosia
Republic of Ur-Gracia
When it was created, the council was a cooperative effort to deal with the threat of monsters, but its purview now extends beyond that.
It has become an organization of great, even absolute power, ruling on international matters between members.
RATTLE
RATTLE
RATTLE

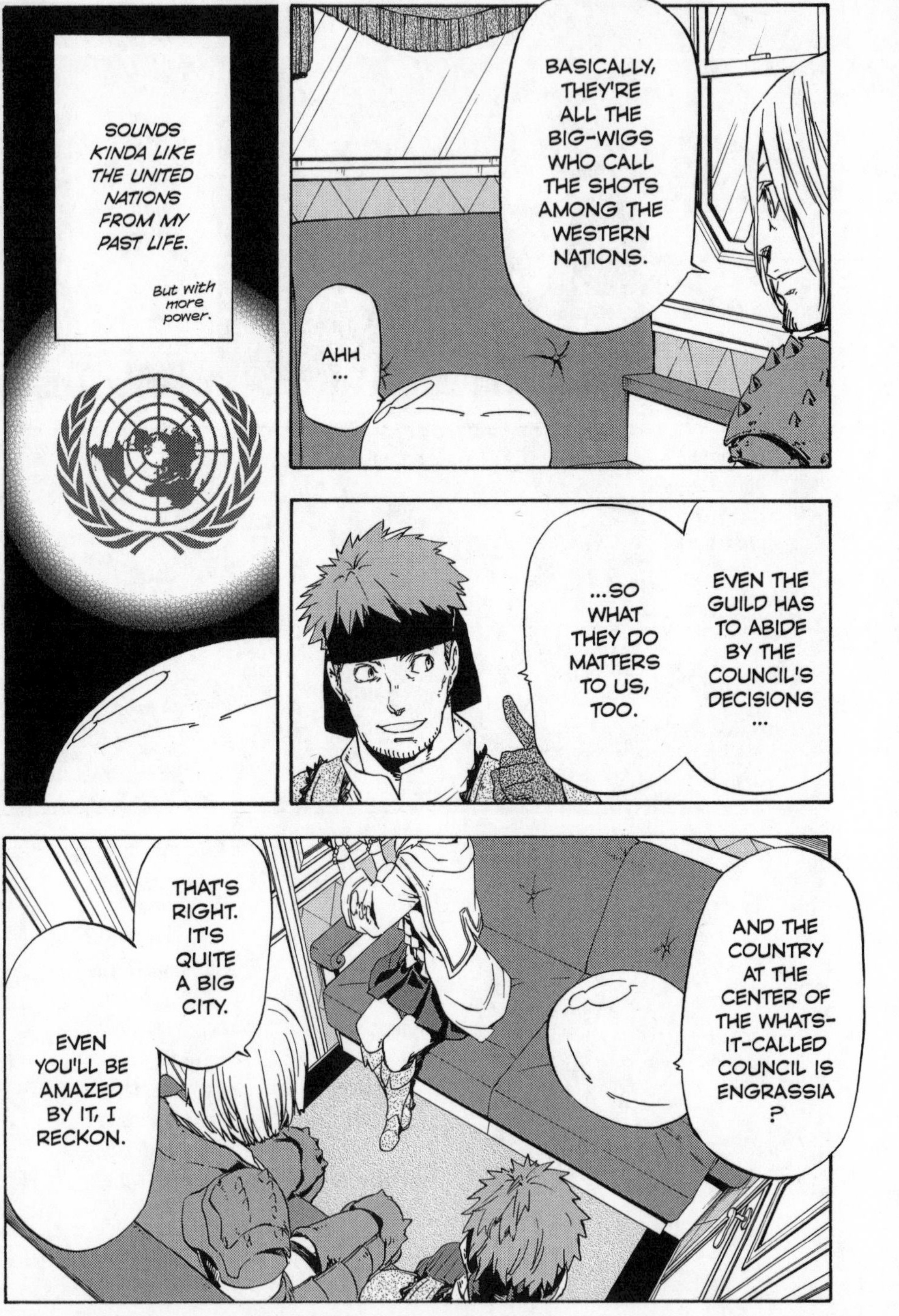
BASICALLY, THEY'RE ALL THE BIG-WIGS WHO CALL THE SHOTS AMONG THE WESTERN NATIONS.
AHH ...
EVEN THE GUILD HAS TO ABIDE BY THE COUNCIL'S DECISIONS ...
...SO WHAT THEY DO MATTERS TO US, TOO.
SOUNDS KINDA LIKE THE UNITED NATIONS FROM MY PAST LIFE.
But with more power.
AND THE COUNTRY AT THE CENTER OF THE WHATS-IT-CALLED COUNCIL IS ENGRASSIA ?
THAT'S RIGHT. IT'S QUITE A BIG CITY.
EVEN YOU'LL BE AMAZED BY IT, I RECKON.

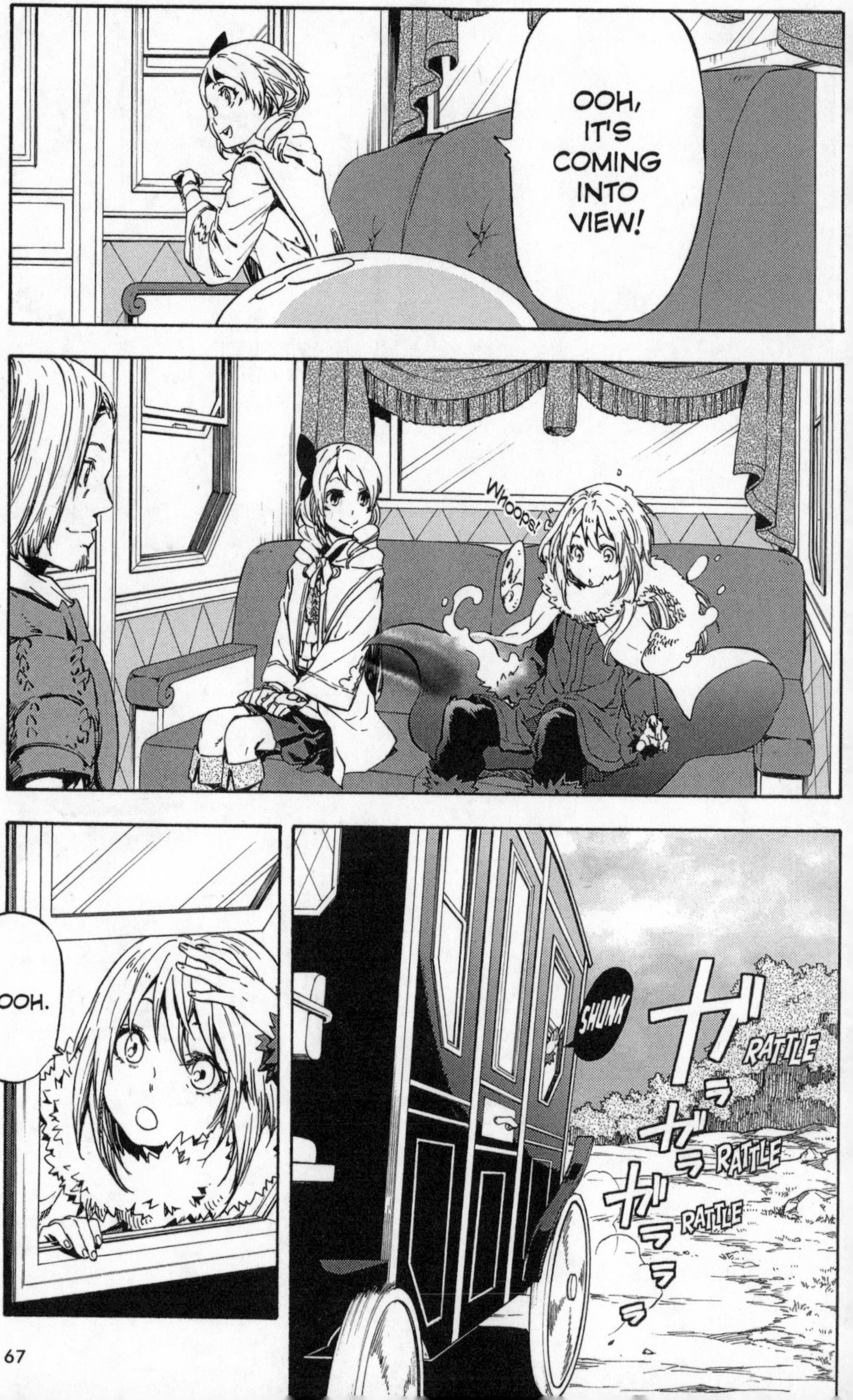
OOH, IT'S COMING INTO VIEW!
Whoops!
SHUNK
ガラ RATTLE
ガラ RATTLE
ガラララ RATTLE
OOOH.

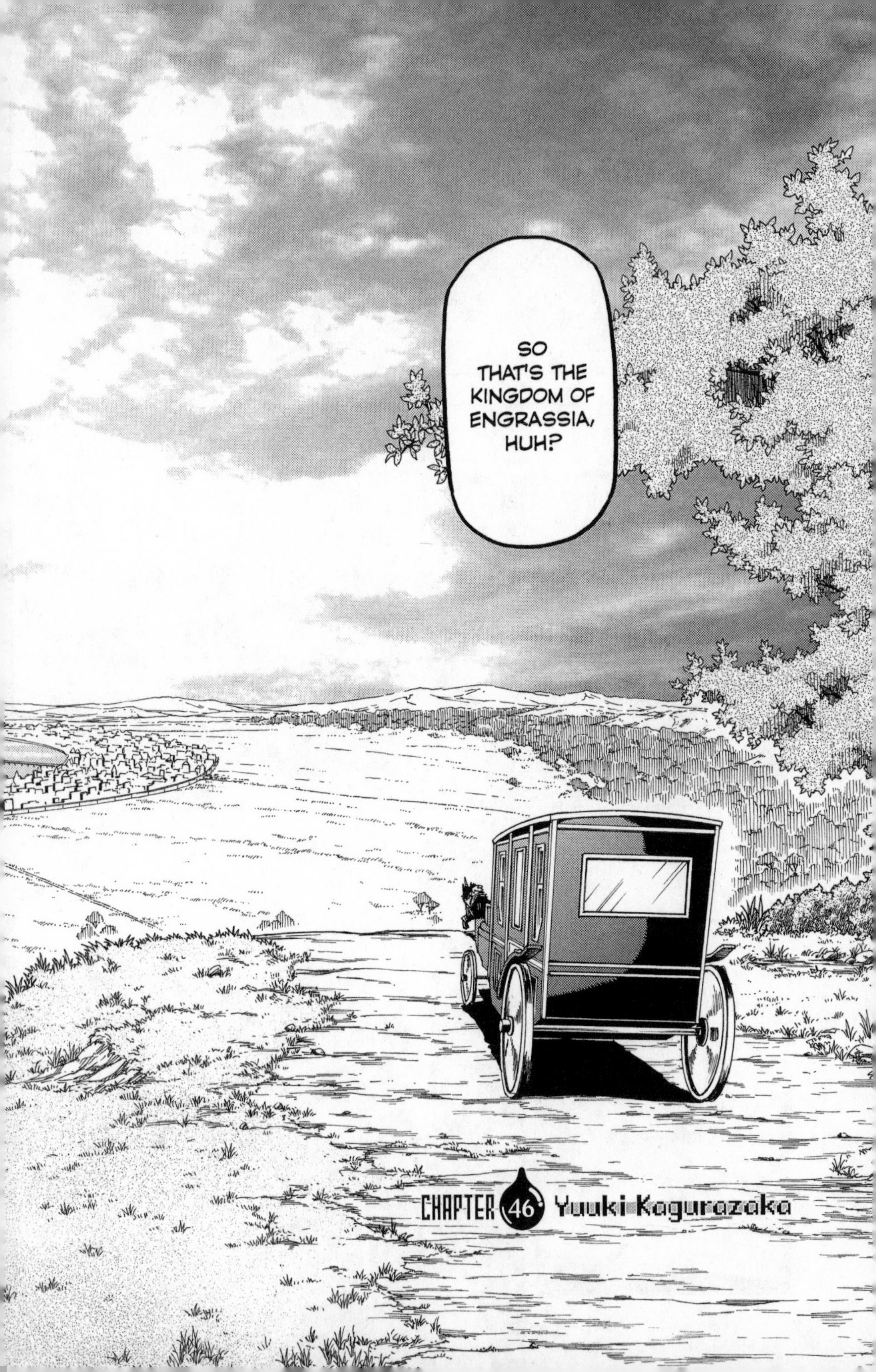
SO THAT'S THE KINGDOM OF ENGRASSIA, HUH?
CHAPTER 46 Yuuki Kagurazaka

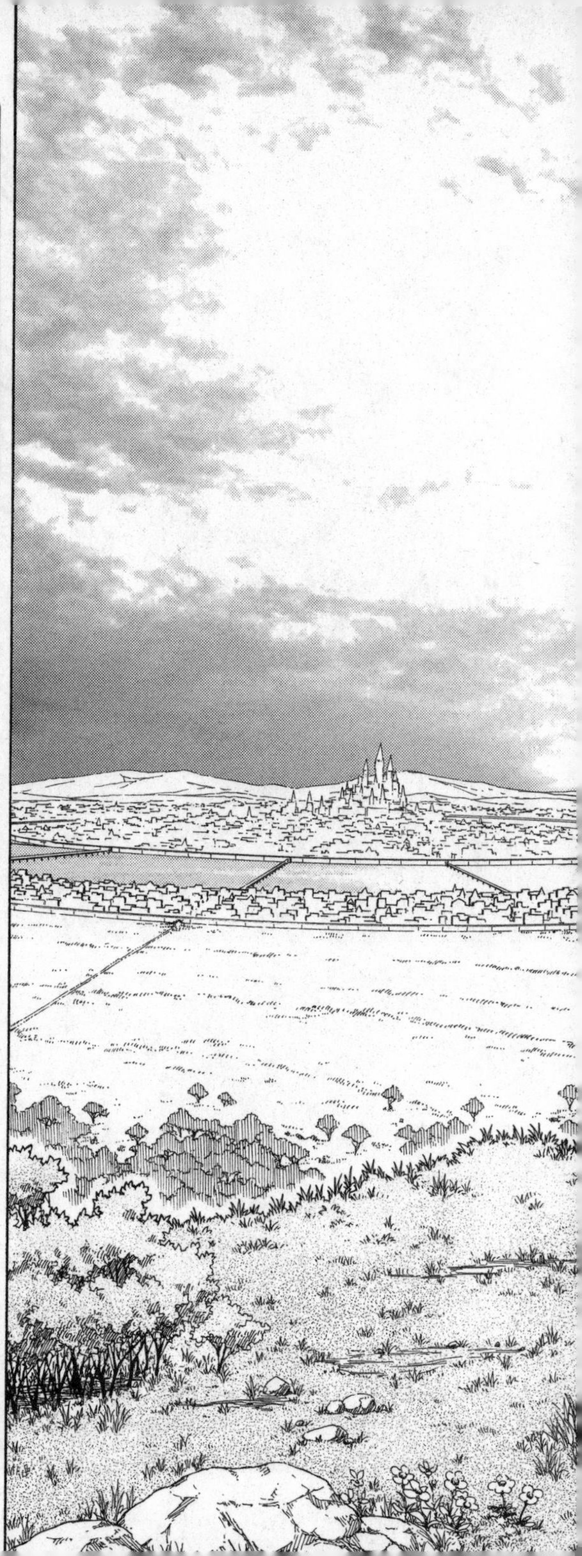

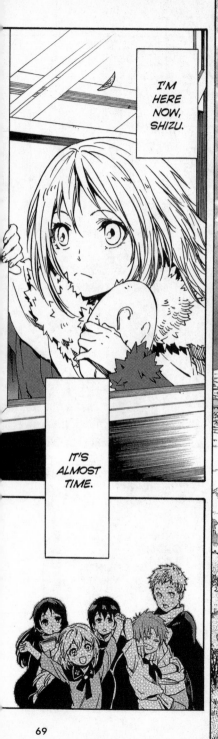

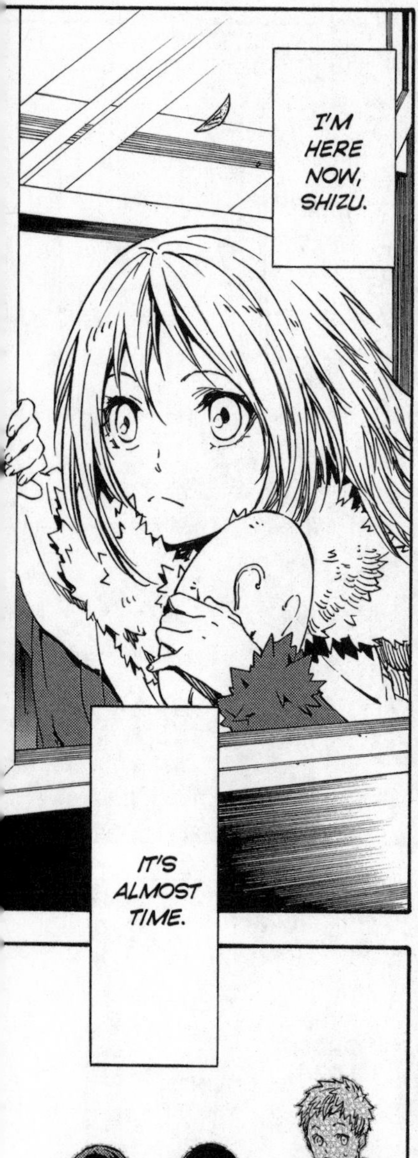
I'M HERE NOW, SHIZU.
IT'S ALMOST TIME.

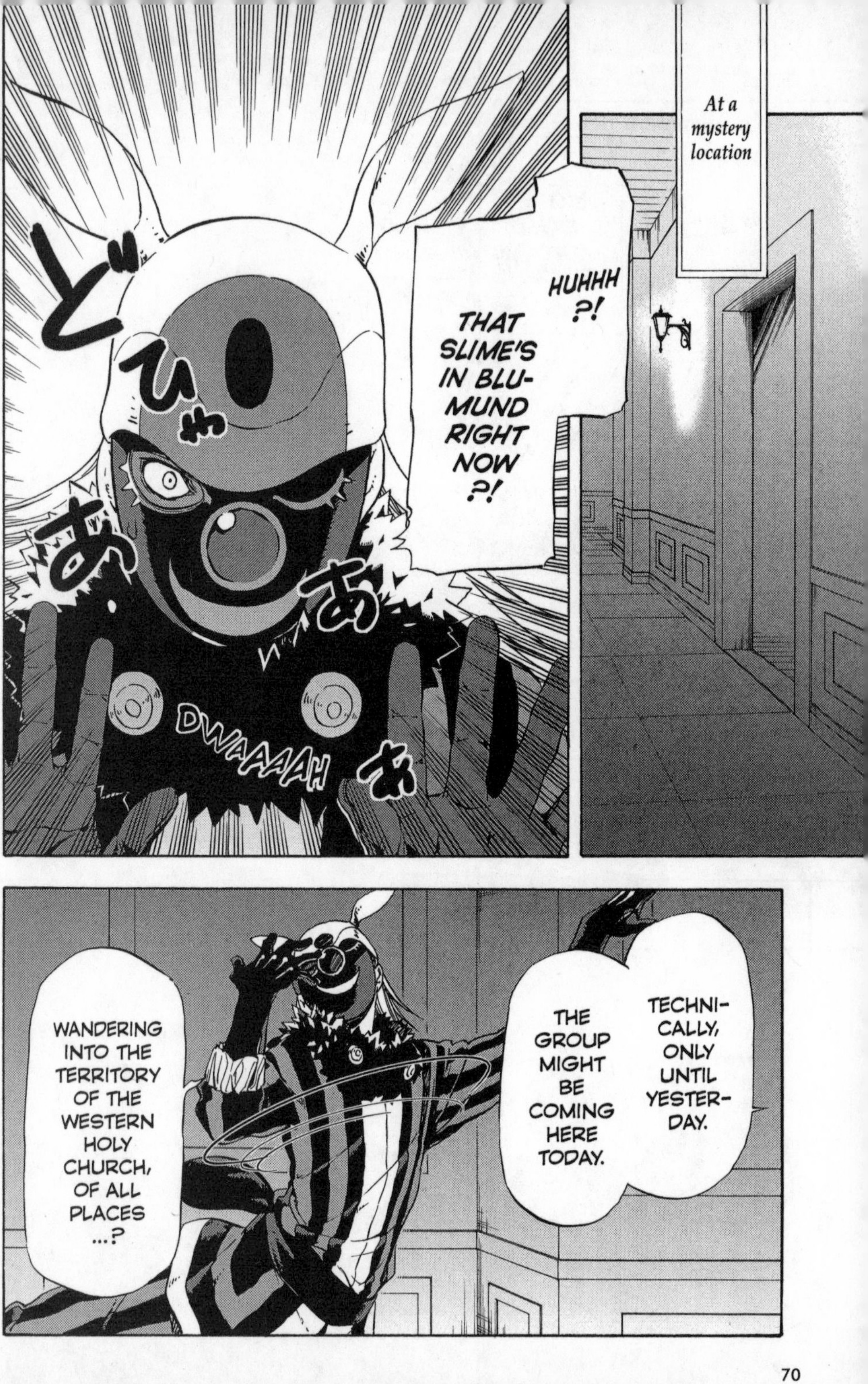
At a mystery location
HUHHH?!
THAT SLIME'S IN BLU-MUND RIGHT NOW?!
DWAAAAH
TECHNI-CALLY, ONLY UNTIL YESTER-DAY.
THE GROUP MIGHT BE COMING HERE TODAY.
WANDERING INTO THE TERRITORY OF THE WESTERN HOLY CHURCH, OF ALL PLACES ...?

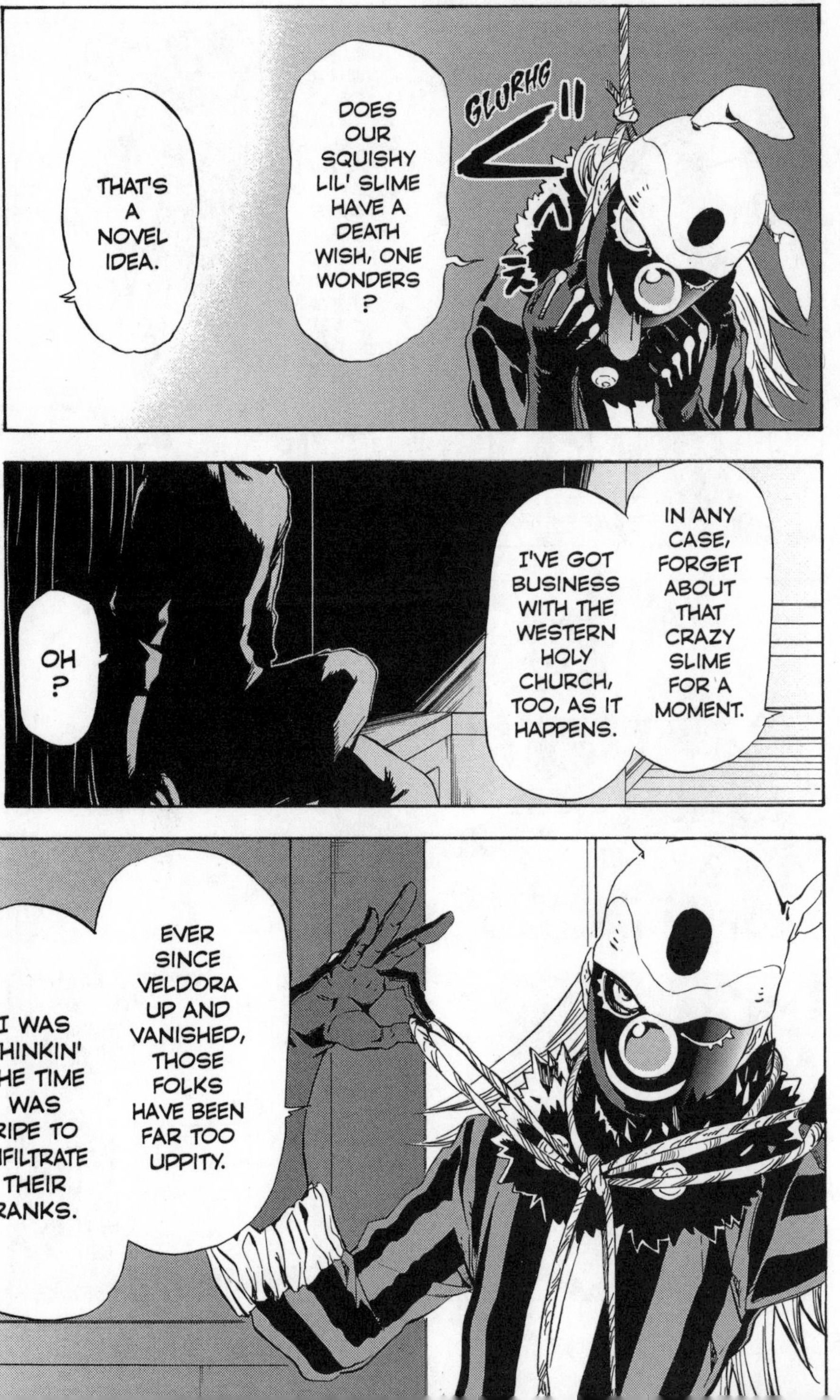
GLURHG
DOES OUR SQUISHY LIL' SLIME HAVE A DEATH WISH, ONE WONDERS?
THAT'S A NOVEL IDEA.
IN ANY CASE, FORGET ABOUT THAT CRAZY SLIME FOR A MOMENT.
I'VE GOT BUSINESS WITH THE WESTERN HOLY CHURCH, TOO, AS IT HAPPENS.
OH?
EVER SINCE VELDORA UP AND VANISHED, THOSE FOLKS HAVE BEEN FAR TOO UPPITY.
I WAS THINKIN' THE TIME WAS RIPE TO INFILTRATE THEIR RANKS.

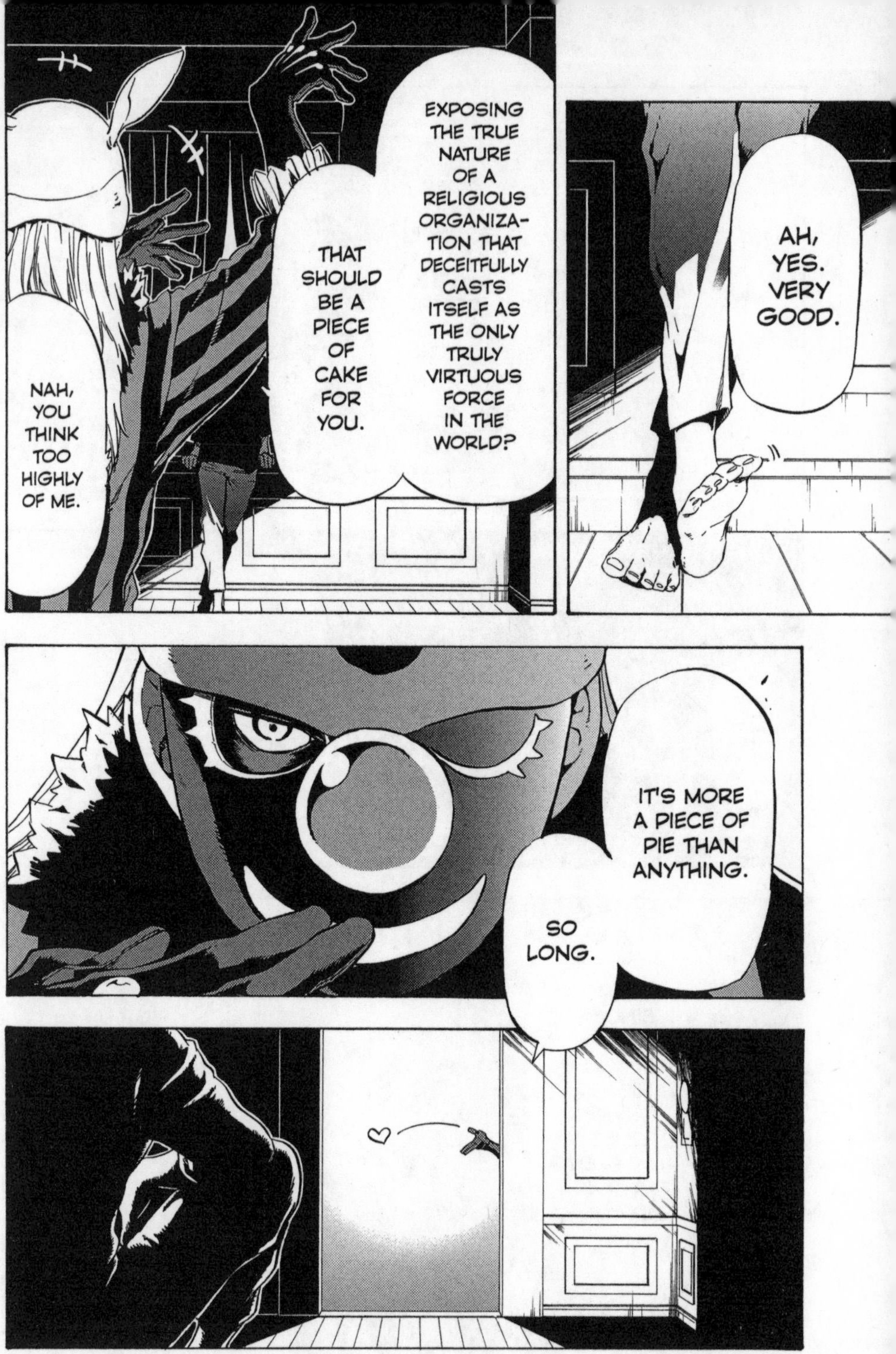
AH, YES. VERY GOOD.
EXPOSING THE TRUE NATURE OF A RELIGIOUS ORGANIZA-TION THAT DECEITFULLY CASTS ITSELF AS THE ONLY TRULY VIRTUOUS FORCE IN THE WORLD?
THAT SHOULD BE A PIECE OF CAKE FOR YOU.
NAH, YOU THINK TOO HIGHLY OF ME.
IT'S MORE A PIECE OF PIE THAN ANYTHING.
SO LONG.

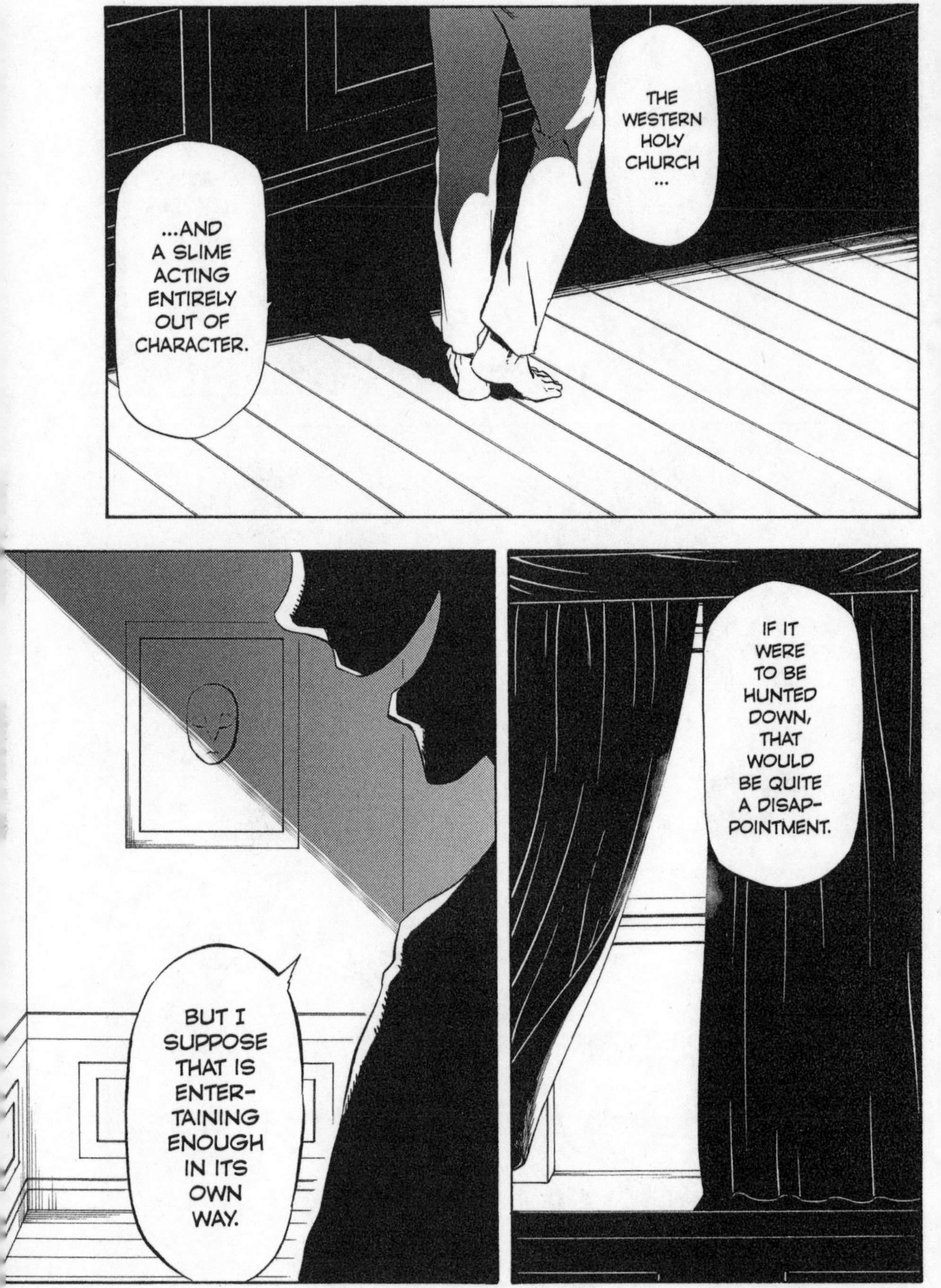
THE WESTERN HOLY CHURCH ...
...AND A SLIME ACTING ENTIRELY OUT OF CHARACTER.
IF IT WERE TO BE HUNTED DOWN, THAT WOULD BE QUITE A DISAP-POINTMENT.
BUT I SUPPOSE THAT IS ENTER-TAINING ENOUGH IN ITS OWN WAY.

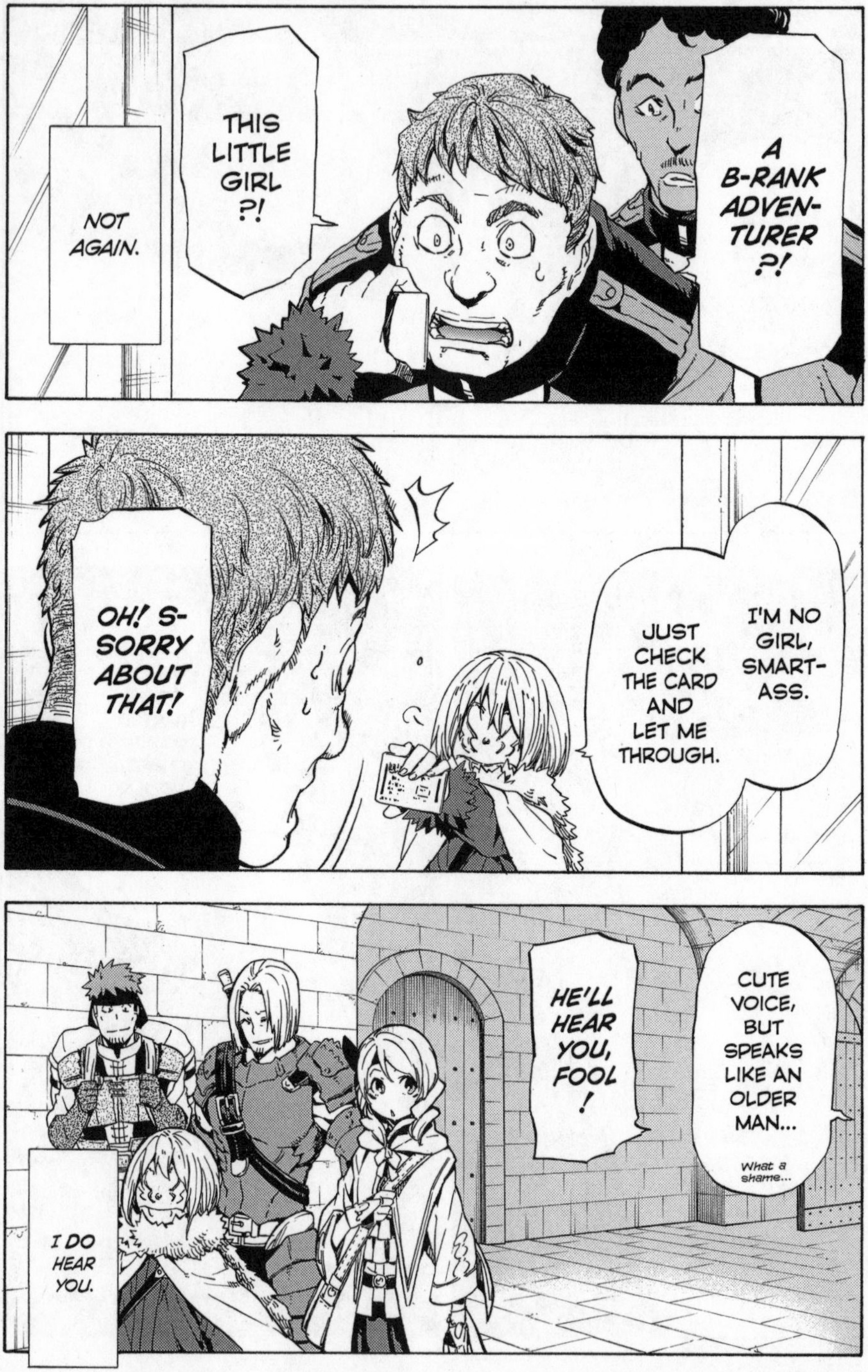
A B-RANK ADVENTURER?!
THIS LITTLE GIRL?!
NOT AGAIN.
I'M NO GIRL, SMART-ASS.
JUST CHECK THE CARD AND LET ME THROUGH.
OH! S-SORRY ABOUT THAT!
CUTE VOICE, BUT SPEAKS LIKE AN OLDER MAN...
What a shame...
HE'LL HEAR YOU, FOOL!
I DO HEAR YOU.

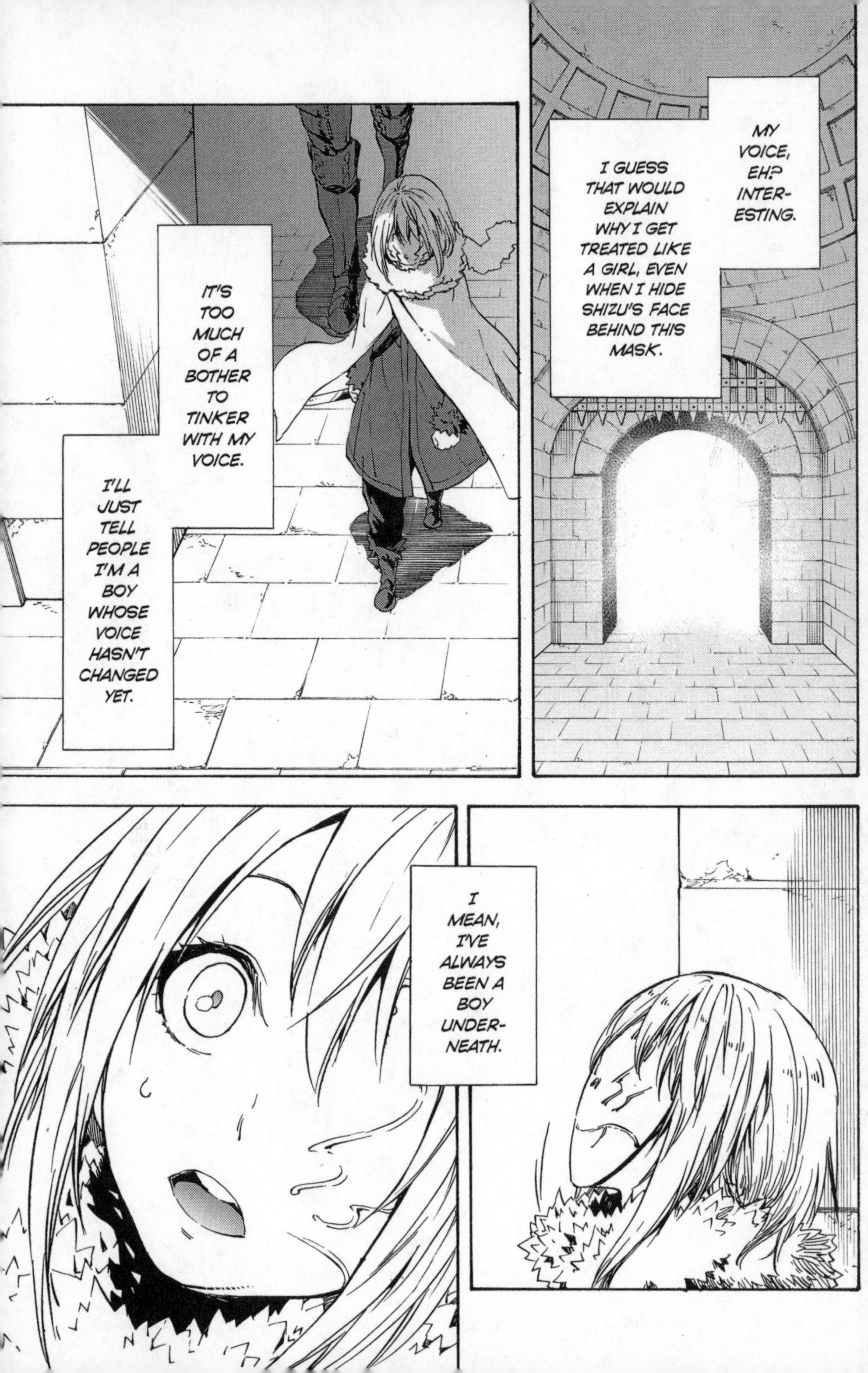
MY VOICE, EH? INTER-ESTING.
I GUESS THAT WOULD EXPLAIN WHY I GET TREATED LIKE A GIRL, EVEN WHEN I HIDE SHIZU'S FACE BEHIND THIS MASK.
IT'S TOO MUCH OF A BOTHER TO TINKER WITH MY VOICE.
I'LL JUST TELL PEOPLE I'M A BOY WHOSE VOICE HASN'T CHANGED YET.
I MEAN, I'VE ALWAYS BEEN A BOY UNDER-NEATH.

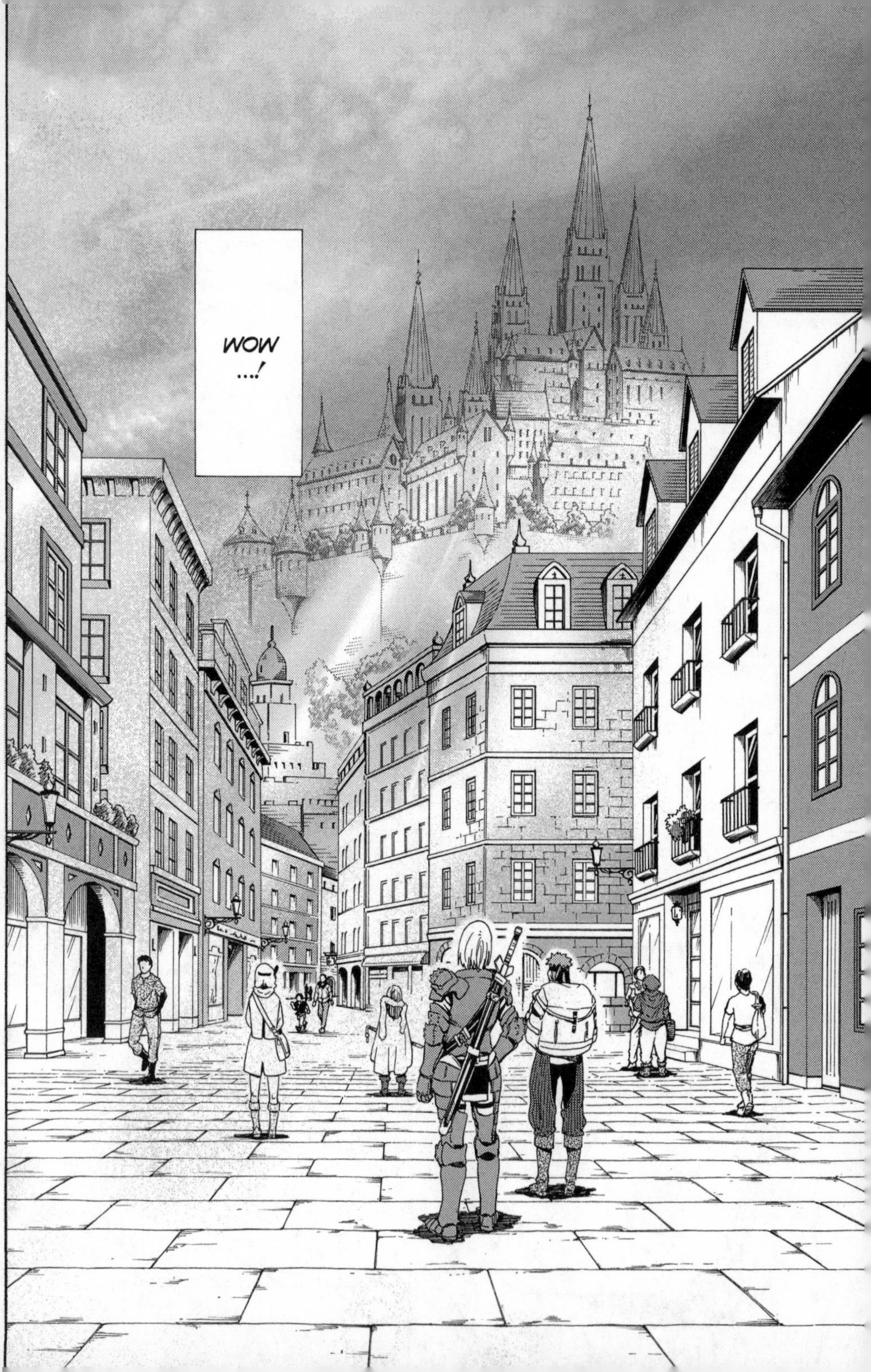
WOW
...!

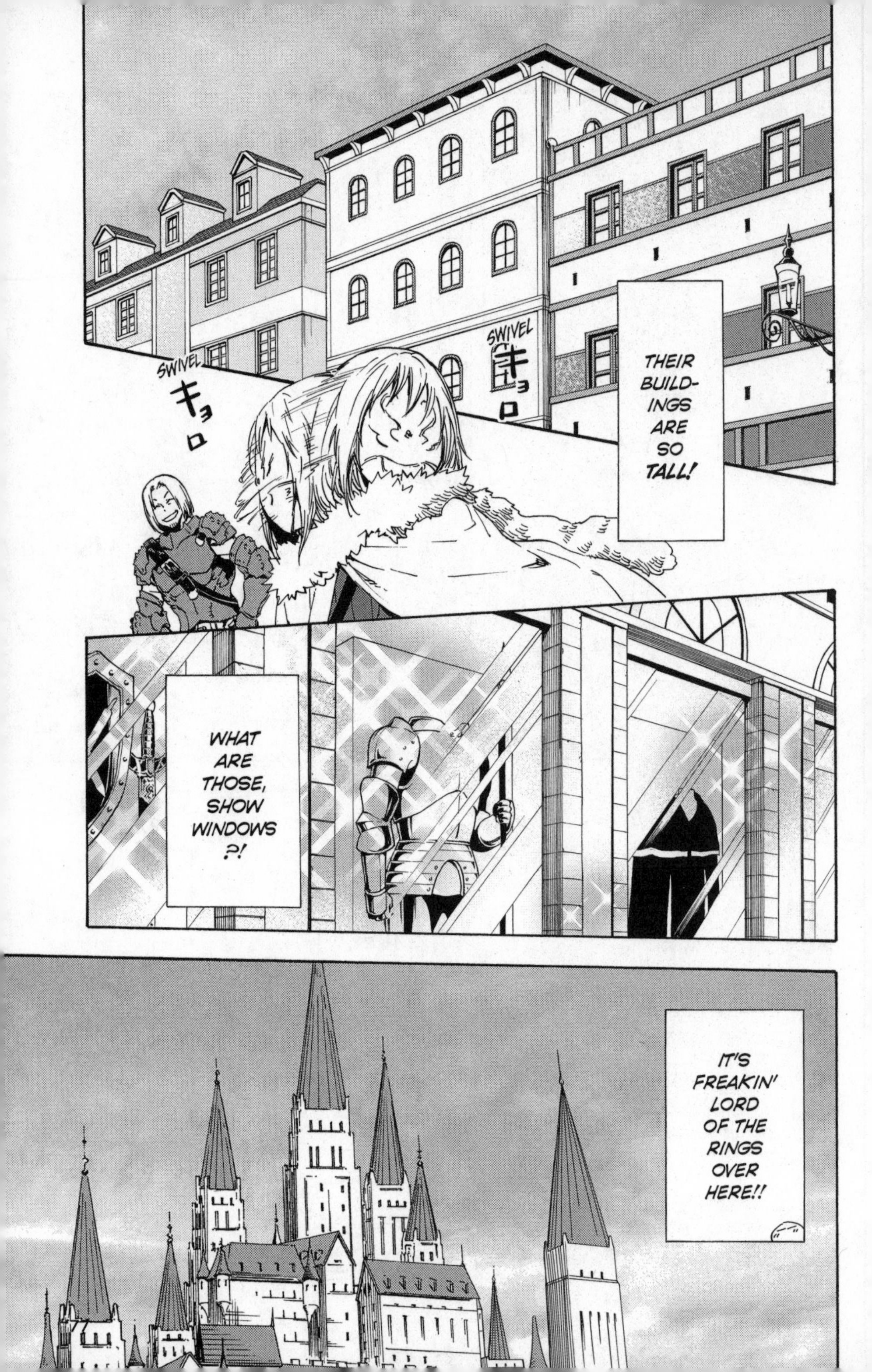
SWIVEL
キョロ
SWIVEL
キョロ
THEIR BUILDINGS ARE SO TALL!
WHAT ARE THOSE, SHOW WINDOWS?!
IT'S FREAKIN' LORD OF THE RINGS OVER HERE!!

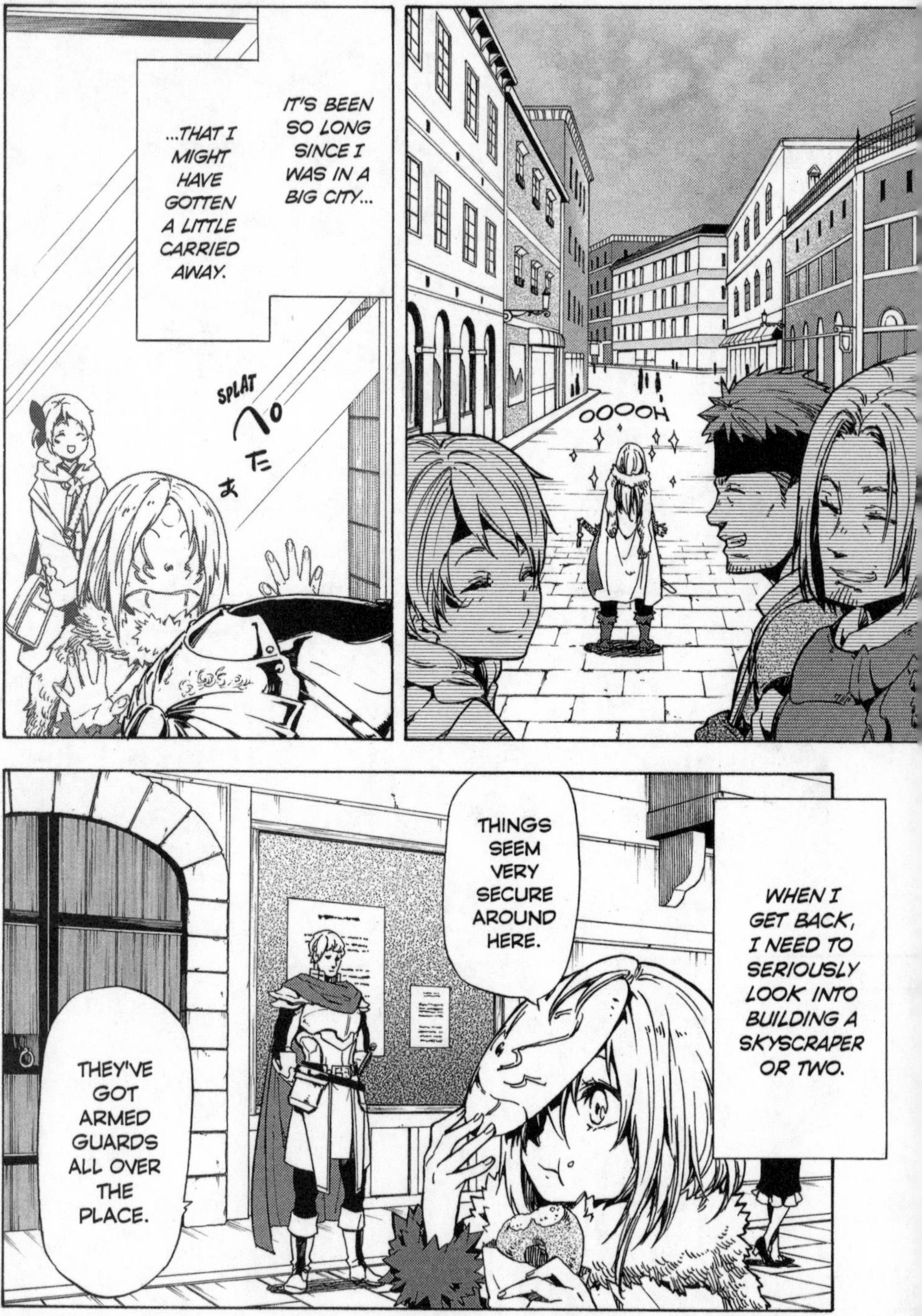
OOOOH
IT'S BEEN SO LONG SINCE I WAS IN A BIG CITY...
...THAT I MIGHT HAVE GOTTEN A LITTLE CARRIED AWAY.
SPLAT
WHEN I GET BACK, I NEED TO SERIOUSLY LOOK INTO BUILDING A SKYSCRAPER OR TWO.
THINGS SEEM VERY SECURE AROUND HERE.
THEY'VE GOT ARMED GUARDS ALL OVER THE PLACE.

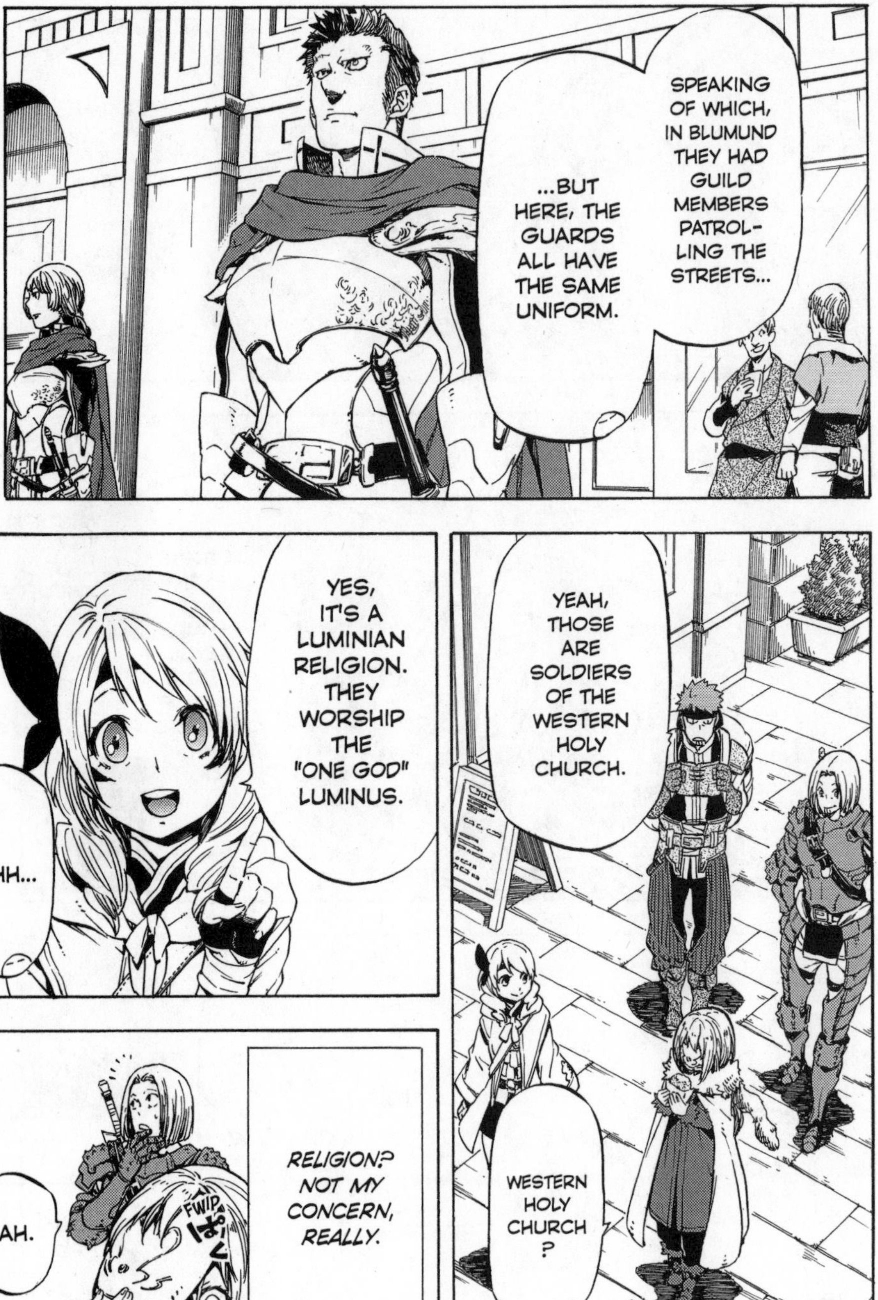
SPEAKING OF WHICH, IN BLUMUND THEY HAD GUILD MEMBERS PATROL-LING THE STREETS...
...BUT HERE, THE GUARDS ALL HAVE THE SAME UNIFORM.
YEAH, THOSE ARE SOLDIERS OF THE WESTERN HOLY CHURCH.
WESTERN HOLY CHURCH?
YES, IT'S A LUMINIAN RELIGION. THEY WORSHIP THE "ONE GOD" LUMINUS.
OHH...
RELIGION? NOT MY CONCERN, REALLY.
FWIP
ぱく
AH.

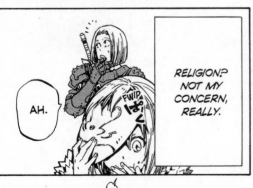

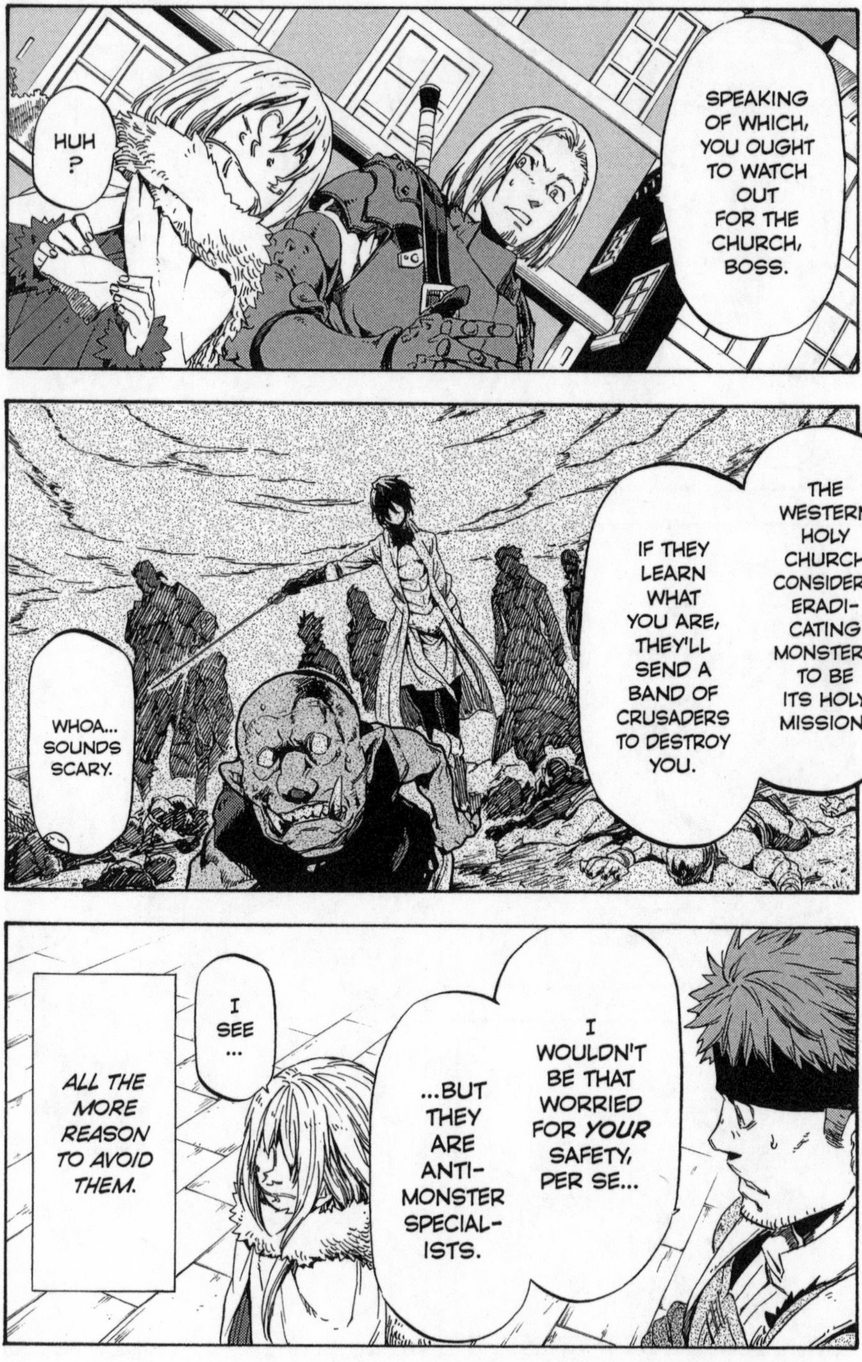
SPEAKING OF WHICH, YOU OUGHT TO WATCH OUT FOR THE CHURCH, BOSS.
HUH?
THE WESTERN HOLY CHURCH CONSIDERS ERADI-CATING MONSTERS TO BE ITS HOLY MISSION.
IF THEY LEARN WHAT YOU ARE, THEY'LL SEND A BAND OF CRUSADERS TO DESTROY YOU.
WHOA... SOUNDS SCARY.
I WOULDN'T BE THAT WORRIED FOR *YOUR* SAFETY, PER SE...
...BUT THEY ARE ANTI-MONSTER SPECIAL-ISTS.
I SEE...
ALL THE MORE REASON TO AVOID THEM.

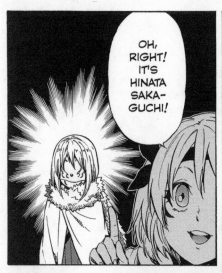

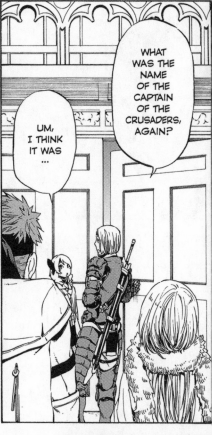

WHAT WAS THE NAME OF THE CAPTAIN OF THE CRUSADERS, AGAIN?
UM, I THINK IT WAS ...
OH, RIGHT! IT'S HINATA SAKA-GUCHI!
HINATA SAKA-GUCHI...
SAKA-GUCHI, AS IN... "HILL" AND "MOUTH"?
ANOTHER JAPANESE NAME, HUH?
FOUR OF YOU?
AND HOW MANY ROOMS WILL YOU NEED?
TWO WILL DO.

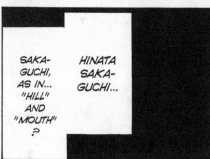

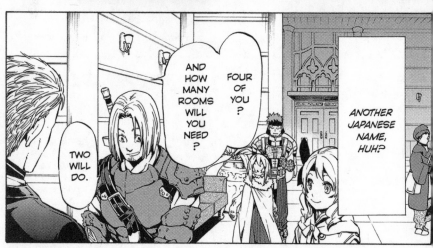

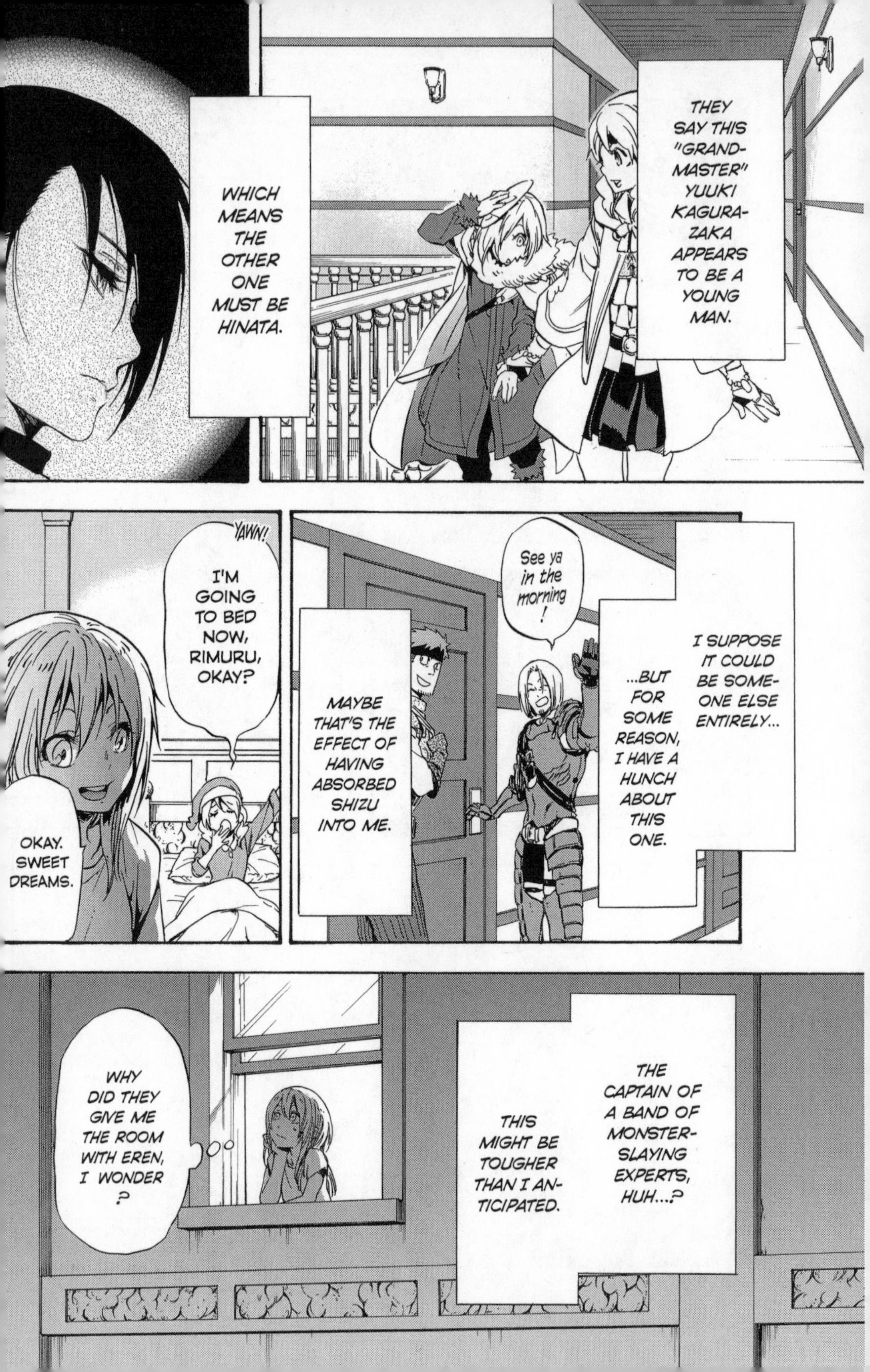
THEY SAY THIS "GRAND-MASTER" YUUKI KAGURA-ZAKA APPEARS TO BE A YOUNG MAN.
WHICH MEANS THE OTHER ONE MUST BE HINATA.
I SUPPOSE IT COULD BE SOME-ONE ELSE ENTIRELY...
See ya in the morning!
...BUT FOR SOME REASON, I HAVE A HUNCH ABOUT THIS ONE.
MAYBE THAT'S THE EFFECT OF HAVING ABSORBED SHIZU INTO ME.
YAWN!
I'M GOING TO BED NOW, RIMURU, OKAY?
OKAY. SWEET DREAMS.
THE CAPTAIN OF A BAND OF MONSTER-SLAYING EXPERTS, HUH...?
THIS MIGHT BE TOUGHER THAN I AN-TICIPATED.
WHY DID THEY GIVE ME THE ROOM WITH EREN, I WONDER?

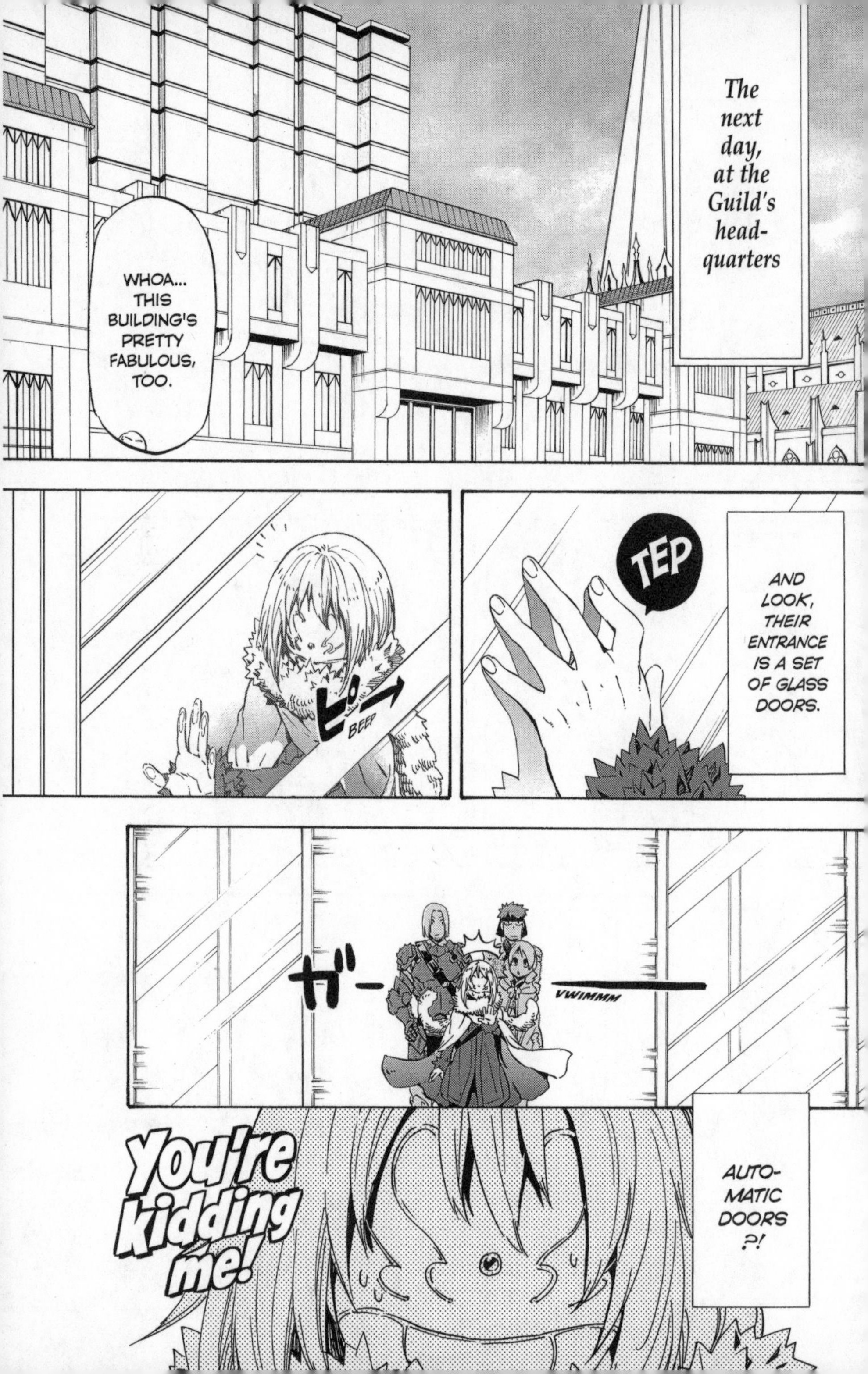
The next day, at the Guild's head-quarters
WHOA... THIS BUILDING'S PRETTY FABULOUS, TOO.
TEP
AND LOOK, THEIR ENTRANCE IS A SET OF GLASS DOORS.
ピー
BEEP
ガー
VWIMMM
AUTO-MATIC DOORS ?!
You're kidding me!

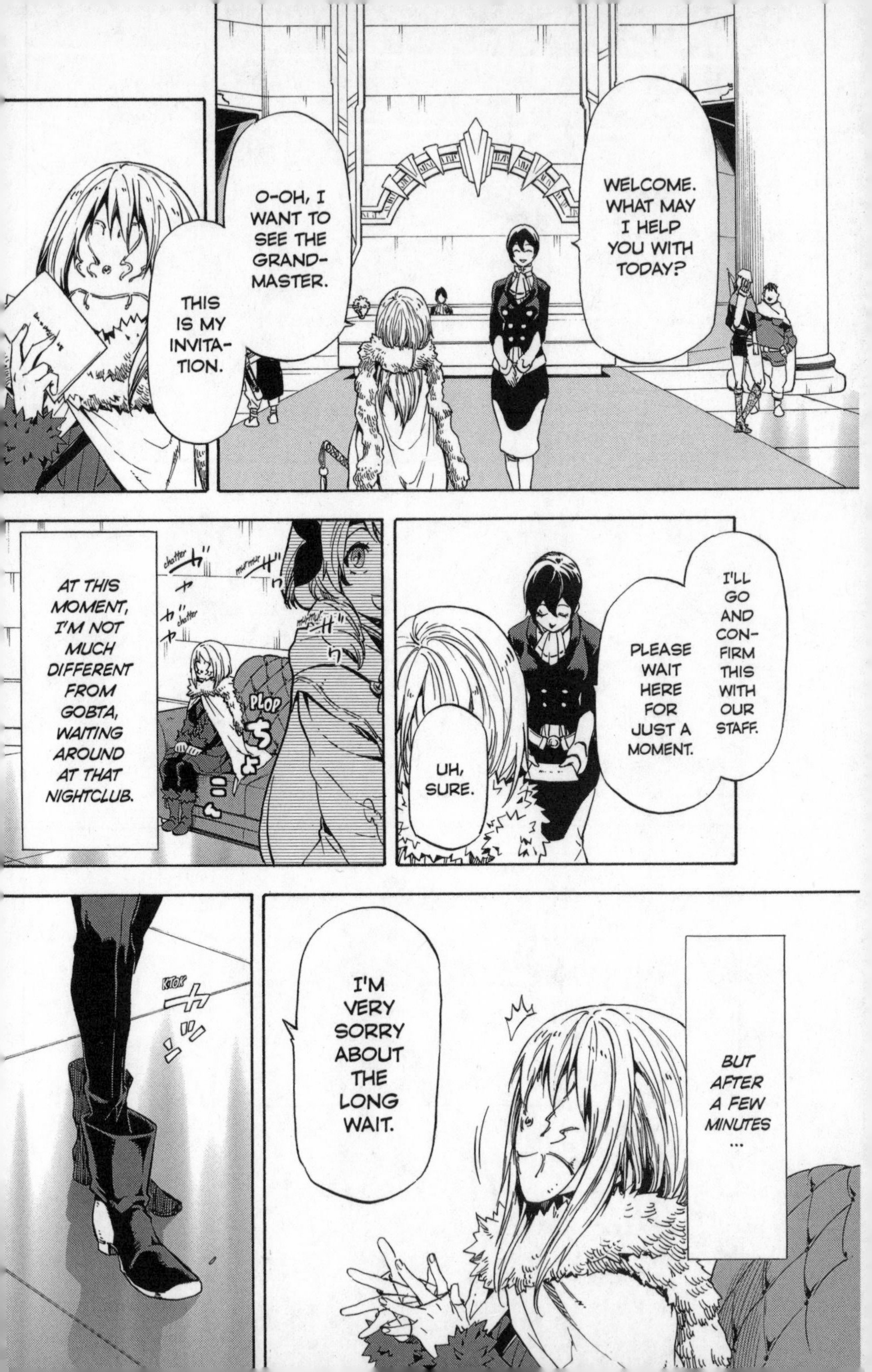
WELCOME. WHAT MAY I HELP YOU WITH TODAY?
O-OH, I WANT TO SEE THE GRAND-MASTER.
THIS IS MY INVITA-TION.
I'LL GO AND CON-FIRM THIS WITH OUR STAFF.
PLEASE WAIT HERE FOR JUST A MOMENT.
UH, SURE.
chatter
murmur
chatter
murmur
PLOP
AT THIS MOMENT, I'M NOT MUCH DIFFERENT FROM GOBTA, WAITING AROUND AT THAT NIGHTCLUB.
BUT AFTER A FEW MINUTES ...
I'M VERY SORRY ABOUT THE LONG WAIT.
KTOK

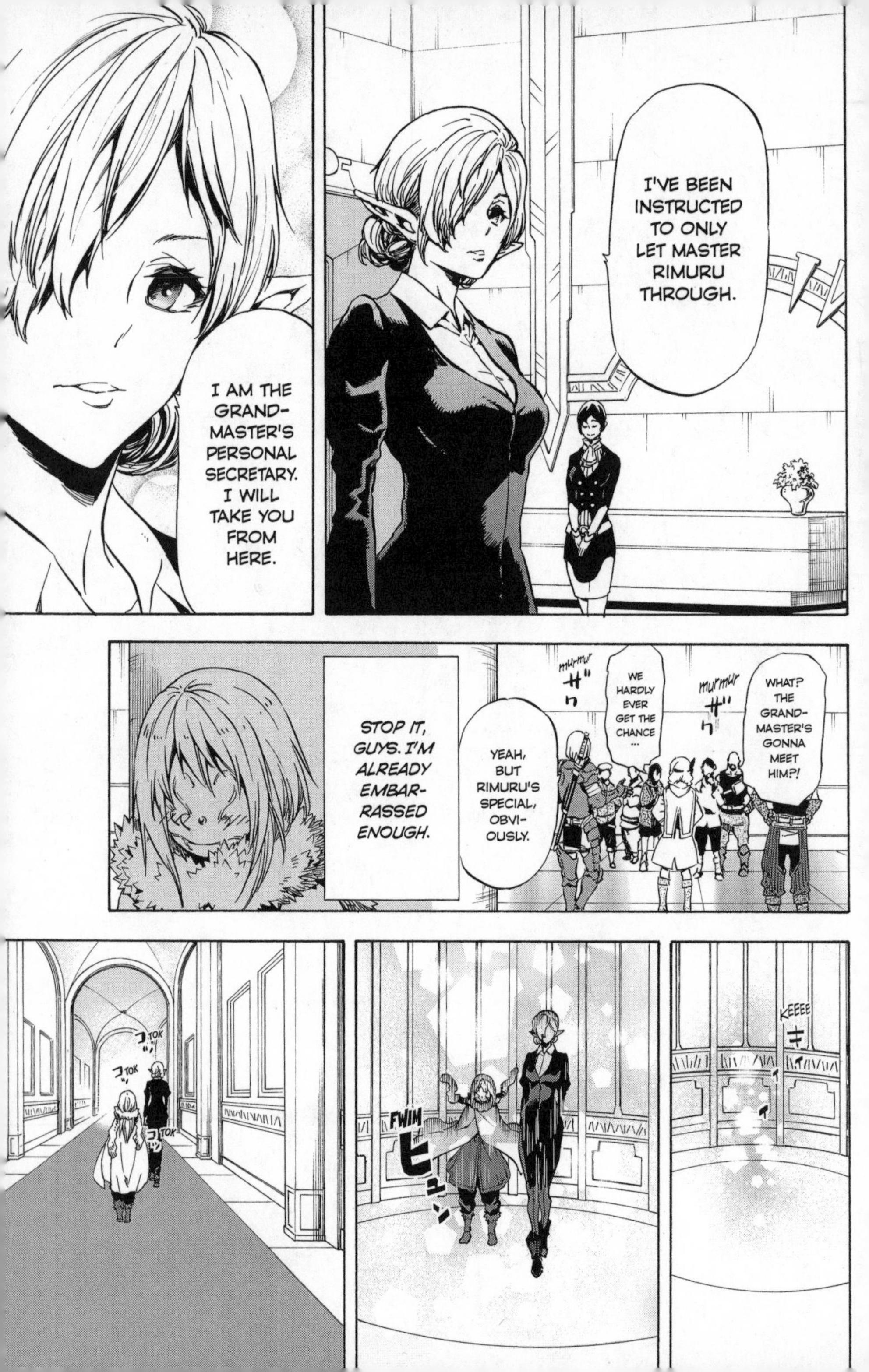
I'VE BEEN INSTRUCTED TO ONLY LET MASTER RIMURU THROUGH.
I AM THE GRAND-MASTER'S PERSONAL SECRETARY. I WILL TAKE YOU FROM HERE.
murmur
WHAT? THE GRAND-MASTER'S GONNA MEET HIM?!
murmur
WE HARDLY EVER GET THE CHANCE ...
YEAH, BUT RIMURU'S SPECIAL, OBVIOUSLY.
STOP IT, GUYS. I'M ALREADY EMBARRASSED ENOUGH.
KEEEE
FWIM
TOK
TOK
TOK

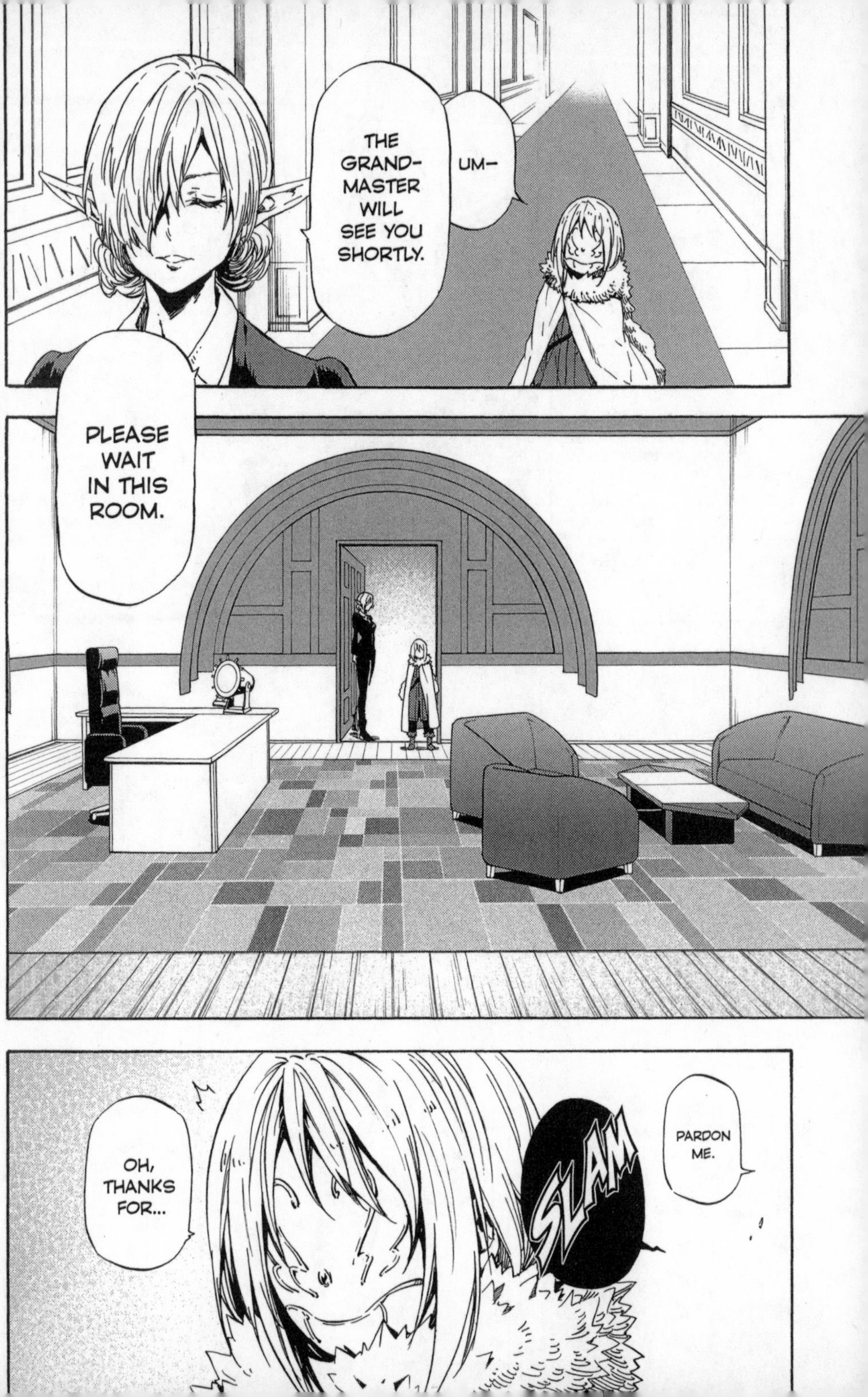
UM—
THE GRAND-MASTER WILL SEE YOU SHORTLY.
PLEASE WAIT IN THIS ROOM.
PARDON ME.
SLAM
OH, THANKS FOR...

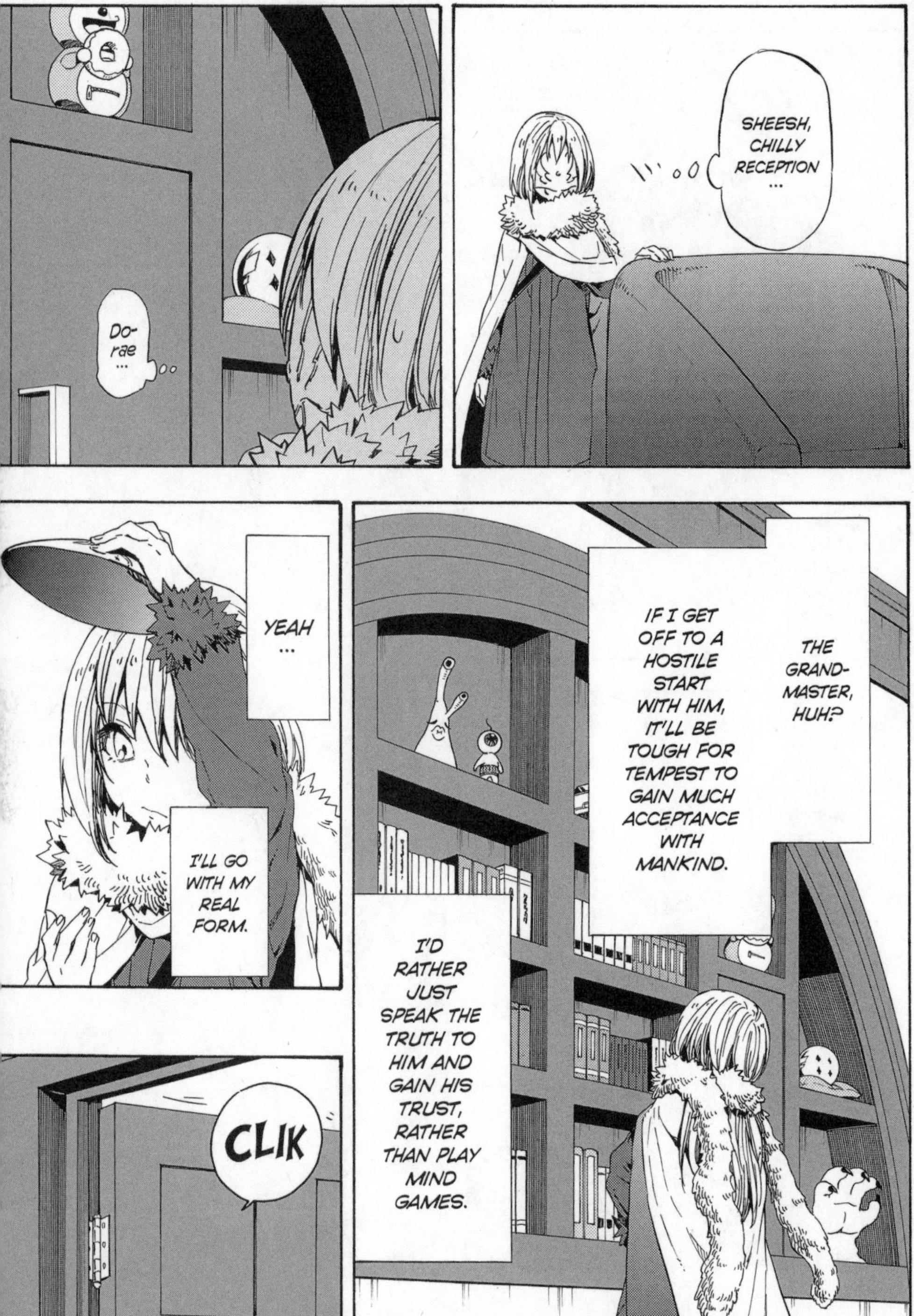
SHEESH, CHILLY RECEPTION ...
Do-rae ...
THE GRAND-MASTER, HUH?
IF I GET OFF TO A HOSTILE START WITH HIM, IT'LL BE TOUGH FOR TEMPEST TO GAIN MUCH ACCEPTANCE WITH MANKIND.
I'D RATHER JUST SPEAK THE TRUTH TO HIM AND GAIN HIS TRUST, RATHER THAN PLAY MIND GAMES.
YEAH ...
I'LL GO WITH MY REAL FORM.
CLIK

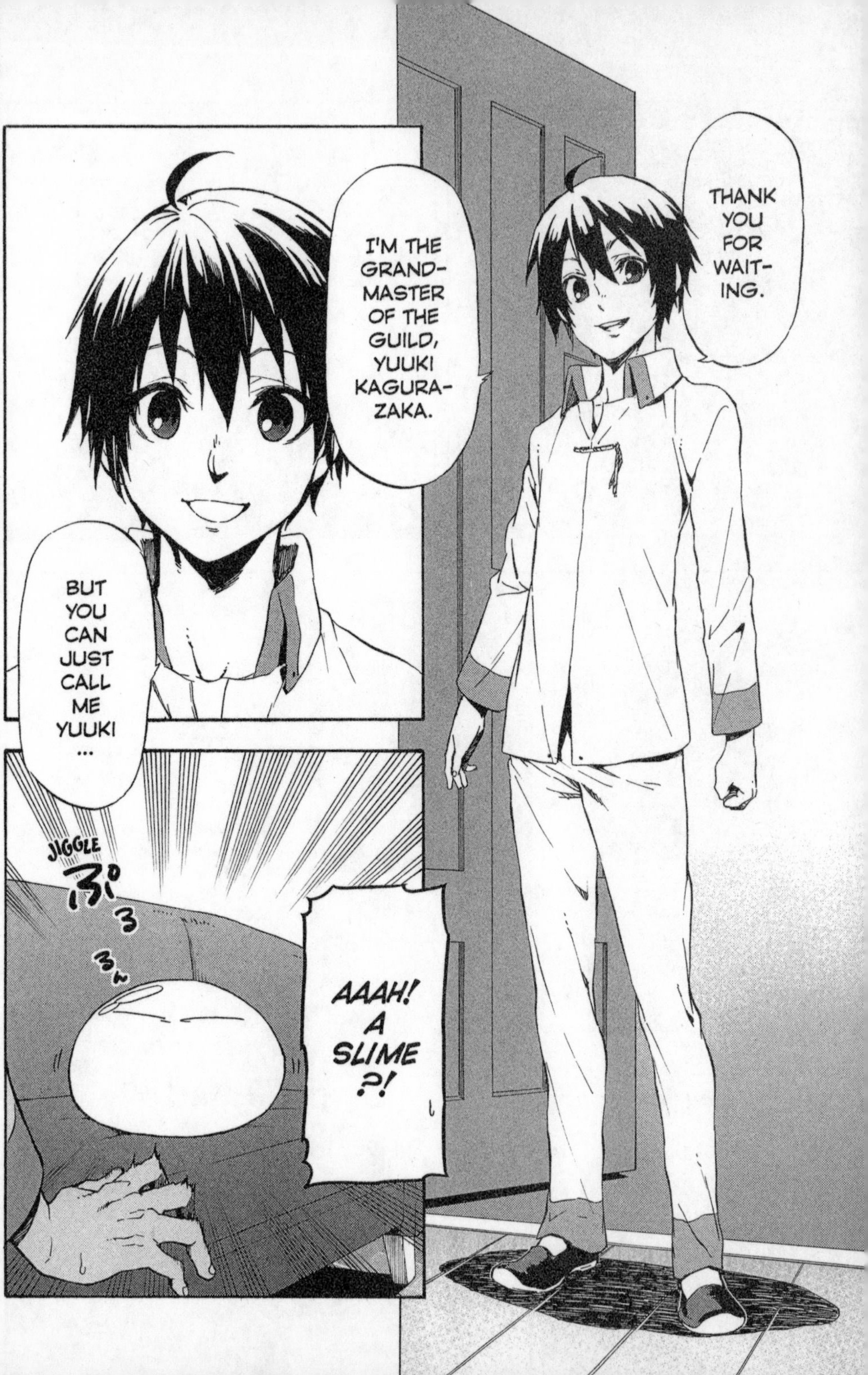
THANK YOU FOR WAIT-ING.
I'M THE GRAND-MASTER OF THE GUILD, YUUKI KAGURA-ZAKA.
BUT YOU CAN JUST CALL ME YUUKI ...
JIGGLE
AAAH! A SLIME ?!

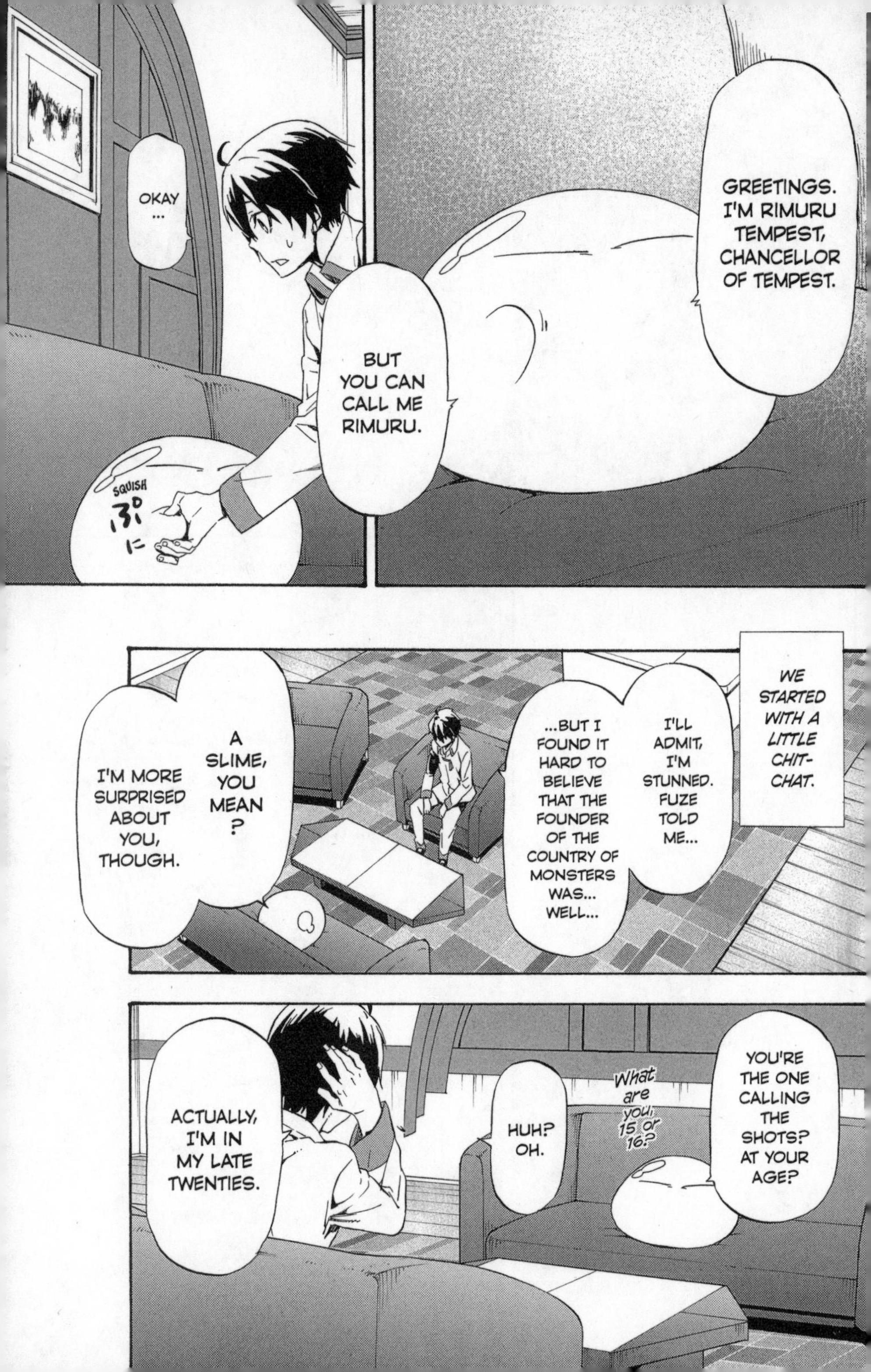
GREETINGS. I'M RIMURU TEMPEST, CHANCELLOR OF TEMPEST.
BUT YOU CAN CALL ME RIMURU.
OKAY...
SQUISH
ぷに
WE STARTED WITH A LITTLE CHIT-CHAT.
I'LL ADMIT, I'M STUNNED. FUZE TOLD ME...
...BUT I FOUND IT HARD TO BELIEVE THAT THE FOUNDER OF THE COUNTRY OF MONSTERS WAS... WELL...
A SLIME, YOU MEAN?
I'M MORE SURPRISED ABOUT YOU, THOUGH.
YOU'RE THE ONE CALLING THE SHOTS? AT YOUR AGE?
What are you, 15 or 16?
HUH? OH.
ACTUALLY, I'M IN MY LATE TWENTIES.

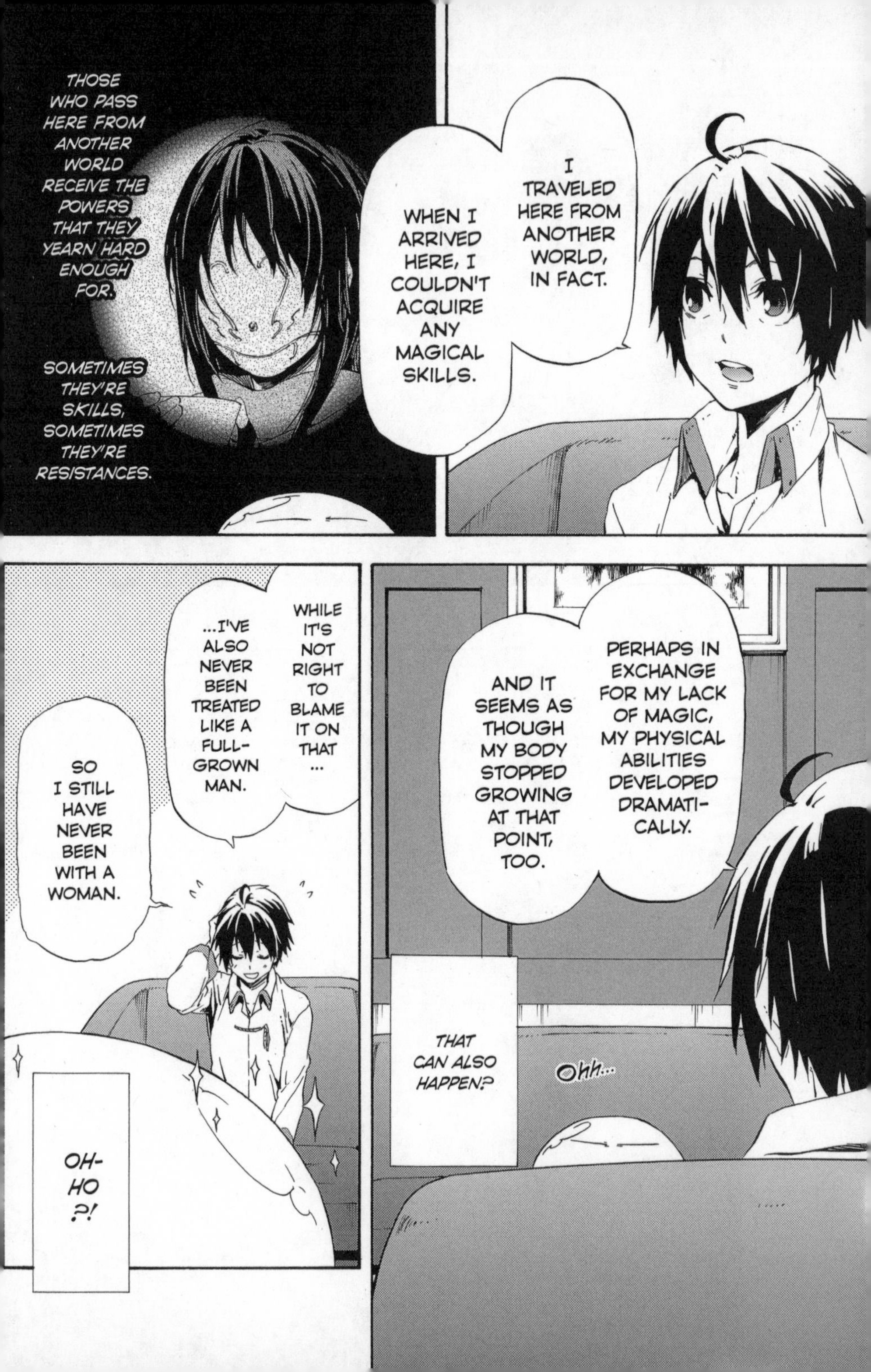
I TRAVELED HERE FROM ANOTHER WORLD, IN FACT.
WHEN I ARRIVED HERE, I COULDN'T ACQUIRE ANY MAGICAL SKILLS.
THOSE WHO PASS HERE FROM ANOTHER WORLD RECEIVE THE POWERS THAT THEY YEARN HARD ENOUGH FOR.
SOMETIMES THEY'RE SKILLS, SOMETIMES THEY'RE RESISTANCES.
PERHAPS IN EXCHANGE FOR MY LACK OF MAGIC, MY PHYSICAL ABILITIES DEVELOPED DRAMATICALLY.
AND IT SEEMS AS THOUGH MY BODY STOPPED GROWING AT THAT POINT, TOO.
Ohh...
THAT CAN ALSO HAPPEN?
WHILE IT'S NOT RIGHT TO BLAME IT ON THAT ...
...I'VE ALSO NEVER BEEN TREATED LIKE A FULL-GROWN MAN.
SO I STILL HAVE NEVER BEEN WITH A WOMAN.
OH-HO ?!

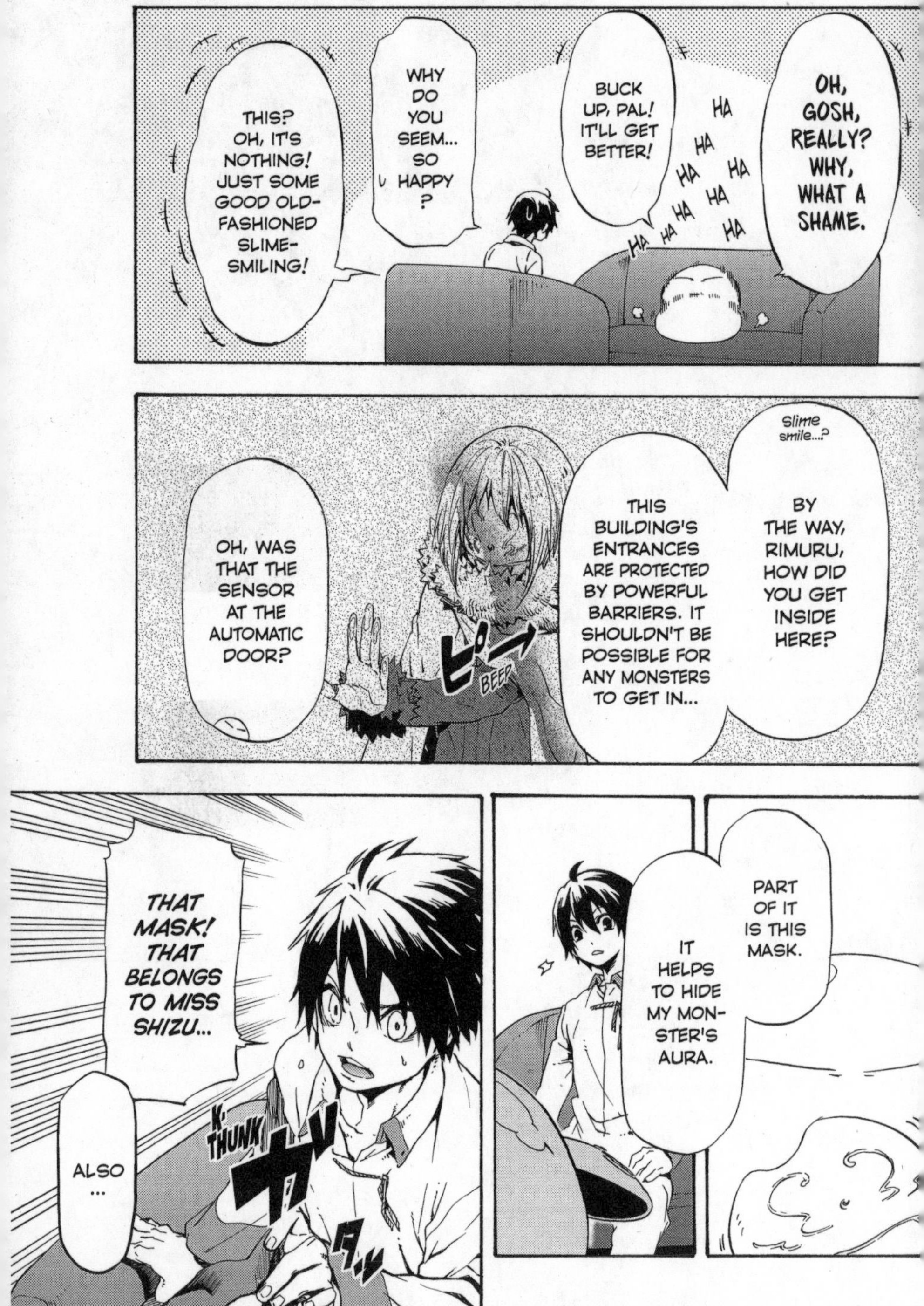
OH, GOSH, REALLY? WHY, WHAT A SHAME.
HA HA HA HA HA HA HA HA HA
BUCK UP, PAL! IT'LL GET BETTER!
WHY DO YOU SEEM... SO HAPPY?
THIS? OH, IT'S NOTHING! JUST SOME GOOD OLD-FASHIONED SLIME-SMILING!
Slime smile...?
BY THE WAY, RIMURU, HOW DID YOU GET INSIDE HERE?
THIS BUILDING'S ENTRANCES ARE PROTECTED BY POWERFUL BARRIERS. IT SHOULDN'T BE POSSIBLE FOR ANY MONSTERS TO GET IN...
BEEP
OH, WAS THAT THE SENSOR AT THE AUTOMATIC DOOR?
PART OF IT IS THIS MASK.
IT HELPS TO HIDE MY MONSTER'S AURA.
THAT MASK! THAT BELONGS TO MISS SHIZU...
K-THUNK
ALSO ...

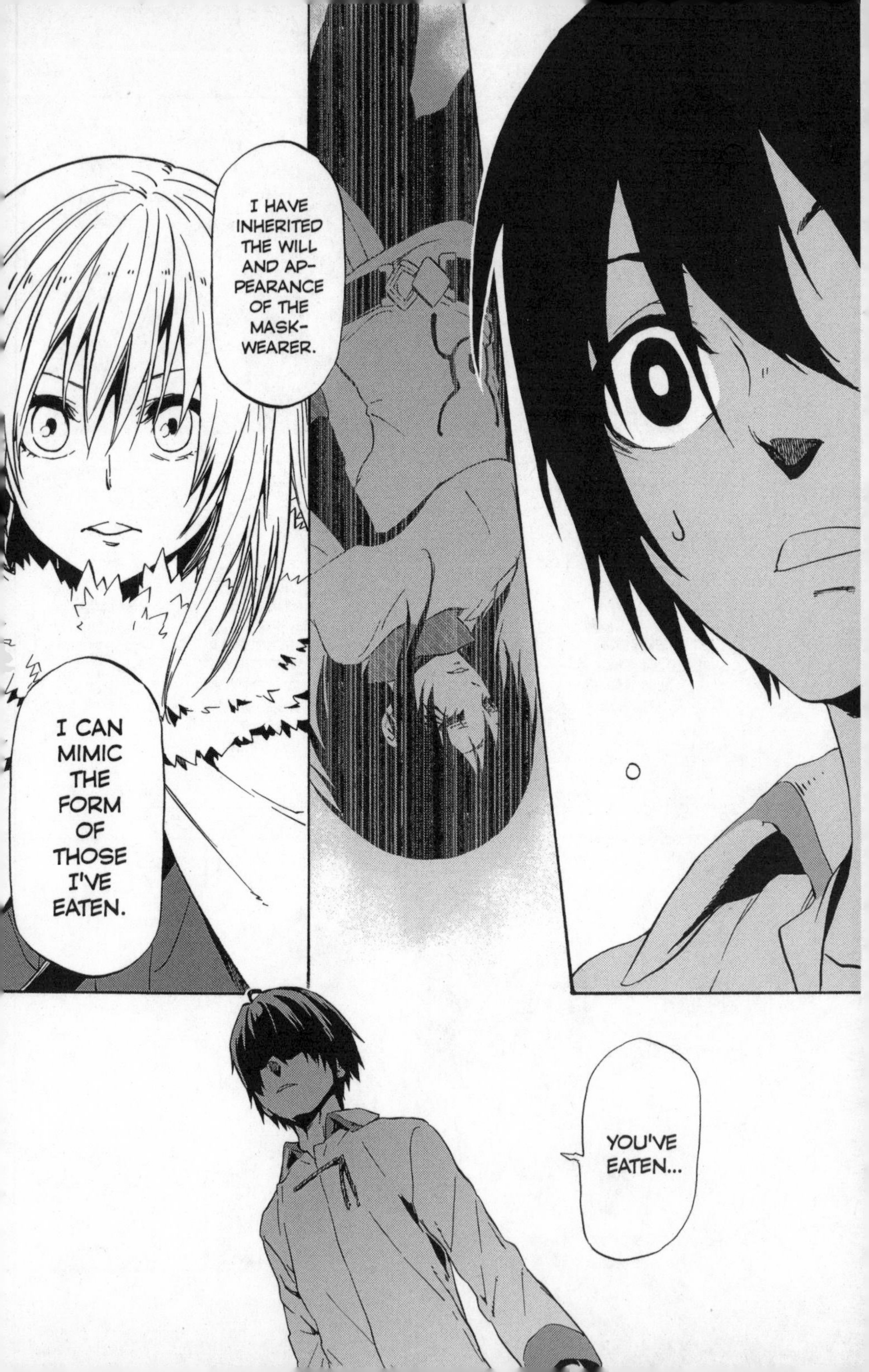
I HAVE INHERITED THE WILL AND AP- PEARANCE OF THE MASK- WEARER.
I CAN MIMIC THE FORM OF THOSE I'VE EATEN.
YOU'VE EATEN...

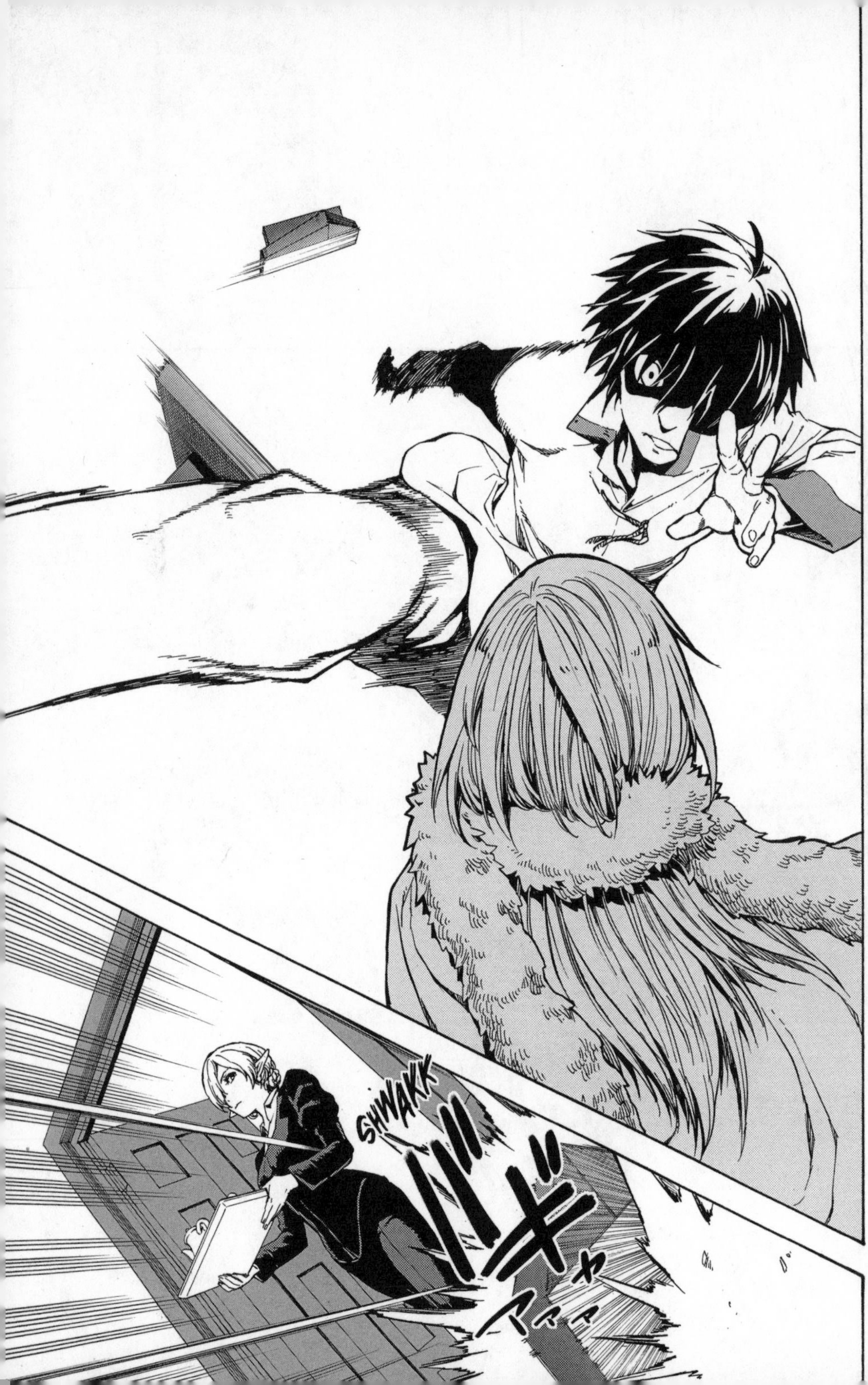
SHWAKK

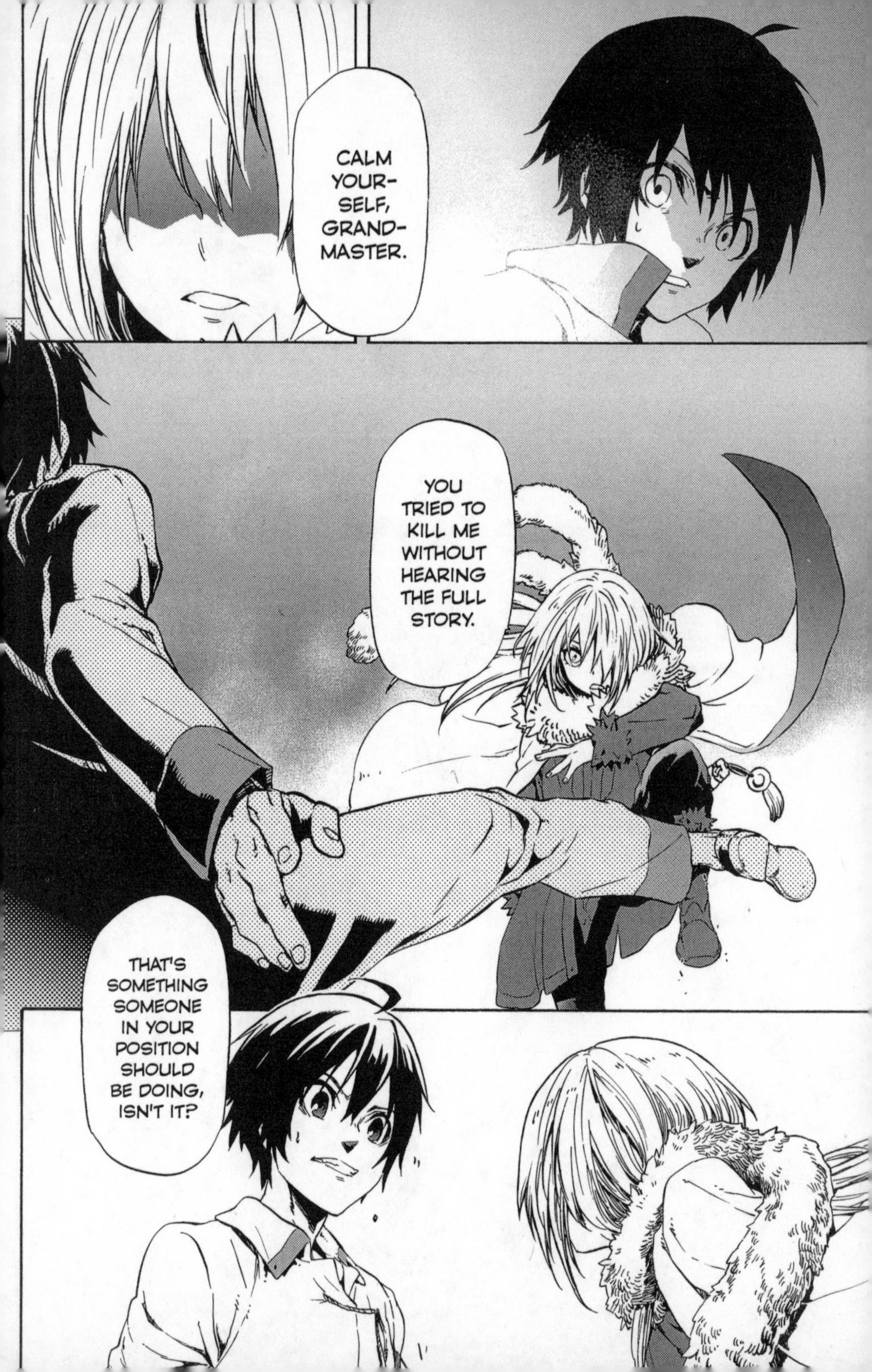
CALM YOURSELF, GRANDMASTER.
YOU TRIED TO KILL ME WITHOUT HEARING THE FULL STORY.
THAT'S SOMETHING SOMEONE IN YOUR POSITION SHOULD BE DOING, ISN'T IT?

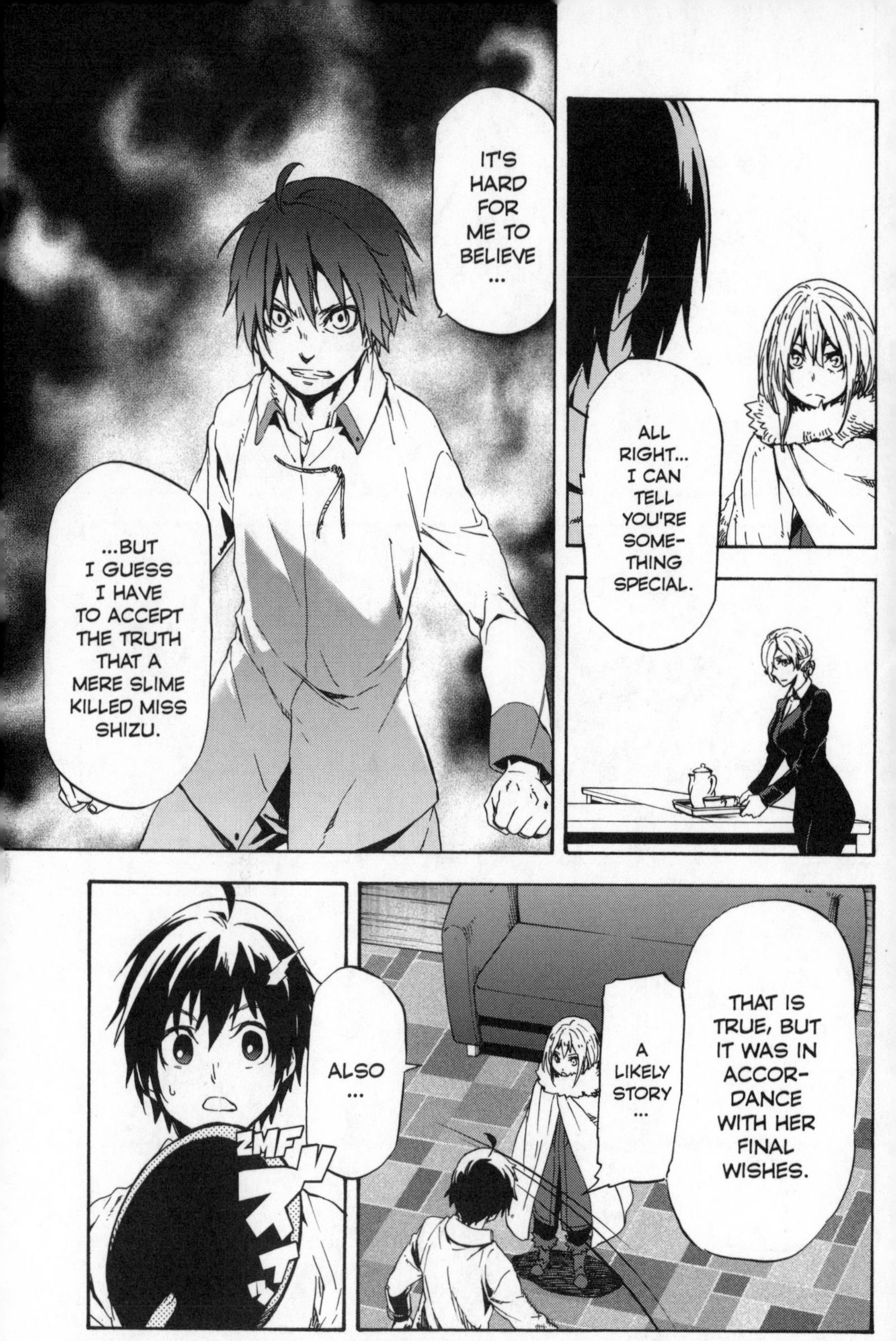
ALL RIGHT... I CAN TELL YOU'RE SOME-THING SPECIAL.
IT'S HARD FOR ME TO BELIEVE ...
...BUT I GUESS I HAVE TO ACCEPT THE TRUTH THAT A MERE SLIME KILLED MISS SHIZU.
THAT IS TRUE, BUT IT WAS IN ACCOR-DANCE WITH HER FINAL WISHES.
A LIKELY STORY ...
ALSO ...
ZMF

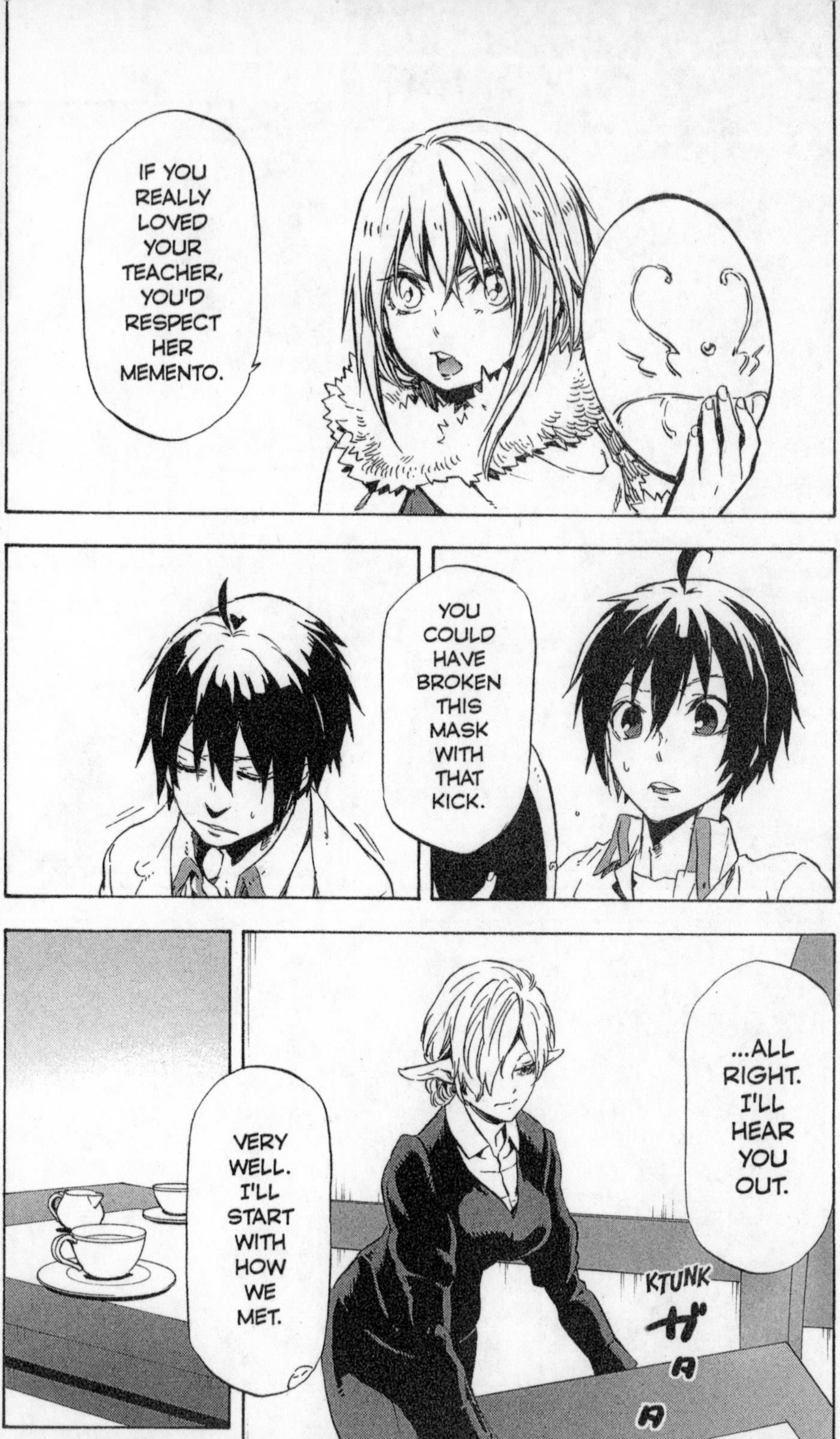
IF YOU REALLY LOVED YOUR TEACHER, YOU'D RESPECT HER MEMENTO.
YOU COULD HAVE BROKEN THIS MASK WITH THAT KICK.
...ALL RIGHT. I'LL HEAR YOU OUT.
KTUNK
ガタタ
VERY WELL. I'LL START WITH HOW WE MET.

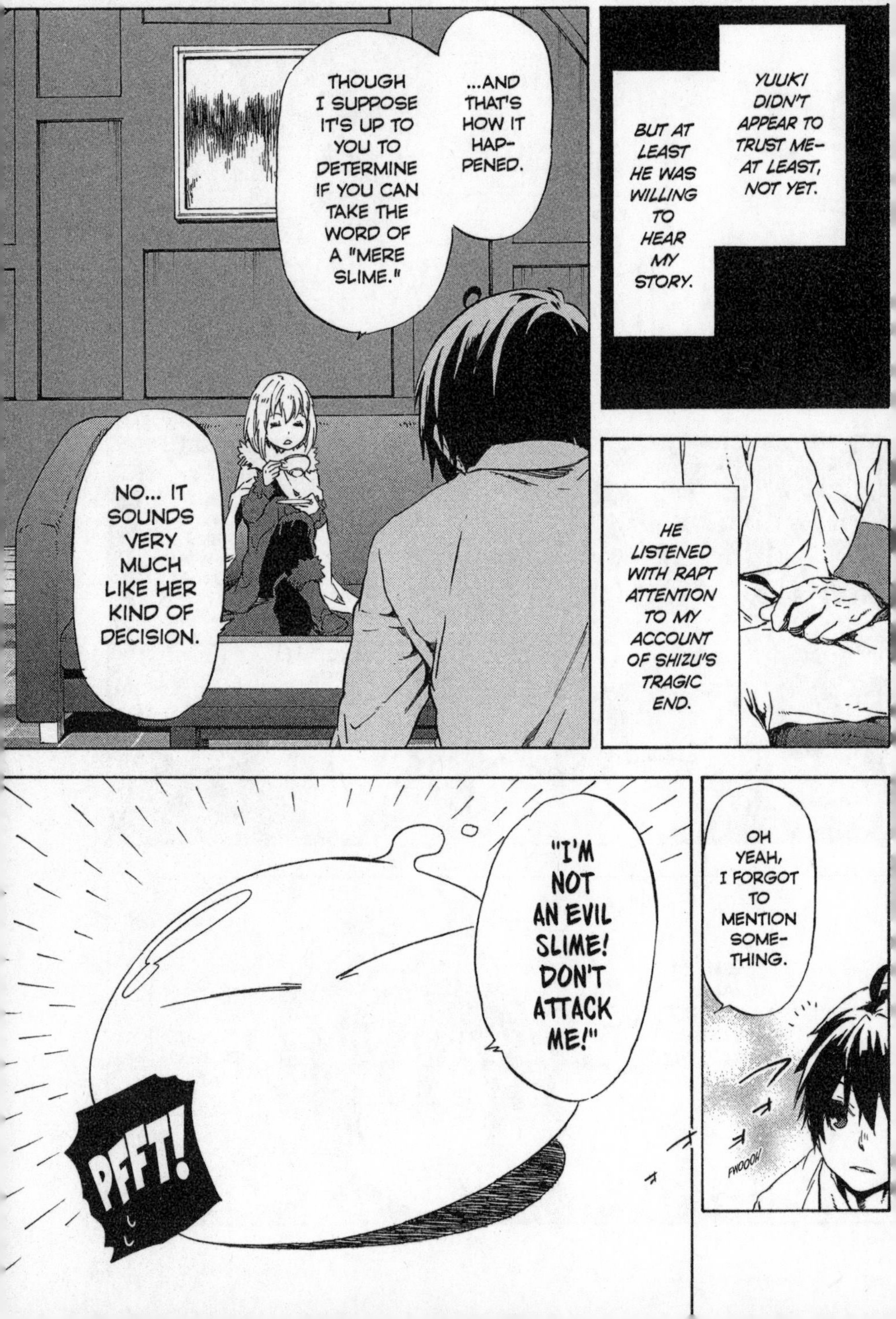
YUUKI DIDN'T APPEAR TO TRUST ME— AT LEAST, NOT YET.
BUT AT LEAST HE WAS WILLING TO HEAR MY STORY.
HE LISTENED WITH RAPT ATTENTION TO MY ACCOUNT OF SHIZU'S TRAGIC END.
...AND THAT'S HOW IT HAP-PENED.
THOUGH I SUPPOSE IT'S UP TO YOU TO DETERMINE IF YOU CAN TAKE THE WORD OF A "MERE SLIME."
NO... IT SOUNDS VERY MUCH LIKE HER KIND OF DECISION.
OH YEAH, I FORGOT TO MENTION SOME-THING.
FWOOOH
"I'M NOT AN EVIL SLIME! DON'T ATTACK ME!"
PFFT!

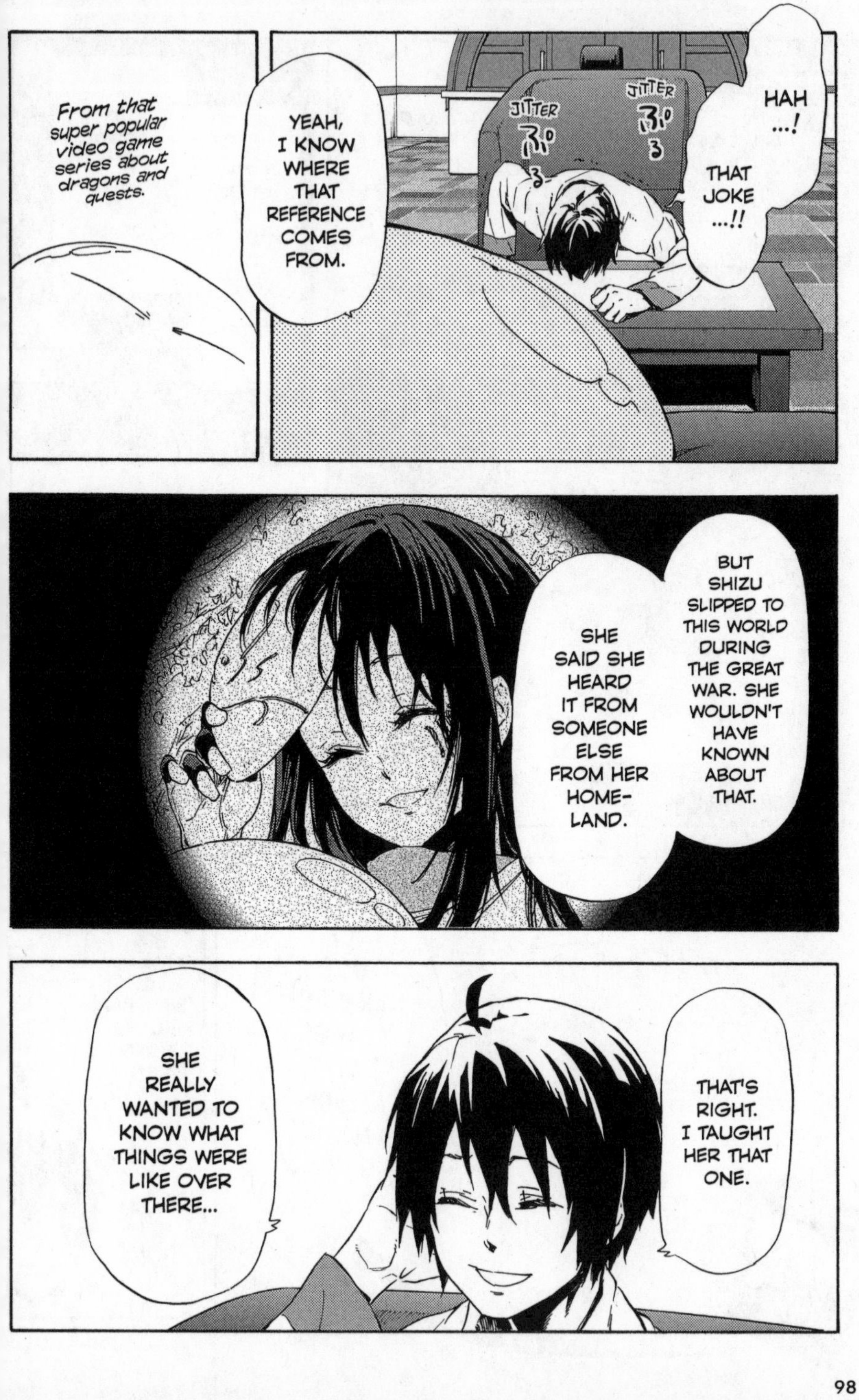
HAH ...!
THAT JOKE ...!!
JITTER
JITTER
YEAH, I KNOW WHERE THAT REFERENCE COMES FROM.
From that super popular video game series about dragons and quests.
BUT SHIZU SLIPPED TO THIS WORLD DURING THE GREAT WAR. SHE WOULDN'T HAVE KNOWN ABOUT THAT.
SHE SAID SHE HEARD IT FROM SOMEONE ELSE FROM HER HOME-LAND.
THAT'S RIGHT. I TAUGHT HER THAT ONE.
SHE REALLY WANTED TO KNOW WHAT THINGS WERE LIKE OVER THERE...

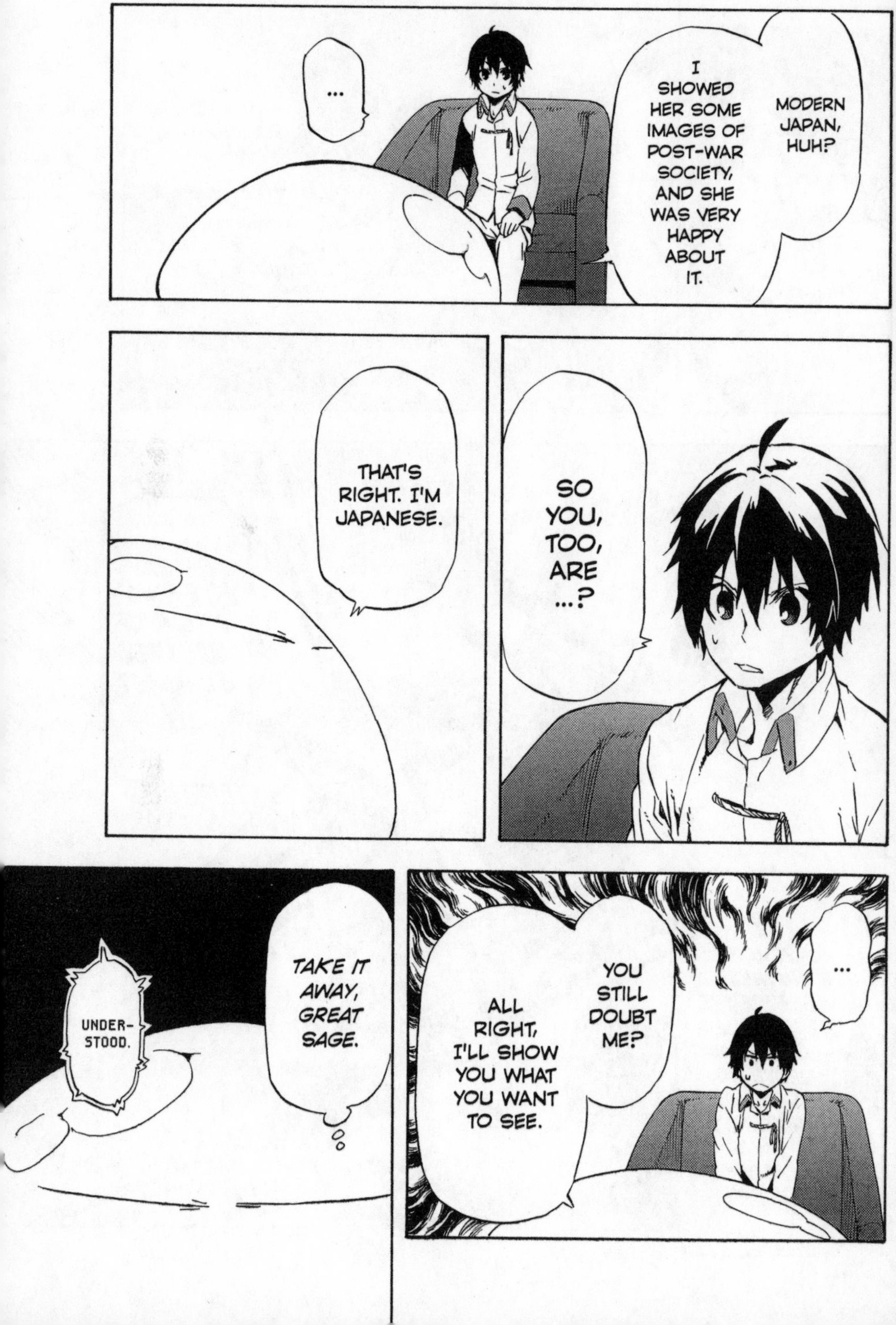
MODERN JAPAN, HUH?
I SHOWED HER SOME IMAGES OF POST-WAR SOCIETY, AND SHE WAS VERY HAPPY ABOUT IT.
...
SO YOU, TOO, ARE ...?
THAT'S RIGHT. I'M JAPANESE.
...
YOU STILL DOUBT ME?
ALL RIGHT, I'LL SHOW YOU WHAT YOU WANT TO SEE.
TAKE IT AWAY, GREAT SAGE.
UNDER-STOOD.

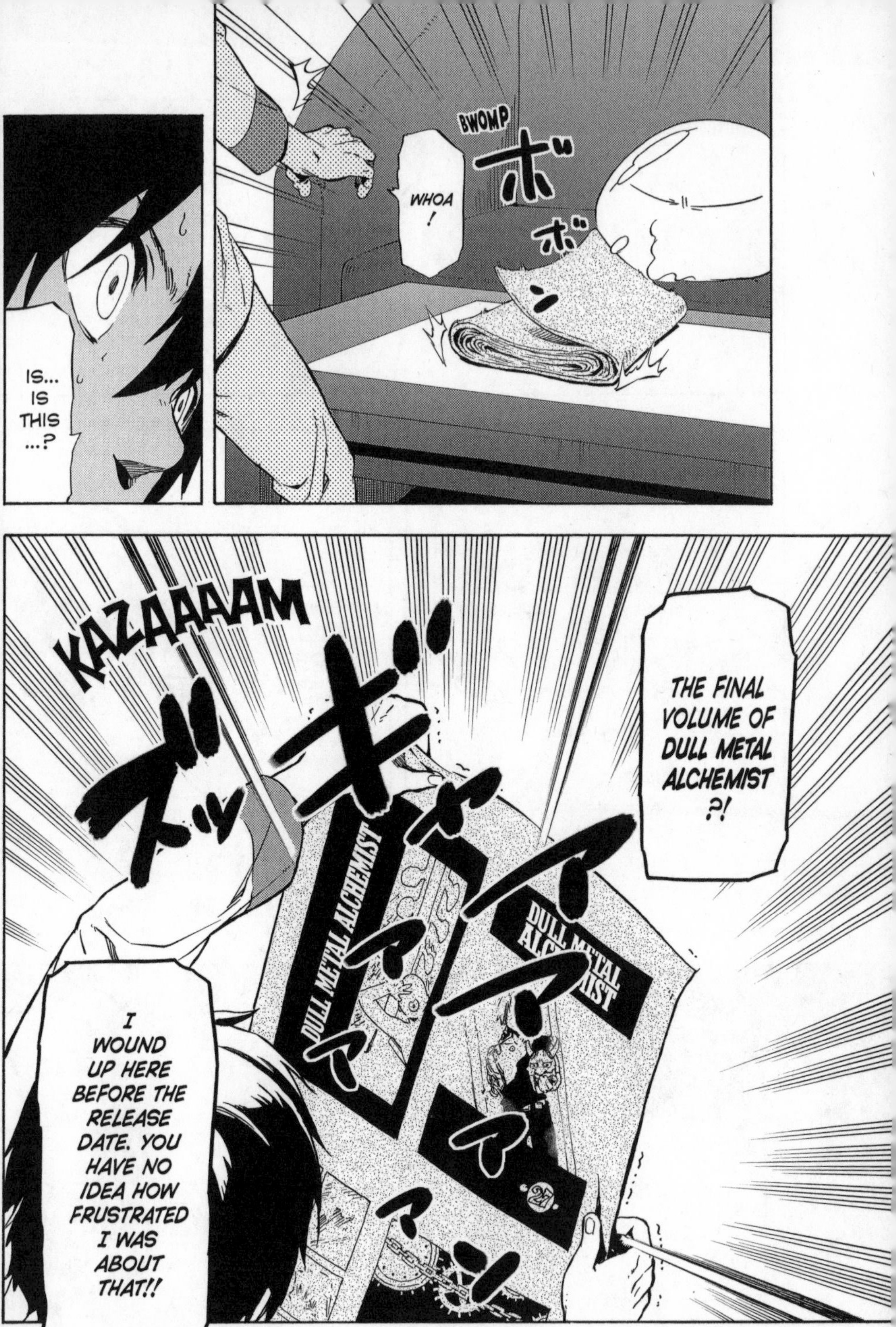
BWOMP
WHOA!
IS... IS THIS ...?
THE FINAL VOLUME OF DULL METAL ALCHEMIST ?!
KAZAAAAM
DULL METAL ALCHEMIST
DULL METAL ALCHEMIST
I WOUND UP HERE BEFORE THE RELEASE DATE. YOU HAVE NO IDEA HOW FRUSTRATED I WAS ABOUT THAT!!

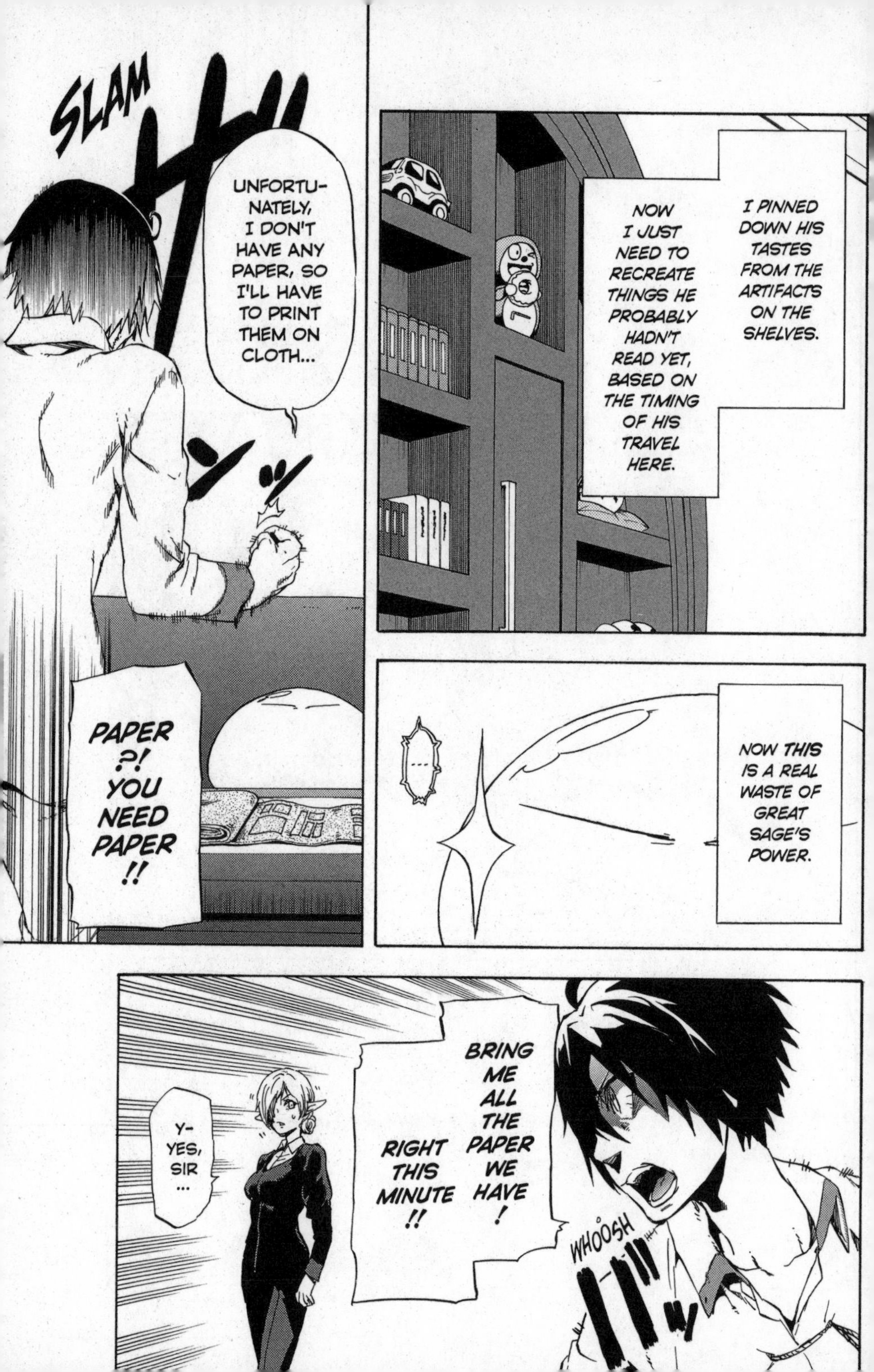
I PINNED DOWN HIS TASTES FROM THE ARTIFACTS ON THE SHELVES.
NOW I JUST NEED TO RECREATE THINGS HE PROBABLY HADN'T READ YET, BASED ON THE TIMING OF HIS TRAVEL HERE.
NOW THIS IS A REAL WASTE OF GREAT SAGE'S POWER.
...
SLAM
UNFORTUNATELY, I DON'T HAVE ANY PAPER, SO I'LL HAVE TO PRINT THEM ON CLOTH...
PAPER?! YOU NEED PAPER!!
BRING ME ALL THE PAPER WE HAVE!
RIGHT THIS MINUTE!!
WHOOSH
Y-YES, SIR...

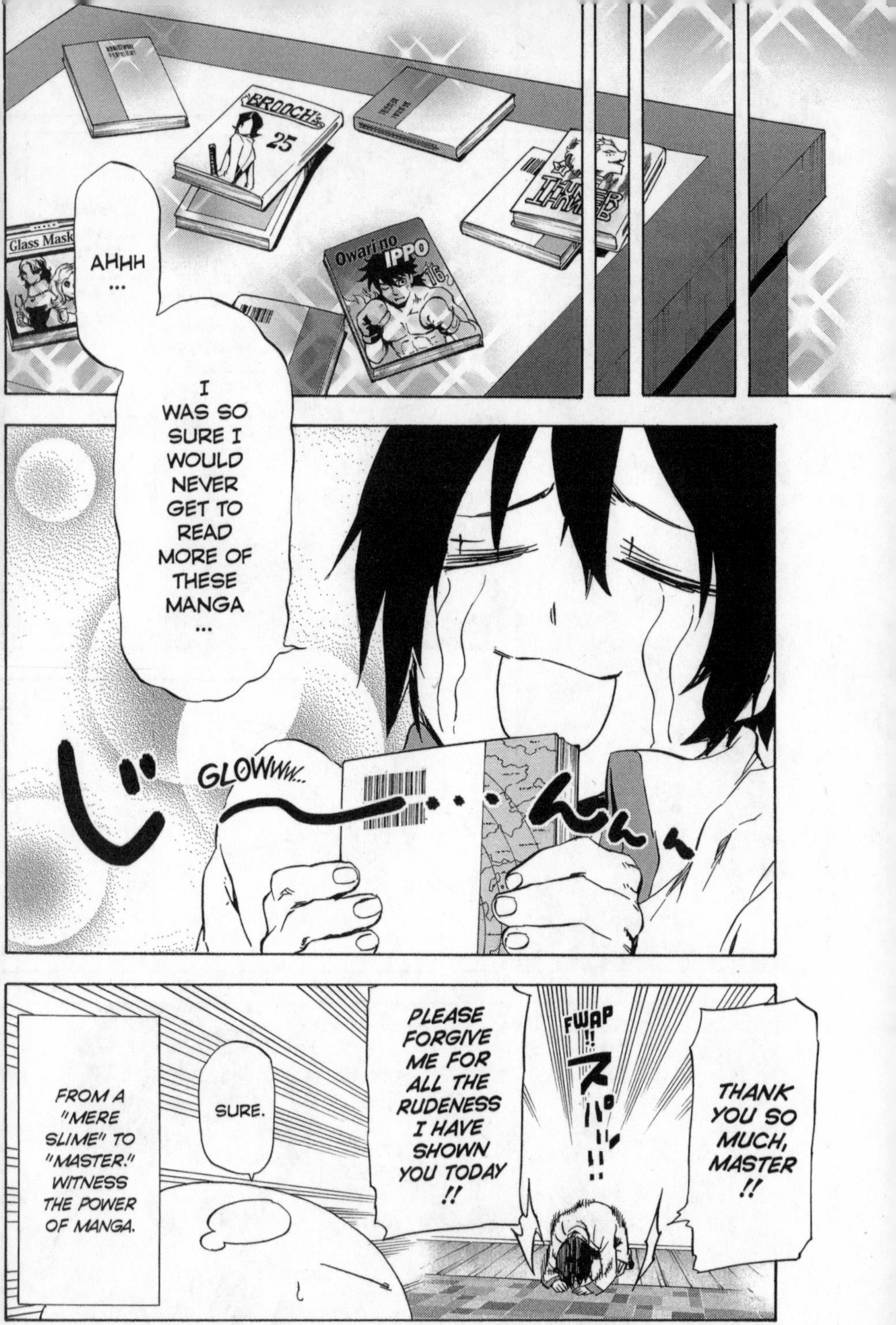
BROOCH's
25
Glass Mask
Owari no IPPO
16
AHHH ...
I WAS SO SURE I WOULD NEVER GET TO READ MORE OF THESE MANGA ...
じ〜ん
GLOWWW...
THANK YOU SO MUCH, MASTER !!
FWAP !!
スパッ!!
PLEASE FORGIVE ME FOR ALL THE RUDENESS I HAVE SHOWN YOU TODAY !!
SURE.
FROM A "MERE SLIME" TO "MASTER." WITNESS THE POWER OF MANGA.

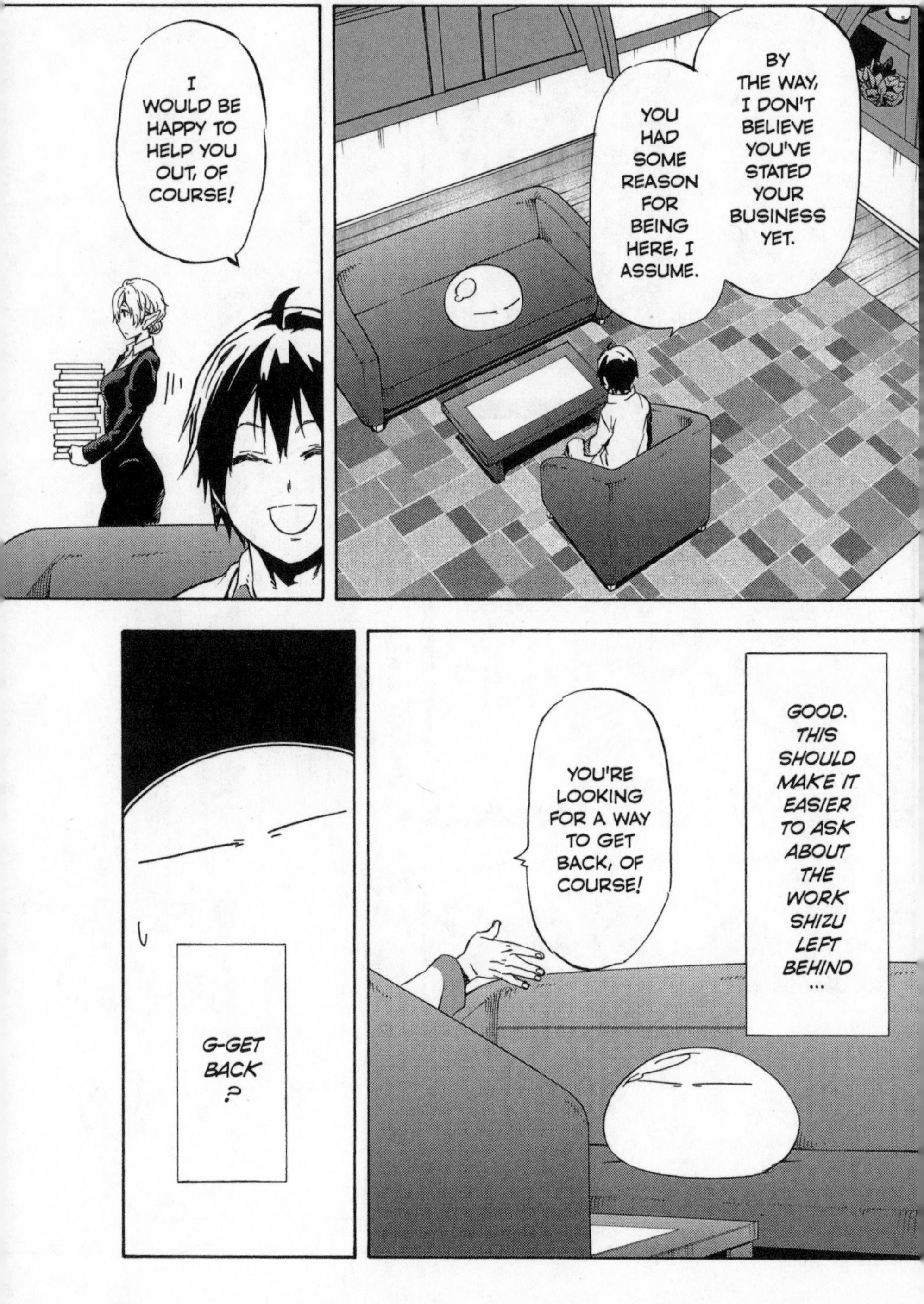
BY THE WAY, I DON'T BELIEVE YOU'VE STATED YOUR BUSINESS YET.
YOU HAD SOME REASON FOR BEING HERE, I ASSUME.
I WOULD BE HAPPY TO HELP YOU OUT, OF COURSE!
GOOD. THIS SHOULD MAKE IT EASIER TO ASK ABOUT THE WORK SHIZU LEFT BEHIND...
YOU'RE LOOKING FOR A WAY TO GET BACK, OF COURSE!
G-GET BACK?

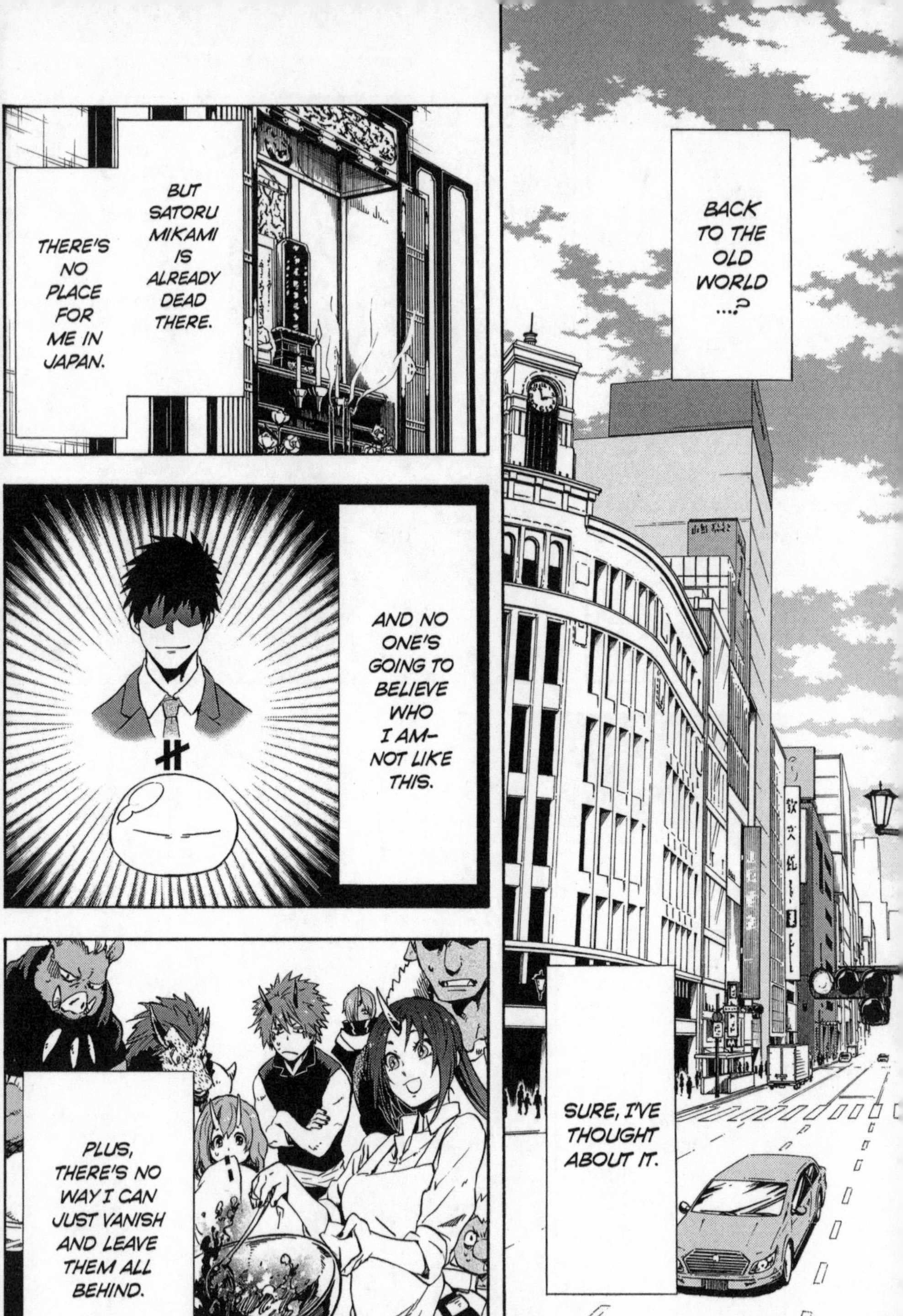
BACK TO THE OLD WORLD ...?
SURE, I'VE THOUGHT ABOUT IT.
BUT SATORU MIKAMI IS ALREADY DEAD THERE.
THERE'S NO PLACE FOR ME IN JAPAN.
AND NO ONE'S GOING TO BELIEVE WHO I AM—NOT LIKE THIS.
PLUS, THERE'S NO WAY I CAN JUST VANISH AND LEAVE THEM ALL BEHIND.

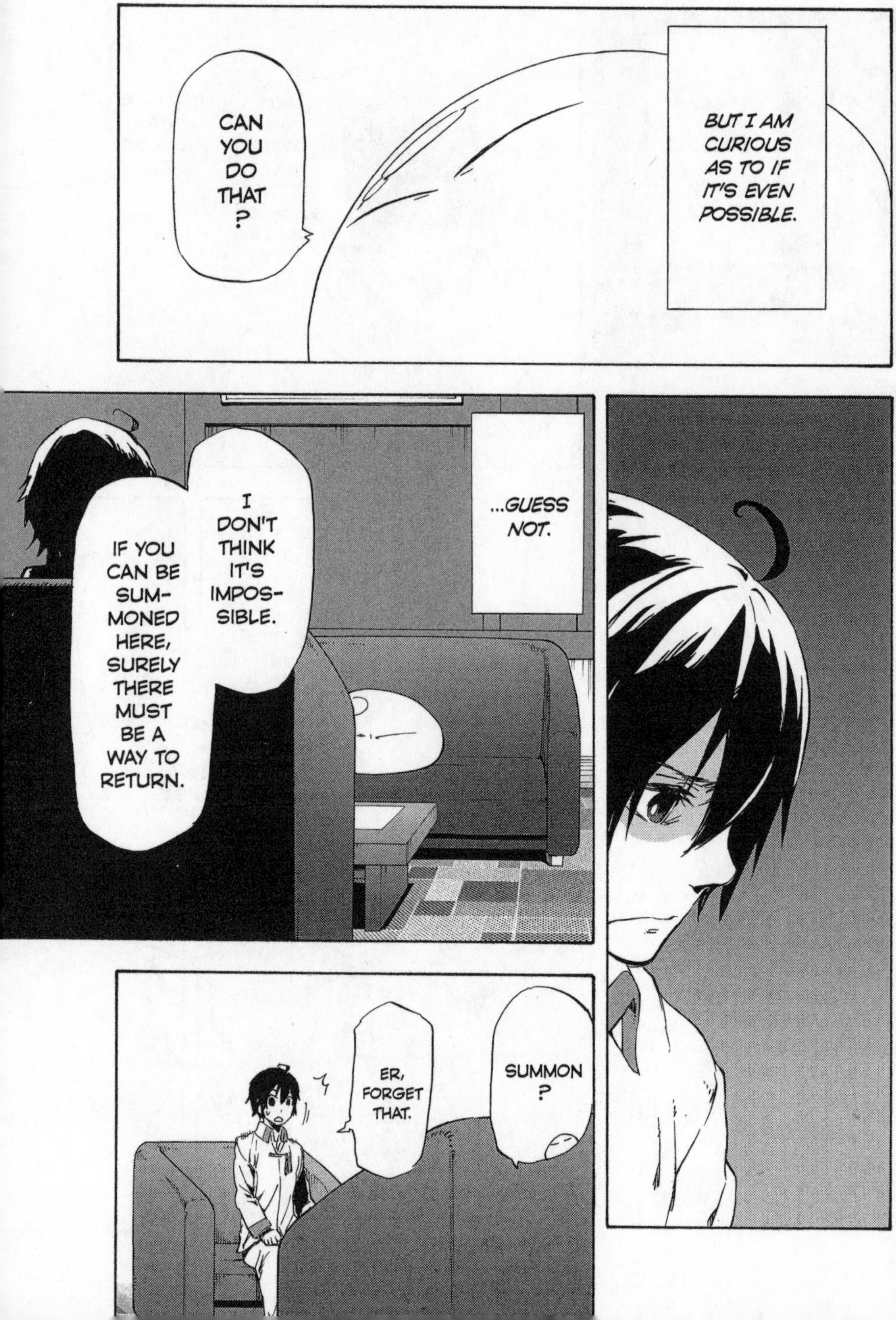
BUT I AM CURIOUS AS TO IF IT'S EVEN POSSIBLE.
CAN YOU DO THAT?
...GUESS NOT.
I DON'T THINK IT'S IMPOSSIBLE.
IF YOU CAN BE SUMMONED HERE, SURELY THERE MUST BE A WAY TO RETURN.
SUMMON?
ER, FORGET THAT.

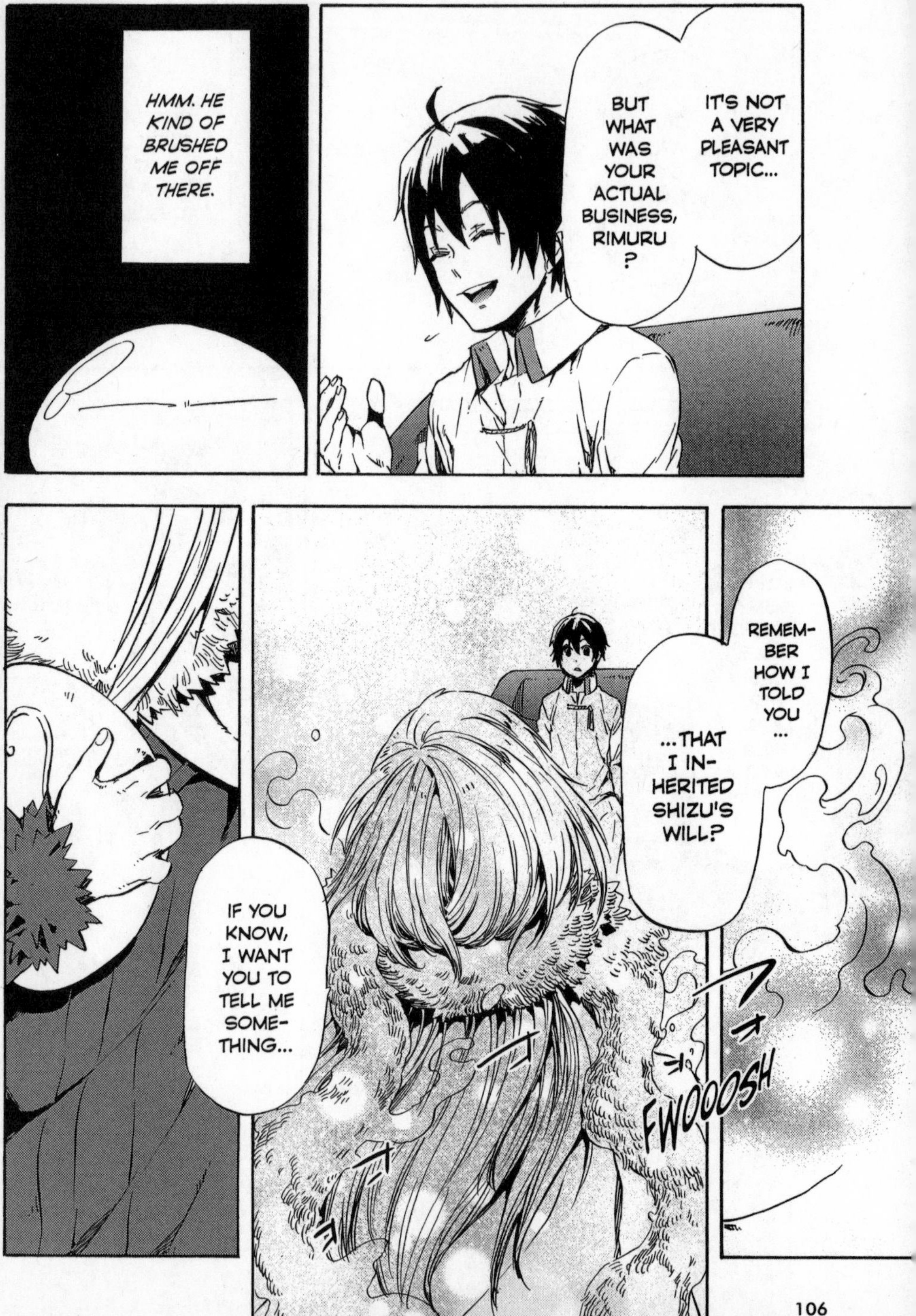
IT'S NOT A VERY PLEASANT TOPIC...
BUT WHAT WAS YOUR ACTUAL BUSINESS, RIMURU?
HMM. HE KIND OF BRUSHED ME OFF THERE.
REMEM-BER HOW I TOLD YOU...
...THAT I IN-HERITED SHIZU'S WILL?
FWOOOSH
IF YOU KNOW, I WANT YOU TO TELL ME SOME-THING...

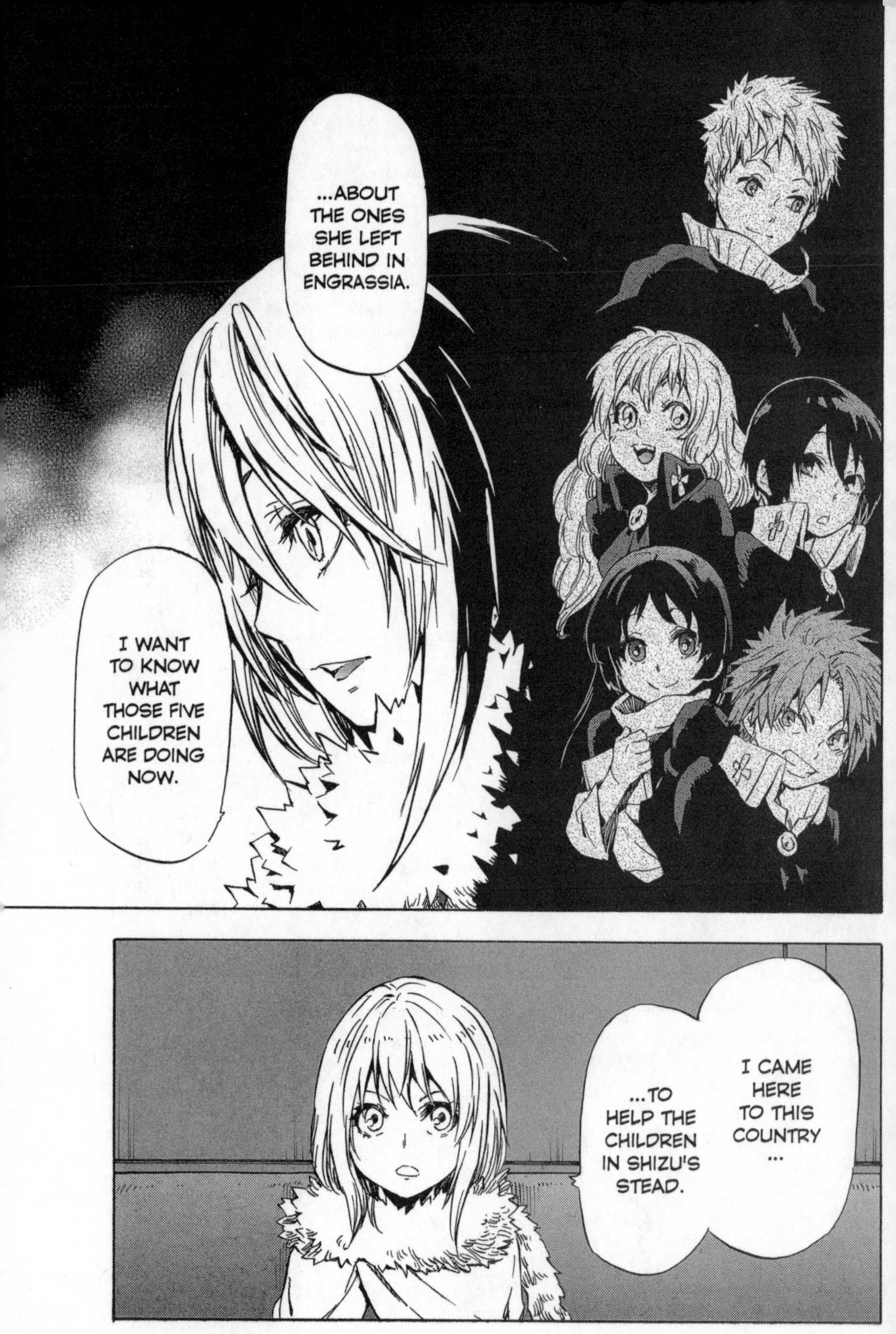
...ABOUT THE ONES SHE LEFT BEHIND IN ENGRASSIA.
I WANT TO KNOW WHAT THOSE FIVE CHILDREN ARE DOING NOW.
I CAME HERE TO THIS COUNTRY ...
...TO HELP THE CHILDREN IN SHIZU'S STEAD.

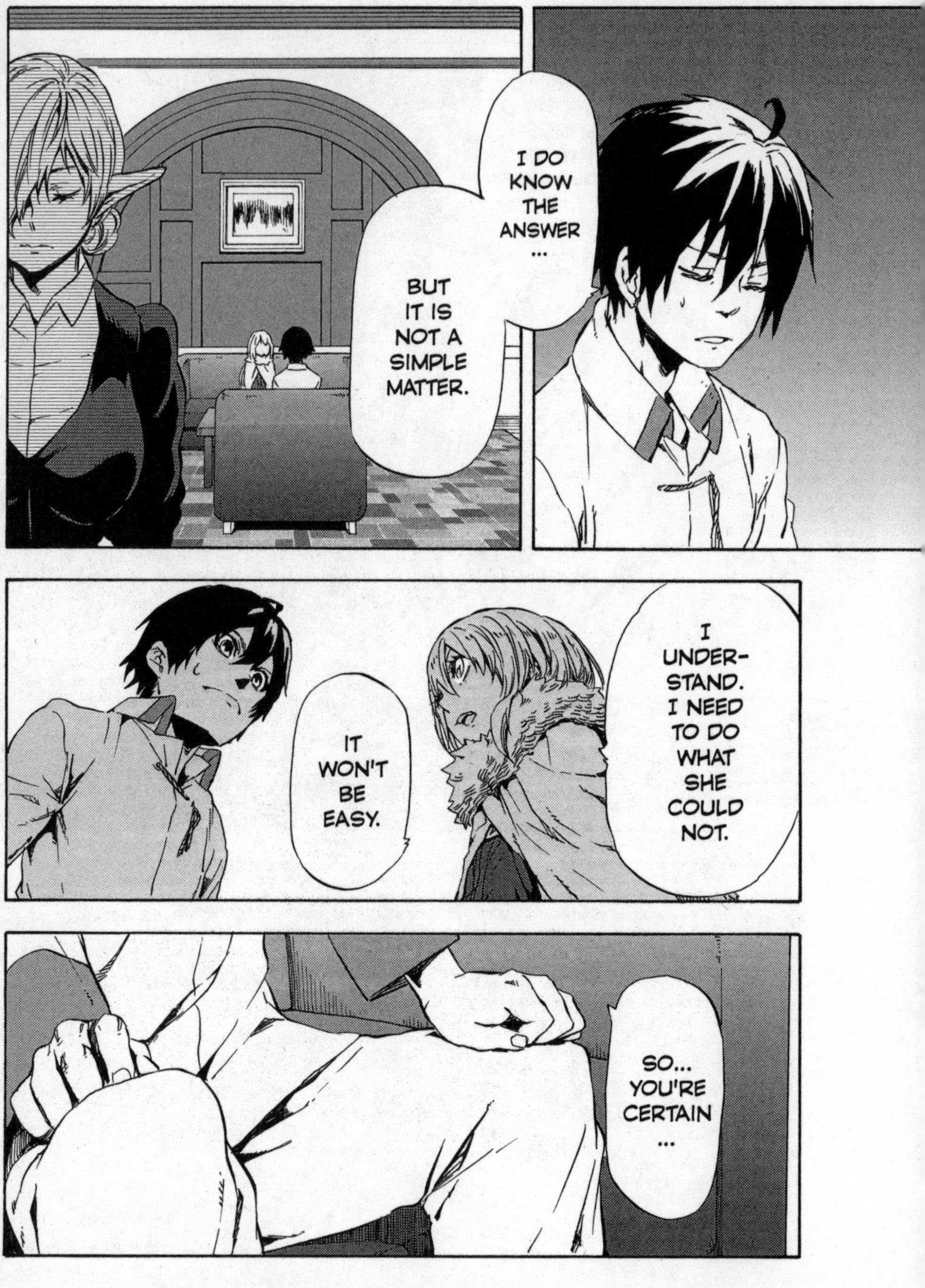
I DO KNOW THE ANSWER ...
BUT IT IS NOT A SIMPLE MATTER.
I UNDER-STAND. I NEED TO DO WHAT SHE COULD NOT.
IT WON'T BE EASY.
SO... YOU'RE CERTAIN ...

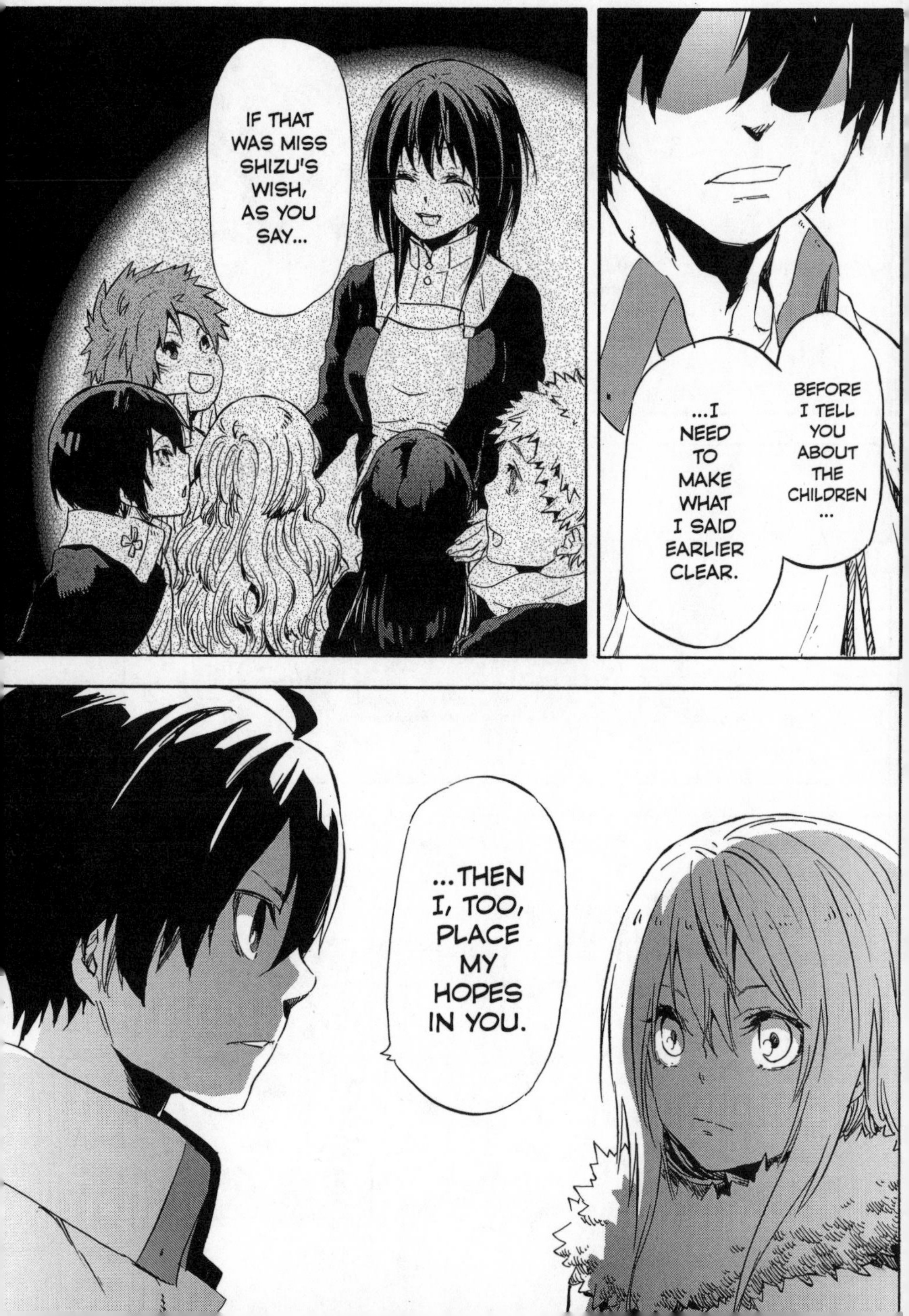
BEFORE I TELL YOU ABOUT THE CHILDREN...
...I NEED TO MAKE WHAT I SAID EARLIER CLEAR.
IF THAT WAS MISS SHIZU'S WISH, AS YOU SAY...
...THEN I, TOO, PLACE MY HOPES IN YOU.

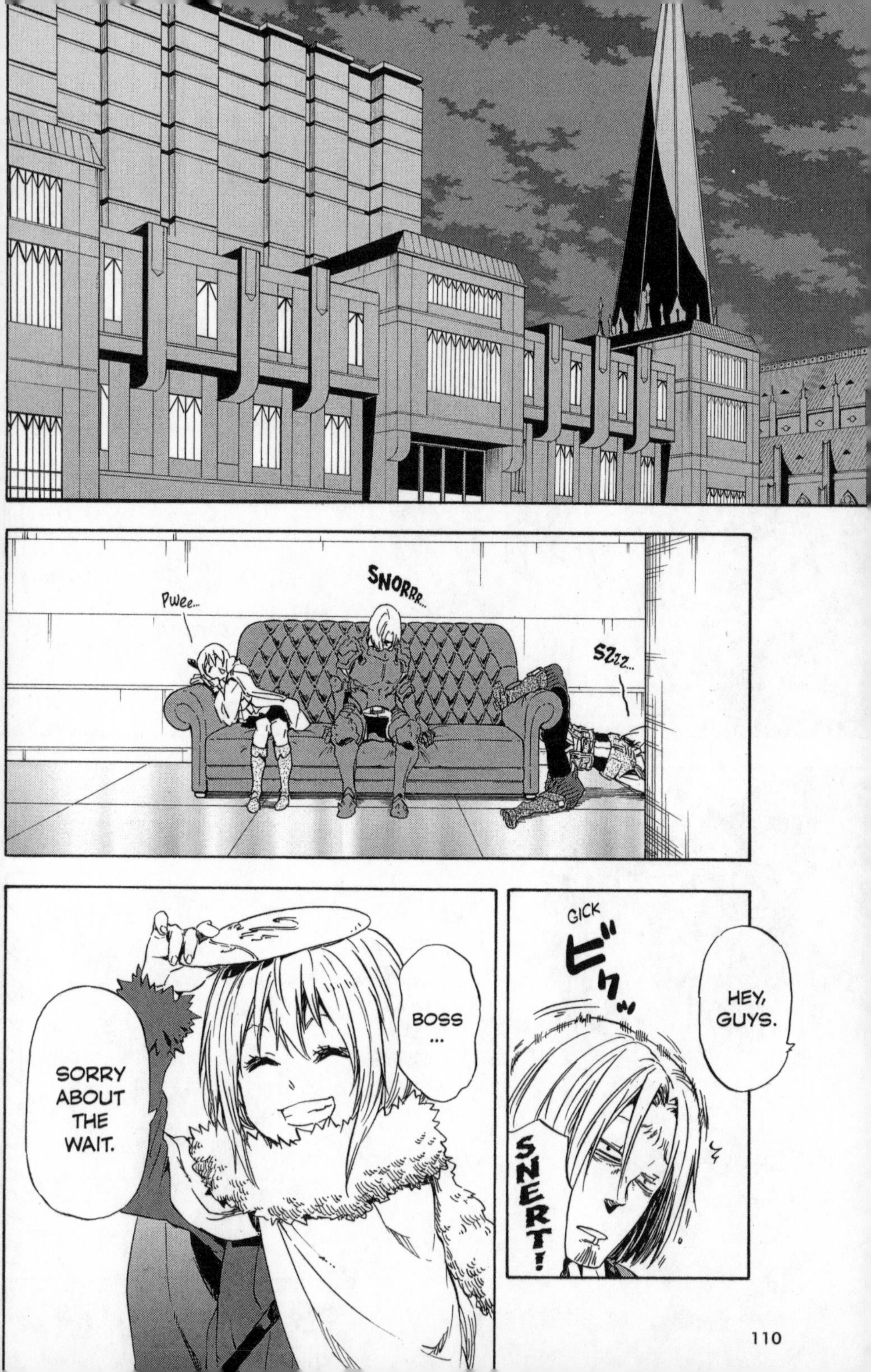
SNORRR...
SZzzz...
Pwee...
HEY, GUYS.
GICK
ビクッ
SNERT!
BOSS...
SORRY ABOUT THE WAIT.

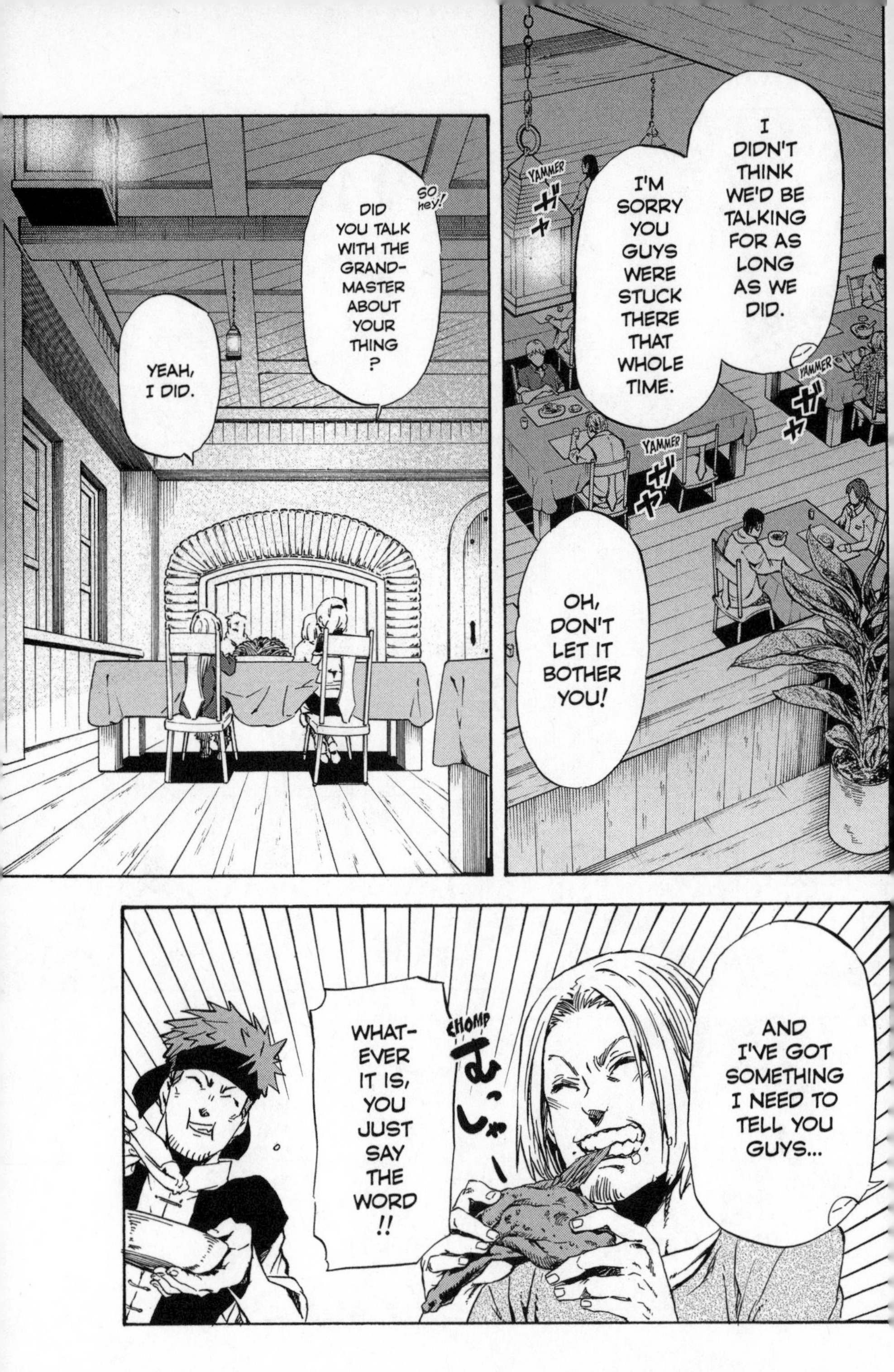
I DIDN'T THINK WE'D BE TALKING FOR AS LONG AS WE DID.
I'M SORRY YOU GUYS WERE STUCK THERE THAT WHOLE TIME.
YAMMER
YAMMER
YAMMER
OH, DON'T LET IT BOTHER YOU!
SO hey!
DID YOU TALK WITH THE GRAND-MASTER ABOUT YOUR THING?
YEAH, I DID.
AND I'VE GOT SOMETHING I NEED TO TELL YOU GUYS...
CHOMP
WHAT-EVER IT IS, YOU JUST SAY THE WORD!!

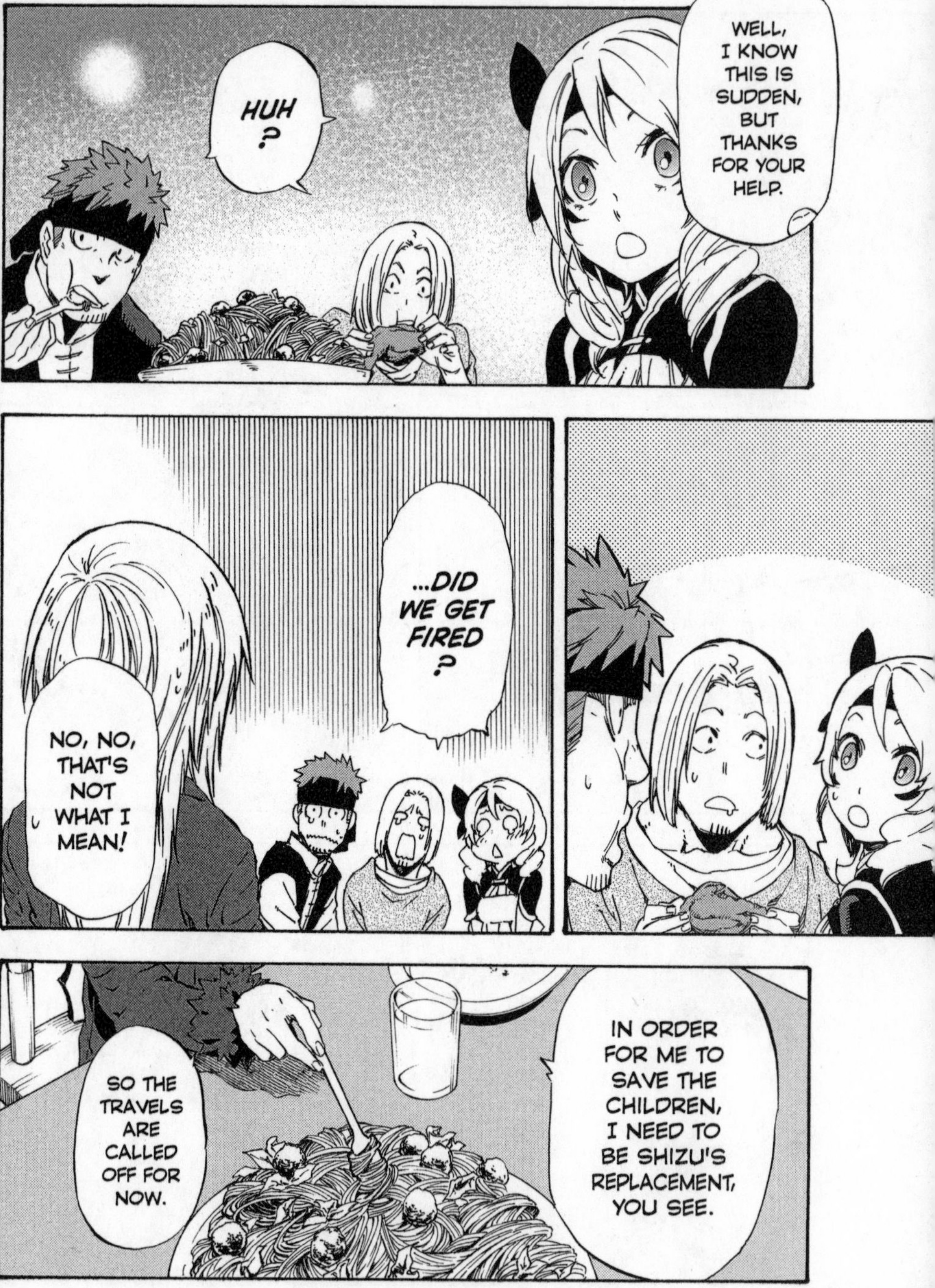
WELL, I KNOW THIS IS SUDDEN, BUT THANKS FOR YOUR HELP.
HUH?
...DID WE GET FIRED?
NO, NO, THAT'S NOT WHAT I MEAN!
IN ORDER FOR ME TO SAVE THE CHILDREN, I NEED TO BE SHIZU'S REPLACEMENT, YOU SEE.
SO THE TRAVELS ARE CALLED OFF FOR NOW.

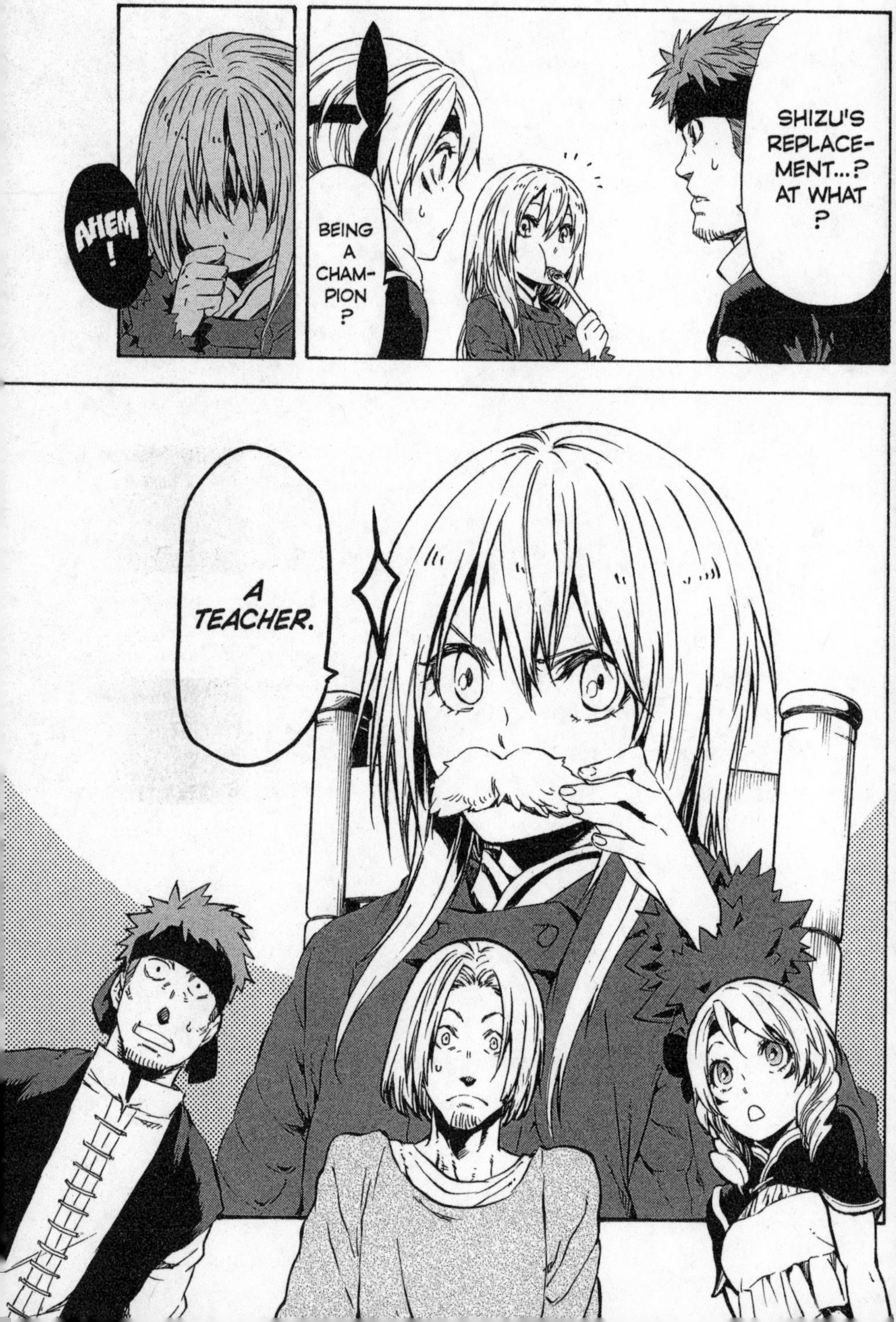
SHIZU'S REPLACEMENT...? AT WHAT?
BEING A CHAMPION?
AHEM!
A TEACHER.

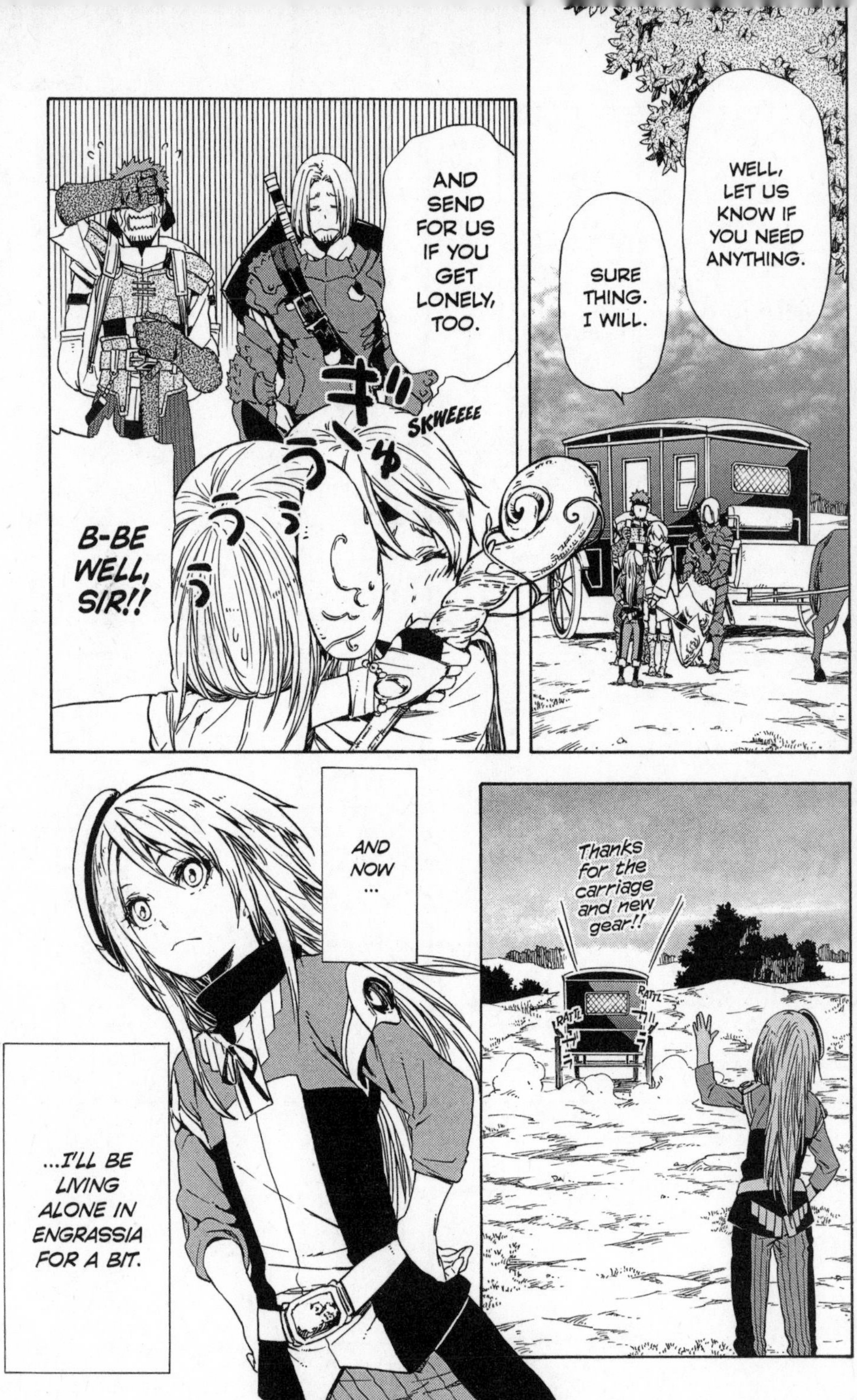
WELL, LET US KNOW IF YOU NEED ANYTHING.
SURE THING. I WILL.
AND SEND FOR US IF YOU GET LONELY, TOO.
SKWEEEE
B-BE WELL, SIR!!
Thanks for the carriage and new gear!!
RATTL
RATTL
AND NOW ...
...I'LL BE LIVING ALONE IN ENGRASSIA FOR A BIT.

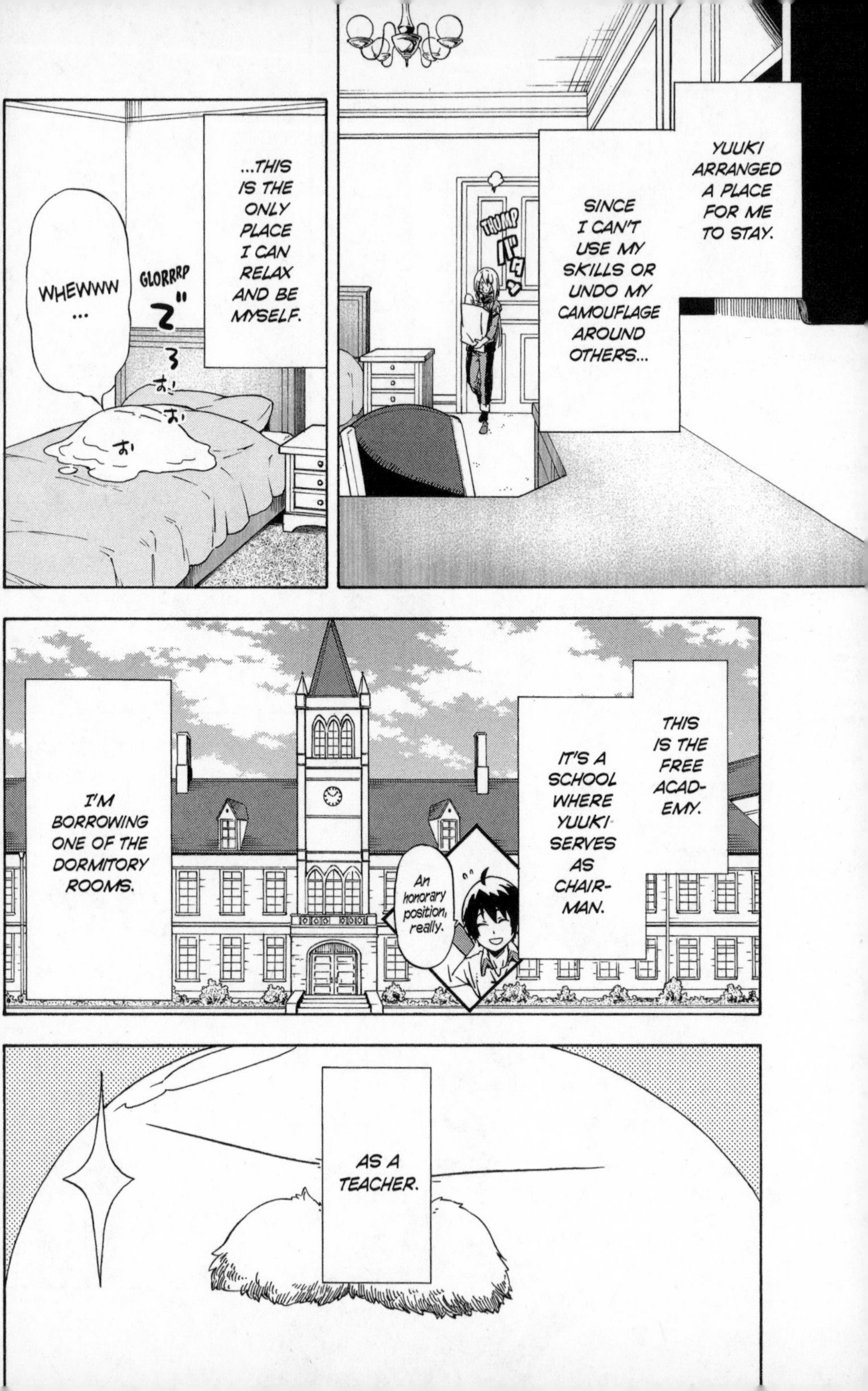
YUUKI ARRANGED A PLACE FOR ME TO STAY.
SINCE I CAN'T USE MY SKILLS OR UNDO MY CAMOUFLAGE AROUND OTHERS...
THUMP
...THIS IS THE ONLY PLACE I CAN RELAX AND BE MYSELF.
GLORRRP
WHEWWW ...
THIS IS THE FREE ACADEMY.
IT'S A SCHOOL WHERE YUUKI SERVES AS CHAIRMAN.
An honorary position, really.
I'M BORROWING ONE OF THE DORMITORY ROOMS.
AS A TEACHER.

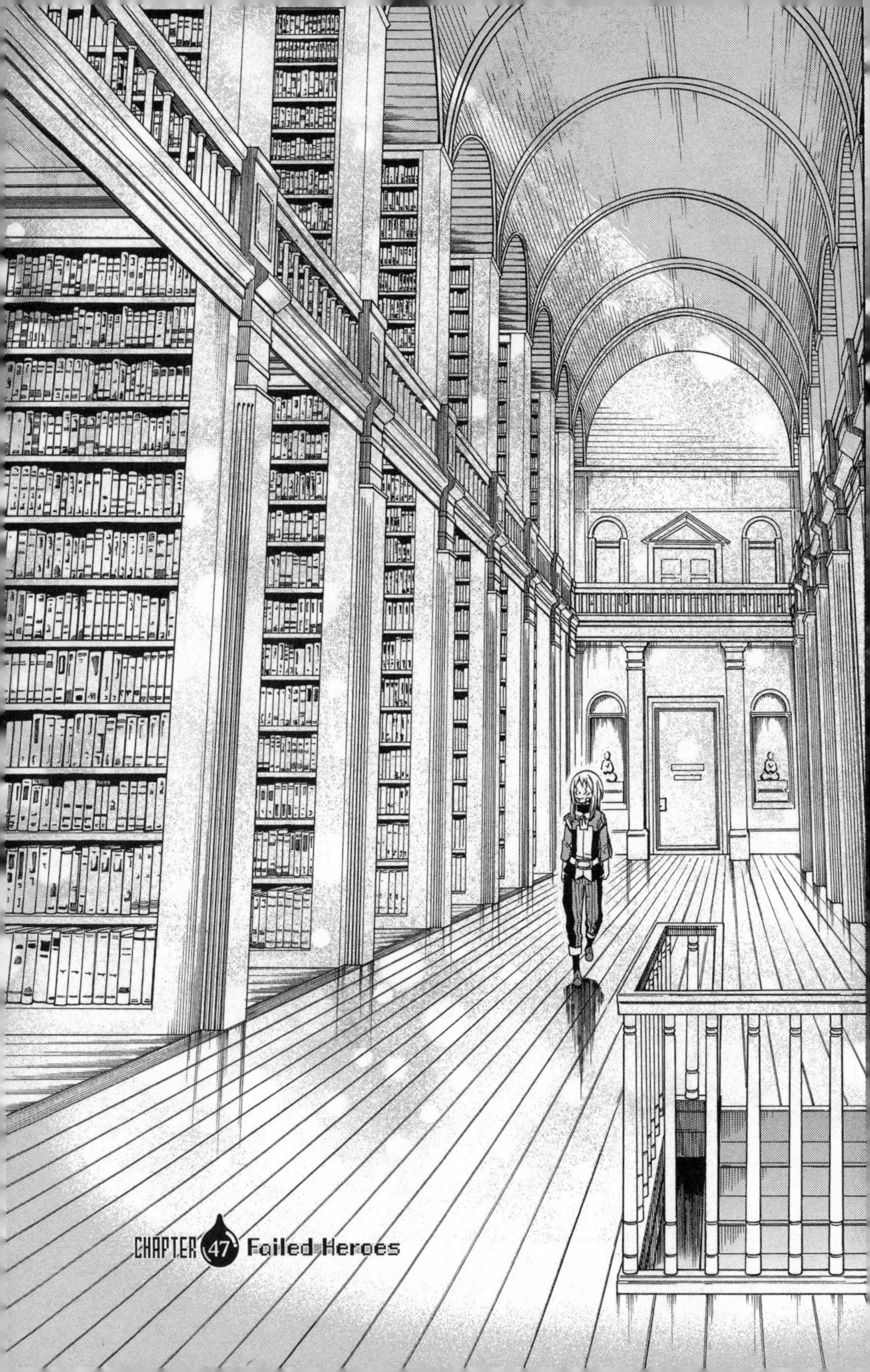
CHAPTER 47 Failed Heroes

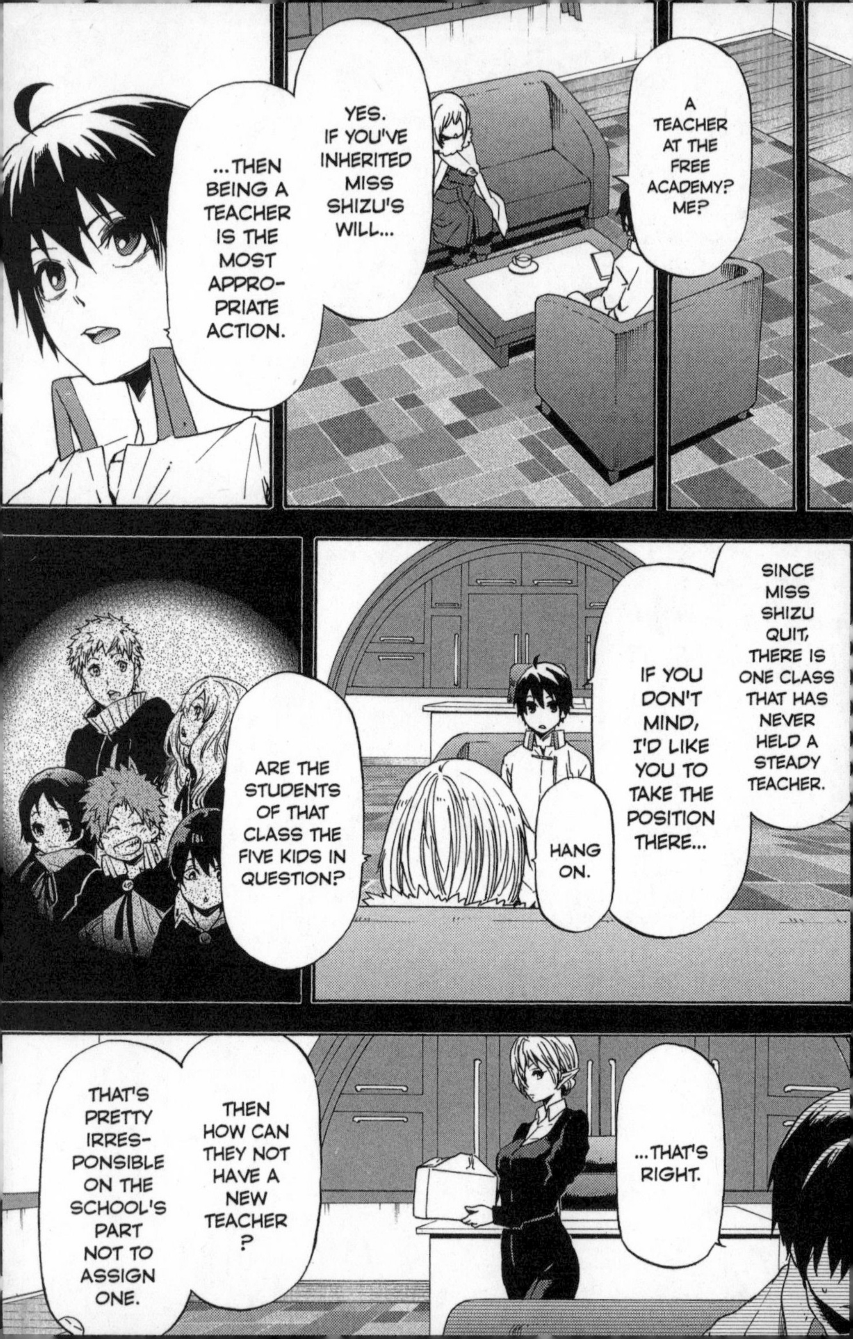
A TEACHER AT THE FREE ACADEMY? ME?
YES. IF YOU'VE INHERITED MISS SHIZU'S WILL...
...THEN BEING A TEACHER IS THE MOST APPROPRIATE ACTION.
SINCE MISS SHIZU QUIT, THERE IS ONE CLASS THAT HAS NEVER HELD A STEADY TEACHER.
IF YOU DON'T MIND, I'D LIKE YOU TO TAKE THE POSITION THERE...
HANG ON.
ARE THE STUDENTS OF THAT CLASS THE FIVE KIDS IN QUESTION?
...THAT'S RIGHT.
THEN HOW CAN THEY NOT HAVE A NEW TEACHER?
THAT'S PRETTY IRRESPONSIBLE ON THE SCHOOL'S PART NOT TO ASSIGN ONE.

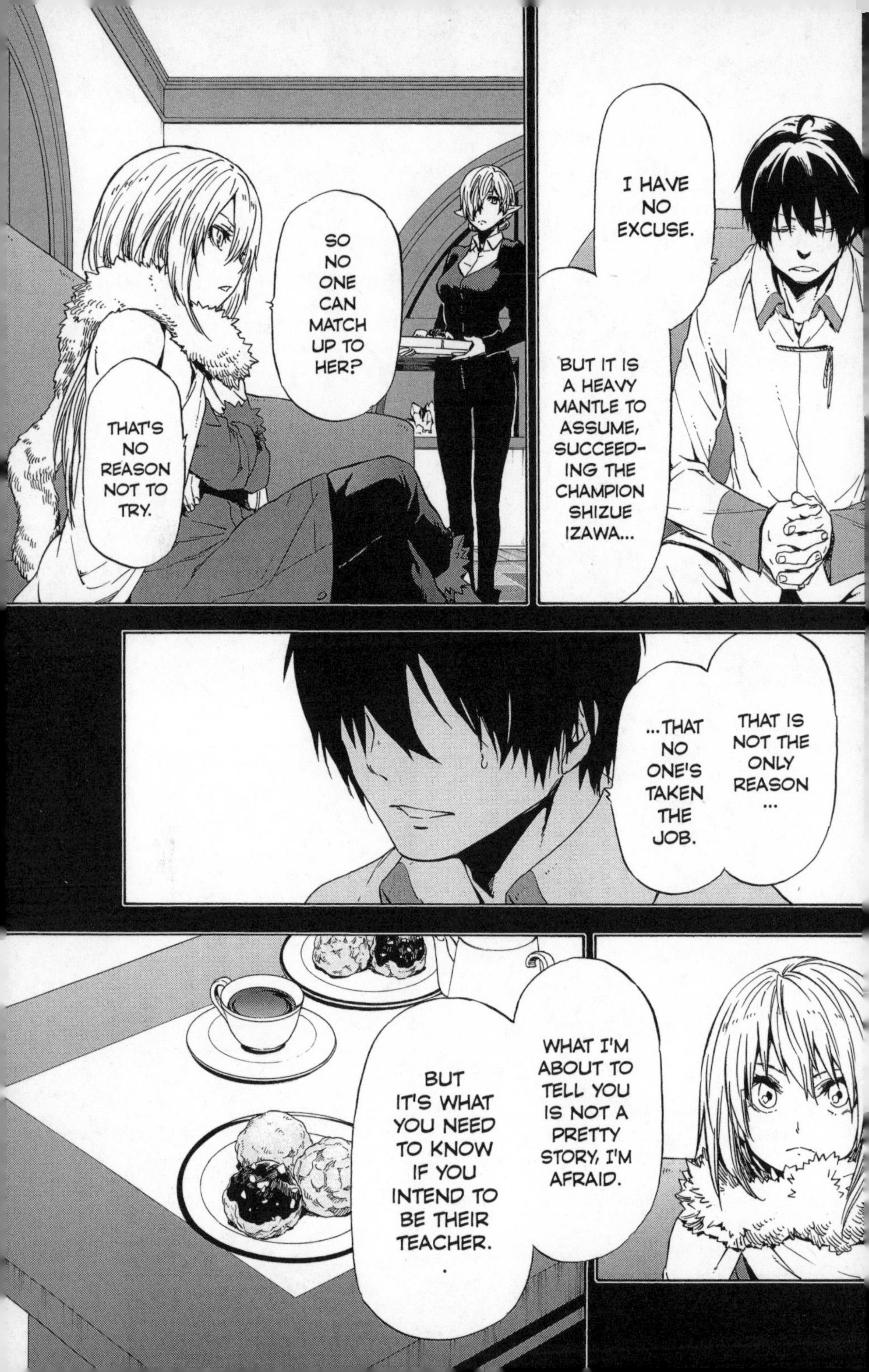
I HAVE NO EXCUSE.
BUT IT IS A HEAVY MANTLE TO ASSUME, SUCCEEDING THE CHAMPION SHIZUE IZAWA...
SO NO ONE CAN MATCH UP TO HER?
THAT'S NO REASON NOT TO TRY.
THAT IS NOT THE ONLY REASON ...
...THAT NO ONE'S TAKEN THE JOB.
WHAT I'M ABOUT TO TELL YOU IS NOT A PRETTY STORY, I'M AFRAID.
BUT IT'S WHAT YOU NEED TO KNOW IF YOU INTEND TO BE THEIR TEACHER.

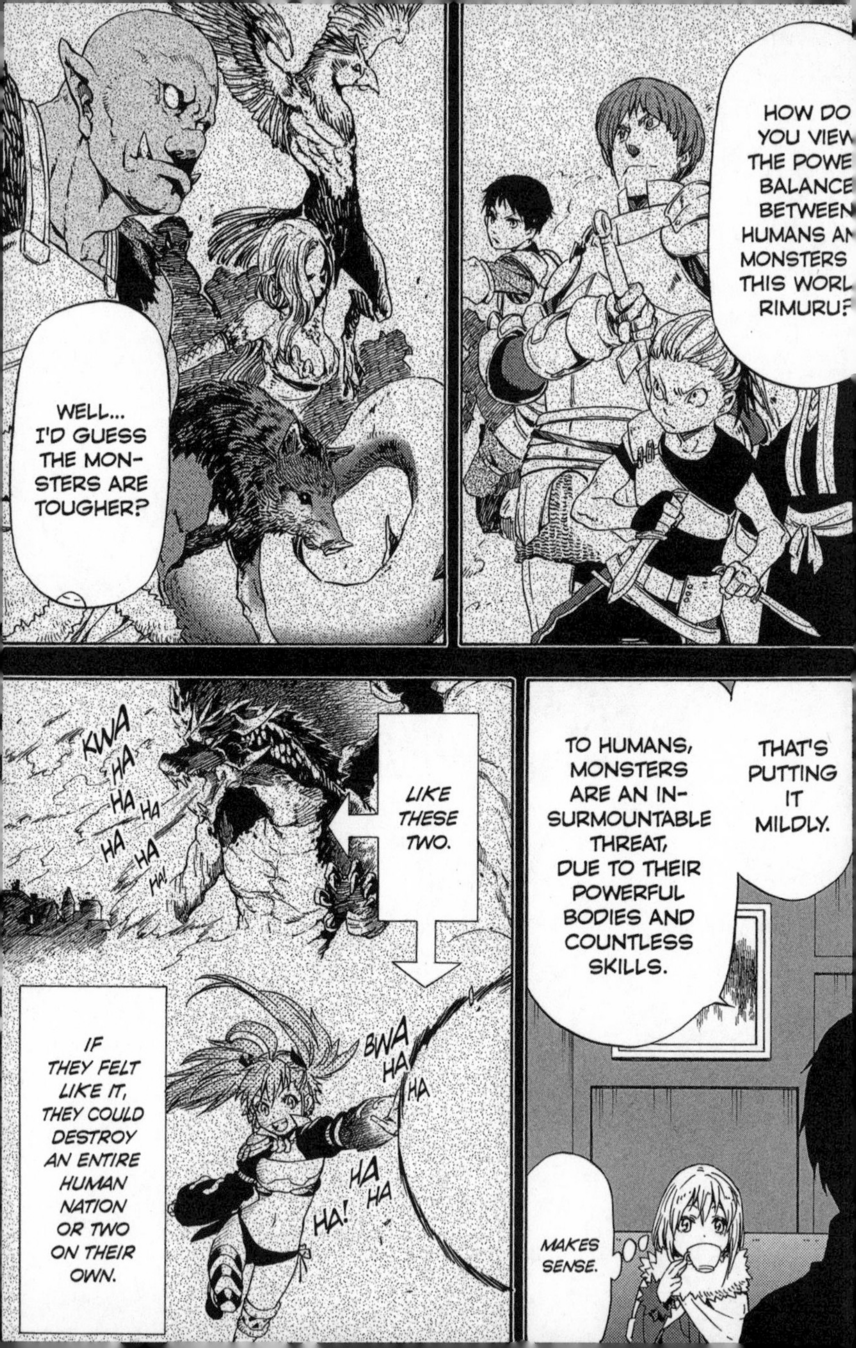
HOW DO YOU VIEW THE POWE BALANCE BETWEEN HUMANS AN MONSTERS THIS WORL RIMURU?
WELL... I'D GUESS THE MON-STERS ARE TOUGHER?
THAT'S PUTTING IT MILDLY.
TO HUMANS, MONSTERS ARE AN IN-SURMOUNTABLE THREAT, DUE TO THEIR POWERFUL BODIES AND COUNTLESS SKILLS.
MAKES SENSE.
KWA HA HA HA HA HA HA!
LIKE THESE TWO.
IF THEY FELT LIKE IT, THEY COULD DESTROY AN ENTIRE HUMAN NATION OR TWO ON THEIR OWN.
BWA HA HA HA HA HA!

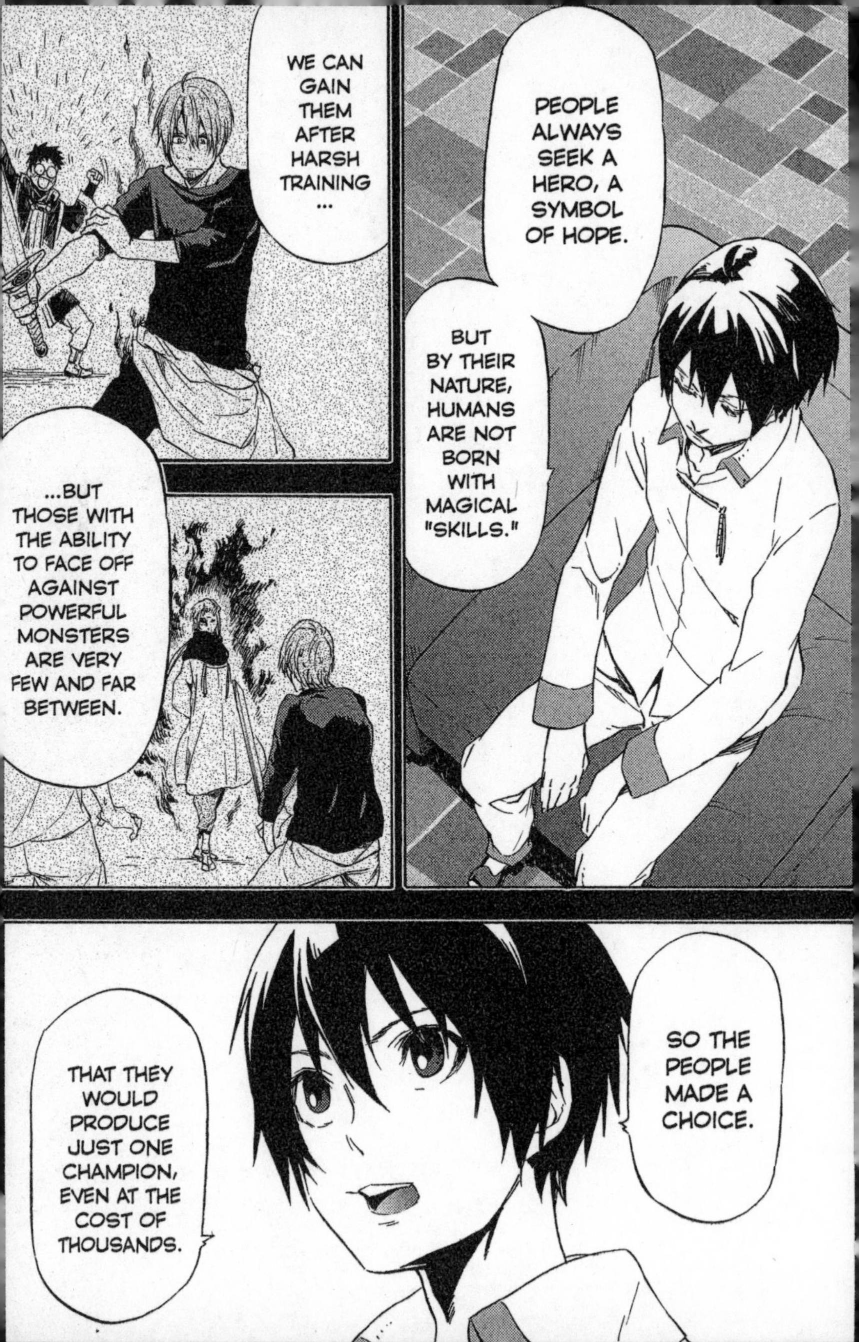
PEOPLE ALWAYS SEEK A HERO, A SYMBOL OF HOPE.
BUT BY THEIR NATURE, HUMANS ARE NOT BORN WITH MAGICAL "SKILLS."
WE CAN GAIN THEM AFTER HARSH TRAINING...
...BUT THOSE WITH THE ABILITY TO FACE OFF AGAINST POWERFUL MONSTERS ARE VERY FEW AND FAR BETWEEN.
SO THE PEOPLE MADE A CHOICE.
THAT THEY WOULD PRODUCE JUST ONE CHAMPION, EVEN AT THE COST OF THOUSANDS.

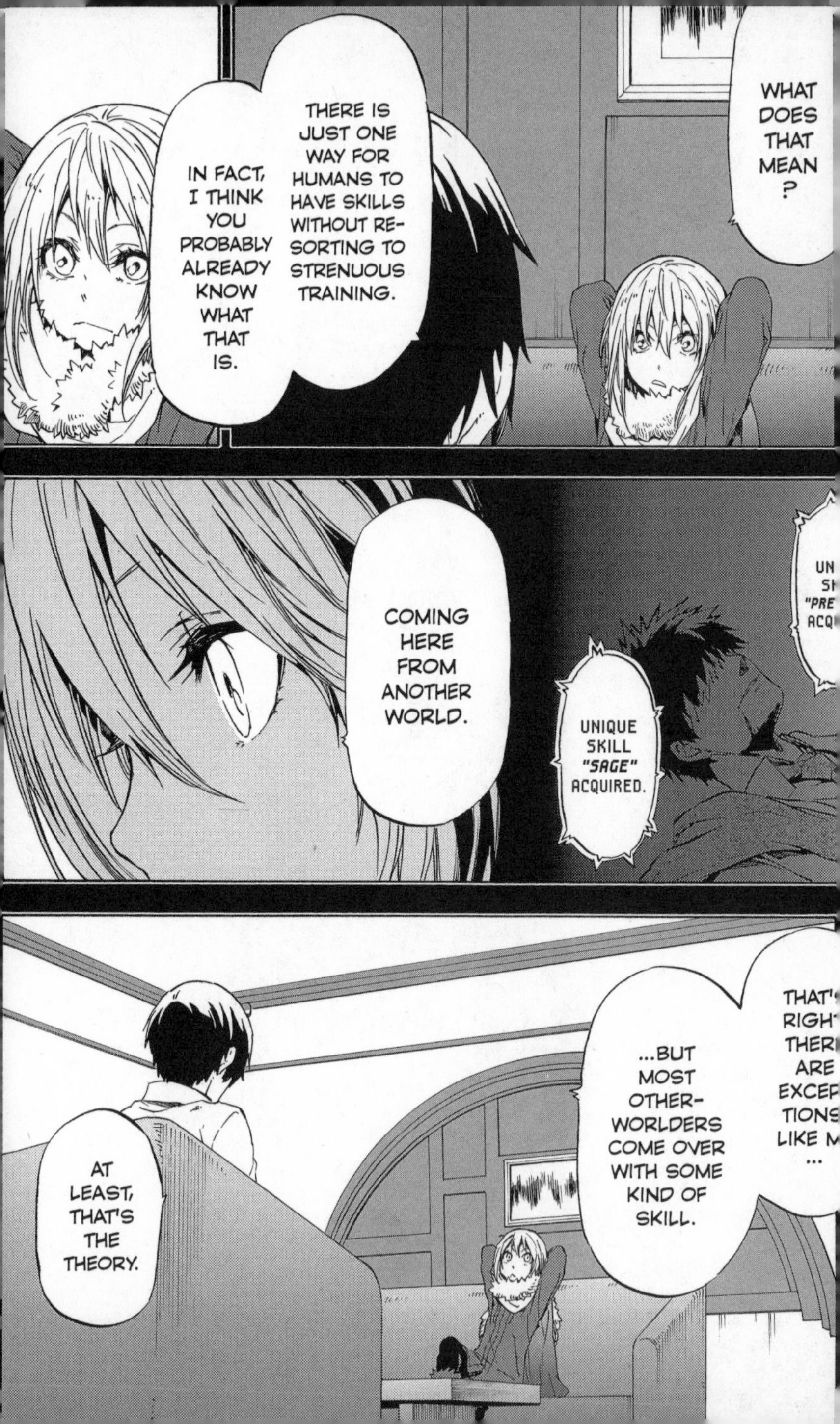
WHAT DOES THAT MEAN?
THERE IS JUST ONE WAY FOR HUMANS TO HAVE SKILLS WITHOUT RE-SORTING TO STRENUOUS TRAINING.
IN FACT, I THINK YOU PROBABLY ALREADY KNOW WHAT THAT IS.
UNIQUE SKILL "SAGE" ACQUIRED.
COMING HERE FROM ANOTHER WORLD.
THAT'S RIGHT THERE ARE EXCEP TIONS LIKE M ...
...BUT MOST OTHER-WORLDERS COME OVER WITH SOME KIND OF SKILL.
AT LEAST, THAT'S THE THEORY.

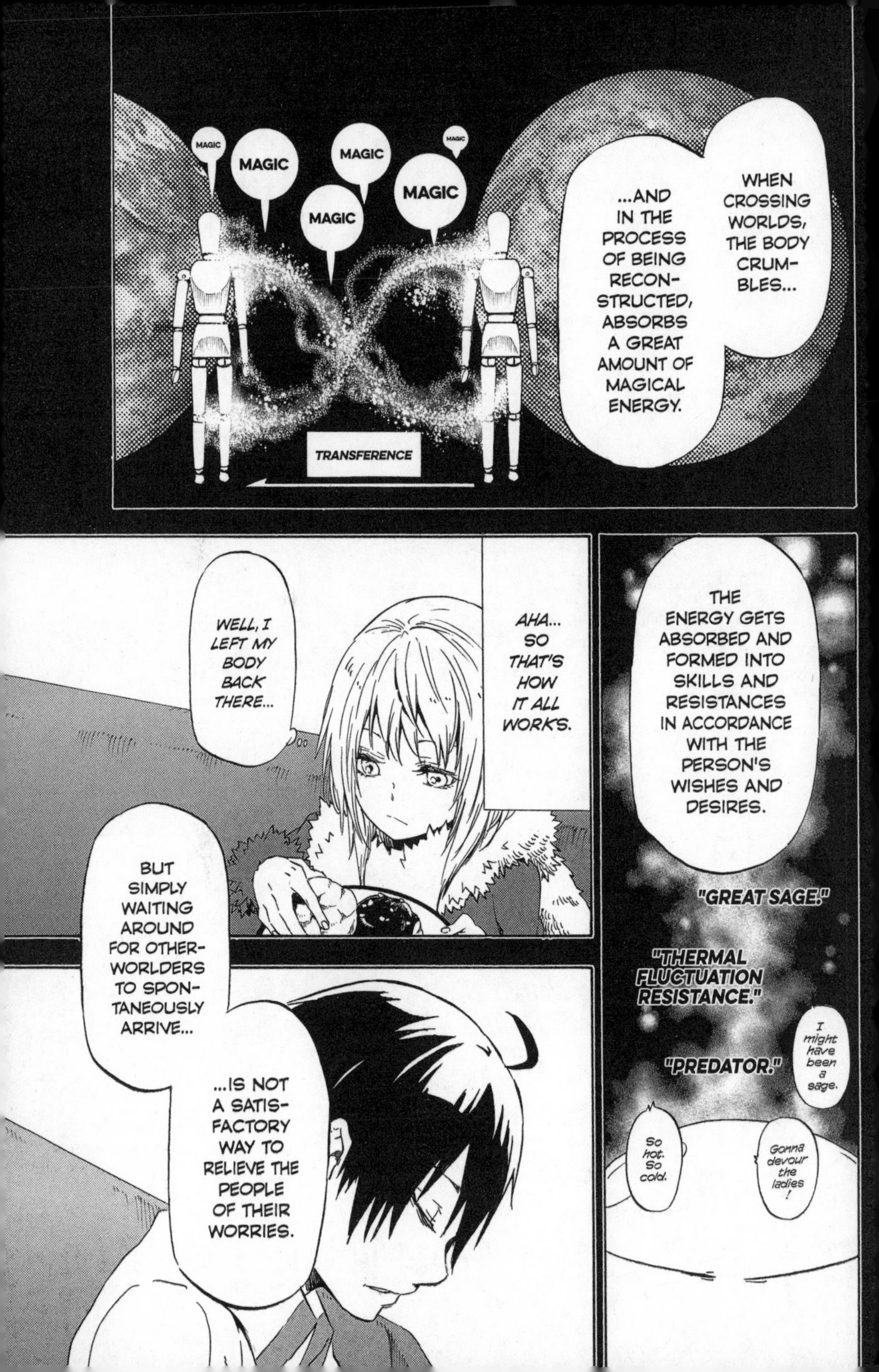
WHEN CROSSING WORLDS, THE BODY CRUMBLES...
...AND IN THE PROCESS OF BEING RECONSTRUCTED, ABSORBS A GREAT AMOUNT OF MAGICAL ENERGY.
MAGIC
MAGIC
MAGIC
MAGIC
MAGIC
MAGIC
TRANSFERENCE
THE ENERGY GETS ABSORBED AND FORMED INTO SKILLS AND RESISTANCES IN ACCORDANCE WITH THE PERSON'S WISHES AND DESIRES.
"GREAT SAGE."
"THERMAL FLUCTUATION RESISTANCE."
"PREDATOR."
I might have been a sage.
Gonna devour the ladies!
So hot. So cold.
AHA... SO THAT'S HOW IT ALL WORKS.
WELL, I LEFT MY BODY BACK THERE...
BUT SIMPLY WAITING AROUND FOR OTHER-WORLDERS TO SPONTANEOUSLY ARRIVE...
...IS NOT A SATISFACTORY WAY TO RELIEVE THE PEOPLE OF THEIR WORRIES.

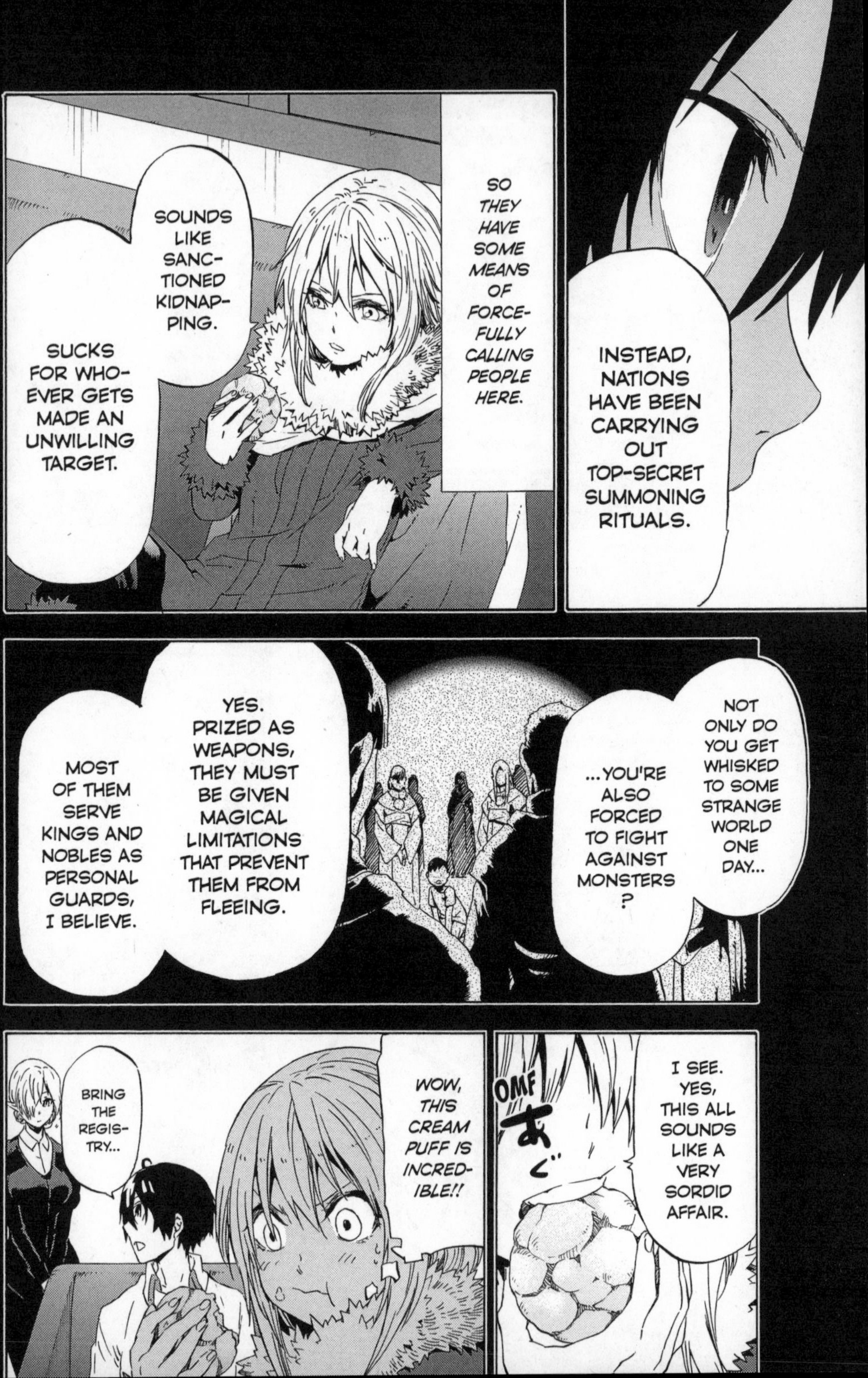
INSTEAD, NATIONS HAVE BEEN CARRYING OUT TOP-SECRET SUMMONING RITUALS.
SO THEY HAVE SOME MEANS OF FORCEFULLY CALLING PEOPLE HERE.
SOUNDS LIKE SANCTIONED KIDNAPPING.
SUCKS FOR WHOEVER GETS MADE AN UNWILLING TARGET.
NOT ONLY DO YOU GET WHISKED TO SOME STRANGE WORLD ONE DAY...
...YOU'RE ALSO FORCED TO FIGHT AGAINST MONSTERS?
YES. PRIZED AS WEAPONS, THEY MUST BE GIVEN MAGICAL LIMITATIONS THAT PREVENT THEM FROM FLEEING.
MOST OF THEM SERVE KINGS AND NOBLES AS PERSONAL GUARDS, I BELIEVE.
OMF
あぐ
I SEE. YES, THIS ALL SOUNDS LIKE A VERY SORDID AFFAIR.
WOW, THIS CREAM PUFF IS INCREDIBLE!!
BRING THE REGISTRY...

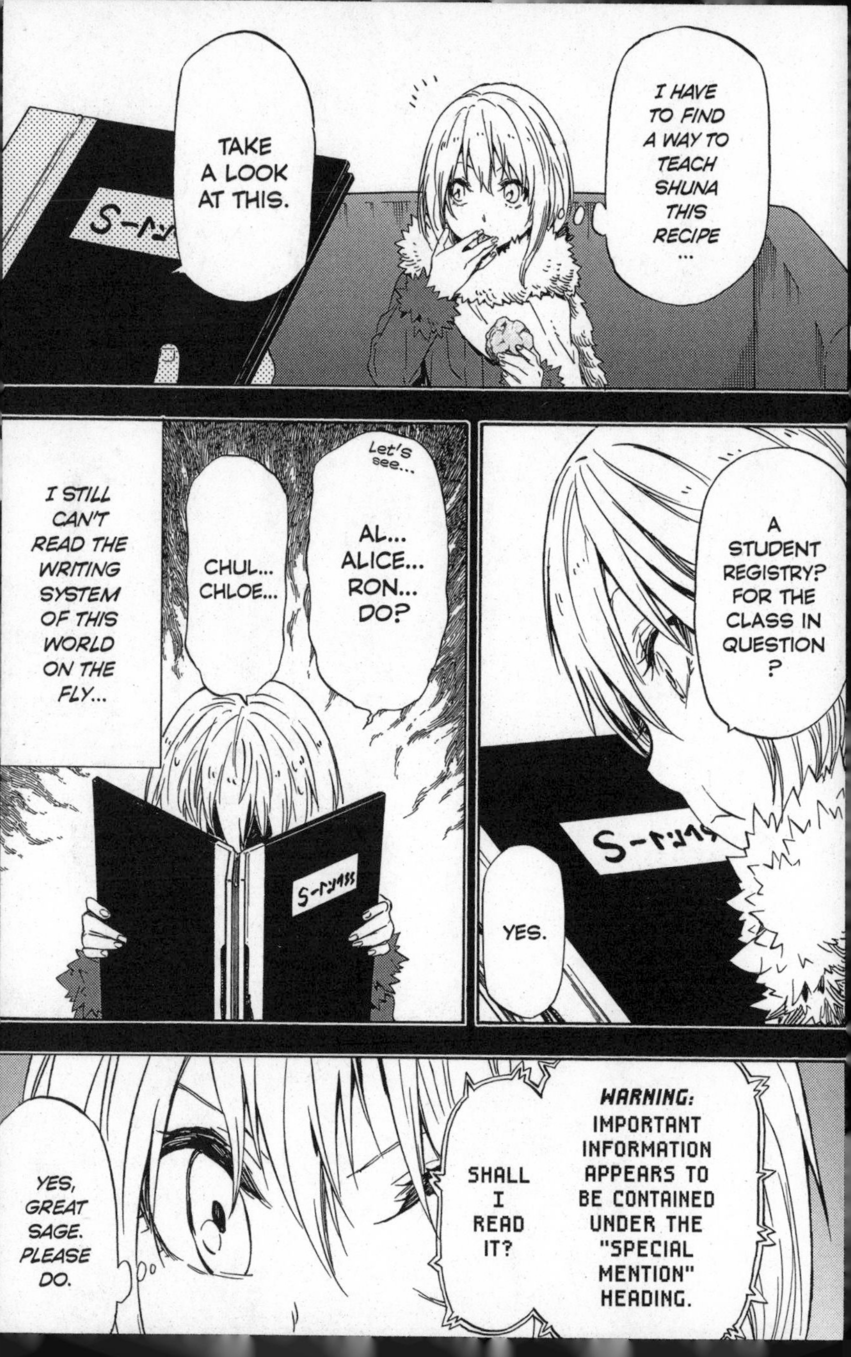
I HAVE TO FIND A WAY TO TEACH SHUNA THIS RECIPE ...
TAKE A LOOK AT THIS.
A STUDENT REGISTRY? FOR THE CLASS IN QUESTION?
YES.
Let's see...
AL... ALICE... RON... DO?
CHUL... CHLOE...
I STILL CAN'T READ THE WRITING SYSTEM OF THIS WORLD ON THE FLY...
WARNING: IMPORTANT INFORMATION APPEARS TO BE CONTAINED UNDER THE "SPECIAL MENTION" HEADING.
SHALL I READ IT?
YES, GREAT SAGE. PLEASE DO.

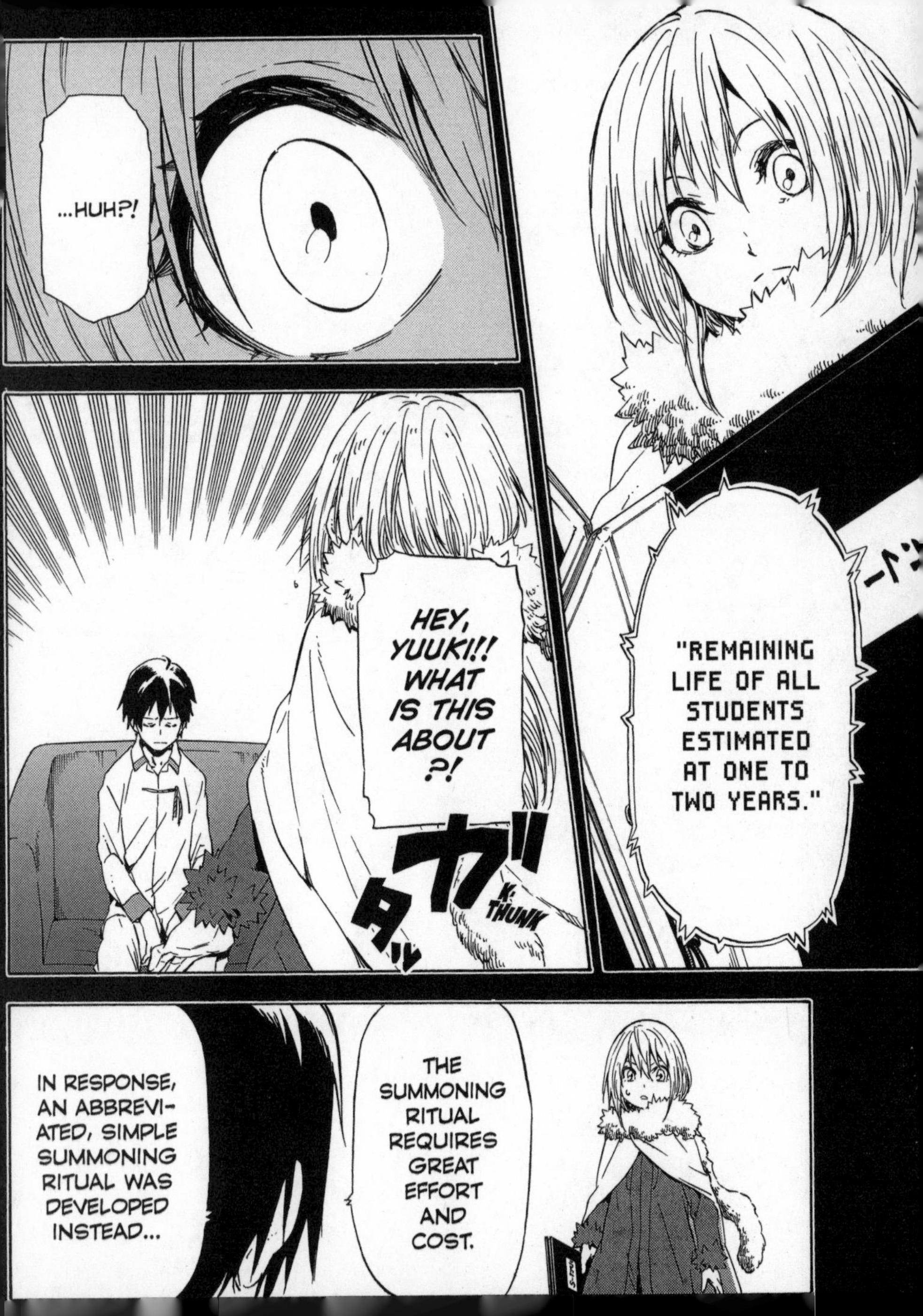
"REMAINING LIFE OF ALL STUDENTS ESTIMATED AT ONE TO TWO YEARS."
...HUH?!
HEY, YUUKI!! WHAT IS THIS ABOUT?!
K-THUNK
THE SUMMONING RITUAL REQUIRES GREAT EFFORT AND COST.
IN RESPONSE, AN ABBREVIATED, SIMPLE SUMMONING RITUAL WAS DEVELOPED INSTEAD...

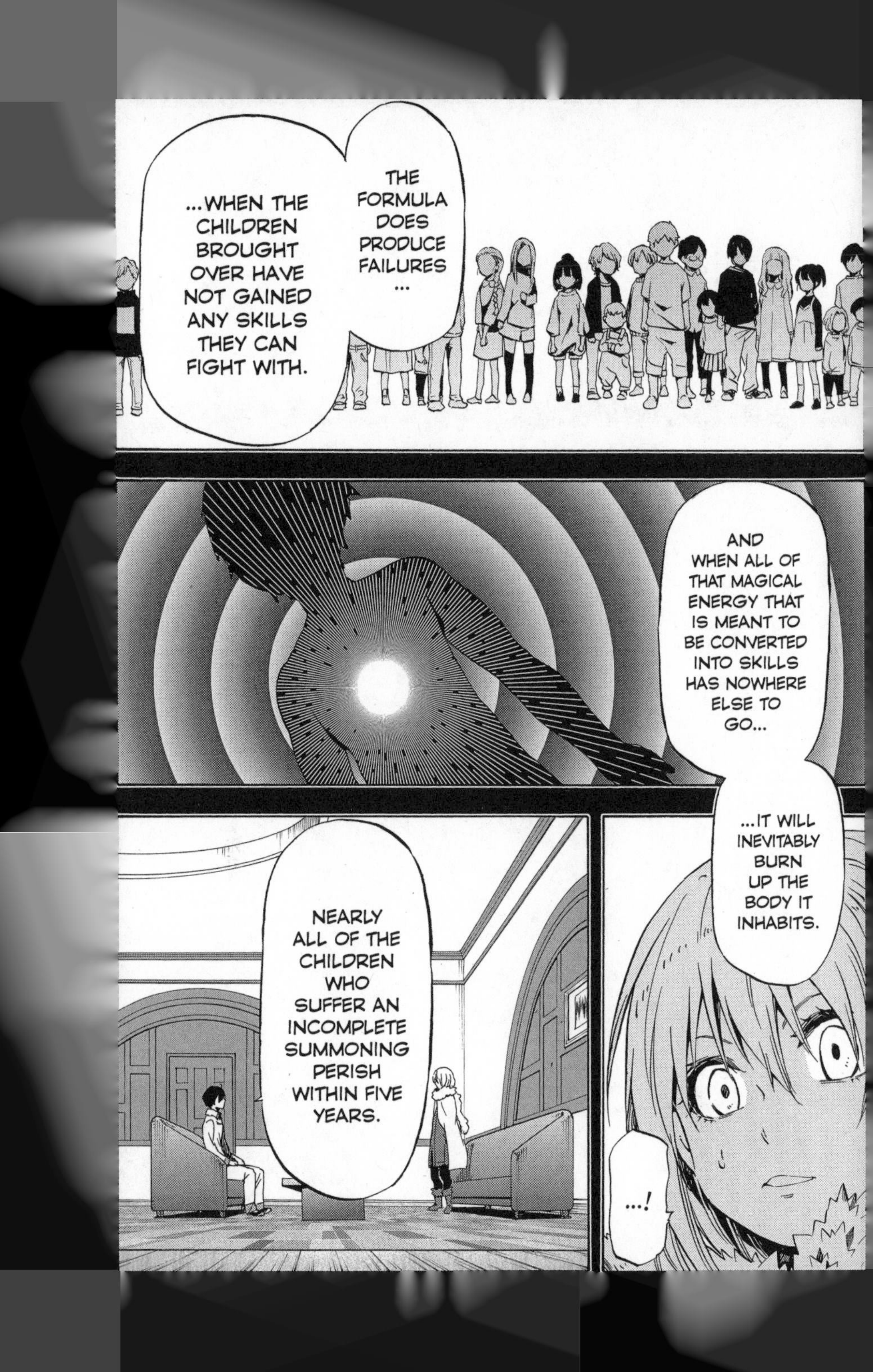
THE FORMULA DOES PRODUCE FAILURES ...
...WHEN THE CHILDREN BROUGHT OVER HAVE NOT GAINED ANY SKILLS THEY CAN FIGHT WITH.
AND WHEN ALL OF THAT MAGICAL ENERGY THAT IS MEANT TO BE CONVERTED INTO SKILLS HAS NOWHERE ELSE TO GO...
...IT WILL INEVITABLY BURN UP THE BODY IT INHABITS.
...!
NEARLY ALL OF THE CHILDREN WHO SUFFER AN INCOMPLETE SUMMONING PERISH WITHIN FIVE YEARS.

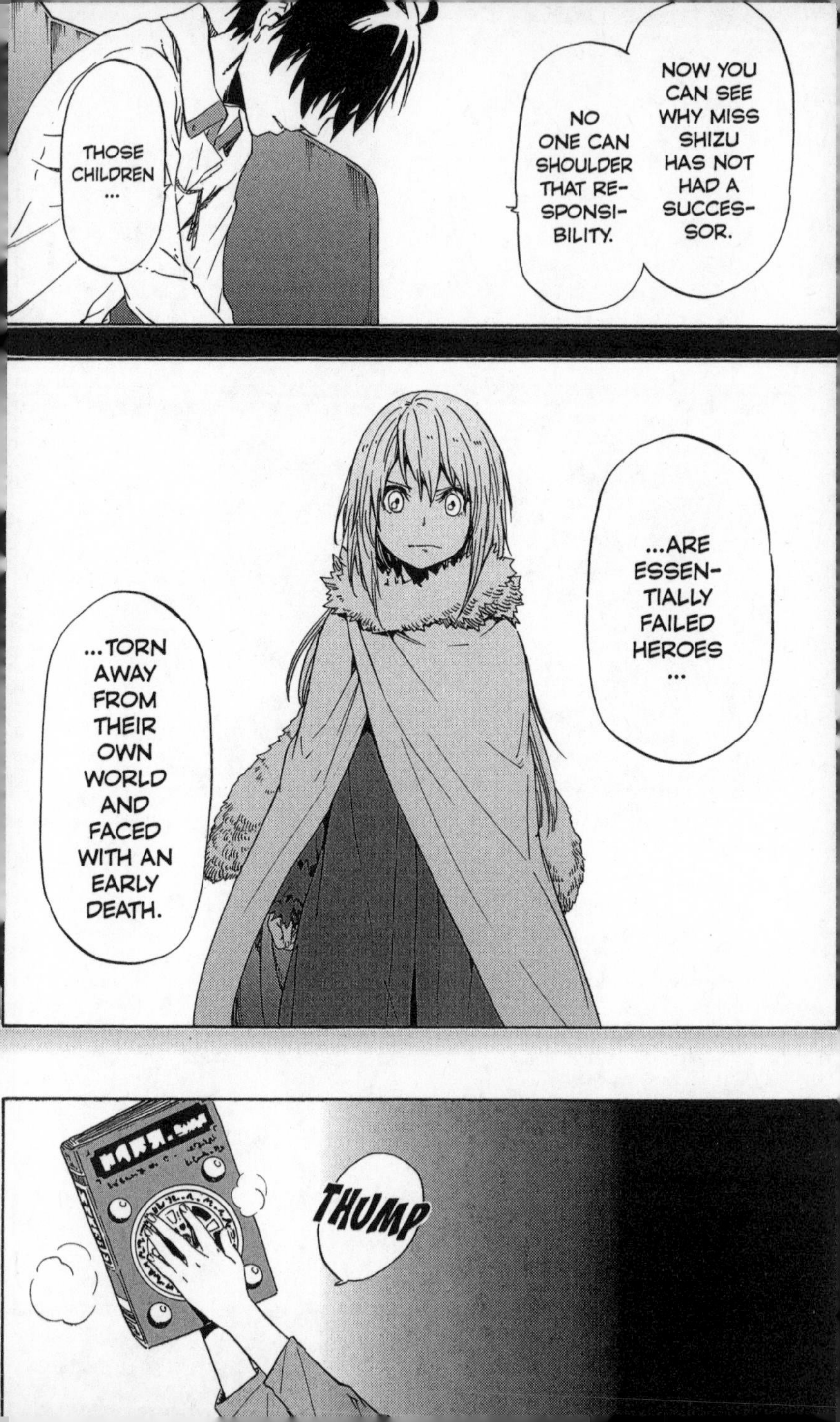
NOW YOU CAN SEE WHY MISS SHIZU HAS NOT HAD A SUCCES-SOR.
NO ONE CAN SHOULDER THAT RE-SPONSI-BILITY.
THOSE CHILDREN ...
...ARE ESSEN-TIALLY FAILED HEROES ...
...TORN AWAY FROM THEIR OWN WORLD AND FACED WITH AN EARLY DEATH.
THUMP

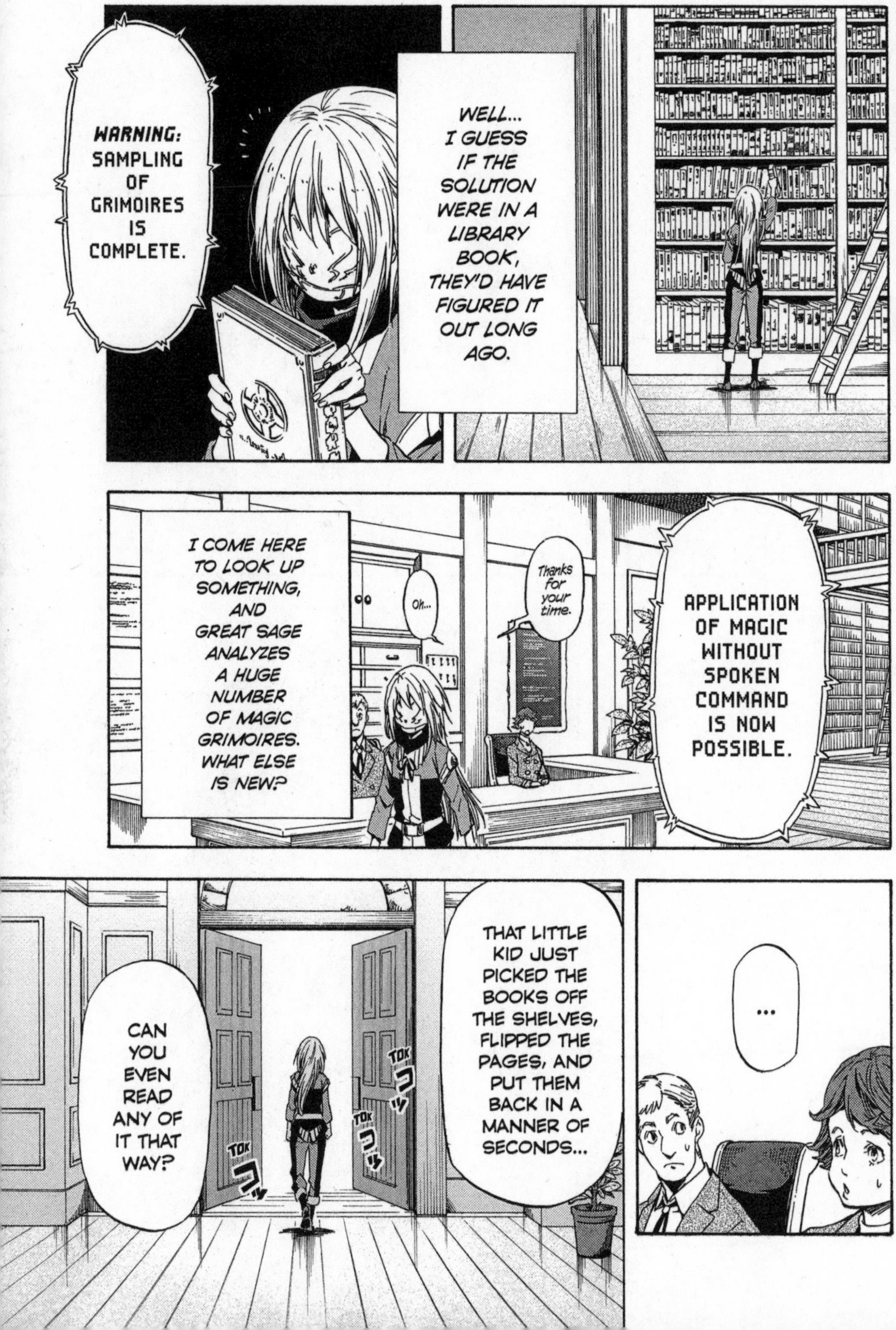
WELL... I GUESS IF THE SOLUTION WERE IN A LIBRARY BOOK, THEY'D HAVE FIGURED IT OUT LONG AGO.
WARNING: SAMPLING OF GRIMOIRES IS COMPLETE.
APPLICATION OF MAGIC WITHOUT SPOKEN COMMAND IS NOW POSSIBLE.
Thanks for your time.
Oh...
I COME HERE TO LOOK UP SOMETHING, AND GREAT SAGE ANALYZES A HUGE NUMBER OF MAGIC GRIMOIRES. WHAT ELSE IS NEW?
...
THAT LITTLE KID JUST PICKED THE BOOKS OFF THE SHELVES, FLIPPED THE PAGES, AND PUT THEM BACK IN A MANNER OF SECONDS...
TOK
TOK
TOK
CAN YOU EVEN READ ANY OF IT THAT WAY?

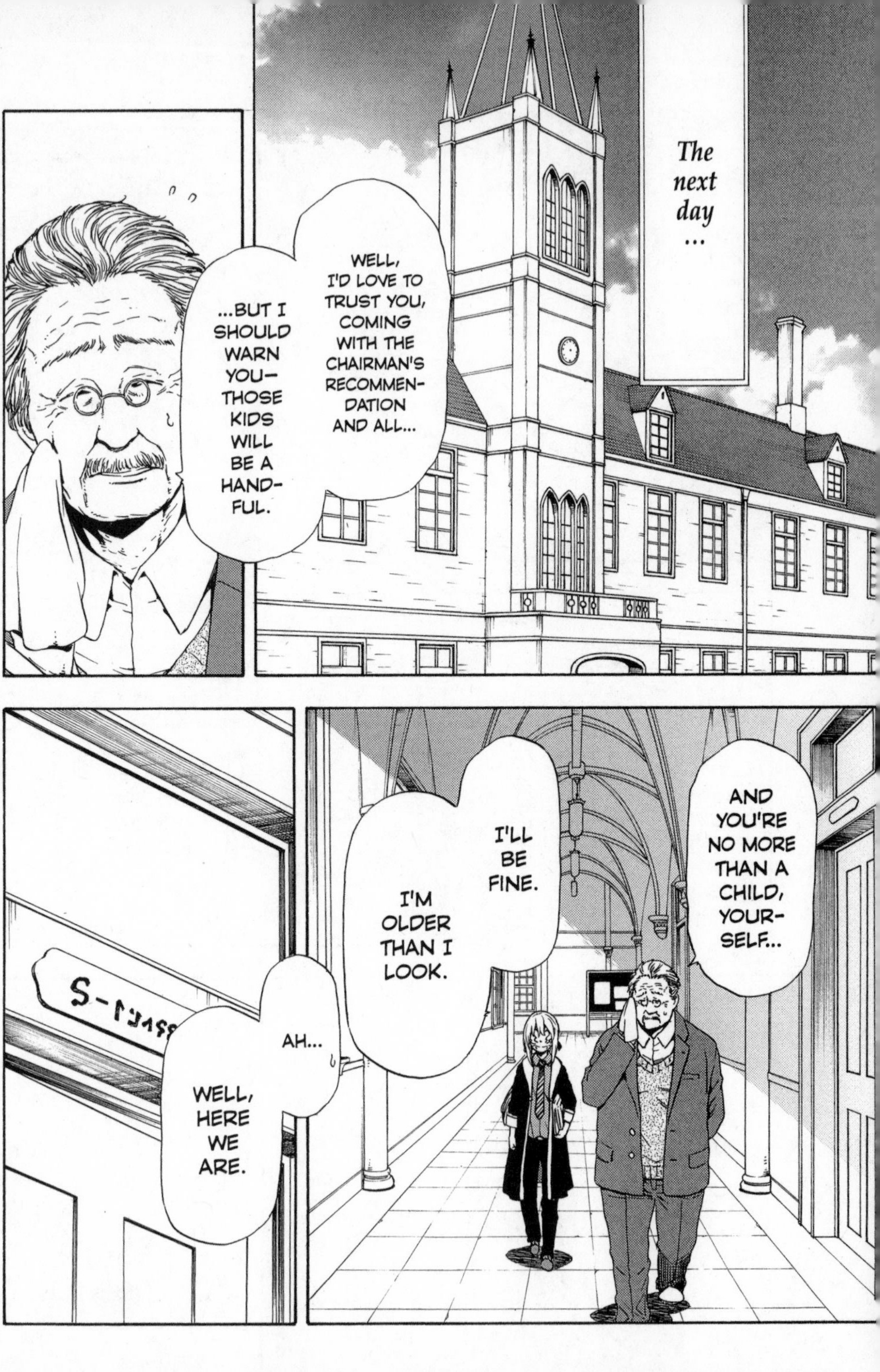
The next day ...
WELL, I'D LOVE TO TRUST YOU, COMING WITH THE CHAIRMAN'S RECOMMEN-DATION AND ALL...
...BUT I SHOULD WARN YOU— THOSE KIDS WILL BE A HAND-FUL.
AND YOU'RE NO MORE THAN A CHILD, YOUR-SELF...
I'LL BE FINE.
I'M OLDER THAN I LOOK.
AH...
WELL, HERE WE ARE.

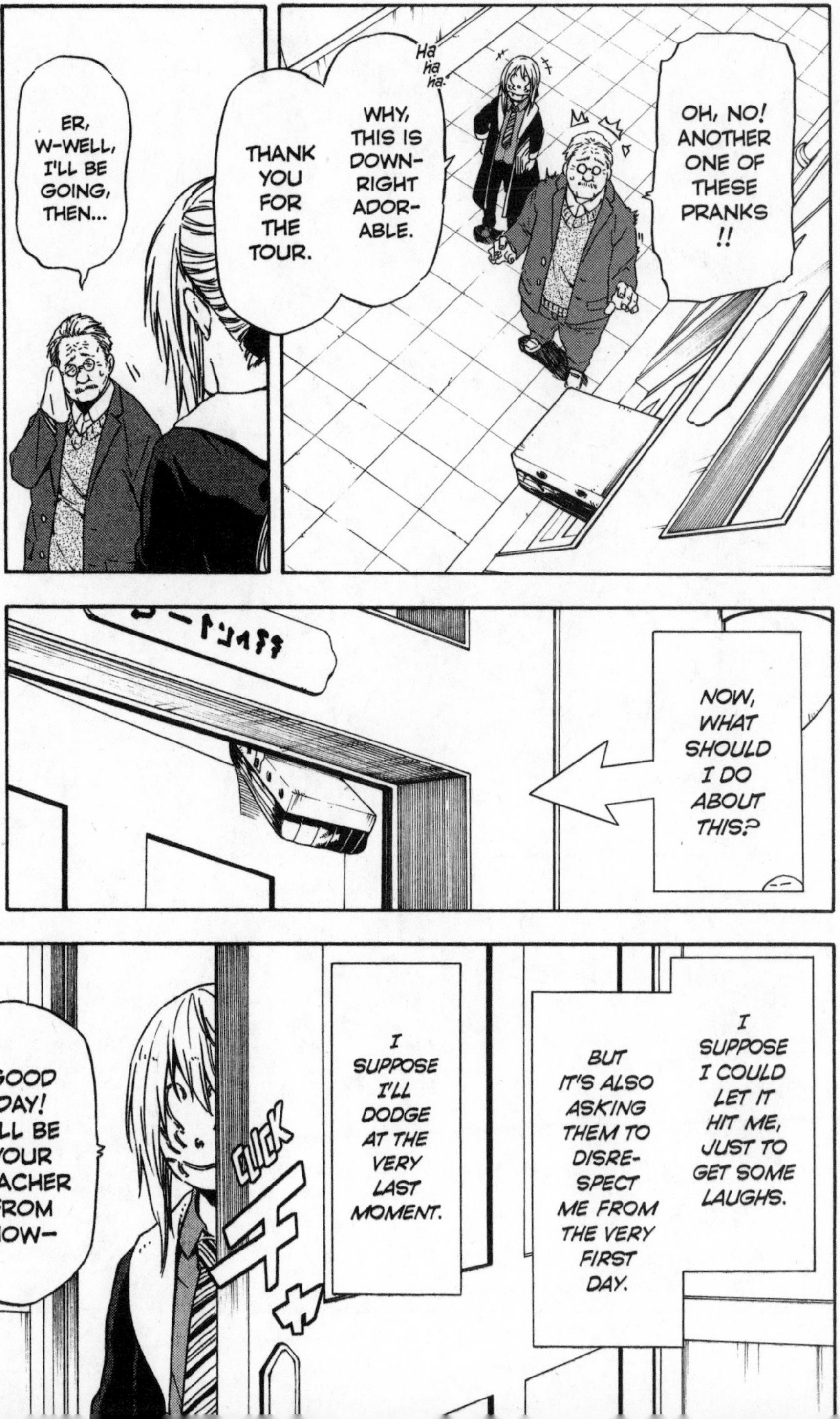
OH, NO! ANOTHER ONE OF THESE PRANKS!!
Ha ha ha.
WHY, THIS IS DOWN-RIGHT ADORABLE.
THANK YOU FOR THE TOUR.
ER, W-WELL, I'LL BE GOING, THEN...
NOW, WHAT SHOULD I DO ABOUT THIS?
I SUPPOSE I COULD LET IT HIT ME, JUST TO GET SOME LAUGHS.
BUT IT'S ALSO ASKING THEM TO DISRESPECT ME FROM THE VERY FIRST DAY.
I SUPPOSE I'LL DODGE AT THE VERY LAST MOMENT.
CLICK
GOOD DAY! I'LL BE YOUR TEACHER FROM NOW-

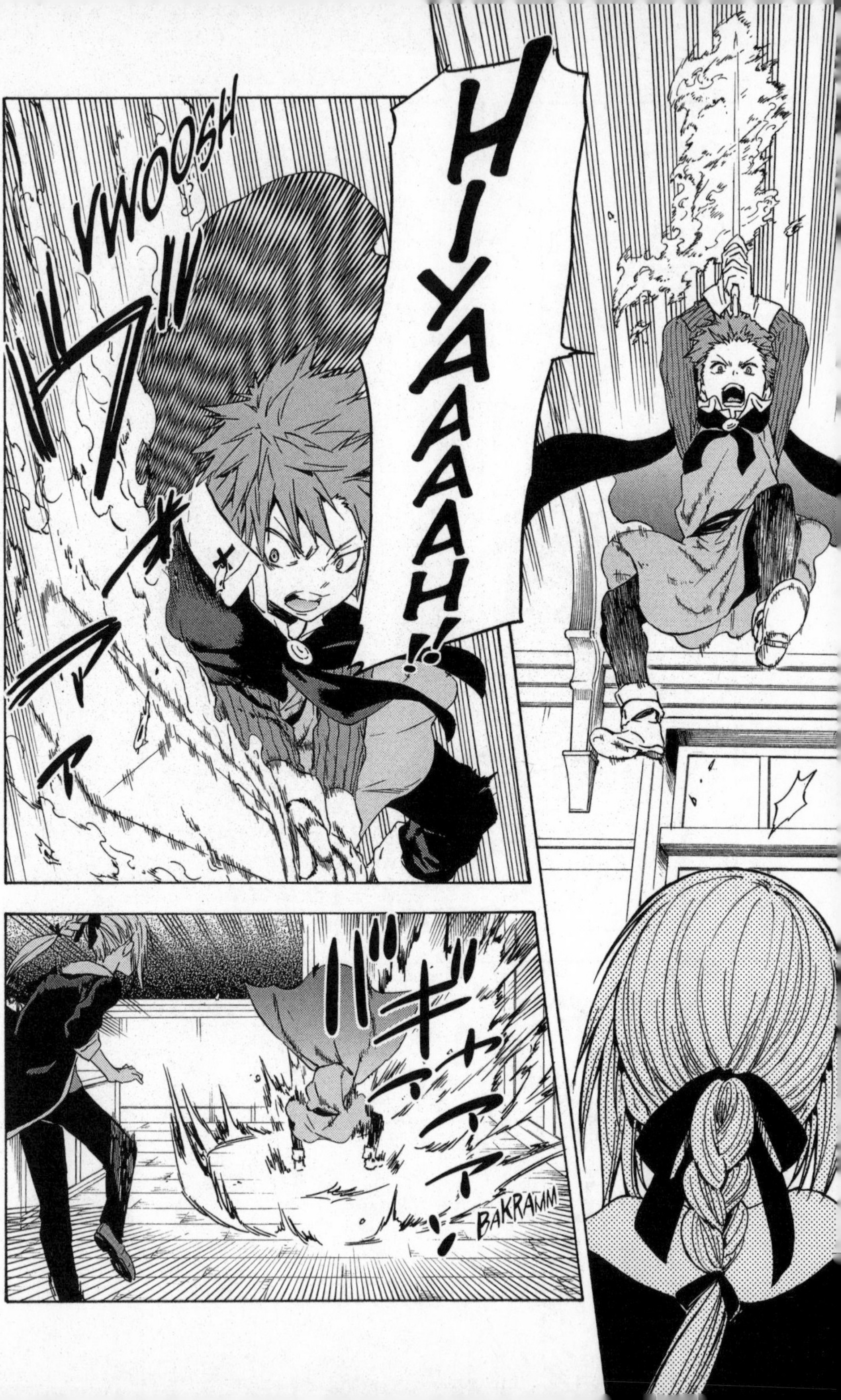
HIYAAAAAH!!
VWOOSH
BAKRAMM

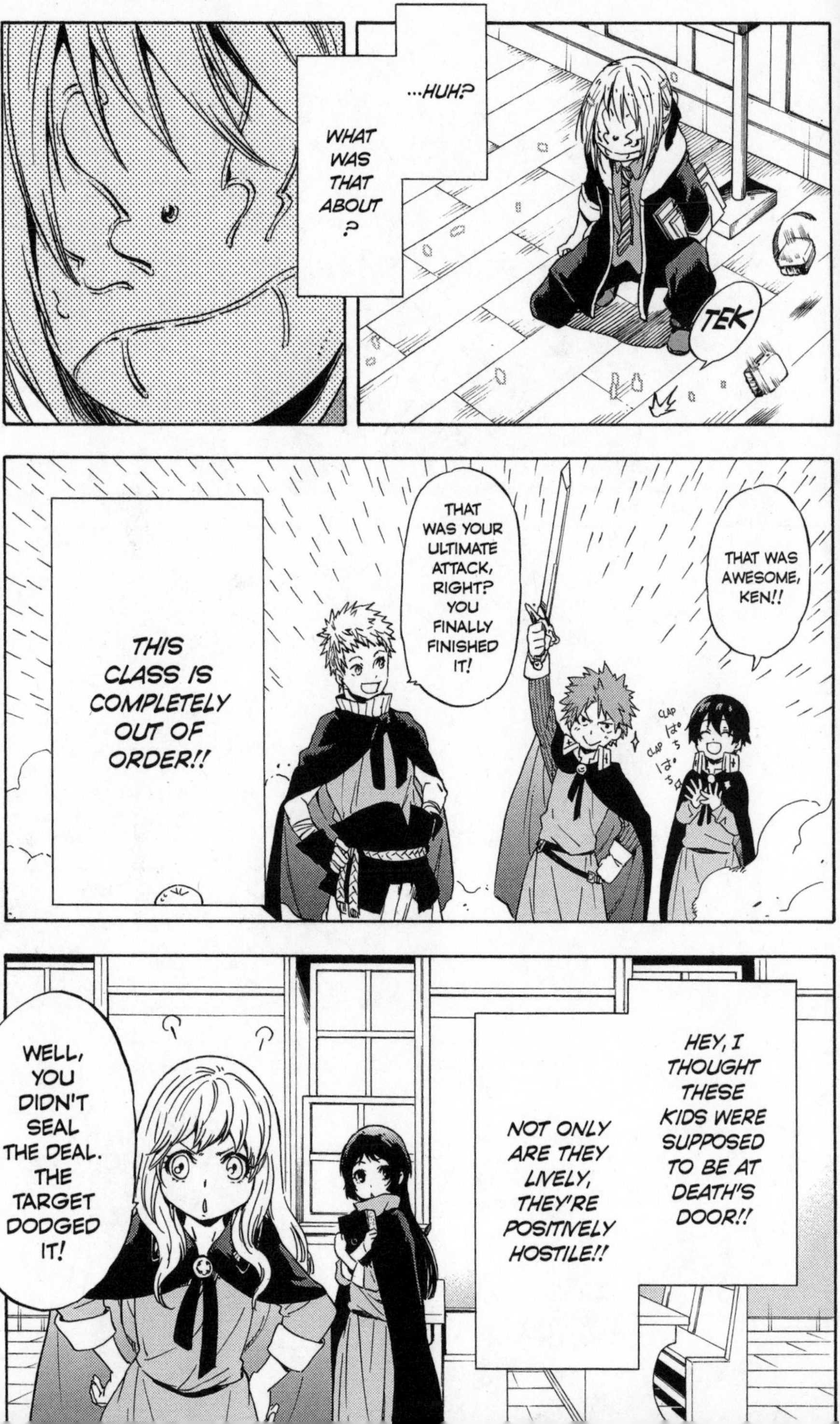
...HUH?
WHAT WAS THAT ABOUT?
TEK
THAT WAS AWESOME, KEN!!
CLAP CLAP
THAT WAS YOUR ULTIMATE ATTACK, RIGHT? YOU FINALLY FINISHED IT!
THIS CLASS IS COMPLETELY OUT OF ORDER!!
HEY, I THOUGHT THESE KIDS WERE SUPPOSED TO BE AT DEATH'S DOOR!!
NOT ONLY ARE THEY LIVELY, THEY'RE POSITIVELY HOSTILE!!
WELL, YOU DIDN'T SEAL THE DEAL. THE TARGET DODGED IT!

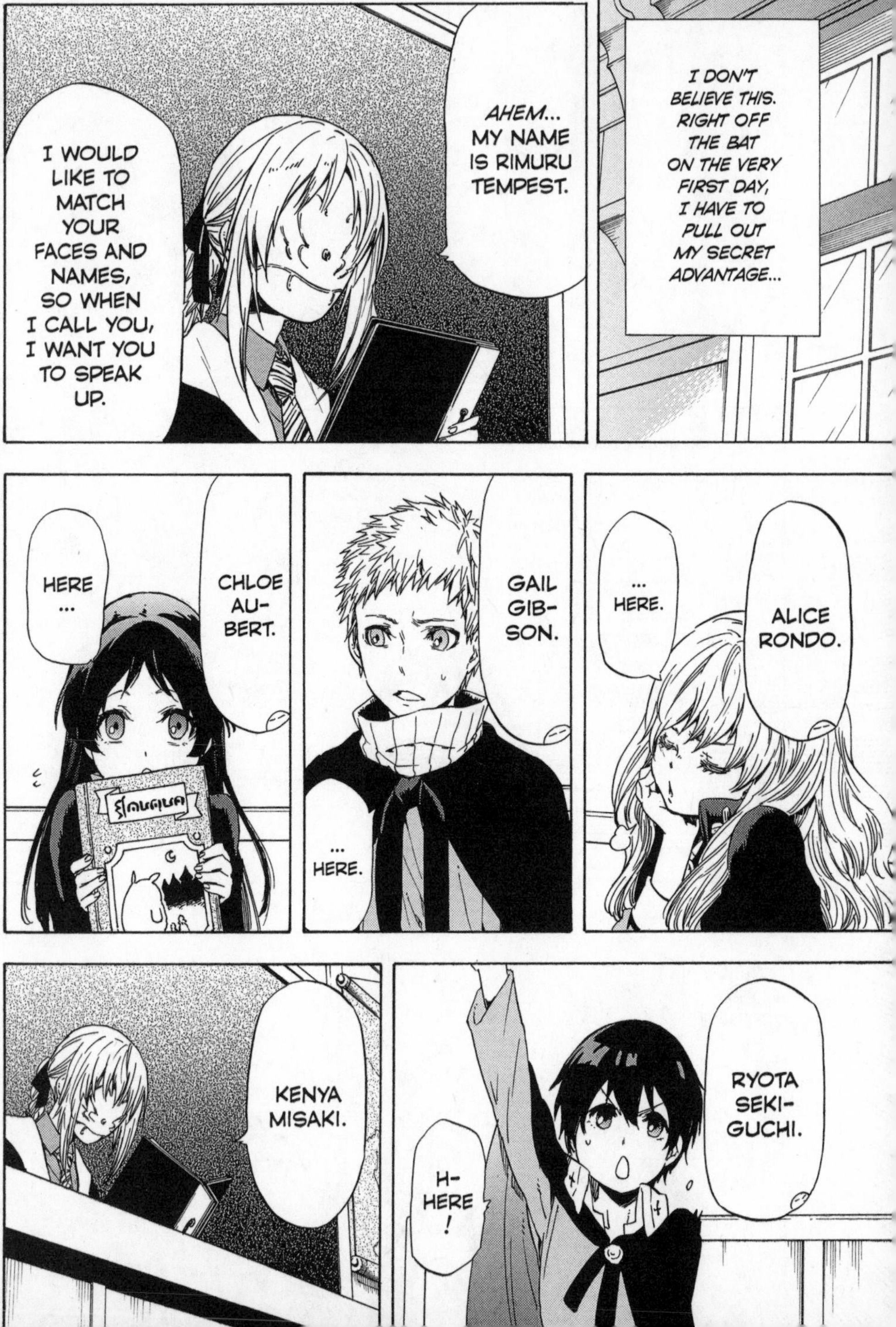
I DON'T BELIEVE THIS. RIGHT OFF THE BAT ON THE VERY FIRST DAY, I HAVE TO PULL OUT MY SECRET ADVANTAGE...
AHEM... MY NAME IS RIMURU TEMPEST.
I WOULD LIKE TO MATCH YOUR FACES AND NAMES, SO WHEN I CALL YOU, I WANT YOU TO SPEAK UP.
ALICE RONDO.
... HERE.
GAIL GIBSON.
... HERE.
CHLOE AUBERT.
HERE ...
RYOTA SEKIGUCHI.
H-HERE!
KENYA MISAKI.

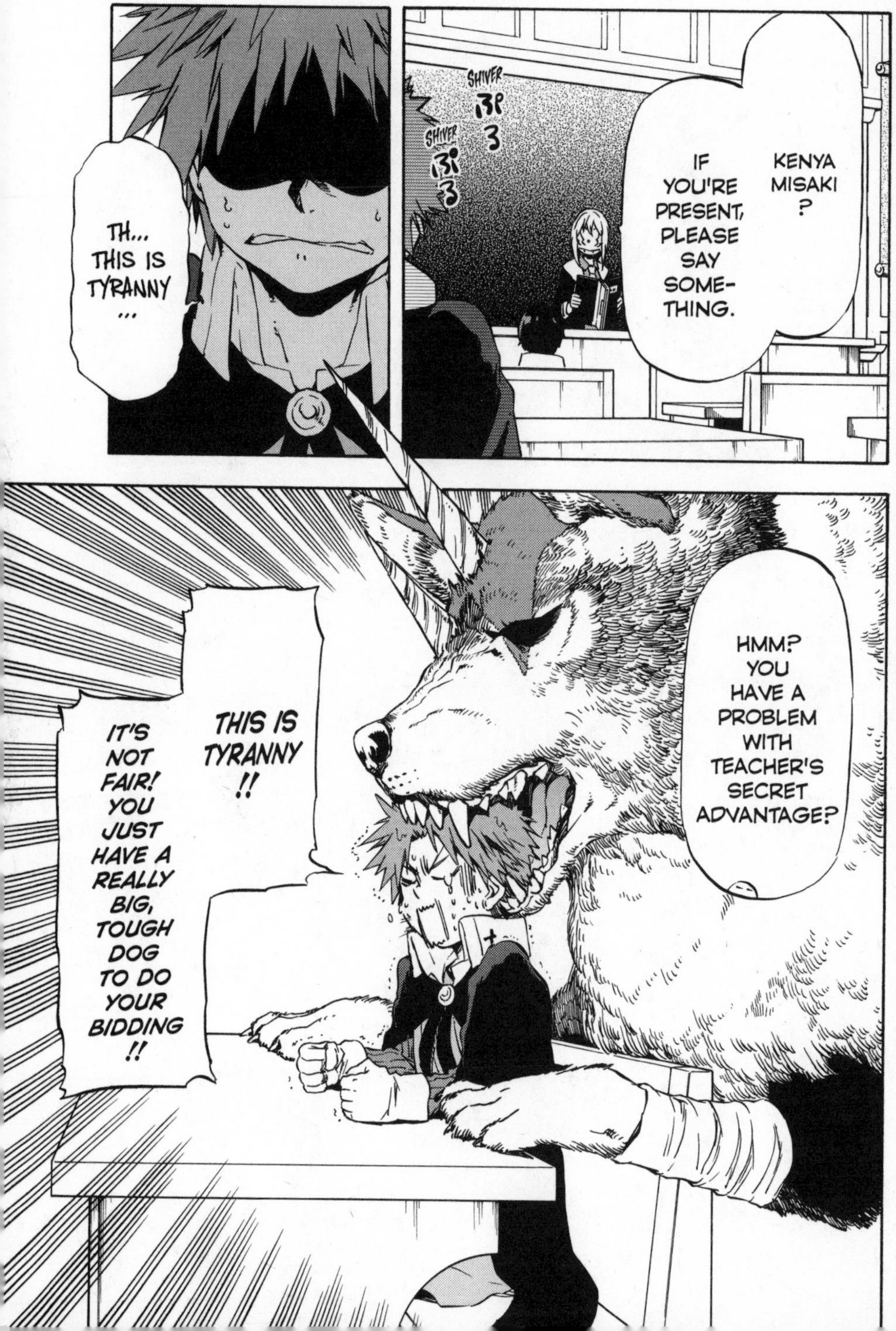
KENYA MISAKI ?
IF YOU'RE PRESENT, PLEASE SAY SOME-THING.
SHIVER ぶる
SHIVER ぶる
TH... THIS IS TYRANNY ...
HMM? YOU HAVE A PROBLEM WITH TEACHER'S SECRET ADVANTAGE?
THIS IS TYRANNY !!
IT'S NOT FAIR! YOU JUST HAVE A REALLY BIG, TOUGH DOG TO DO YOUR BIDDING !!

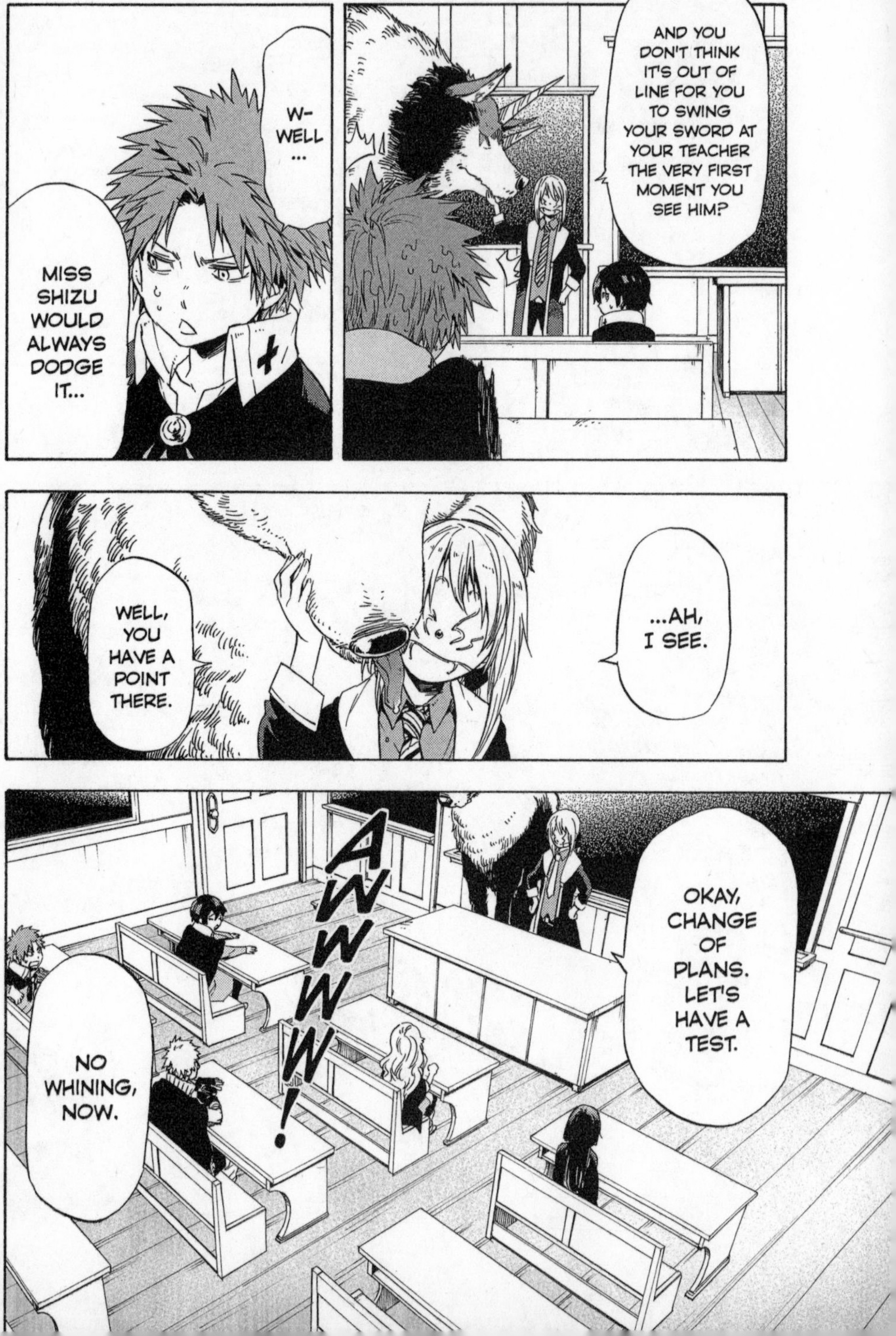
AND YOU DON'T THINK IT'S OUT OF LINE FOR YOU TO SWING YOUR SWORD AT YOUR TEACHER THE VERY FIRST MOMENT YOU SEE HIM?
W-WELL ...
MISS SHIZU WOULD ALWAYS DODGE IT...
...AH, I SEE.
WELL, YOU HAVE A POINT THERE.
OKAY, CHANGE OF PLANS. LET'S HAVE A TEST.
AWWWW!
NO WHINING, NOW.

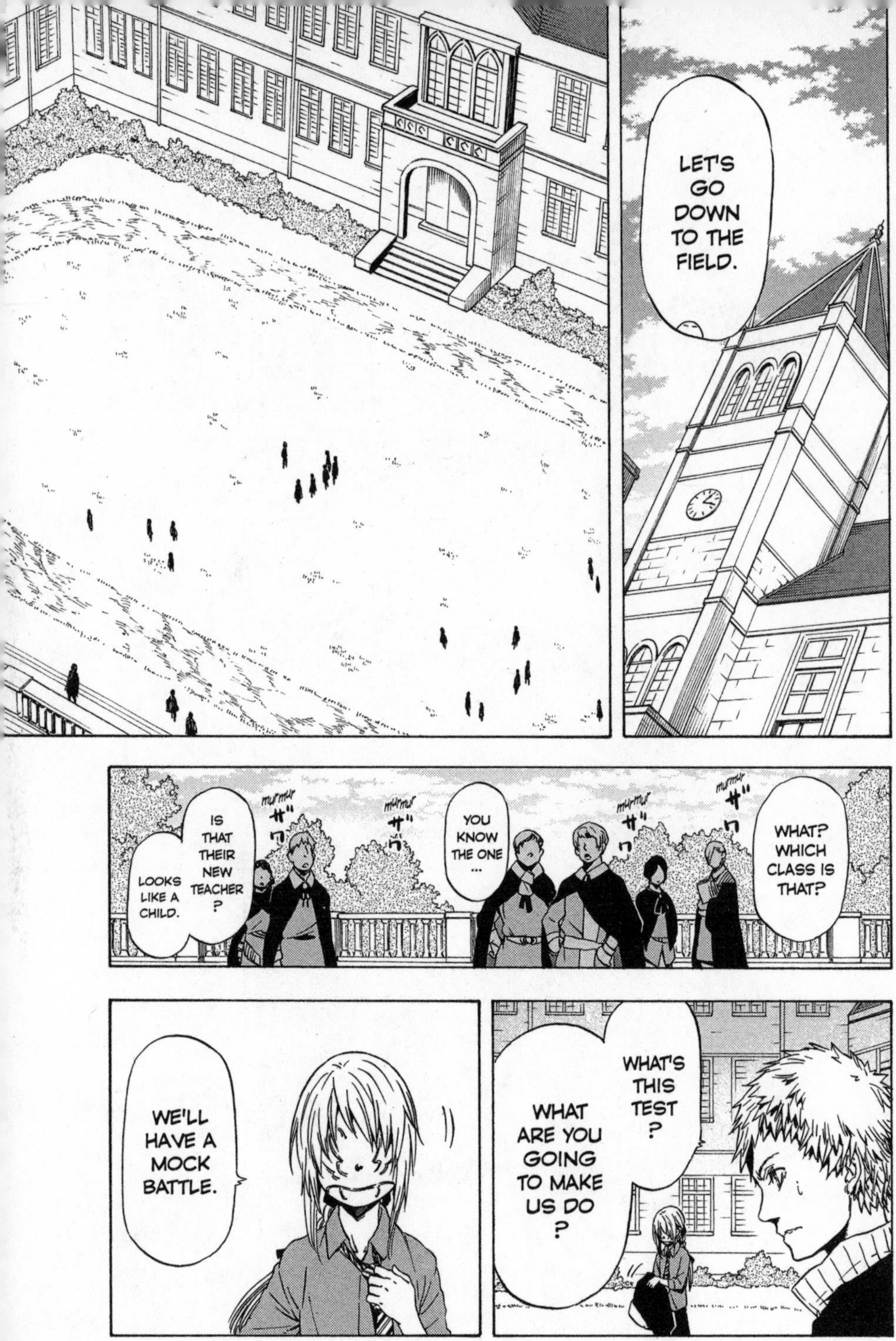
LET'S GO DOWN TO THE FIELD.
murmur ザワ
WHAT? WHICH CLASS IS THAT?
murmur ザワ
YOU KNOW THE ONE ...
murmur ザワ
IS THAT THEIR NEW TEACHER?
LOOKS LIKE A CHILD.
WHAT'S THIS TEST?
WHAT ARE YOU GOING TO MAKE US DO?
WE'LL HAVE A MOCK BATTLE.

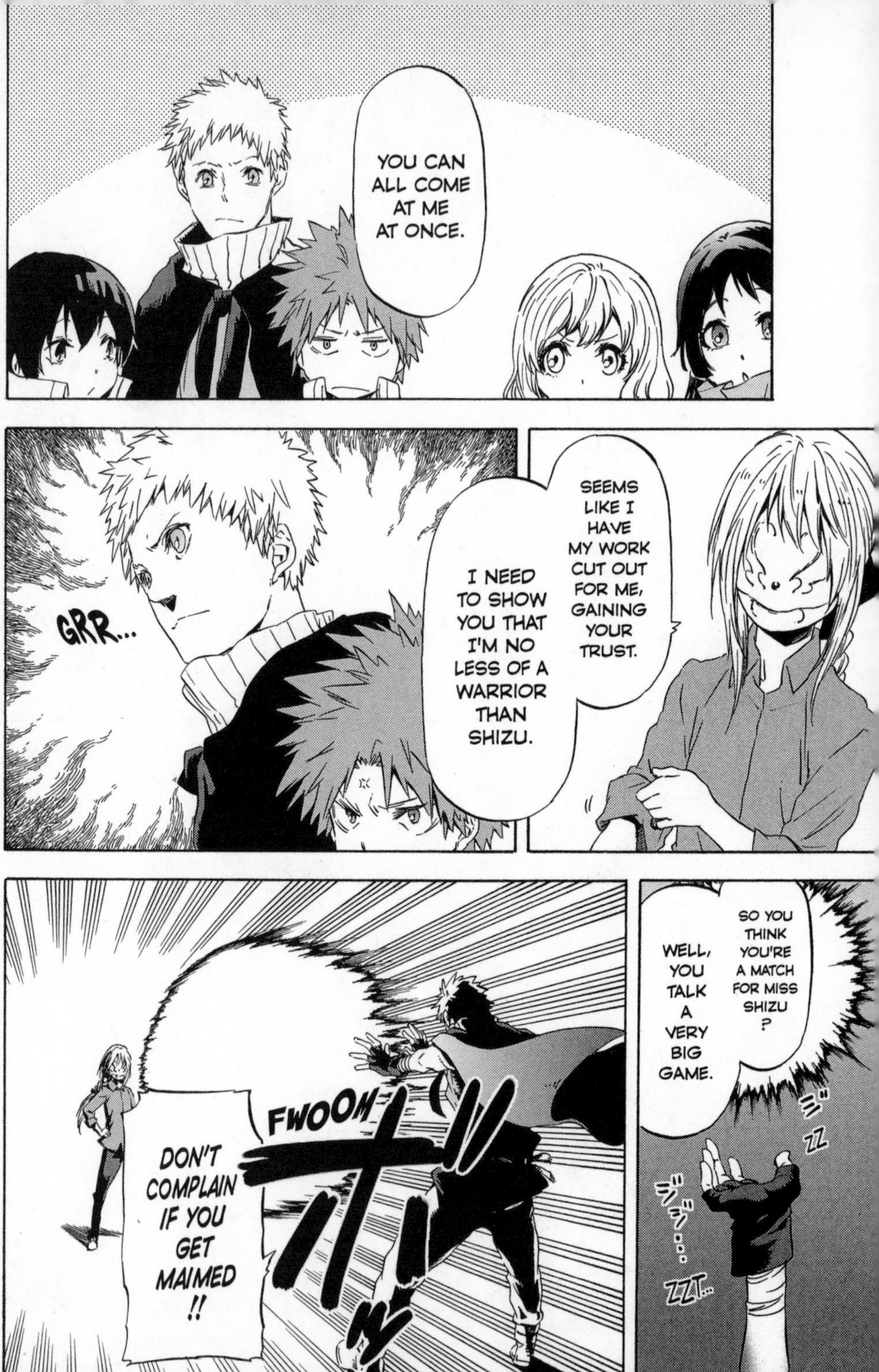
YOU CAN ALL COME AT ME AT ONCE.
SEEMS LIKE I HAVE MY WORK CUT OUT FOR ME, GAINING YOUR TRUST.
I NEED TO SHOW YOU THAT I'M NO LESS OF A WARRIOR THAN SHIZU.
GRR...
SO YOU THINK YOU'RE A MATCH FOR MISS SHIZU?
WELL, YOU TALK A VERY BIG GAME.
ZZ
ZZT...
FWOOM
DON'T COMPLAIN IF YOU GET MAIMED!!

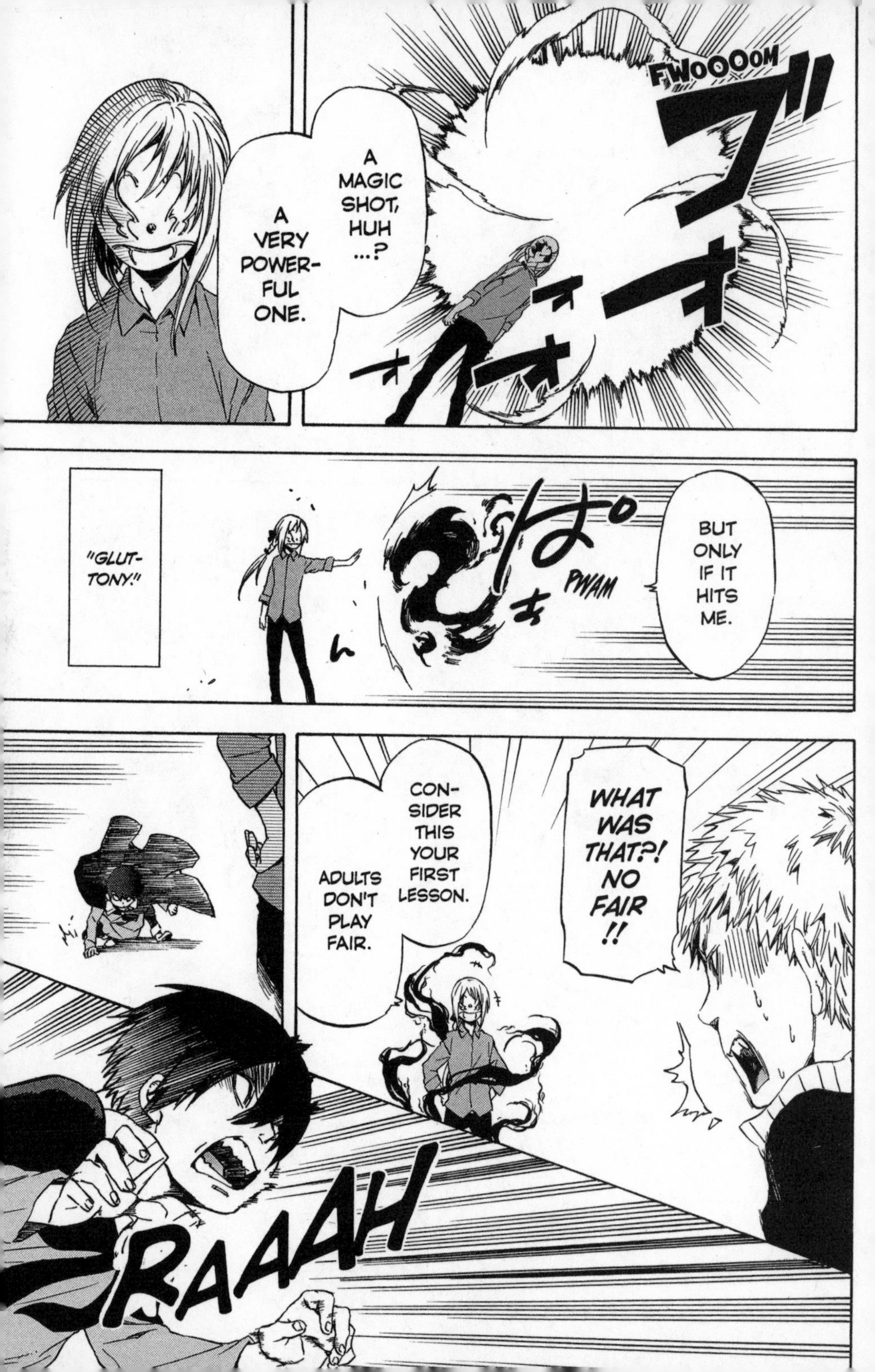
FWOOOOM
A MAGIC SHOT, HUH ...?
A VERY POWER-FUL ONE.
BUT ONLY IF IT HITS ME.
PWAM
"GLUT-TONY!"
WHAT WAS THAT?! NO FAIR !!
CON-SIDER THIS YOUR FIRST LESSON.
ADULTS DON'T PLAY FAIR.
RAAAH

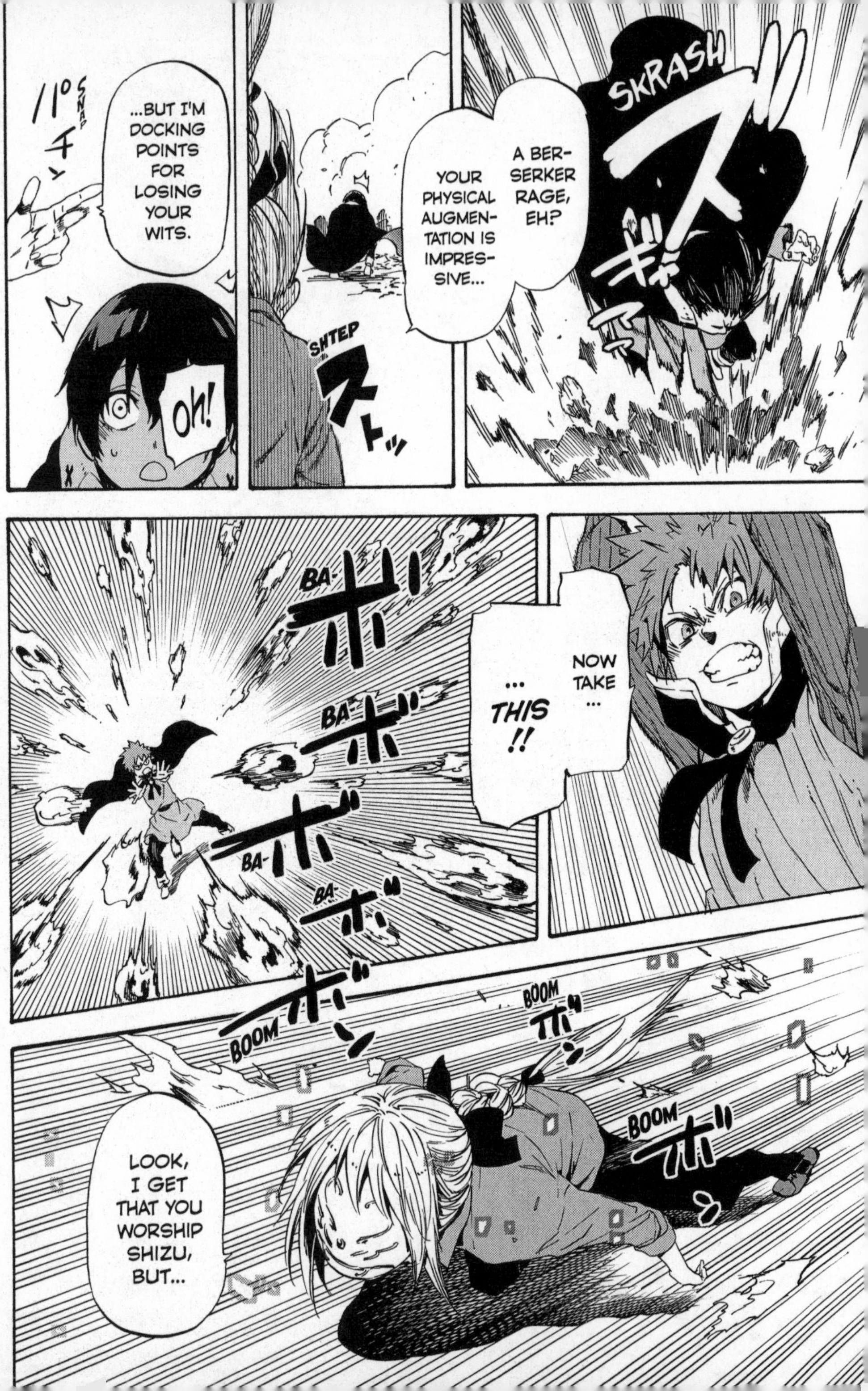
SKRASH
A BER-SERKER RAGE, EH?
YOUR PHYSICAL AUGMENTATION IS IMPRESSIVE...
SHTEP
SNAP
...BUT I'M DOCKING POINTS FOR LOSING YOUR WITS.
Oh!
NOW TAKE ...
... THIS!!
BA-
BA-
BA-
BA-
BOOM
BOOM
BOOM
LOOK, I GET THAT YOU WORSHIP SHIZU, BUT...

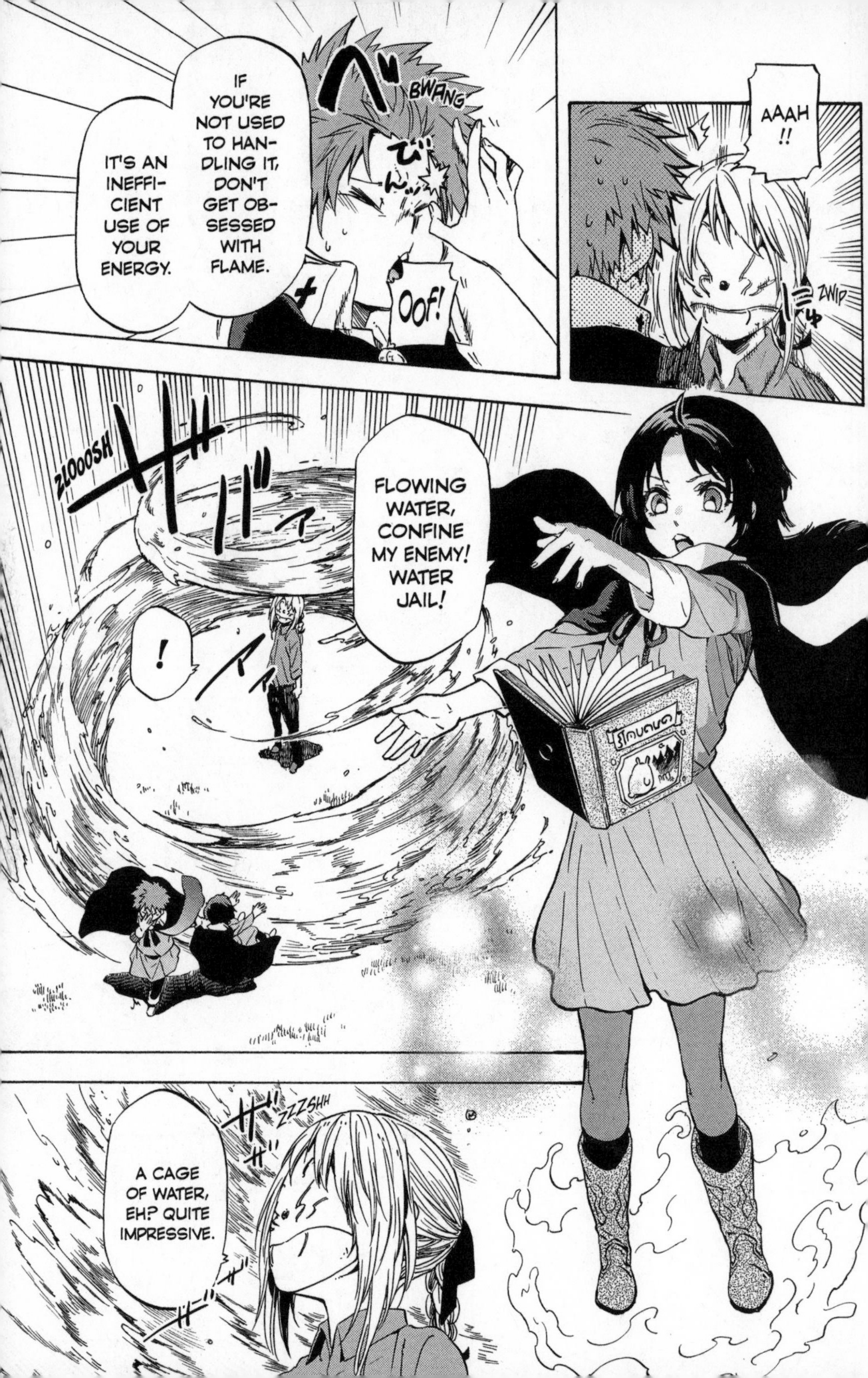
AAAH !!
ZWIP
BWANG
IF YOU'RE NOT USED TO HAN-DLING IT, DON'T GET OB-SESSED WITH FLAME.
IT'S AN INEFFI-CIENT USE OF YOUR ENERGY.
OOF!
FLOWING WATER, CONFINE MY ENEMY! WATER JAIL!
ZLOOOSH
!
ZZZSHH
A CAGE OF WATER, EH? QUITE IMPRESSIVE.

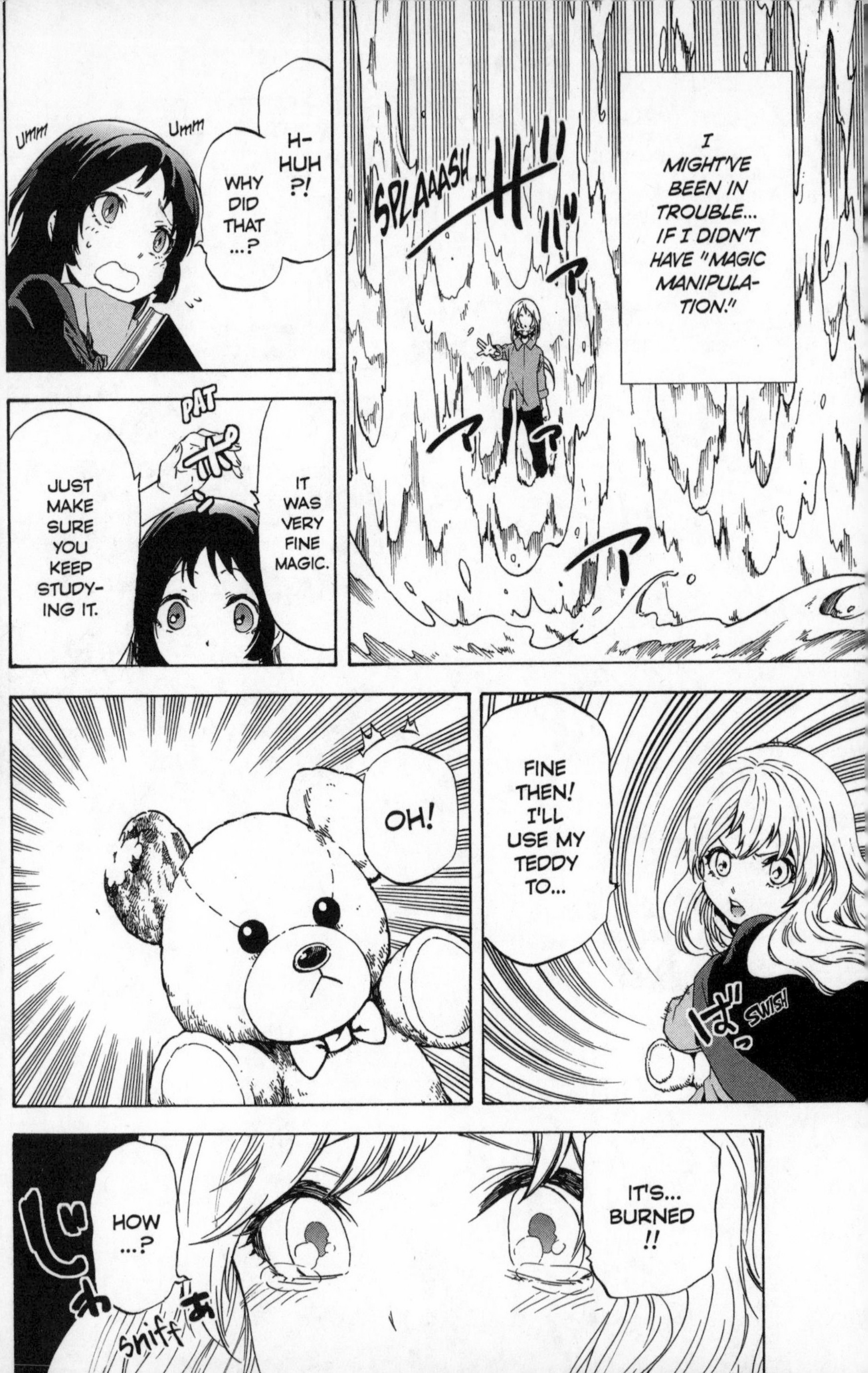
I MIGHT'VE BEEN IN TROUBLE... IF I DIDN'T HAVE "MAGIC MANIPULATION."
SPLAAASH
H-HUH?!
WHY DID THAT...?
Umm
Umm
PAT
IT WAS VERY FINE MAGIC.
JUST MAKE SURE YOU KEEP STUDYING IT.
FINE THEN! I'LL USE MY TEDDY TO...
SWISH
OH!
IT'S... BURNED!!
HOW...?
sniff

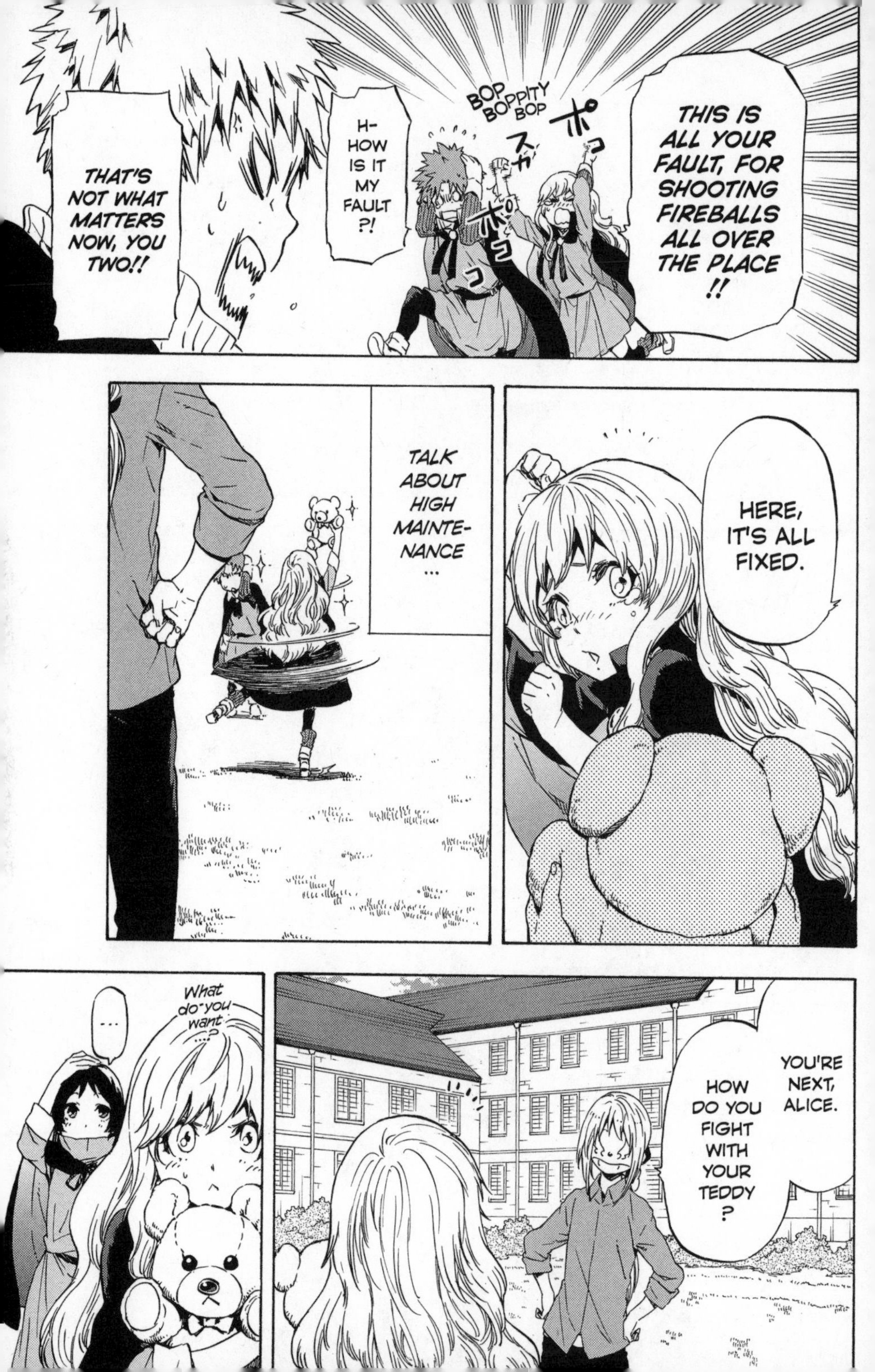
THIS IS ALL YOUR FAULT, FOR SHOOTING FIREBALLS ALL OVER THE PLACE!!
BOP BOPPITY BOP
H-HOW IS IT MY FAULT?!
THAT'S NOT WHAT MATTERS NOW, YOU TWO!!
HERE, IT'S ALL FIXED.
TALK ABOUT HIGH MAINTE-NANCE...
YOU'RE NEXT, ALICE.
HOW DO YOU FIGHT WITH YOUR TEDDY?
What do-you want...?
...

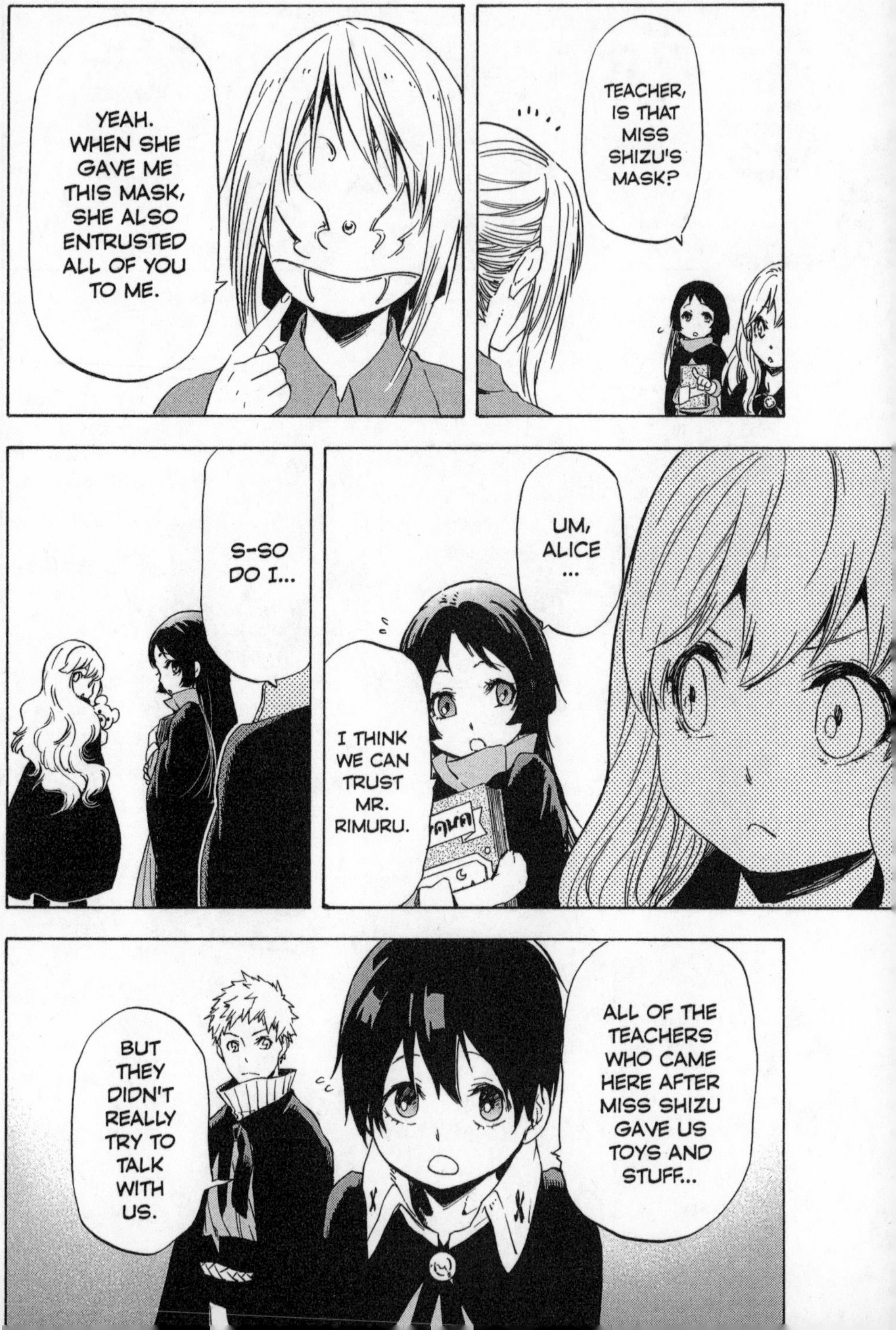
TEACHER, IS THAT MISS SHIZU'S MASK?
YEAH. WHEN SHE GAVE ME THIS MASK, SHE ALSO ENTRUSTED ALL OF YOU TO ME.
UM, ALICE ...
I THINK WE CAN TRUST MR. RIMURU.
S-SO DO I...
ALL OF THE TEACHERS WHO CAME HERE AFTER MISS SHIZU GAVE US TOYS AND STUFF...
BUT THEY DIDN'T REALLY TRY TO TALK WITH US.

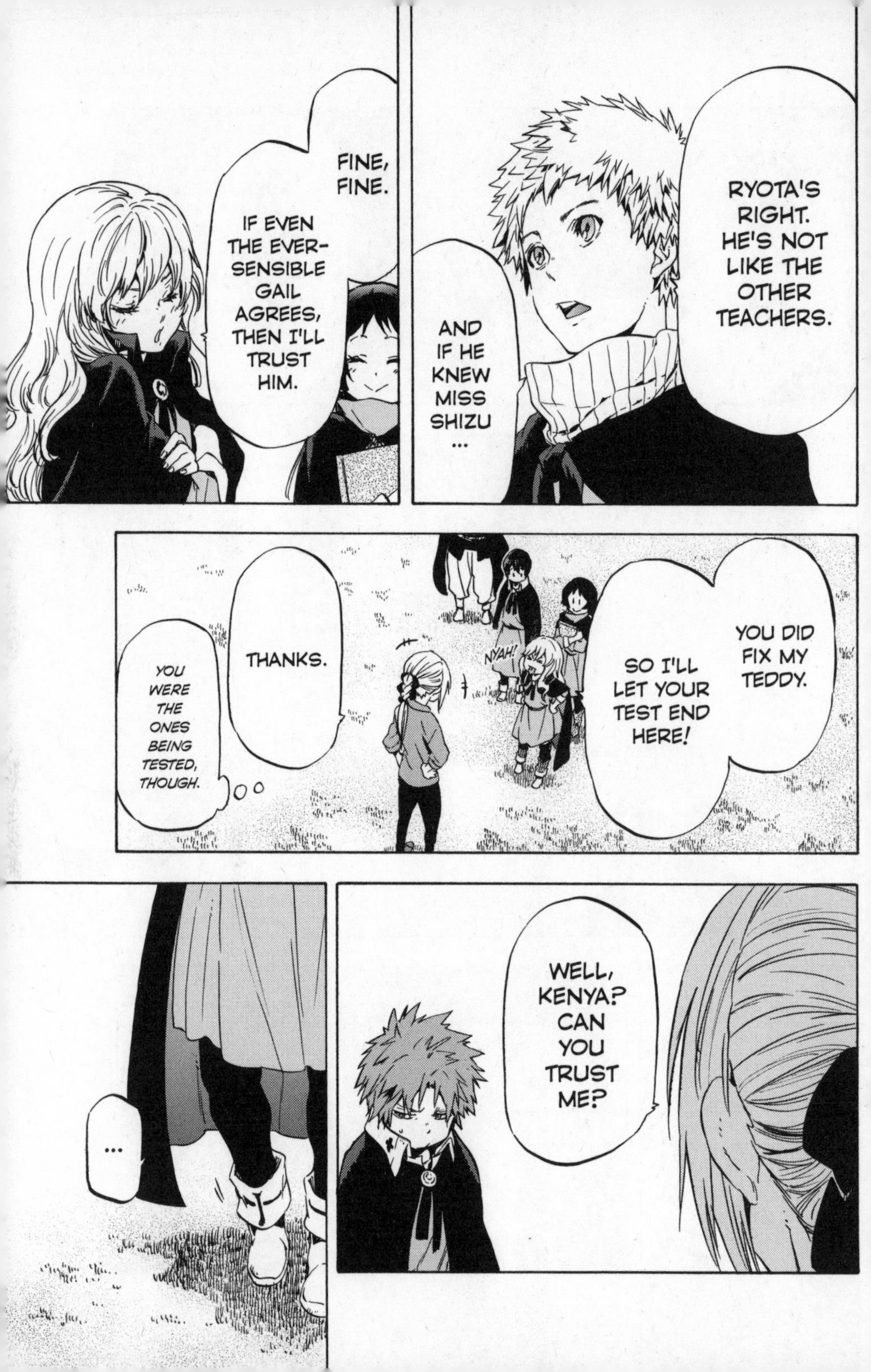
RYOTA'S RIGHT. HE'S NOT LIKE THE OTHER TEACHERS.
AND IF HE KNEW MISS SHIZU ...
FINE, FINE.
IF EVEN THE EVER-SENSIBLE GAIL AGREES, THEN I'LL TRUST HIM.
YOU DID FIX MY TEDDY.
SO I'LL LET YOUR TEST END HERE!
NYAH!
THANKS.
YOU WERE THE ONES BEING TESTED, THOUGH.
WELL, KENYA? CAN YOU TRUST ME?
...

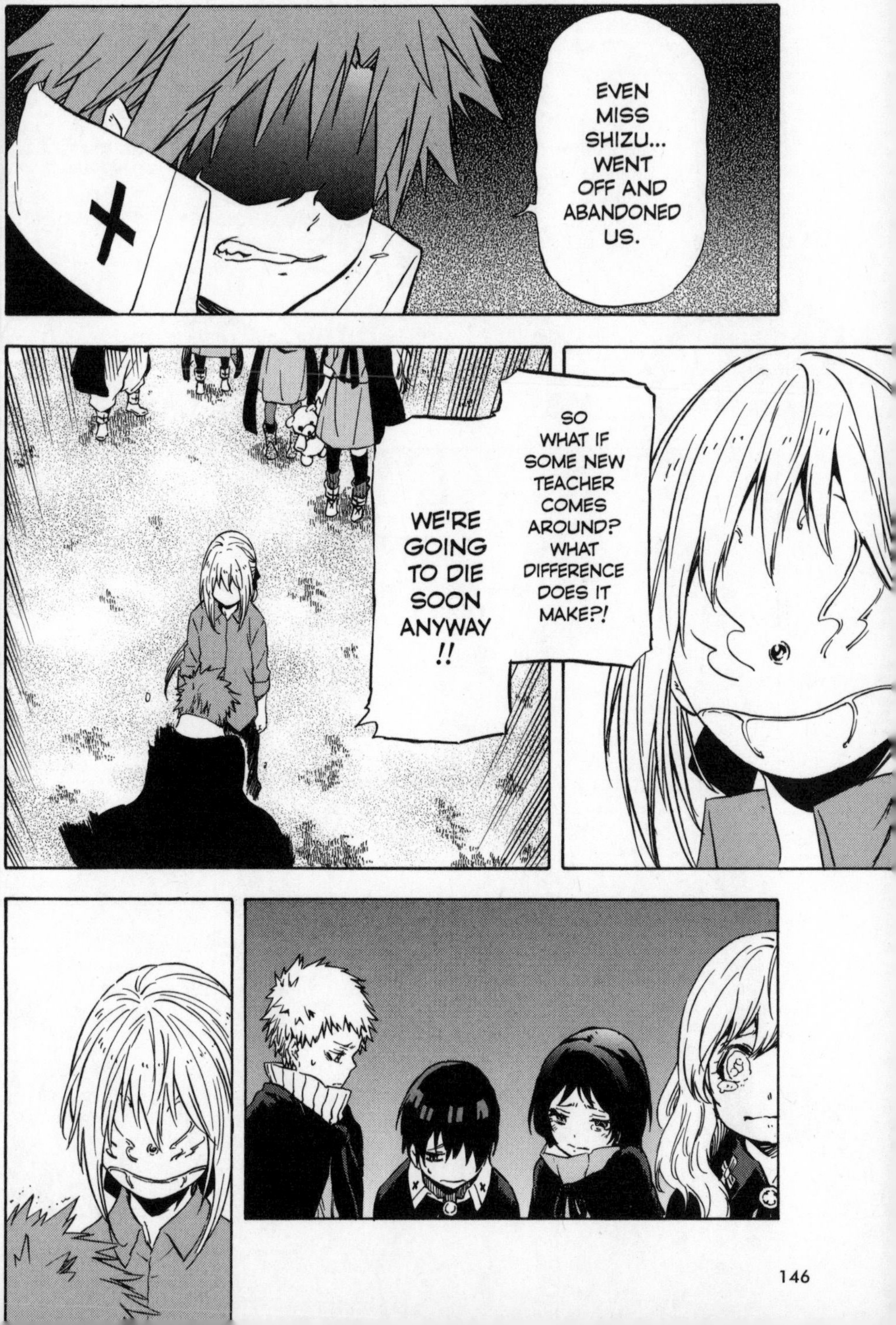
EVEN MISS SHIZU... WENT OFF AND ABANDONED US.
SO WHAT IF SOME NEW TEACHER COMES AROUND? WHAT DIFFERENCE DOES IT MAKE?!
WE'RE GOING TO DIE SOON ANYWAY!!

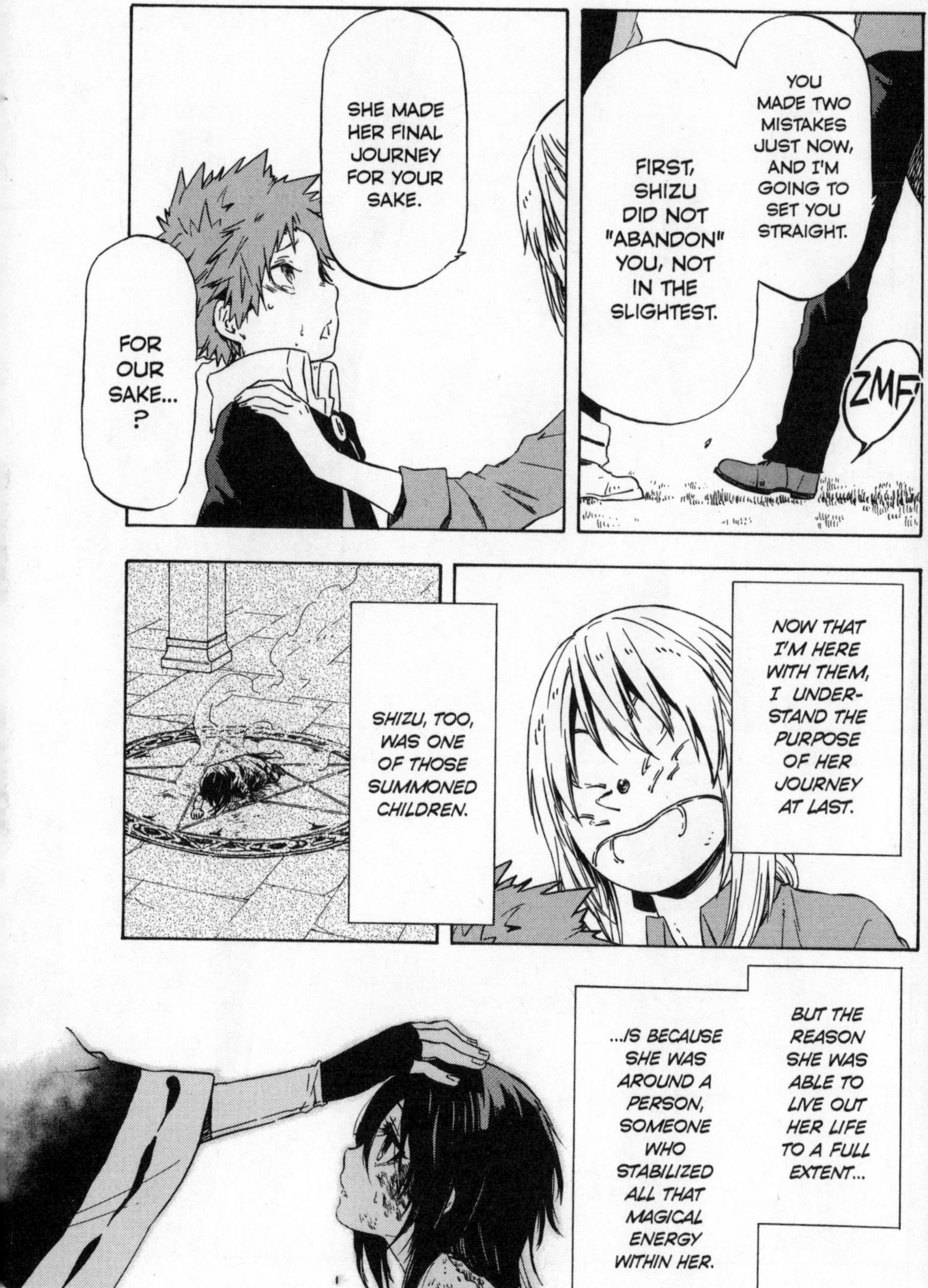
YOU MADE TWO MISTAKES JUST NOW, AND I'M GOING TO SET YOU STRAIGHT.
FIRST, SHIZU DID NOT "ABANDON" YOU, NOT IN THE SLIGHTEST.
ZMF
SHE MADE HER FINAL JOURNEY FOR YOUR SAKE.
FOR OUR SAKE...?
NOW THAT I'M HERE WITH THEM, I UNDERSTAND THE PURPOSE OF HER JOURNEY AT LAST.
SHIZU, TOO, WAS ONE OF THOSE SUMMONED CHILDREN.
BUT THE REASON SHE WAS ABLE TO LIVE OUT HER LIFE TO A FULL EXTENT...
...IS BECAUSE SHE WAS AROUND A PERSON, SOMEONE WHO STABILIZED ALL THAT MAGICAL ENERGY WITHIN HER.

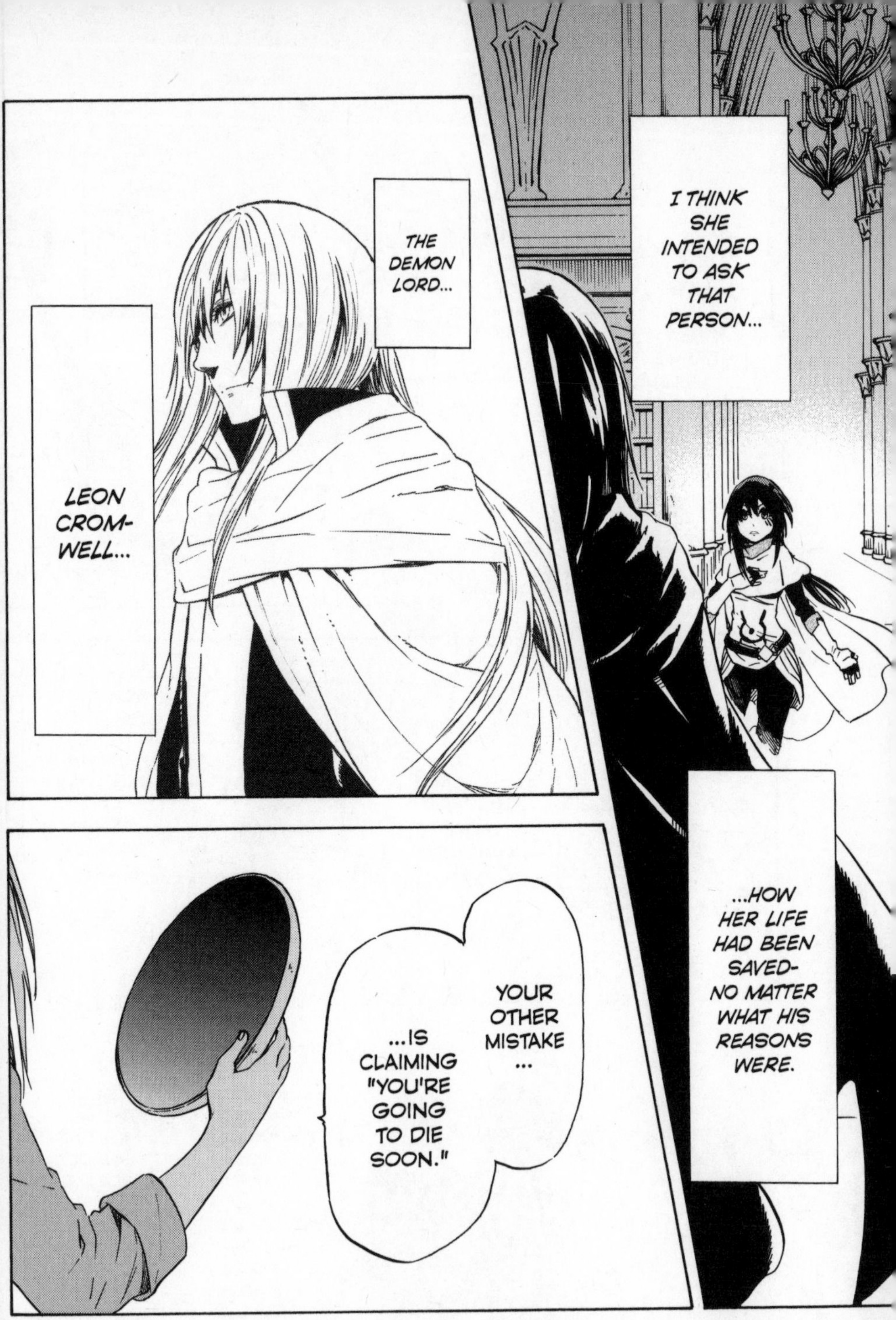
I THINK SHE INTENDED TO ASK THAT PERSON...
...HOW HER LIFE HAD BEEN SAVED- NO MATTER WHAT HIS REASONS WERE.
THE DEMON LORD...
LEON CROM-WELL...
YOUR OTHER MISTAKE ...
...IS CLAIMING "YOU'RE GOING TO DIE SOON."

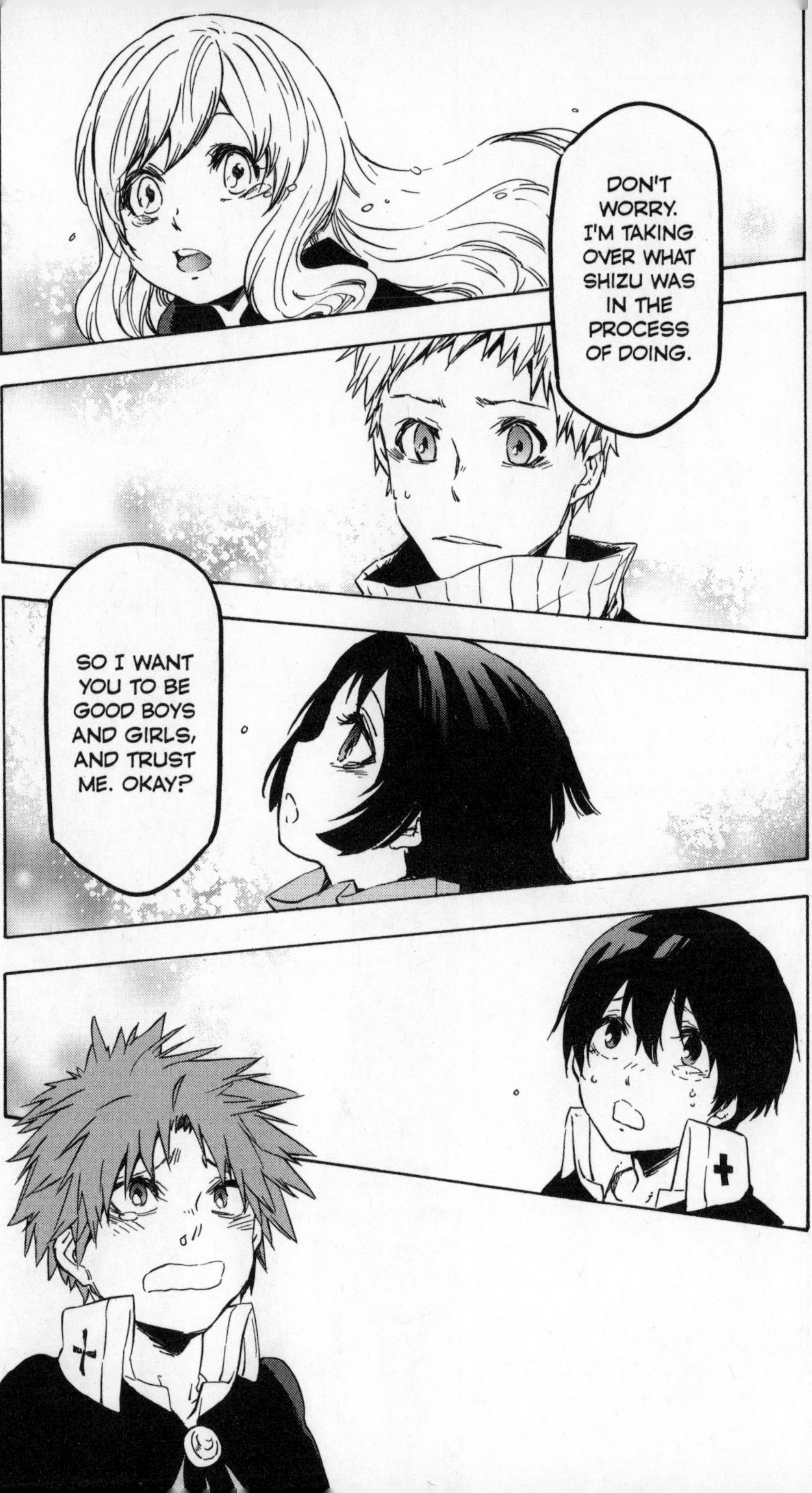
DON'T WORRY. I'M TAKING OVER WHAT SHIZU WAS IN THE PROCESS OF DOING.
SO I WANT YOU TO BE GOOD BOYS AND GIRLS, AND TRUST ME. OKAY?

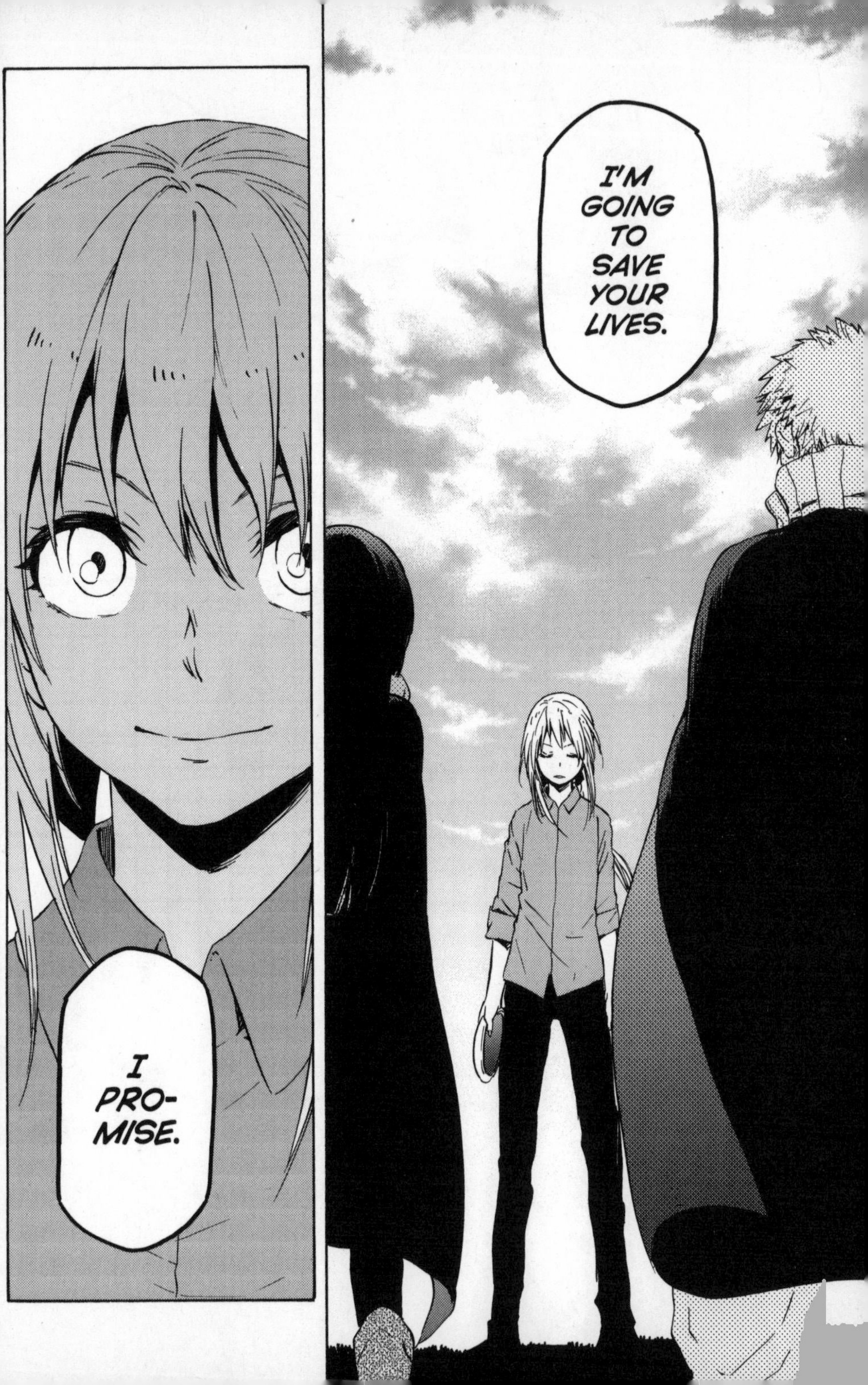
I'M GOING TO SAVE YOUR LIVES.
I PRO-MISE.

Reincarnate
in Volume 11?

→YES

NO

Bonus Short Story

Veldora's Slime Observation Journal
~ADVENTURE~

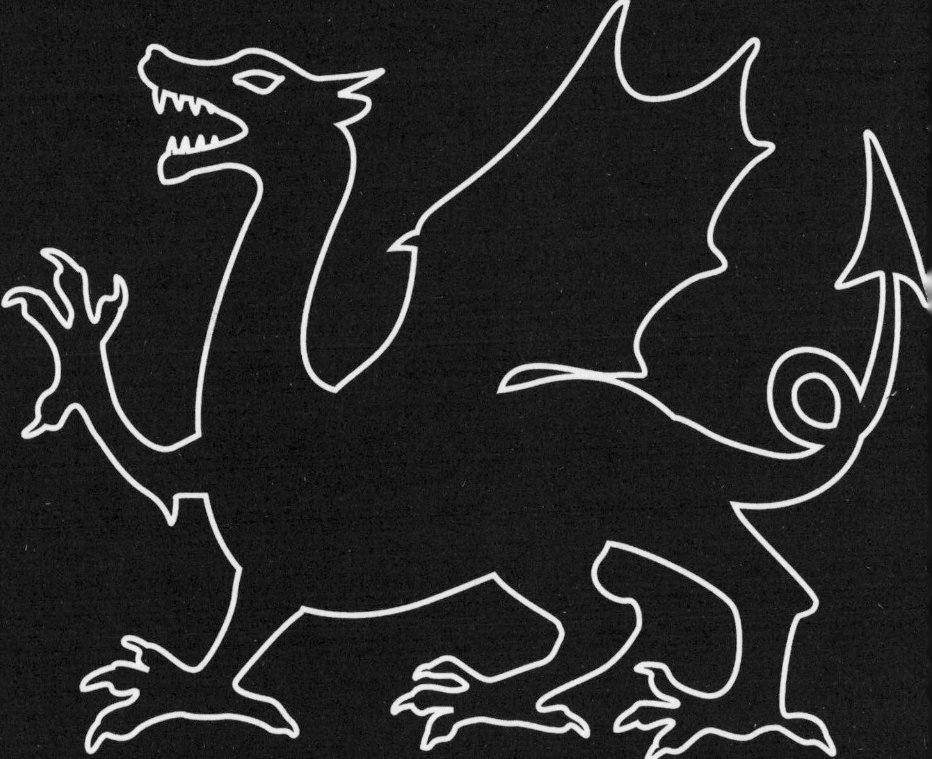

Veldora's Slime Observation Journal
~ADVENTURE~

♦ IN THE KINGDOM OF BLUMUND (PART ONE) ♦

Ah, yes, things are grand. Very grand, indeed!

I am productive! I am efficient! I am cool and suave at my job!!

Those cheers follow me everywhere in my head these days. Life is good and enjoyable. Now that we have mastered the timing of Rimuru's towering rages, Ifrit and I have nothing to fear anymore. Now we can slack off when appropriate, and use our time for leisurely matters.

"..."

B-but I am doing my job, of course.

"...*Understood.*"

Phew, that was frightening.

And yet I have won once again. It is a good winning streak, and shows no sign of ending soon. I feel good, and I believe I shall engage in my daily observation of Rimuru's affairs, as has become my habit.

Rimuru was in a city today. He traveled through the forest and arrived at the human kingdom of Blumund.

As I suspected, his purpose on this trip was not just to drum up sales. He is carrying on the will of the woman named Shizu, whose form he now assumes. There are children whom Shizu left behind, children she cared about, and he wants to find and take care of them.

To do so, he is on his way to the great kingdom of Engrassia, the center of the Western Nations.

"We can have our guildmaster write you a recommendation letter," suggested Eren.

Apparently, the highest position in the free guild, known as the "grandmaster," was an apprentice of Shizu's. Fuze knew her as well, and it is for that reason that he claims to have an "in" with this grandmaster, who goes by the name of Yuuki Kagurazaka.

Even here, it's all about who you know.

"Connections are very valuable things. So, Ifrit: you were fused with Shizu. Wouldn't you know a thing or two about her apprentices and these children she cared for?" I said, turning to the fire spirit.

Instead, Ifrit complained, "Well, you see, at the time I did not have as established a personality as I do now. I acted automatically, without interest in the mortal world... There were times that I resonated with my host, Shizue Izawa, and learned information, but for the most part, I was no more conscious of what was happening than if I were having a dream..."

Hmph. So the short answer is that he does not know.

"However, I do have some memory of her two apprentices."

"Oh?"

I was prepared to be disappointed, but it turns out that Ifrit does remember. So, what kind of people were Shizu's apprentices? Let us hear it from the mouth of the spirit himself!

"What I remember was the training method. They were apprentices of hers, but technically, the power of me and Shizu fused together was not beyond theirs."

"Both of them?"

"Actually, there was a male and a female, but I am speaking more of the female. The male, Yuuki Kagurazaka, did not strike me as a threat. His physical advancement was tremendous, enough to be on a level with Shizu, but he exclusively dealt in physical damage. Without magical support, or some kind of magical weapon or tool, he could not harm my body of flames."

Ah, I see. Shizu was able to "fuse" with Ifrit, preventing her from suffering physical attack damage. Then indeed, this Yuuki and his physical-only blows would not represent a threat.

"But his mind was extremely nimble, and I recall him being very adept at methods of managing an organization."

Ifrit's memory on this point was vague, as he had little interest in that subject. But even then, by the sound of it, this fellow has climbed the ranks with alarming speed. I suppose this Yuuki is better suited to the ways of politics than warfare and combat.

"And what about the woman?"

If she was greater in power than Shizu fused with Ifrit, then this woman would have to be far beyond the limits of humanity. It sounded to me like she might even harbor the potential to be a demon lord.

"To me, she seemed like a true monster."

"That powerful?"

"Yes. As a matter of fact, Shizu and I repelled one another, so we only exhibited our true combined power on a handful of occasions. But in the span of less than a single month, that woman succeeded in gaining the maximum potential fighting power that we possessed. And in her case, this power was utterly unfettered, guided by her will alone..."

This is more impressive than I imagined. Still inferior to me, of course, but she might perhaps be even mightier than Rimuru is today.

For his part, Rimuru seems to be wary about meeting the female; perhaps he can innately sense the danger she poses.

I would hope that he will be cautious of this possible encounter.

With Fuze's letter of recommendation in hand, Rimuru went ahead and registered himself as an adventurer, whatever that is. Apparently, being registered with the guild is a form of identification, and that is supposed to be a very useful thing to have.

Humans are a cowardly lot, and constantly cautious of those they do not know. Therefore, when traveling to a different country, they must undergo a customs process.

This means nothing to great beings like myself, and other monsters who can fly, but since Rimuru is transformed into a human at the moment, it is a necessary chore to undergo. If his identity were to be revealed, it would certainly cause quite a stir. If the guild guarantees his identity, there is no reason not to go through with it.

For one thing, the majority of the Western Nations have branch offices of the guild. Being an adventurer means smooth travel from country to country. Rimuru realized this as well, and decided to register. Before he even went to see Fuze, he was off undertaking the test to become an adventurer.

But that aside, I was more curious about a different conversation.

"A-are these phantomflowers?! And look how many there are…"

At this particular moment, Kaval's trio was up to more entertaining business.

"Those are the plants that Geld gave to them," said Ifrit. "I heard them talking about sales of rare plants—they must command quite a sum."

"You noticed too, Ifrit? We were concerned about the topic of raising funds, and here is a hint right under our noses."

"Yes. They've been taking home the monster materials that had already been disposed of, and using them…"

"To make money."

Ifrit and I stared at one another and nodded. *When I am freed, I will become an adventurer!* I decided. Then I realized I had better listen to a description of what an adventurer actually does.

The term is a title, and is applied to official members of the free guild. There are many kinds of membership, but only those in three divisions that venture outside of town—harvesting, exploration, and combat—are called "adventurers."

Because these three divisions involve danger, applicants must be tested to gauge their skill. Rimuru chose "combat." This is the most dangerous test, apparently, but Rimuru chose it because of the convenience of taking the test in that same building.

One day, I, too, shall take the combat division test and become an adventurer.

"Of course, if there is a job that makes money and is easier, I might dabble in that area as well!"

"I know. It all depends on Lord Rimuru's wishes."

That is correct. In essence, I speak of allowance money.

For if Ifrit and I wish to relax and spend our lives in leisure, there is no need to go out of our way to work a job.

"Well, I suppose we shall need money for a variety of things in the future. It was a stroke of fortune that we caught wind of this idea of becoming adventurers."

"The more means of gaining income, the better, after all."

"Rimuru's town does not yet have any system of currency. Barter trade is the main form of commerce, so one cannot work for a wage, so to speak. And if one were to make a mistake, I feel that scolding and retribution would come swiftly. So in that sense, being an adventurer should be a painless and reliable method."

"A wise decision, Master. Thinking back on it now, Shizu made quite an adequate living as an adventurer."

"If I earn an income, I might even send some of it your way, Ifrit. Look forward to that."

"Thank you, Master. I will."

Very good.

If I threaten Rimuru—give me allowance, or I will engage in deviant behavior!—he will surely consider it. And if not, I can just run away from home and become an adventurer. A trip for two, just me and Ifrit. It does not sound bad.

Of course, I would need to give Ifrit a physical body and be revived, but I am sure that Rimuru will do all of that for me. Thanks in advance, Rimuru.

I look forward to all of the things that he will do for the sake of our bright future. And now, I believe I shall cheer him on in his trial.

Now, the real question is about the content of the test.

The test proctor, a summoner named Thegis, will summon monsters. If the monster is defeated, the subject passes the test.

There stands Rimuru, atop a magic circle. This particular circle casts a special magical barrier around it, to ensure that no magical effects can pass beyond its threshold. And naturally, the summoned creatures cannot exit the boundary of the barrier.

It has no effect on humans, so that help can be extended in an emergency...but I doubt that Rimuru will have need of any such thing.

The Hound Dog and Dark Goblin that Thegis first summoned were child's play. Rimuru dispatched them in moments, swiftly climbing the ranks. Eventually the man wised up and skipped Rimuru ahead to the B-rank test.

In this case, the summoned beast was a Lesser Demon.

The adventurers wailed and warned that it was uniquely suited to taking advantage of Rimuru's type, but this is not a foe to worry about. Behold Rimuru's mighty swordcraft! He cut the spiritual being in twain, when no physical attacks should have any effect.

"Is that…a sword of magic?"

"Indeed. A very clever trick. He used his own battle aura to manipulate the magicules around him, adding a magical effect to his blade."

"Affirmative: This is correct. It is a skill called Magic Aura that combines magic and arts."

Rimuru can do just about anything.

He is beyond simply executing magic without an incantation, but can create his own magical flows on a conceptual level.

"We cannot let him take all the glory."

Aha! Listen to Ifrit, burning with ambition. Yes, that is very true. I cannot rest on my laurels while this sterling example is present.

"Then I shall incorporate this idea into my Veldora-style Killing Arts. Can you keep up, Ifrit?"

"Of course!"

That's what I like to hear!

"Understood: Now activating strengthening program."

H-huh?

No, no, no, you need not bother!

"Warning: Estimating remaining power of individuals named 'Veldora' and 'Ifrit'...Confirmed."

Gyaii! I-I've been found out!!

"Suggestion: Undertaking workload just before limit, or beyond limit, will lead to greater gains."

No! Wait!!

"No waiting period required. Beginning now."

This was the beginning of a new hell...

◆ IN THE KINGDOM OF BLUMUND (PART TWO) ◆

Dazed and reeling, I opened my bleary eyes. The first thing I saw was Ifrit, whose own eyes appeared dead.

"You're awake, Master Veldora?"

"Y-yes. It is the first time in ages that I have felt true fear."

"I quite understand. And how did it go for you?"

"Very well," I grinned.

"I'm glad to hear it. It was worth planning for such an eventuality, then."

I nodded wisely. As a matter of fact, we expected that Rimuru would learn that we were slacking off. Once you've been caught, it's too late to panic. But only one as wise and omniscient as me would think to prepare for such eventualities ahead of time.

I split my unique skill Inquirer's resources in such a way that Rimuru spotting my slacking off would not harm me. I have simply transitioned my conscious mind to the extra partition that I set aside!

Well? Are you quaking in awe at my intellect? I can feel the joy welling up from the very core of my being.

If only more were here to praise my greatness. But alas, the only one with me is Ifrit. I shall have to be satisfied with the success of my plan for now.

"And how long have I been without consciousness?"

"About two evenings have passed."

"And, er, you were...fine?"

"No," said Ifrit, his eyes nearly dead. Upon closer examination, the spirit was faded here and there, as if barely capable of maintaining humanoid form. "All of the load was placed not upon my calculations, but upon my astral form itself... Having my mind entirely conscious for the duration only made it more frightening..."

"A-ah, I see. That must have been quite an ordeal..." I said kindly, and not at all awkwardly, to break the heavy, uncomfortable silence.

I had been through a terrible ordeal, too, but as I merely went unconscious, I suppose I should consider myself lucky. Why, I might even find myself sympathizing with Ifrit. Unlike me, Ifrit has no means of hiding his power. Rimuru can read all of his information, and there is no way to hide it.

He shall simply have to wean off bits of the power he gains in the future, and embezzle them away safely... Hang in there, Ifrit! You have me in your corner.

And now, it is time to ascertain the situation.

"So what happened after it started?"

"I was ordered to maintain a clear mind, even if my flesh should be exhausted. So I kept my mind focused on the outside world the entire time," said Ifrit sadly.

From what he told me, Rimuru's group received a scolding from Fuze, and it is possible that he might have treated us more harshly than needed out of misplaced frustration. He seemed an unfair and cruel man to me.

At any rate, I must make full use of my hidden processing power to find a solution to our quandary. It was with this in mind that I focused on Rimuru's present situation.

I found that he was dressed to the nines. He was preparing to meet some fancy person, and seemed nervous about it.

"What is the situation?"

"When he asked Fuze for a letter of recommendation yesterday, he was forced to arrange a meeting with the king of this country. The meeting is planned for two days' time, but he will be holding a practice dialogue with a minister before that."

"I see. The humans do prize their customs and formality, after all. So he requires advance planning before he may meet this king."

"That's right. It should be worthwhile to learn these things."

In the meantime, Rimuru and his counterpart began their meeting. The other fellow is Veryard, one of the ministers of this kingdom. Apparently, he has known Fuze since childhood.

"I am not familiar with the local customs, so please excuse me if I happen to cause offense," said Rimuru, very politely.

"Based on power alone, this fellow would be no match for Lord Rimuru."

"Don't be a fool, Ifrit. What have you been watching all this time?"

"S-sorry, Master."

"Take Milim, for example. If she used sheer power to attempt to put him under her thumb, do you think she could have forced Rimuru to obey?"

"No, I don't. Lord Rimuru is a fearsome person. He would pretend to obey, but secretly plot his revenge."

"That is correct. These humans are the same. Strength alone does not decide a negotiation. If you seek results, then mutual trust is important."

What do you think about that?! I watched for Ifrit's reaction. He stared back at me in obvious admiration.

Kwa ha ha ha ha! It feels very good.

At this rate, I suspect Rimuru's negotiations will go very well, indeed. I had no basis for this expectation, but I held it all the same as I listened in on their conversation.

Their dreadfully long and boring discussion lasted into the night.

I understood the contents because I am very smart, but normally one would give up listening long before that point.

They have apparently agreed that for Tempest and Blumund to be open to each other, two conditions must be met.

One, a guarantee of mutual security.
Two, a guarantee of free passage.

To sum up Veryard's statements, if the Kingdom of Blumund should fall into a perilous situation, they will seek help from Rimuru and his country.

Because Blumund is a small nation, it barely has any military power to speak of. An attack from a single A-rank monster could pose an existential threat. According to the Kingdom of Blumund, my being gone has thrown the Great Forest of Jura into a state of chaos. For that reason, they seek to use Rimuru and his people as a defensive structure.

"Humans are crafty and cautious creatures. Have they really learned to trust Lord Rimuru, just like that?"

"Oh, I very much doubt that they have. But they also have no choice but to trust him."

Regardless of what Rimuru may be thinking, the national strength of Tempest is enough to easily topple Blumund. From Blumund's perspective, it is a waste of effort to even try being wary of Tempest.

"What did I tell you? Trust is a major factor. Blumund will trust Rimuru, and will keep their word in turn. If we betrayed them, what would happen?"

"Rimuru and Tempest itself would lose trust?"

"That is right. Blumund would lambast them, and spread the word of that treachery to other neighboring lands. In any case, we represent a potential foe they cannot defeat. So to drum up allies, they will be prepared to suffer first."

"I see… So if Lord Rimuru were to decide to invade Blumund, the humans would all band up together as one."

"I doubt that such a thing would ever happen, but at the very least, Veryard has to consider it a possibility."

At that rate, he probably would prefer to use Rimuru's nation instead. Depending on their future relationship, if they can build up a slow and steady trust, it might turn out beneficial for both countries.

And then I shall reap a greater allowance… Heh heh heh.

That part depends entirely on the matter of free passage. "Increased tax yields" is such an intoxicating phrase. Only Rimuru could win such a prize in negotiation. I believe we can say this process has been a success.

♦

Two days later.

Rimuru is dressed in his ceremonial best in preparation for
meeting the King of Blumund. Because they had that negotiation session ahead of time, today's meeting is really more
of a ceremonial formality. It all proceeds quite smoothly.

Both sides have signed the ceremonial sheet, officially ratify-
ing the treaty.

"And if the Eastern Empire should invade, we will certainly
appreciate all the help you can give us," whispered the King
of Blumund to Rimuru, after they had shared a friendly
handshake.

This was the true aim of Blumund. In other words, the guarantee of military aid will apply not just to monster attacks,
but invasions from hostile nations.

As Baron Veryard smiled pleasantly, Rimuru held his head in
his hands. But my eyes cannot be fooled. He is not lamenting,
but holding back his laughter! What an actor that Rimuru is.
He pretends that he was just fooled, but he certainly would
have been aware of this cheap ploy from the start.

"Why do you say that? It looked to me like Lord Rimuru was
rather deftly manipulated…"

"Hah, you fool!" I spat. Ifrit is still so immature. He might be
my equal in the game of shogi, but he has much yet to learn
in the tactical arts.

"Er, actually…I win many more of our shogi—"

"Silence!!" I demanded, shutting up the babbling Ifrit. The
issue of winning percentage at shogi would go unaddressed.
Instead, I adopted a teacherly tone. "Now listen to me, Ifrit.
Think hard about this."

"Y-yes…?"

"Keeping the location of Tempest in mind, recall Blumund
and its neighboring countries," I said, thoughtfully drawing

up a conceptual map of the world. Then I pointed to it and explained. (Ah, how I love to show off.)

"In life, as in shogi, it is important to put yourself in the opponent's position. Blumund borders a number of nations, but most of them are in a cooperative arrangement. Given that, which direction should they be most wary of?"

"Um, the Great Forest of Jura?"

"Precisely. So if any enemy were to invade from that direction, they would first come into contact not with the Kingdom of Blumund…"

"Oh!"

"Figured it out? Yes, first they would come across Tempest."

"Meaning…"

"Yes. Regardless of the treaty with Blumund, Rimuru would be bearing the brunt of any invasion."

In other words, by preying on Veryard's unease, Rimuru was able to earn an owed favor for something that he would never have gained in the first place. I can barely contain my disbelief at his brilliant trickery.

"Well done, Lord Rimuru. And I can see that I have much to learn from you yet, Master Veldora. You saw through that clever twist when I could not."

"Ah, yes, indeed! That is entirely accurate. *Kwaaa ha ha ha!!* I hollered.

After that, Rimuru's trade plans lined up brilliantly. He gave his test proctor Thegis a "full-potion," which regrew the man's lost foot.

"That's impossible!!"

"Regeneration?!" shouted Thegis and Veryard.

It is understandable.

Full-potions are occasionally discovered in ancient ruins, but even the dwarven kingdom's engineers have been unable to re-create them. It is baffling that anyone should have hundreds of them like Rimuru does.

In most cases, it happens when recovery potions are placed for long periods of time in locations with extremely high-density magical fields. And even then, a large part of the process is luck.

So in a sense, their shock is quite natural. Of course, there is no fixed market price for such a thing. Those who truly need one would likely spend any amount of money. Naturally, Thegis' joy was immeasurable, having such a gift bestowed upon him out of the blue.

Veryard lost his calculating cool, and struck up a deal exactly as Rimuru requested without haggling.

"So everything went according to Lord Rimuru's plan, then?"

"It did. Blumund thinks that they have come out ahead in this deal, but this might as well have been free gains for Rimuru. It was perfect negotiation. And now…"

Ifrit and I were all smiles and nods. The negotiations were a great success, and now I can hardly wait to find out how much allowance I will receive.

◆YUUKI KAGURAZAKA◆

Rimuru's group left the Kingdom of Blumund. They head for the center of the Western Nations: the great Kingdom of Engrassia.

"It is just as you expected, Master Veldora," said Ifrit, while I was actually concentrating on my work for once. I decided that I had earned myself a little break, so I got into a nice, relaxed position.

"Hrm? How so?"

"I mean, about the countries Blumund was worried about. Those adventurers were explaining that nearly all of the surrounding countries are part of the Council of the West."

By adventurers, he is referring to Kaval's trio. And the Council of the West is basically the official name for the agreement that binds together what we call the Western Nations.

This is where my knowledge can sometimes be limited. As the names of things can evolve over time, it is enjoyable to find out the latest customs.

Whoops, I must be careful. If I am not, Rimuru might punish me once again.

So I decided to resume my work. Only not at full capacity this time. As I worked on decoding my Unlimited Imprisonment, the portion of my processing power I set aside allowed me to observe Rimuru's actions.

I can sense Ifrit gazing upon me with envy. Heh heh heh. But I will not help you. If you are chagrined, Ifrit, then grow stronger! I ignored him and focused on Rimuru.

Rimuru's special Ranga-pulled carriage is so advanced, it absorbs all of the rumbling of the unkempt road. No other vehicle could proceed to Engrassia at this breakneck pace.

Even for me, it is painful to keep my mind split in two parts like this. So I think that I shall have to alternate between slacking off and doing my work as I observe Rimuru's travels.

"You're very dexterous like that, Master Veldora."

"Silence, fool! I know you are envious of me, but this is actually extremely difficult."

But I have no intention of stopping. I will make any effort necessary to gain my entertainment.

As I suffered for this noble goal, the carriage moved onward. At last, the imposing sight of Engrassia came around the bend.

There was an inspection to enter the kingdom first, but there is an even more stringent process to enter the capital city. Rimuru, however, is a B-rank adventurer now. They let him in right away, just for showing his identification. This only bolstered my desire to become an adventurer.

From there, he headed through the great gate into the vast urban city. Rimuru was stunned by the sight—and so was I. The last time I was in this place was over three centuries ago. Engrassia was a great nation back then, but it had not advanced this far by half.

From what I saw flying overhead, they had many two-story buildings of wood and stone, and only a handful of taller structures. The homes of the peasants had glass windows, but none as pristine and clear as these.

The march of civilization is astonishing. I had known this as a fact, but actually seeing it for myself is a different and over-whelming experience. Just look at how the glass reflects the sunlight, sparkling and blue.

Rimuru clearly finds it fascinating as well. The adventurer trio is escorting him about the city; he is clearly taking ideas and inspiration from what he sees.

I am excited about this too, Rimuru, but have you noticed yet? Danger lurks all over the town.

They are affiliated with the Western Holy Church. One of the reasons I so rarely visited the Western Nations is because of the zealous eye of their church.

I would have beaten them in a fight, but they are a tenacious lot. They come out in a horde, and attack repeatedly and re-lentlessly, leaving their foes no chance to rest. I have no idea why they would hate me, but for some strange reason, they did.

"Oh, I'm certain they do."

"What?"

"I'm absolutely certain."

Damn you, Ifrit. Why do you state this so forcefully? I hate that I am unable to prove him wrong. But Rimuru's companions are giving him a proper lecture on the danger of the Western Holy Church, so I will let the topic go.

The next day, Rimuru headed for the headquarters of the free guild, his destination for this trip. Their large glass doors move automatically. They are the same automated doors from Rimuru's past memories—one of those fruits of scientific technology, moving with electricity as though by magic.

Only here, they are re-creating the effect with actual magic. In any case, it is a good thing to live in greater comfort and ease. The desire for convenience is the great engine of culture's advancement. I think this worthy of praise.

After a wait, Rimuru was allowed to meet with the guild's grandmaster.

They took him through several magical defensive walls and to a meeting room protected by a special magical barrier. There he had to wait even longer, but I was more curious about the various items displayed around the room.

In fact, they looked like things from Rimuru's memory...

Speaking of which, this apprentice of Shizu's was also supposed to be from Rimuru's home. Seeing the evidence firsthand must have been more than enough proof to believe it.

"Thank you for waiting," said a man who came into the room, though he looked no more than a boy.

"Ifrit, is that Yuuki?"

"It is he. Yuuki's appearance has not changed since I first met him."

Oh?

Rimuru and Yuuki exchanged greetings and personal introductions. In the light conversation that followed, Yuuki revealed that he does not physically age. He also possesses no special skills, and claims to have excellent physical growth instead.

"Very suspicious."

"What is?"

"This Yuuki boy. How does a person so skilled at politics speak so openly about himself? That does not happen."

"Sometimes you have the most insightful commentary, Master Veldora."

"I cannot fathom why you would use the qualifier, 'sometimes.'"

"Pardon me."

As we chatted, I continued a close observation of Yuuki. There was one thing I noticed in particular.

Rimuru was in his slime form for this meeting, and for whatever reason, he transformed into human form right before Yuuki's eyes. When the young man saw Rimuru's face, he turned pale.

"I can mimic the form of those I've eaten."

"You've eaten...?" Yuuki mumbled, and immediately launched into a kick. Rimuru blocked it with his own leg.

But my keen eye cannot be fooled!

"What did you see just now, Ifrit?"

"I can understand the reason for Yuuki's emotional distress, and why he would feel the desire to attack Lord Rimuru."

"Is that all?"

"Meaning what, Master?"

"Was Yuuki's attack a true attempt?"

"Now that you mention it…the kick was tremendous, but it seemed to be far from his full ability."

"Indeed."

So my view was correct. Yuuki already has information on Rimuru, through means unknown to me.

I suppose it makes sense. It would be unnatural for him not to investigate the chancellor of a monster nation who defeated the Orc Lord. I am not certain of how much Fuze and Kaval's party were passing back to Yuuki, but it seems fairly clear that he possesses some level of information already.

So his show of anger was probably meant to gauge Rimuru's reaction. On top of that, he has the option of stifling his hostility in a sign of trust. In this way, he can win Rimuru's trust in return, which I suspect is his true intention.

"I-if that is the case, are you saying that all of what Yuuki just did is an act?"

"I believe so. You have much to learn if you cannot figure out that much."

"That's not fair…b-but I suppose you're right… Even Shizu was impressed by Yuuki's intellect. Perhaps your assessment is the correct one, Master Veldora…"

Ifrit seems unable to agree wholeheartedly, but also is not capable of ruling my opinion out. Of course, it is possible that I am wrong, but it is safer to be cautious of the man regardless. And Rimuru surely knows that as well.

Now behaving properly, Yuuki is prepared to hear out Rimuru's story. That too is part of his act, I'm sure, but it is a very keen act indeed.

"So you, too, are…?"

"That's right, I'm Japanese."

Even this far in, Yuuki is dedicated to his skeptical act. Surely he has already investigated and is certain of this information—so what trap is he preparing to spring on Rimuru?

That was when the slime took action.

I can scarcely believe it. He printed his holy "manga" text on cloth, and handed it over to Yuuki!!

I want that. I want that, too!!

This was the point that Yuuki's act dropped away. "Is…is this the final volume of *Dull Metal Alchemist*?!" he shouted, holding it up with reverence to gaze upon it. I am so jealous that I might shed tears of blood.

Rimuru told Yuuki that he had to use cloth, because there was no paper. And then Yuuki reacted exactly as I expected him to.

"Paper?! You need paper!!" he shouted, and called for all the paper he had.

Paper is a luxury item, but manga is more important. I am keenly, painfully aware of just how he feels.

This incident caused a remarkable change in Yuuki's cautious attitude. Now he calls Rimuru "Master," and has apologized for his rudeness. Of course he has. The crime of doubting Rimuru is not so easily forgiven.

But Rimuru is an understanding person. He forgave Yuuki right away, and the two got along quickly.

"Is this an act, too?"

"Don't be a fool, Ifrit. No one who loves manga can be evil. It is simply a fact."

Just look at the tears in Yuuki's eyes as he partakes in the masterpiece that is *Dull Metal Alchemist*. Such a reaction cannot possibly be an act! Therefore, I believe we can trust him now.

"O...kay..."

Ifrit appears as if he cannot fathom what I mean. What a dense spirit he is, not to respond to such impassioned testimonials. Oh well. He is simply lacking in the necessary experience. Work on your worldly wisdom, that you might one day reach my level of enlightenment.

But unlike Ifrit, Rimuru is a clever man.

He saw through Yuuki's act, and used the power of manga to ensnare him. Now Yuuki trusts Rimuru. And the end result is that Rimuru is one step closer to the end goal of this journey.

Thus assured, Yuuki is able to entrust in Rimuru the children Shizu left behind with her death.

Rimuru is to be a teacher in this land.

◆ FAILED HEROES ◆

With Rimuru's acceptance of the teaching position, Kaval, Gido and Eren have been officially dismissed.

As reward for their service, Rimuru gave them a carriage and new equipment. It seems extravagant to me, but they are friends, so I suppose this is acceptable.

Rimuru now studies new things for his next challenge. The children have but a few years left to live. He is poring through texts, searching for anything that might help him save them.

But the summoning tool, which was hoped to produce effective weapons, turned out to be rigid and inconvenient. In the case of these children, they were failed examples of a simplified, abbreviated version of summoning.

Fortunately for them, they are not ruled over by a summoner, but as a side effect of an imperfect summons, the massive energy produced is beyond their control. Ultimately, it is destined to devour their bodies and lead to collapse.

This, it seems, is beyond even Rimuru's "Gluttony" skill to fix. That magical energy resides in the children's souls, and there is no means to separate it from them. This is why he is spending his time in the library, in search of an answer…but to no avail.

I am not surprised. Even with my great knowledge, I am aware of no means to calm a power that resides in the soul. Surely no dusty tome in some fussy library will have that answer…

But Rimuru will not give up. The next day, he headed to this "school" with a determined look on his face. With the vice principal's guidance, he went to Class S, where the children in question were placed.

Even I was a little worried. I wondered what state these children would be in. According to the vice principal's story, there was no one to look after the children. The other teachers shunned them. Given their situation, and their bleak outlook ahead, I assumed the children would be downcast and miserable with their lot in life.

But I needn't have worried about that.

It became quite clear that they are healthy and hearty. They've identified anyone aside from themselves as an enemy, and launched an attack on Rimuru the moment he met them.

"Hiyaaaah!" one said, bearing down on Rimuru with an attack that might whallop a lesser monster. Of course, he did not let it hit him, but it surely caught him off-guard. If he did not have B-rank power, he might have been seriously injured. In light of this, Rimuru removed his kid gloves.

He returned the favor at full power—summoning Ranga from the shadows to terrify the children.

"Th...this is...tyranny..."

"Hmm? You have a problem with Teacher's secret advantage?"

The children complained, but it fell on Rimuru's deaf ears.

You see, Rimuru is a dreadful person. How much terror have Ifrit and I felt on his account...? How many tears have we shed at his tyranny?! A little threat from Ranga is but the tip of his iceberg.

"I think it is perilous to slack off around Rimuru."

"Yes, and this is a good reminder of why. I will continue my discipline with the utmost diligence."

"Heh heh heh. You have grown, Ifrit."

"I wish you would grow too, Master Veldora."

I do not understand. I have grown so much, I am barely recognizable anymore.

"How rude. Now I am able to split my conscious mind into parts. I cannot imagine a greater sign of growth."

Most likely only a few people in the world can achieve such a feat. I told Ifrit off in this way to encourage him to praise me more.

But Ifrit only looked at me with dull, exasperated eyes. "I've been thinking about this too, you know. Why doesn't Lord Rimuru come to monitor us lately?"

"Because he believes that we are working hard at our job, of course."

"But is that really true?"

What? Ifrit, what are you talking about?

"Master Veldora, think about it. Let's set aside the matter of whose benefit we're working toward. Splitting your mind like this is placing a great amount of strain on you, Master. Isn't that correct?"

"But of course. I am taking an unbearable amount of information for any other mind, and working hard to filter it with a limited span of processing power!"

In other words, I would be unable to withstand such agony if it were not in the service of slacking off!

"Right there. That's what I'm suspicious of."

"What?"

"In other words, Master Veldora, you are fulfilling your normal amount of work, while also handling a far more strenuous processing task. Isn't that actually expanding your operational span?"

Hrmm?!

Now that he says it, I do understand what he means. Compared to when I first split my consciousness, I do feel as if I have grown just slightly accustomed to the sensation.

"Then you think that Rimuru has been intentionally going easy on me?"

"The possibility is high, I surmise."

"Madness..."

"As a matter of fact, recently I have been able to control multiple body doubles, while in the process of conversation. Eventually, I noticed how abnormal that level of growth is."

"What...did you say...?!"

"If you've been growing in the same way, Master Veldora, then wouldn't you say that was exactly what Lord Rimuru wanted from you?"

Wait a moment.

I do believe Rimuru said something to me about "undertaking a workload beyond one's limits"...

So could this mean—?!

"Then...then you think we've been dancing on Rimuru's palm all this time...?"

Terrifying.

Is there nothing that Rimuru cannot make us do?

I glanced at the outside world for a moment, only to see the little children being pounded flat. Of course they are. If even we do not stand a chance against him, how would these children ever emerge victorious?

"I'm going to save your lives. I promise," Rimuru announced, after displaying his power to them. How powerful and heartening those words are. And coming from Rimuru, I cannot help but believe them to be true. So that tells me...

"Shall we take our work seriously?"

"I believe it to be the wise decision, Master."

I decided it would be best to strive toward my goal in earnest. It was not because I was terrified of Rimuru, that I assure you.

To be reincarnated in Volume 11!

THE OTHER ONE IS CONSOMMÉ

FOR SOME REASON, THE DRYADS LOVE MY POTATO CHIPS.
I love the sea-weed and salt flavor...
No, lightly salted is best.
LORD RIMU-RU!
Whoa!
JEEZ, YOU LIKE TO POP UP OUT OF NO-WHERE...
...LIGHTLY SAL... I MEAN, TREYNI.
Uh-oh.
ARE YOU SUGGESTING THAT YOU REFER TO US BY OUR FAVORITE POTATO CHIP FLAVORS?
Because I do love lightly salted flavor.
NOPE.
NOPE.
NOPE.
NOPE.
NOPE.
SHAKE ぶ
SHAKE ぶ
SHAKE ぶ
SHAKE ぶ

LIST OF ACKNOWLEDGMENTS

AUTHOR:
Fuse-sensei

CHARACTER DESIGN:
Mitz Vah-sensei

TRAVEL GUIDE:
Sho Okagiri-sensei

REINCARNATED SLIME DIARY:
Shiba-sensei

ASSISTANTS:
Muraichi-san
Daiki Haraguchi-san
Masashi Kiritani-sensei
Taku Arao-sensei

Everyone at the editorial department

AND YOU!!

SPECIAL THANKS

Hiromu Arakawa-sensei

Garden Eel Slime

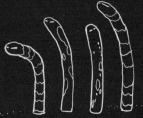

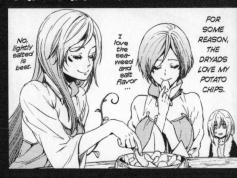

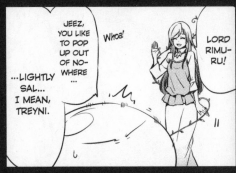

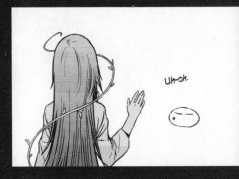

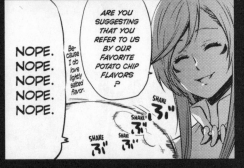

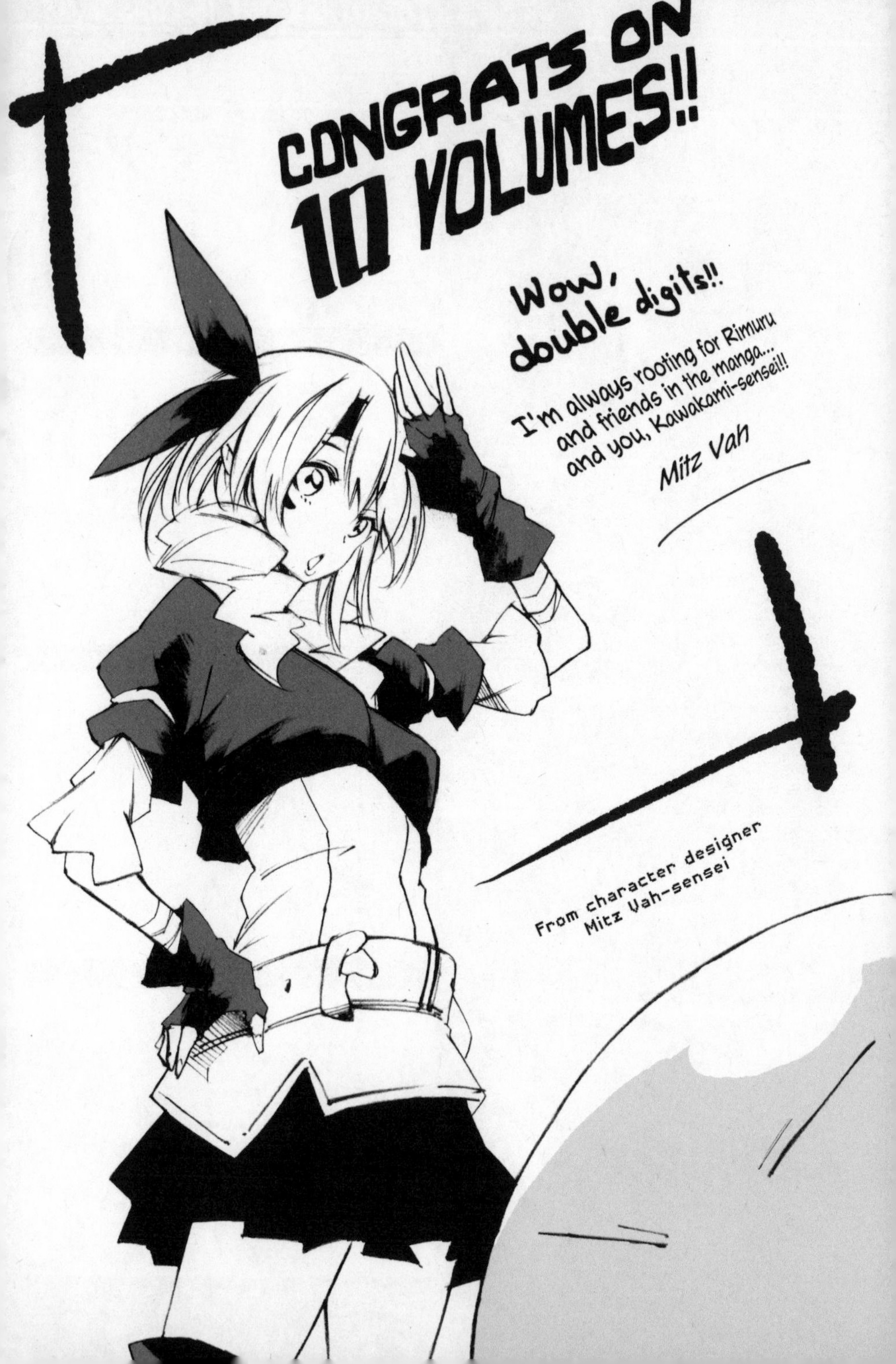
CONGRATS ON 10 VOLUMES!!
Wow, double digits!!
I'm always rooting for Rimuru and friends in the manga... and you, Kawakami-sensei!!
Mitz Vah
From character designer Mitz Vah-sensei

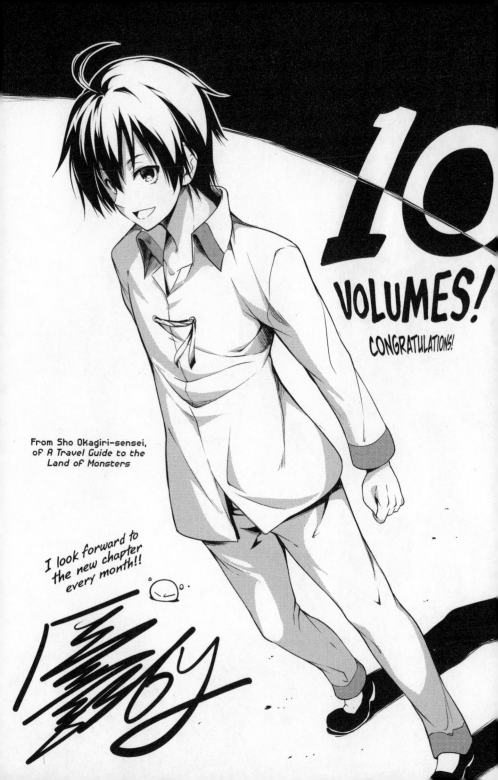

10 VOLUMES!

CONGRATULATIONS!

From Sho Okagiri-sensei, of A Travel Guide to the Land of Monsters

I look forward to the new chapter every month!!

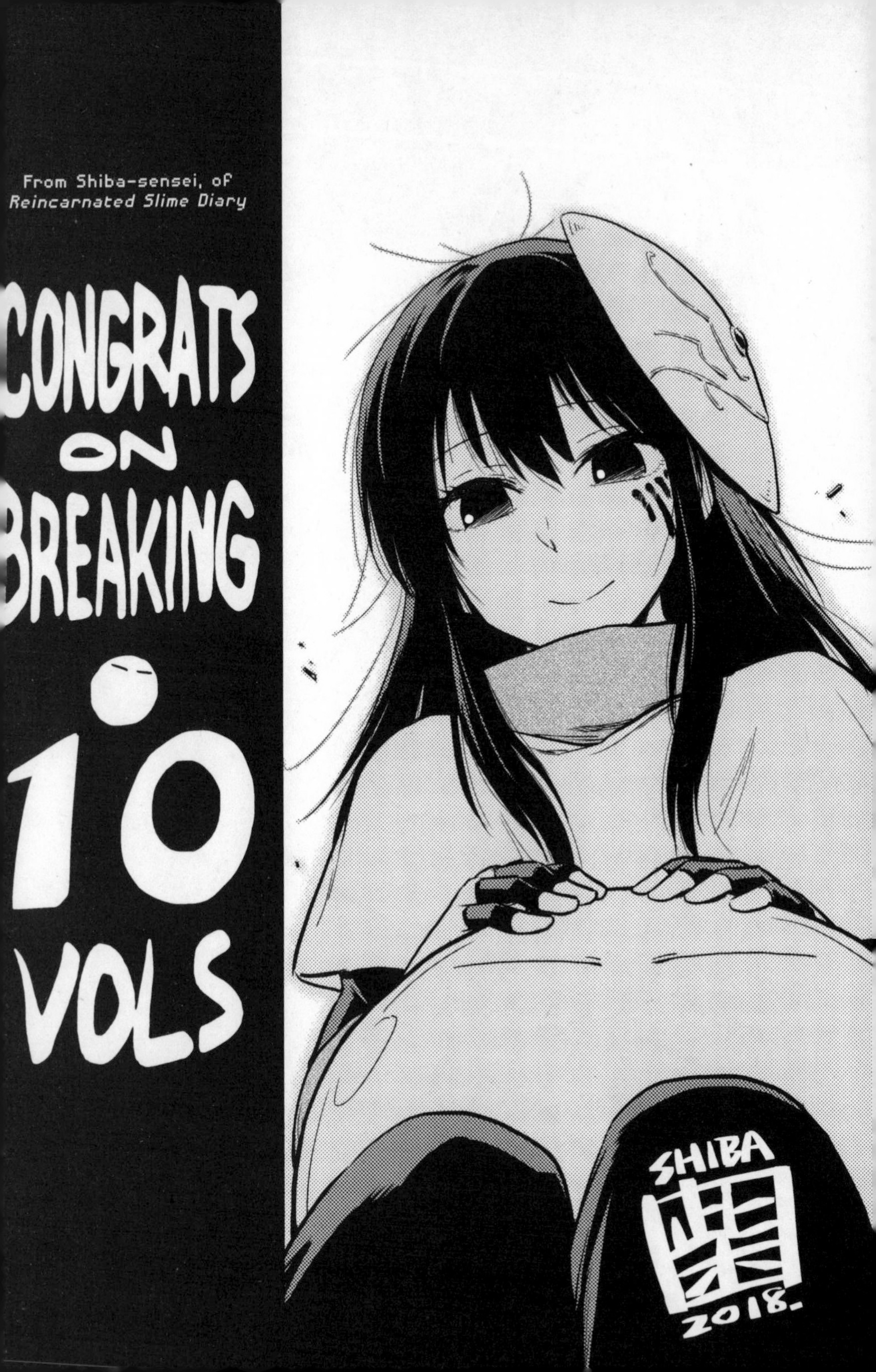
From Shiba-sensei, of
Reincarnated Slime Diary
CONGRATS ON BREAKING 10 VOLS
SHIBA
2018.

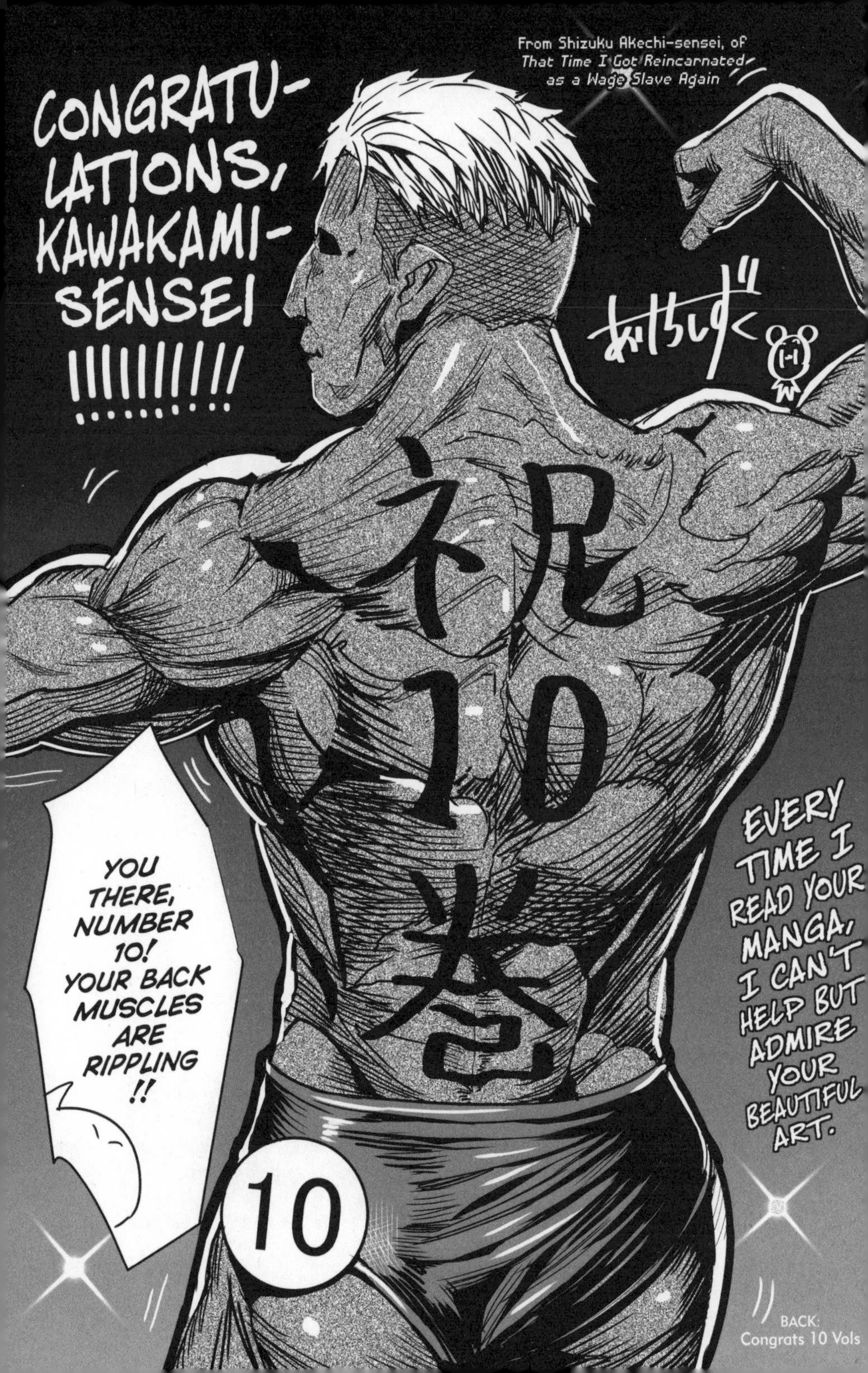
From Shizuku Akechi-sensei, of *That Time I Got Reincarnated as a Wage Slave Again*
CONGRATU-LATIONS, KAWAKAMI-SENSEI !!!!!!!!!!!.........!!
あけちしずく
祝10巻
EVERY TIME I READ YOUR MANGA, I CAN'T HELP BUT ADMIRE YOUR BEAUTIFUL ART.
YOU THERE, NUMBER 10! YOUR BACK MUSCLES ARE RIPPLING!!
10
BACK: Congrats 10 Vols

To commemorate the airing of each episode of the *Reincarnated as a Slime* anime, the *Shonen Sirius* official Twitter account (@shonen_sirius) made a series of promotional tweets. Here are the various congratulatory illustrations from other artists in the Sirius magazine, uploaded before November 26th!

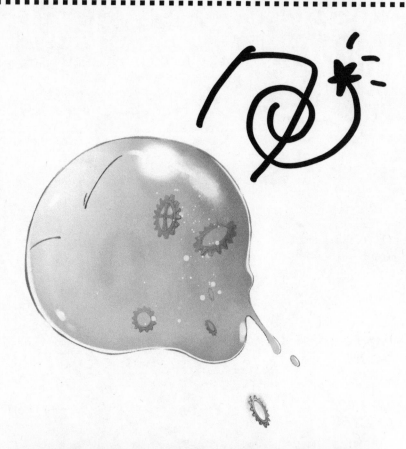

October 8th, 2018

Kuro-sensei (@oyasaismaba)

Artist of *Revisions* in *Monthly Shonen Sirius*

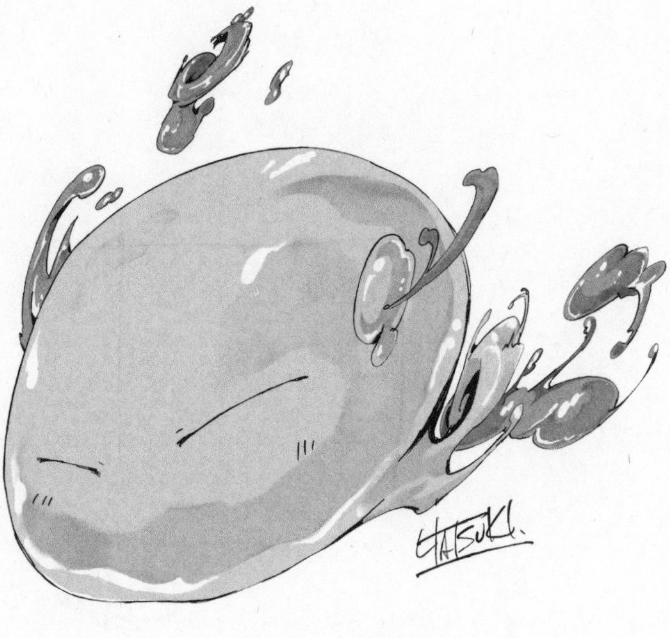
YATSUKI.

October 15th, 2018

Yatsuki-sensei (@yatsuki)

Artist of *Slave Princess* in *Monthly Shonen Sirius*

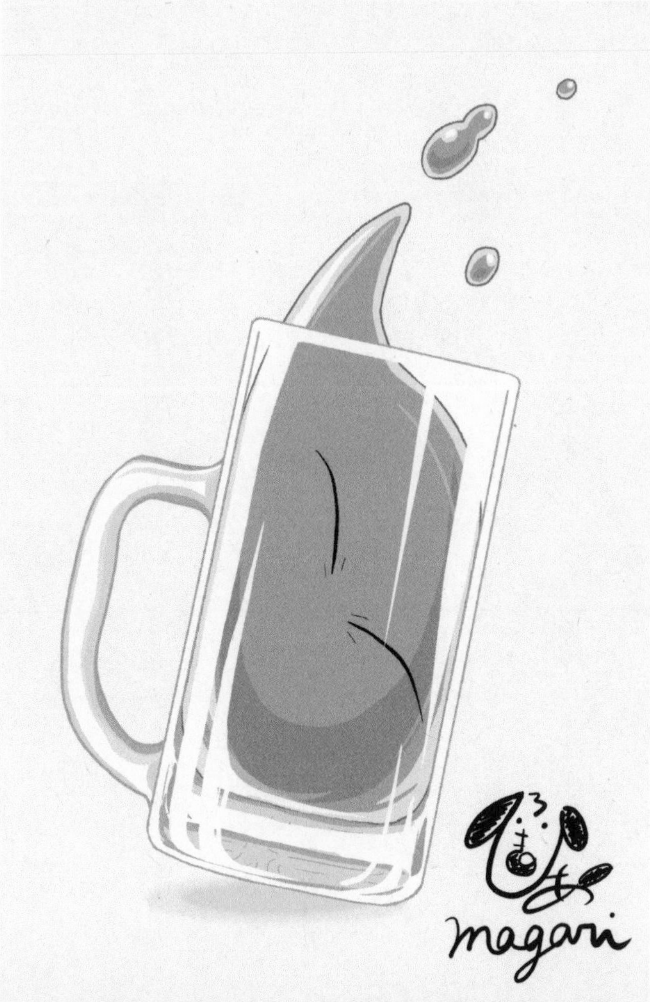
magari

October 22nd, 2018

Hiroaki Magari-sensei (@magarihiroaki)

Artist of *Ten ni Mukatte Tsubakuro* in
Nico Nico Seiga's *Sirius Wednesday*

October 29th, 2018

Tae Tono-sensei (@t0nofnh)

New series coming soon!

November 5th, 2018

Masaya Shimoda-sensei (@MY96249116)

Artist of *Ishio Kushiyama's Bludgeon Record in Magazine Pocket*

November 26th, 2018

Hiiro Akikaze-sensei (@undeadstar)

Artist of *Seija Muso* in Nico Nico Seiga's *Sirius Wednesday* and *Pixiv Comics*

『That Time I Got Reincarnated as an Ogre Girl』

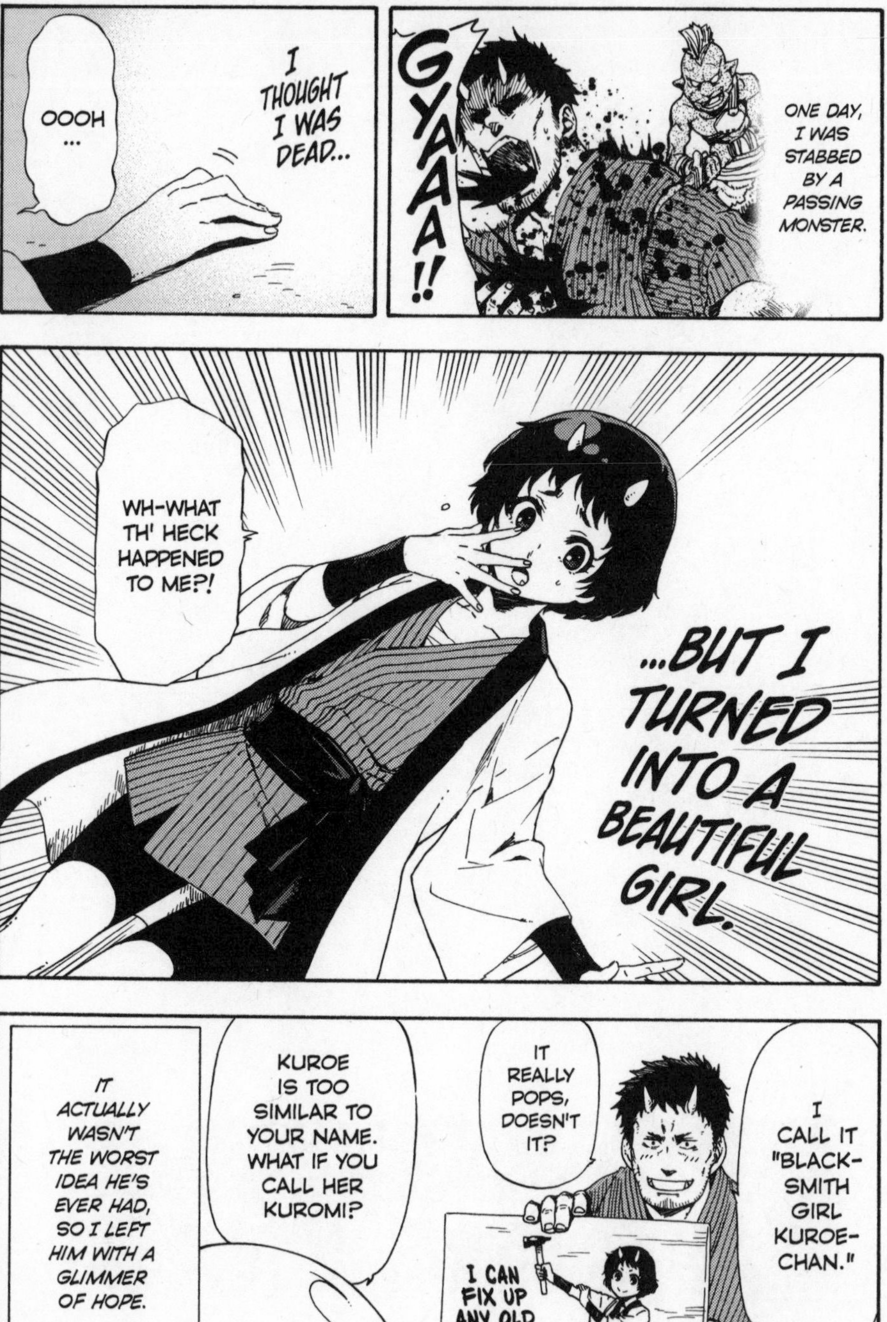
ONE DAY, I WAS STABBED BY A PASSING MONSTER.
GYAAAA!!
I THOUGHT I WAS DEAD...
OOOH ...
WH-WHAT TH' HECK HAPPENED TO ME?!
...BUT I TURNED INTO A BEAUTIFUL GIRL.
I CALL IT "BLACK-SMITH GIRL KUROE-CHAN."
IT REALLY POPS, DOESN'T IT?
I CAN FIX UP ANY OLD HUNK O' LEAD!
KUROE IS TOO SIMILAR TO YOUR NAME. WHAT IF YOU CALL HER KUROMI?
IT ACTUALLY WASN'T THE WORST IDEA HE'S EVER HAD, SO I LEFT HIM WITH A GLIMMER OF HOPE.

Slime tempura.

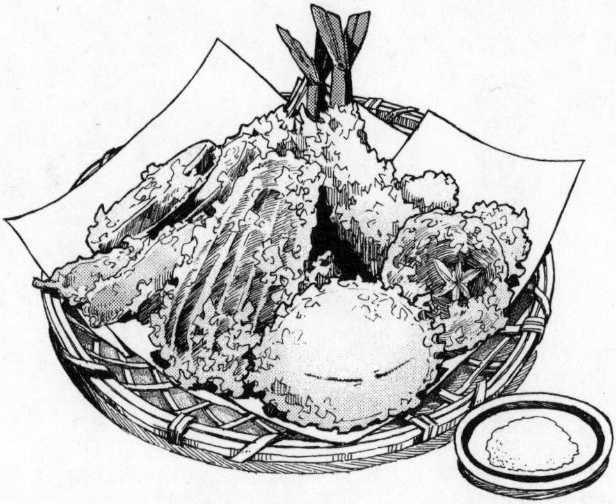

AKA "Teslimpura."

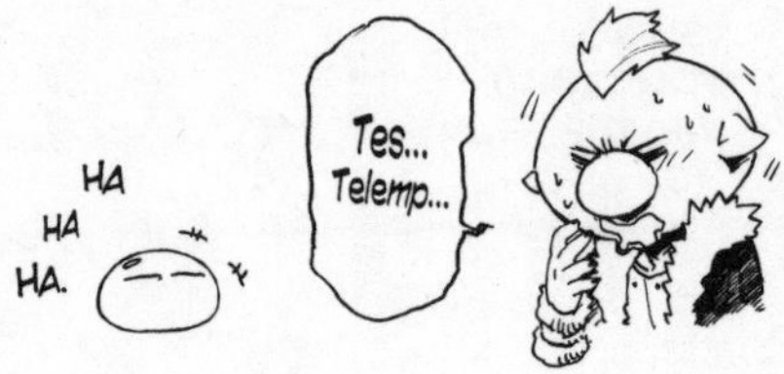
Tes... Telemp...
HA HA HA.

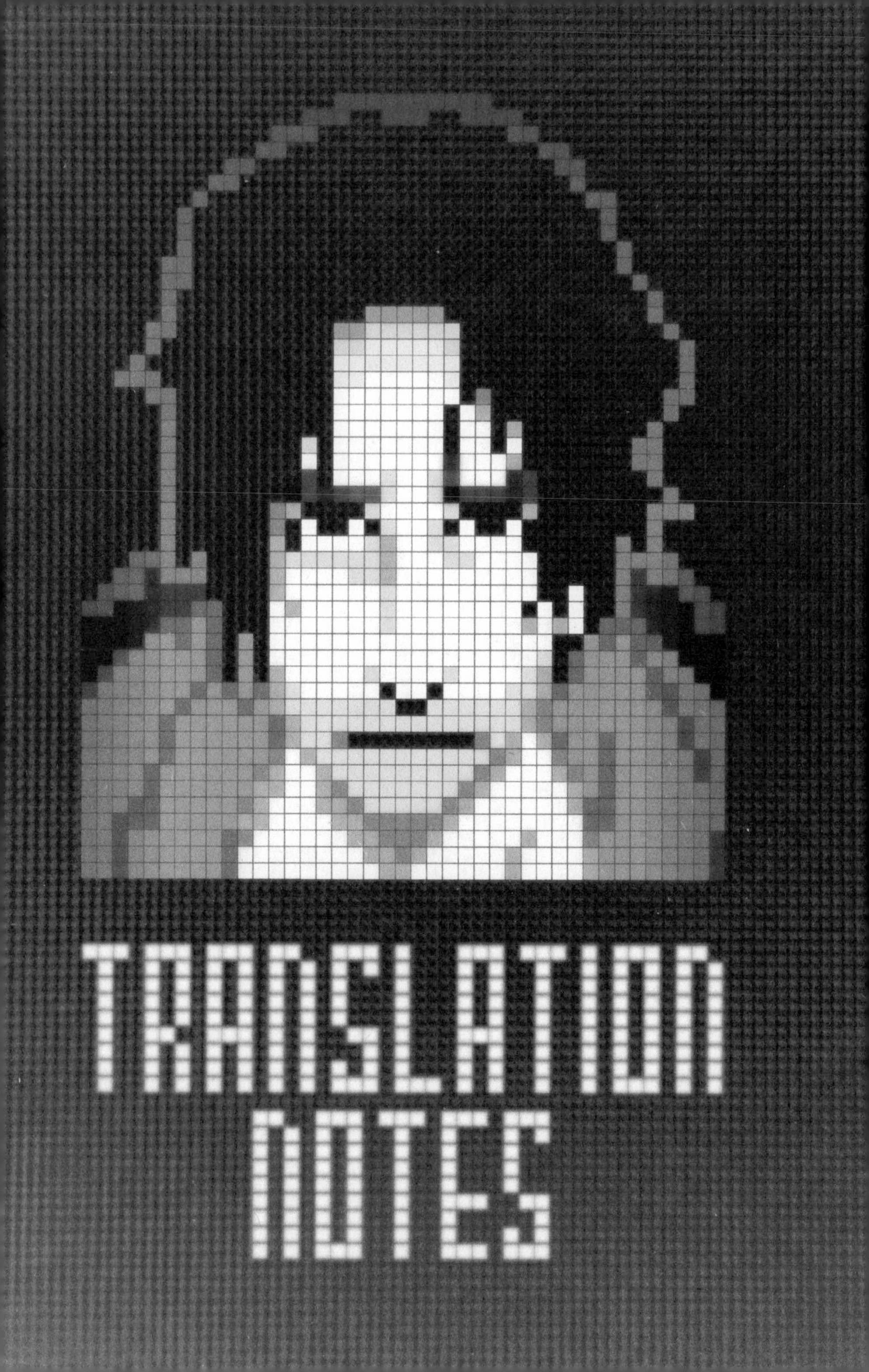
TRANSLATION
NOTES

DORAEMON

page 87

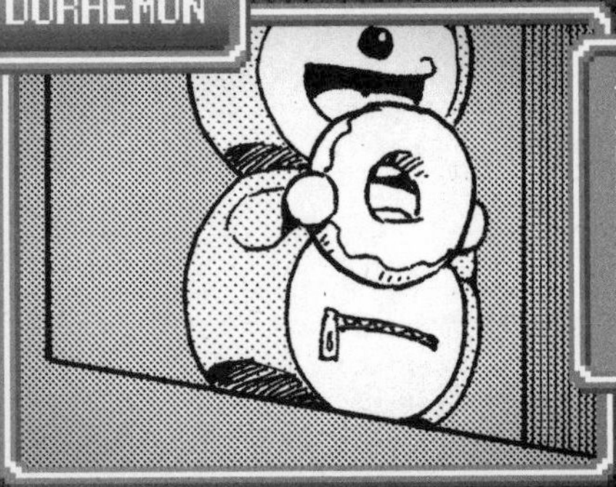

The beloved blue cat robot character and Japanese cultural icon created by Fujiko Fujio and made famous around the world through its long-running manga and anime series. Also visible in this scene are what appear to be one of the titular balls from *Dragon Ball*, the eyeball character "Medama Oyaji" from *GeGeGe no Kitaro*, and the alien "Migi" from *Parasyte*.

DULL METAL ALCHEMIST

page 100

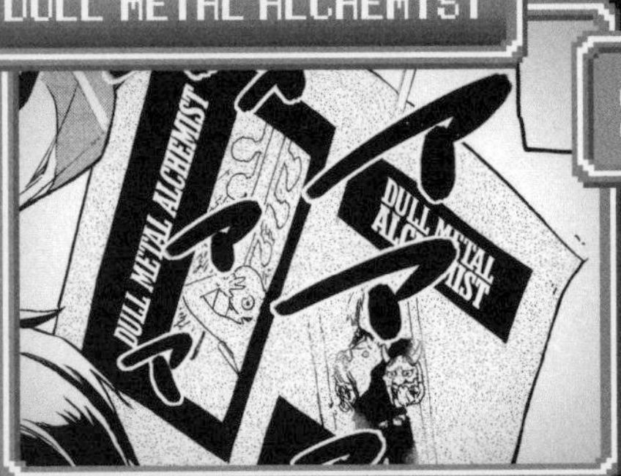
DULL METAL ALCHEMIST
DULL METAL ALCHEMIST

A parody of Hiromu Arakawa's popular fantasy manga/anime series, *Full Metal Alchemist*.

MANGA PARODIES

page 102

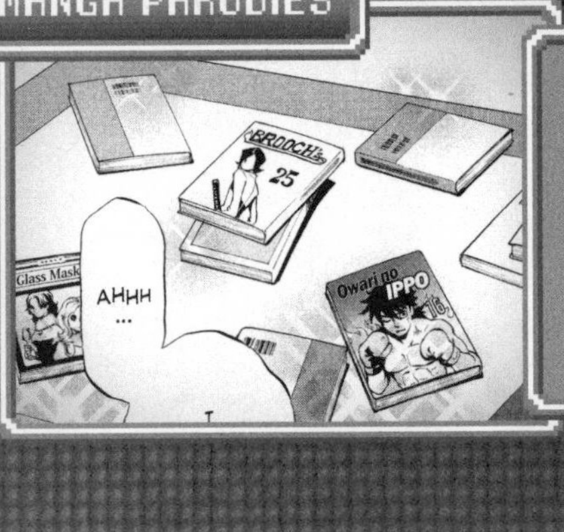
BROOCH
25
Glass Mask
AHHH ...
Owari no IPPO

The manga volumes visible on the desk include *ThunderxThunder*, a parody of the *Shonen Jump series HunterxHunter*; *Brooch*, a parody of *Bleach*; *Owari no Ippo*, a parody of boxing series *Hajime no Ippo*, which makes the title sound like "Last Step" instead of the original "First Step"; and *Glass Mask*, a parody of the shojo manga about theater acting, except that the word "glass" in the title refers to a beverage glass rather than the material.

‹ KAMOME ›
SHIRAHAMA

Witch Hat Atelier

A magical manga
adventure for
fans of Disney
and Studio
Ghibli!

The magical adventure that took Japan by storm is finally here, from acclaimed DC and Marvel cover artist Kamome Shirahama!

In a world where everyone takes wonders like magic spells and dragons for granted, Coco is a girl with a simple dream: She wants to be a witch. But everybody knows magicians are born, not made, and Coco was not born with a gift for magic. Resigned to her un-magical life, Coco is about to give up on her dream to become a witch…until the day she meets Qifrey, a mysterious, traveling magician. After secretly seeing Qifrey perform magic in a way she's never seen before, Coco soon learns what everybody "knows" might not be the truth, and discovers that her magical dream may not be as far away as it may seem…

KC
KODANSHA
COMICS

Magus of the Library

Mitsu Izumi

MITSU IZUMI'S STUNNING ARTWOR[K] BRINGS A FANTASTIC[] LITERARY ADVENTU[RE] TO LUSH, THRILLING LIFE!

Young Theo adores books, bu[t] prejudice and hatred of his v[illage] keeps them ever out of his [reach.] Then one day, he chances to [meet] Sedona, a traveling librarian [who] works for the great library [of] Aftzaak, City of Books, and his life changes forever...

The award-winning manga about what happens inside you!

"Far more entertaining than it ought to be... what kid doesn't want to think that every time they sneeze a torpedo shoots out their nose?"

–Anime News Network

Strep throat! Hay fever! Influenza! The world is a dangerous place for a red blood cell just trying to get her deliveries finished. Fortunately, she's not alone…she's got a whole human body's worth of cells ready to help out! The mysterious white blood cells, the buff and brash killer T cells, even the cute little platelets— everyone's got to come together if they want to keep you healthy!

Cells at Work!

はたらく細胞

By Akane Shimizu

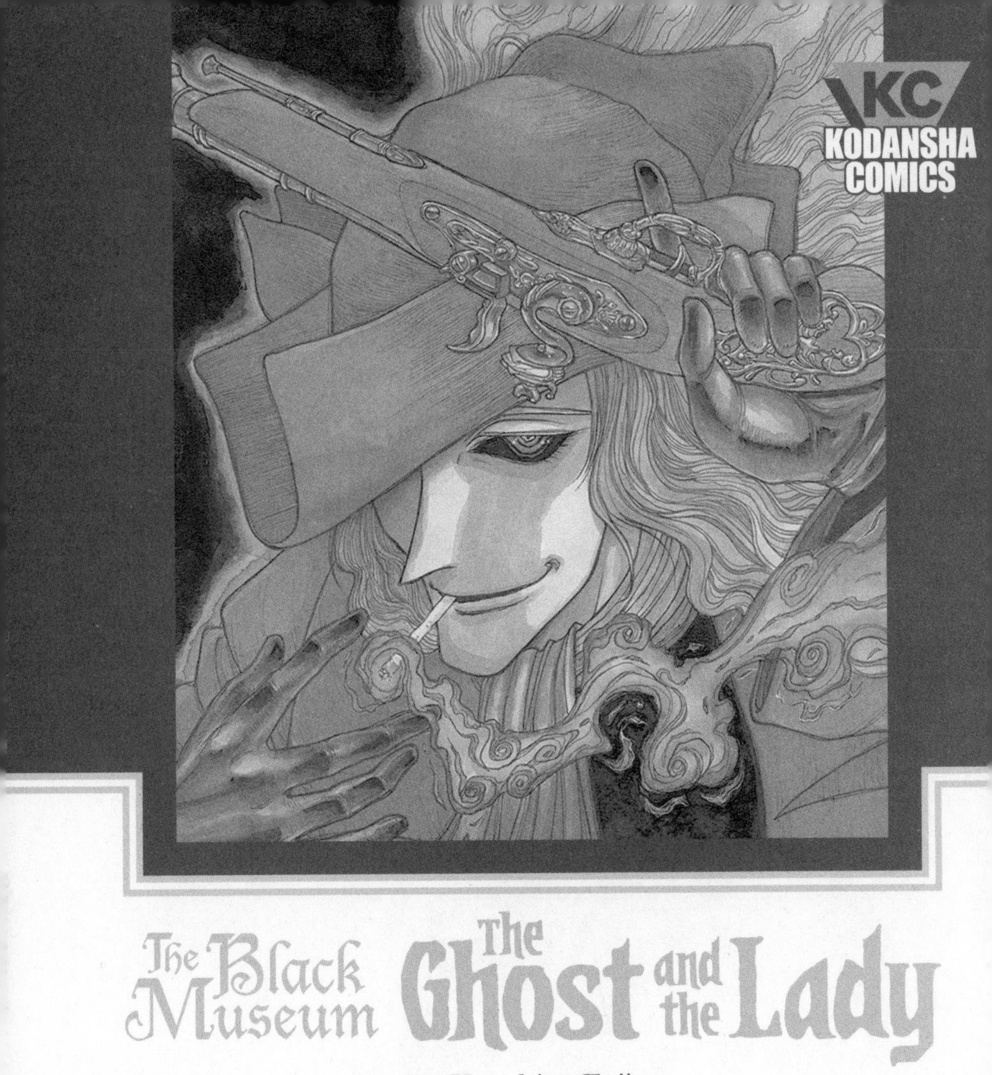
KODANSHA
COMICS

The Black Museum: The Ghost and the Lady

By Kazuhiro Fujita

Deep in Scotland Yard in London sits an evidence room dedicated to the greatest mysteries of British history. In this "Black Museum" sits a misshapen hunk of lead–two bullets fused together–the key to a wartime encounter between Florence Nightingale, the mother of modern nursing, and a supernatural Man in Grey. This story is unknown to most scholars of history, but a special guest of the museum will tell the tale of The Ghost and the Lady...

Praise for Kazuhiro Fujita's *Ushio and Tora*

"A charming revival that combines a classic look with modern depth and pacing... **Essential viewing both for curmudgeons and new fans alike.**" — Anime News Network

"**GREAT!** The first episode of Ushio and Tora captures the essence of '90s anime." — IGN

H·A·P·P·I·N·E·S·S

——ハピネス——

By **Shuzo Oshimi**

From the creator of *The Flowers of Evil*

Nothing interesting is happening in Makoto Ozaki's first year of high school. His life is a series of quiet humiliations: low-grade bullies, unreliable friends, and the constant frustration of his adolescent lust. But one night, a pale, thin girl knocks him to the ground in an alley and offers him a choice. Now everything is different. Daylight is searingly bright. Food tastes awful. And worse than anything is the terrible, consuming thirst...

Praise for Shuzo Oshimi's *The Flowers of Evil*

A shockingly readable story that vividly—one might even say queasily—evokes the fear and confusion of discovering one's own sexuality. Recommended." —The Manga Critic

A page-turning tale of sordid middle school blackmail." —Otaku USA Magazine

A stunning new horror manga." —Third Eye Comics

KC KODANSHA COMICS

Japan's most powerful spirit medium delves into the ghost world's greatest mysteries!

Story by Kyo Shirodaira, famed author of mystery fiction and creator of *Spiral*, *Blast of Tempest*, and *The Record of a Fallen Vampire*.

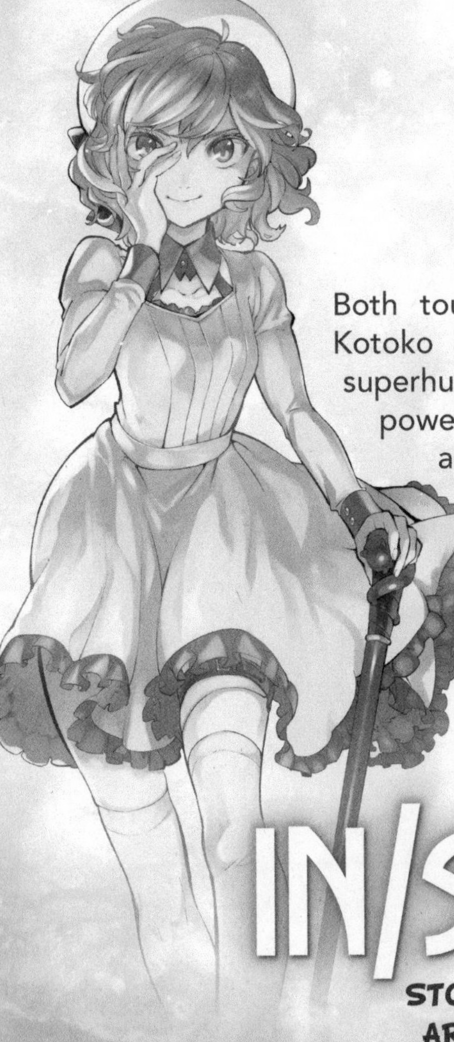

Both touched by spirits called yôkai Kotoko and Kurô have gained unique superhuman powers. But to gain he powers Kotoko has given up an ey and a leg, and Kurô's persona life is in shambles. S when Kotoko suggest they team up to dea with renegades from the spirit world, Kur doesn't have many othe choices, but Kotoko might jus have a few ulterior motives...

IN/SPECTRE

STORY BY KYO SHIRODAIR

ART BY CHASHIBA KATAS

KC
KODANSHA COMICS

New action series from Hiroyuki Takei, creator of the classic shonen franchise Shaman King!

In medieval Japan, a bell hanging on the collar is a sign that a cat has a master. Norachiyo's bell hangs from his katana sheath, but he is nonetheless a stray — a ronin. This one-eyed cat samurai travels across a dishonest world, cutting through pretense and deception with his blade.

Nekogahara

STRAY CAT SAMURAI

By
Hiroyuki Takei

Having lost his wife, high school teacher Kōhei Inuzuka is doing his best to raise his young daughter Tsumugi as a single father. He's pretty bad at cooking and doesn't have a huge appetite to begin with, but chance brings his little family together with one of his students, the lonely Kotori. The three of them are anything but comfortable in the kitchen, but the healing power of home cooking might just work on their grieving hearts.

"This season's number-one feel-good anime!" —Anime News Network

"A beautifully-drawn story about comfort food and family and grief. Recommended." —Otaku USA Magazine

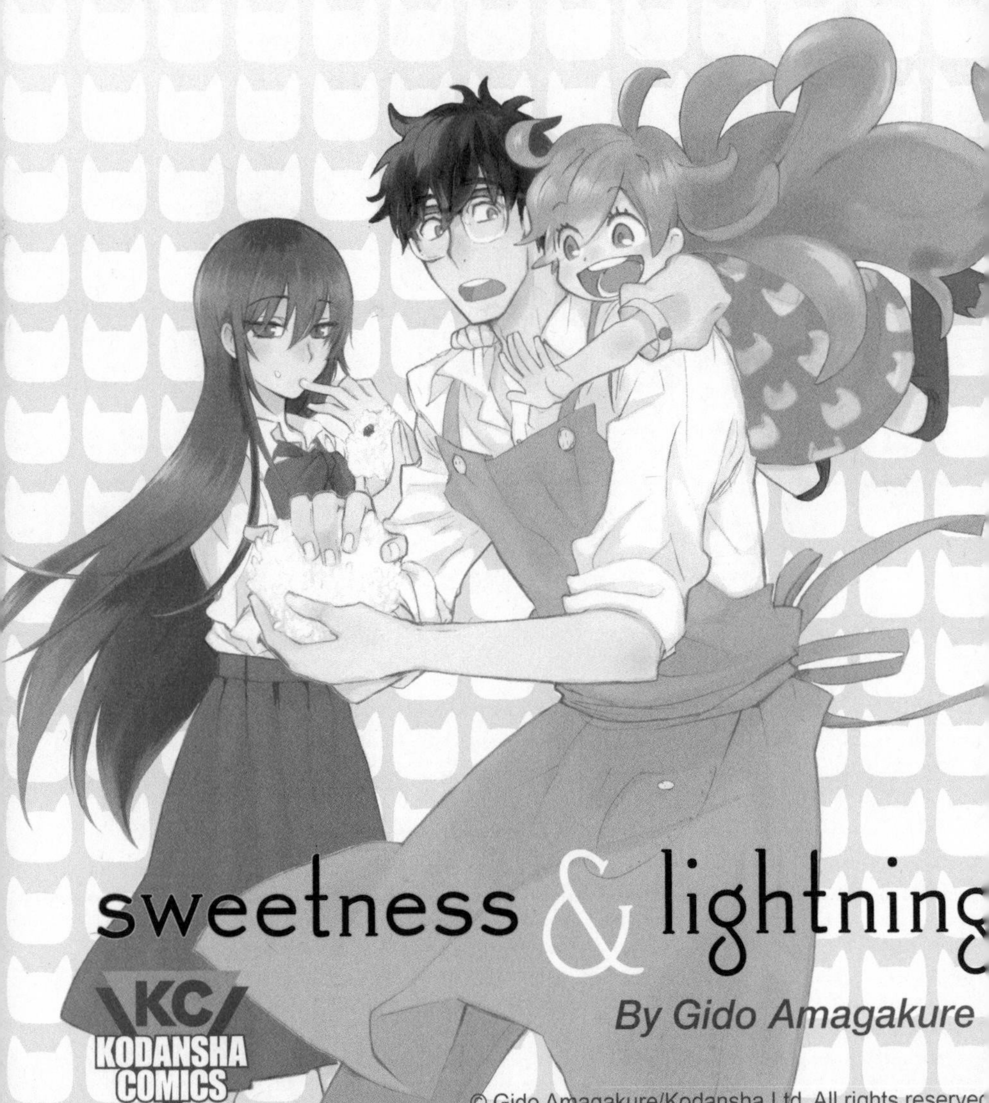
sweetness & lightning
By Gido Amagakure
KC
KODANSHA COMICS

Based on the critically acclaimed classic horror manga

The first new *Parasyte* manga in over 20 years!

NEO PARASYTE f

BY ASUMIKO NAKAMURA, EMA TOYAMA, MIKI RINNO, LALAKO KOJIMA, KAORI YUKI, BANKO KUZE, YUUKI OBATA, KASHIO, YUI KUROE, ASIA WATANABE, MIKIMAKI, HIKARU SURUGA, HAJIME SHINJO, RENJURO KINDAICHI, AND YURI NARUSHIMA

A collection of chilling new *Parasyte* stories from Japan's top shojo artists!

Parasites: shape-shifting aliens whose only purpose is to assimilate with and consume the human race... but do these monsters have a different side? A parasite becomes a prince to save his romance-obsessed female host from a dangerous stalker. Another hosts a cooking show, in which the real monsters are revealed. These and 13 more stories, from some of the greatest shojo manga artists alive today, together make up a chilling, funny, and entertaining tribute to one of manga's horror classics!

KC KODANSHA COMICS

KC
KODANSHA
COMICS

"I'm pleasantly
surprised to find
modern shojo using
cross-dressing as a
dramatic device to deliver
social commentary...
Recommended."

-Otaku USA
Magazine

The prince in his dark days

By **Hico Yamanak**

A drunkard for a father, a household of poverty... For 17-year-old Atsuk
misfortune is all she knows and believes in. Until one day, a chanc
encounter with Itaru–the wealthy heir of a huge corporation–change
everything. The two look identical, uncannily so. When Itaru curiousl
goes missing, Atsuko is roped into being his stand-in. There, in his shoe
Atsuko must parade like a prince in a palace. She encounters many ne
experiences, but at what cost...?

That Time I Got Reincarnated as a Slime volume 10 is a work of fiction. Names, characters, places, and incidents are the products of the author's imagination or are used fictitiously. Any resemblance to actual events, locales, or persons, living or dead, is entirely coincidental.

A Kodansha Comics Trade Paperback Original.

Published in the United States by Kodansha Comics,
an imprint of Kodansha USA Publishing, LLC, New York.

Publication rights for this English edition arranged through Kodansha Ltd., Tokyo.

First published in Japan in 2018 by Kodansha Ltd., Tokyo, as *Tensei Shitara Suraimu Datta Ken* volume 10.

ISBN 978-1-63236-748-8

Printed in the United States of America.

www.kodansha.us

9 8 7 6 5 4

Translation: Stephen Paul
Lettering: Evan Hayden
Editing: Ajani Oloye
Kodansha Comics edition cover design: Phil Balsman